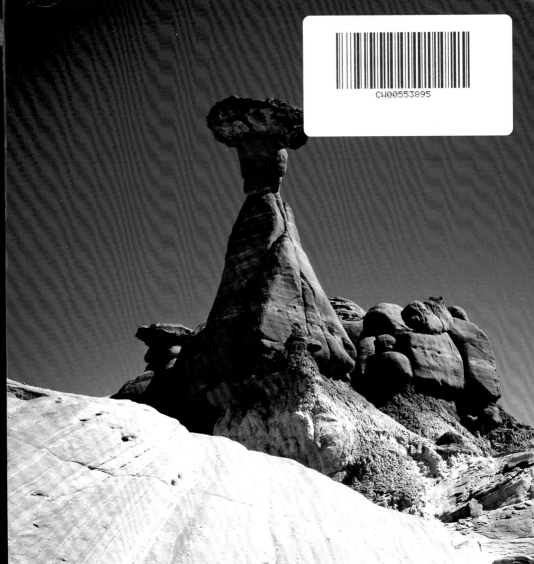

Photographing the
Southwest

Third Edition
Volume 1– A guide to the natural landmarks of Southern Utah

Laurent Martrès

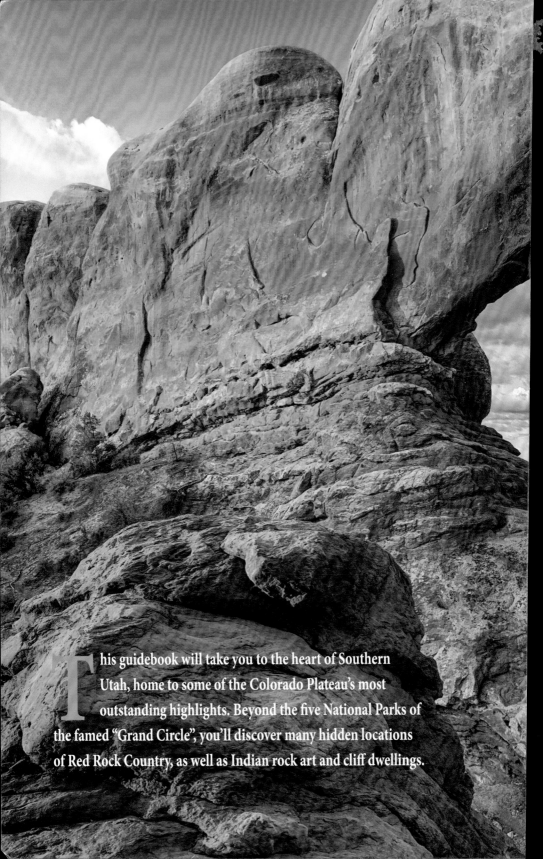

This guidebook will take you to the heart of Southern Utah, home to some of the Colorado Plateau's most outstanding highlights. Beyond the five National Parks of the famed "Grand Circle", you'll discover many hidden locations of Red Rock Country, as well as Indian rock art and cliff dwellings.

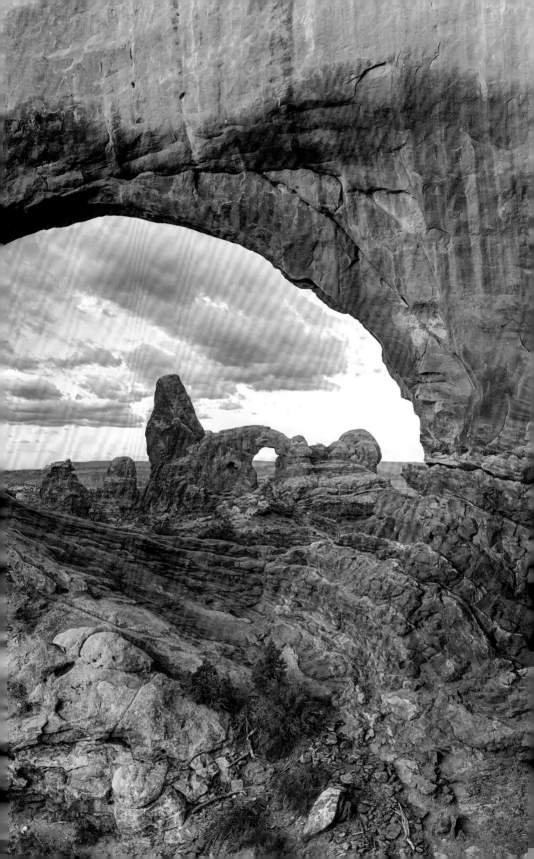

PHOTOGRAPHING THE SOUTHWEST (3RD EDITION)
Volume 1 - Southern Utah

Published by PhotoTripUSA Publishing
An imprint of

GRAPHIE
INTERNATIONAL, INC.
8780 19th Street, Suite 199
Alta Loma, CA 91701, USA

Executive Publisher: Laurent Martrès
Editor-in-Chief: Philippe Schuler
Editors: John Stottlemyer & Greg Vaughn
Cover Design: Sioux Bally-Maloof, Heartstone Arts

Cover photo: Angel Arch (Canyonlands Nat'l Park)
Title page photo: Toadstool Hoodoo (Grand Staircase-Escalante Nat'l Monument)
Overleaf photo: Turret Arch through North Window (Arches Nat'l Park)

Visit our web site: **www.phototripusa.com**
Laurent's web site: **www.martres.com**

Printed in China

Disclaimer
Some of the locations described in this book require travel through remote areas, where footpaths and 4-wheel drive trails can be difficult, even dangerous. Travel at your own risk and always check conditions locally before venturing out. The author and publisher decline all responsibility if you get lost, stranded, injured, or otherwise suffer any kind of mishap as a result of following the advice and descriptions in this book. Furthermore, the information contained herein may have become outdated by the time you read it; the author and publisher assume no responsibility for outdated information, errors, and omissions.

Publisher's Cataloging-in-Publication

Martrès, Laurent.
Photographing the Southwest. Volume 1, Southern Utah
/ Laurent Martrès. -- 3rd edition.
pages cm
Includes bibliographical references and index.
ISBN-13: 978-0-916189-23-5
ISBN-10: 0-916189-23-6

1. Utah--Guidebooks. 2. Landscape photography--Utah
--Guidebooks. I. Title.

F824.3.M37 2015   917.9204'34
                          QBI14-600152

Acknowledgements

As with any book of this scope, many individuals have contributed one way or another to a better experience for the reader. They are two many to name here, but I want to acknowledge a few for their special contribution.

My deepest gratitude goes to Philippe Schuler, whose careful editing of the manuscript and innumerable enhancements to its contents have resulted in a much better book. Philippe brought to these guidebooks a level of precision and excellence that I would not have been able to achieve on my own. He co-wrote several sections and contributed informative textual and pictorial content throughout the various volumes and chapters of the *Photographing the Southwest* series. He also spent countless hours verifying the relevance and accuracy of the practical information and helped immensely in restructuring the presentation of this Third Edition.

Tom Till's exraordinary body of work on the American Southwest and UNESCO World Heritage Sites has been my biggest source of inspiration throughout my career and my admiration for his imagery still perdures. I'm proud to have had the privilege to act as Tom's publisher and editor for his very inspiring book *Photographing the World.*

John Stottlemyer and Greg Vaughn have spent many hours combing through this book for typos and other blunders. I'm very thankful for their help in making the book a better read

Momo Vuyisich logged many hours tirelessly piloting the plane during our aerial photography expeditions. He is a very special person and it's an honor for me to be his friend.

Contributing photographers

Many thanks to my friends and hiking partners. It wouldn't have been nearly as fun without you guys.

Jerry Day - darkskydreams.com
Ron Flickinger - ronflickinger.com
Gene Mezereny - mezereny.com
Denis Savouray - americainmyheart.com
Rick Schafer - theanasazi.com
Philippe Schuler - phschuler.com
John Stottlemyer - worldviewphotography.zenfolio.com
Isabel & Steffen Synnatschke - synnatschke.com
Tom Till - tomtillphotography.com
Momo Vuyisich - wildwestgallery.com
Scott Walton - scottwaltonphotographs.com
Charles Wood - cdwood.zenfolio.com

TABLE OF CONTENTS

About this Book ...

Welcome to the Third Edition of Photographing the Southwest - Vol. 1. Simply stated, this book is a location resource for photographers and casual visitors alike. It supplements other—more traditional—travel guides, describing how and when to enjoy these locations under the best conditions, and of course how to get the best shots.

The present Volume 1 in the Southwest series covers Southern Utah; Volume 2 is about Arizona and a bit of Nevada; Volume 3 deals with Colorado & New Mexico. All three share the same visual and photographic perspective.

Many of the natural landmarks I describe are well known; others are off the beaten path. The majority are easily accessible, others may be a bit harder to get to. All will provide you with unforgettable images and memories.

This guidebook has something very unique, although others may have picked up on the idea. I provide a rating system, whereby I rate from 1 to 5 the scenic value and photographic value, as well as the level of difficulty to access the location by car and on foot.

Even if you're not a photographer, you'll find lots of information that traditional guides leave out. The location of a hidden site, the most beautiful angle to shoot it, and especially the best time of day to view it. This information is as valuable for seeing and enjoying a site with your own eyes as it is for photography. These books are written for everyone with a passion for the Southwest.

May this book bring you a slew of new ideas for your creative photography of the Southwest.

... and some thoughts on Photography

There is a non-palpable, but none the less essential ingredient to successful landscape photography: An unbridled love for nature and strong emotional connection to the land and your subject. Photographing should be an extension of that love, to record the memories and share with others the joy of being there. If your fascination with camera equipment or the physics of optics take precedence over your love of nature, it is doubtful that you'll ever achieve your full creative potential. Your craft may become technically excellent and you may acquire a nice portfolio to impress friends and family, but you won't be able to communicate emotions if they weren't present when you took the picture. Most people I know who seriously pursue photography of the Southwest have this love of the land within them. Sometimes, however, I meet folks who are more interested in 'shooting' than in enjoying the beauty around them.

Over the years I have taken pleasure in asking people whether they would do a particularly strenuous hike to a beautiful spot if they had to leave their camera at home. I have had a few people flatly—and honestly—tell me that they wouldn't.

This isn't necessarily a criticism; photography doesn't have to equate to love of nature to be enjoyed as a hobby. I do say, however, that simply being there, quietly enjoying the place and the moment, is far more important than bringing back a few pictures.

Another important axiom of good landscape photography is that it seldom happens by accident. In all probability, you'll need to visit a location several times, seeing it under different light and in different seasons—perhaps even a few times without a camera—to start pre-visualizing your image. As you observe, ponder, and feel during your time there, you begin to refine your past experience, to anticipate a change of light or a break in the clouds. Your best images—those which carry the most emotional content—will be the result of careful planning and pre-visualization.

Finally, with your pre-visualized image in mind, you'll rise early—very early—and drag your sleepy body inside your freezing car. You'll drive on the edge of your seat to the now familiar location, peering through the darkness to spot deer on the road through the still partially icy windshield, nervously glancing at the clock and worrying about the changing light on the horizon. Perhaps you'll be biting on a hard power bar between nervous sips of coffee, to warm you up a bit and get your mind in gear. You will walk to your location briskly, plant your tripod firmly, ready-up filters and lenses. You'll wait, floating in a dual state of serene peace and nervous anticipation. And then, the momentous event you came for will happen: Glorious, unspeakably beautiful sunrise. The land will be bathed in hues of yellow and red and you will feel vindicated for all the effort you put into your journey.

But there is little time for reflection. There is a job to be done—photos to be taken. The adrenaline kicks in and you become totally focused. You shoot like a maniac, oblivious to everything else but your subject, annoyed if a laggard suddenly shows up. You shoot and shoot until the incredible light finally becomes a little too bright, a little too crude. When you're done, you smile and bask in the joy that overtakes you as you feel one with this place that you love so much. You linger a while to make the moment last, letting the sun warm you up, your body still weary from lack of sleep. As you walk back to the trailhead, you let your mind wander and play like a puppy. You're proud and ecstatic at having experienced this cosmic moment. You suddenly become part of the great brotherhood of early-rising nature lovers, and, unbeknownst to you, you've just bonded with the fly fisherman in Montana, the ice fisherman in Minnesota, and the deer hunter in Idaho!

Months later you sit in your living room looking at the big, majestic enlargement hanging on your wall and you grin happily at the beloved landscape basking in the morning sun. But you also feel something deeper—a special connection. The memories that you bring back from such incredibly poignant and precious moments are treasured as much as the print itself. You may not have the words to express it, but that's OK. The picture will speak for you.

-- Laurent Martrès

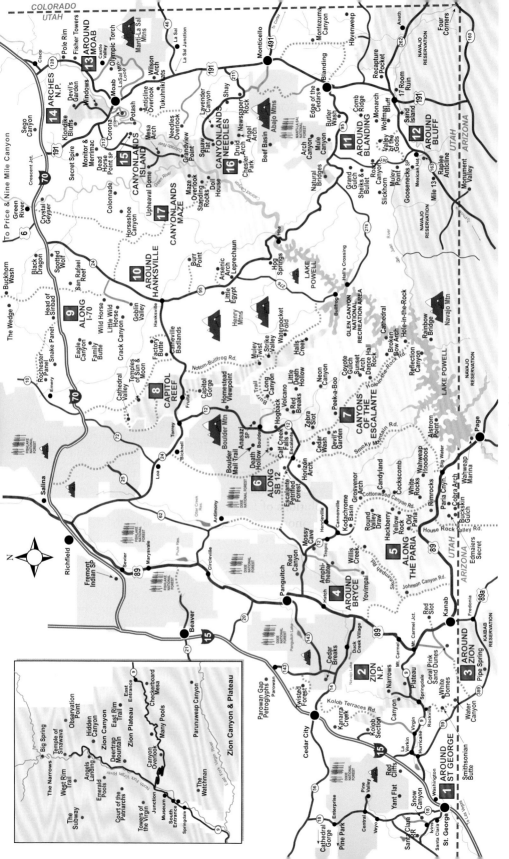

Territory covered in this volume

INTRODUCTION

Important information about Maps

You may be surprised that this book doesn't contain any detailed maps other than the simple one to the left, which describes the general location of the chapters and some of the more prominent sections. Had I chosen to illustrate with numerous maps the locations covered in the three volumes of *Photographing the Southwest*, it would have dramatically increased the size, weight and price of the books, making them impractical to carry on a trip. But most importantly, any number of small maps I could have included would still not substitute for the real thing. The fact is you will need several different kinds of maps to effectively use the information.

Maps play a huge role in several respects. Large scale maps are necessary to get a global perspective of your trip and make initial decisions. Detailed road maps are necessary in order to follow the instructions in the "*Getting there*" sections of the book. You'll find a list of recommended maps in the *Appendix*, along with a short description of each. Let me point out that one particular map—the *AAA Indian Country* map—stands out as an excellent asset in the preparation and enjoyment of your trips. This remarkable map covers almost all the territory of *Volume 1* and about half the terrain of *Volumes 2* and *3*.

Additionally, since many of the locations I describe are off the beaten path, 7.5 minute US-Geological Survey maps are absolutely necessary. Although the information on these maps is sometimes outdated, they are an indispensable tool for locating remote sites and navigating the backcountry. There are a number of applications for desktop/laptops or mobile devices that allow you to download, display, and print various resolutions of Digital Rasterized Graphic files for specific locations. This is a very economical and practical way to go.

Thanks to mobile computing, a new even more powerful tool has emerged. One you can easily take in the field; in fact, one you should always bring in the field. I'm talking about maps for mobile phones and tablets. Once installed on your mobile device equipped with a GPS, you can track your precise location in real time while driving on remote dirt roads or hiking on trails. Consider this simple scenario: Driving back from your sunset shoot, you find yourself at a fork and do not remember which branch you came in on earlier. The digitized map(s) that you downloaded on your mobile device makes it extremely easy to track your location and hence the correct turn to return home. While it's true that you can do this with a mapping GPS alone, tracking your progress on a mobile device with all the fine detail of a USGS 7.5' topographic map provides a degree of accuracy and comfort that is not possible with the GPS' tiny screen. Entering waypoints from a larger keyboard is also easier and navigating the maps on a large screen provides a better understanding of the topology—hills to climb, canyons to bypass, etc.—especially if you use relief shading or, better yet, 3-dimensional viewing.

And now for the 'coup de grace'. Enter the most extraordinary, game-changing tool: terrain mapping from satellite. This is the most important recent development for photographers and anybody needing to navigate remote areas. Google Earth and TPE (The Photographer's Ephemeris) have emerged at the vanguard of new tools allowing us not only to plot our trips using actual aerial photography of the terrain, but to project sun and moon rise and set anytime in the future, and see how it affects a particular feature of the terrain.

GPS considerations

In the first edition, I considered it inappropriate to give away GPS points. My philosophy at the time was that readers needed to make their own adventure, performing a minor amount of effort in researching locations. I also considered, and still consider, GPS usage fraught with dangers in the hands of inexperienced users. Knowing GPS coordinates is one thing, but it is no substitute for a topographic map, particularly when it comes to understanding relief.

I have noticed that novice users tend to rely on the "GOTO" function of their GPS, without consideration for the topography. Rarely can one follow the straight line indicated on the GPS. Gullies too deep for crossing and cliffs too high for climbing are common occurrences.

In the previous decade, a majority of friends and government agency officials shared my concern. The consensus at the time was that giving away GPS coordinates could make things too easy and perhaps dangerous for novice users.

Circumstances have changed drastically since then: GPS coordinates can be found on the Internet for just about any location of interest and the information is freely exchanged between peers with similar pursuits. In this new context, it would be counterproductive to force readers to seek GPS information outside of this book.

I do not want to entice readers to rely exclusively on their GPS unit, however. Instead, you'll find coordinates whenever they are truly useful, or sometimes indispensable.

I'll reiterate my warning here: The GPS is no substitute for a topographic map and a compass, and in some cases for plain old instinct and navigational skills. Batteries eventually die, but the compass will continue to indicate your direction. You should always carry spare batteries, a compass and a map... and of course know how to use them.

If you are a novice user, I suggest that you attend a clinic. GPS clinics are available for free at many outdoor equipment stores in cities across the country.

One last bit of advice: do not walk with your eyes riveted to your GPS. Instead, try finding your way around by observing landmarks and following natural paths. Not only will you become a better routefinder, but you'll enjoy your surroundings a lot more. Your GPS is not a toy; use it only when necessary, to make sure that you are on course. Once you've mastered its use and are aware of its potential pitfalls, you may wonder how you got along without it.

The coordinate system used in this book is Degrees, Minutes, Seconds in WGS84 datum. It is the simplest to understand for novice users. It is also the best choice in terms of readability and ease of input. The popular UTM system may have some pluses, but it is not as immediately descriptive when comparing two waypoints. Coordinates expressed in UTM are also easier to mistype. Once typed into your GPS unit, tablet, or on-line web site, you can simply switch the WGS84 coordinates to your preferred reference system.

Driving around

The question of the best vehicle to use may naturally arise when you visit an area as vast as the American Southwest. In this *Volume 1* of *Photographing the Southwest*, about 56% of the sites are accessible via paved roads or tracks adequate for passenger cars. An additional 18% of the sites can be accessed via rougher tracks that are still potentially passable by passenger cars if driven with caution in dry weather. The rest necessitate an SUV or some kind of high-clearance vehicle. In a number of cases (not the majority) use of a four-wheel drive (4WD) vehicle and some experience with this kind of driving is required. High-clearance is generally associated with larger tires than on the typical passenger car and is often necessary to negotiate the irregularities of a track, prevent damage to the undercarriage, and avoid becoming high-centered. Complementing high clearance, 4WD, especially in low-range, is useful on sandy or muddy tracks or tracks presenting rock steps and/or particularly steep angles—a small minority of locations in this book.

Road difficulty is examined in detail for each location in the text, as well as in the Ratings section at the end of the book. I rate the difficulty of vehicular access under "normal" conditions, i.e. always in dry weather and long after a rain. In wet conditions or after violent thunderstorms, a track rated accessible by passenger car can become impassable even to a high-clearance 4WD vehicle. The ratings provided should always be confirmed with visitor centers or local authorities, as track conditions change frequently based on recent weather and the elapsed time since the last road maintenance. Don't take any unnecessary risks. Towing may cost hundreds or even thousands of dollars should you become stranded in some remote location.

Undoubtedly, using an SUV with good ground clearance to explore the locations in this guidebook (even if it isn't 4WD) provides a degree of flexibility and comfort not offered by passenger cars and limits the risk of damage to your vehicle. If you are considering car camping on your trip, you may even be able to sleep in your vehicle. Assuming you have a flat surface after folding down the rear seats, a person of average height can usually sleep in the back. If you own a pick-up, a shell will provide inexpensive and effective protection against the elements.

If you are traveling in your own SUV or pick-up truck, you should always carry a tow strap, a shovel, a tire repair kit (with plugs), and a small air compressor. The latter will allow you to reinflate your tires after airing down in particularly sandy terrain. If you fly in from another part of the country (or the world) and rent an SUV from a major rental company, be aware that it will rarely offer 4WD. Furthermore, your rental agreement usually prohibits taking the rental vehicle off paved roads, so think twice about where you want to go, as you'll be assuming a major financial risk. One last piece of advice concerning rental vehicles: Always verify the presence of an adequate spare tire and tools to change it. You don't want to be stuck on a remote road just because the crank to operate the jack is missing.

Hiking

I'm often asked about the level of difficulty of the hikes involved in visiting various locations. The answer depends on a plurality of factors. Many readers are not necessarily avid hikers. While a majority are probably content to carry a lightweight camera, some may be hauling heavy photographic gear. At the other end of the spectrum, some folks prefer long hikes so they can "get away from the crowds". In this book, about 51% of the locations can be visited and photographed with almost no hiking at all or else an easy stroll lasting less than an hour round-trip. An additional 23% of the sites should be accessible to most readers, requiring between one to three hours round-trip with moderate difficulty. About 16% are more demanding, as they require up to six hours round-trip and/or involve some kind of difficulty such as elevation change, orienteering, tougher terrain, obstacles or other risks. A minority require longer, more strenuous hiking or backpacking (mentioned only marginally in this guidebook).

In addition to the descriptions in the text, hiking difficulty is summed up in detail at the end of the book, with ratings on difficulty of access on foot for each location. These ratings are done with the average hiker in mind. My 'average' hiker is neither a person with mobility problems nor a marathon runner. S/he is in average physical shape (exercising regularly, preferably walking) and having a reasonably good sense of orientation, under normal hiking conditions (in dry weather and average temperatures).

Reading this guidebook, you'll find out that visiting the Southwest—even off the beaten track—is not the exclusive domain of hard-core hikers. You'll come to realize that ordinary city folks can find plenty of trips to satisfy their photographic pursuits with only a modest amount of effort. Obviously, you need to set reasonable goals for yourself. Begin your trip with easy hikes, increasing your mileage progressively and alternating hard and easy days. Pay particular attention to the duration of your hikes. Some people tend to be overly optimistic, especially if taking lots of pictures.

Always heed the advice of park rangers and professional guides, even if it feels a little too conservative. This is particularly important when hiking in canyon country. Flash floods may happen in any season, although they tend to happen much more frequently during summer. You don't want to find yourself trapped in a slot canyon when that happens.

Hiking equipment should also be considered carefully. It can make a significant difference in terms of security and comfort. Security should not be taken lightly, as there is a very real risk of getting lost on backcountry hikes without trails. Although a minority, there are a few such hikes in this guidebook. Start with the Ten Essentials:

- ❐ A first aid kit
- ❐ Waterproof matches or a small lighter
- ❐ A pocket knife
- ❐ A headlamp (there are very small, lightweight LED models)
- ❐ Sunglasses (polarized types are nice for photography)
- ❐ A loud whistle (so you can be located by your party or a rescue team in case of mishap)
- ❐ High-energy food (trail mix or energy bars)
- ❐ A topographic map of the area
- ❐ A compass and if possible a GPS unit (always take a waypoint of your vehicle's location)
- ❐ Extra clothing in case of a sudden change in weather.

Your digital camera can also be a useful tool when hiking in the backcountry, where there is no trail or no obvious landmark and you'll be returning the same way you came. At each strategic location (such as a spot where you need to go down or ascend a cliff, an intersection of side canyons, or when leaving the course of a wash) turn around and take a snapshot, taking care to place the direction to be followed on returning in the center of the frame. If you have any doubt as to the correct course when you return, just examine the shots you took on your camera's LCD. Including a finger on the side of these shots will allow you to locate them easily.

A good pair of hiking shoes with good ankle support is essential for hiking in the Southwest. Ankle support and soles with good traction are essential on small pebbles and slickrock. Sneakers are definitely inadequate for the trail and should stay in your car. If you're going to wade inside streambeds—this book offers several opportunities to do so—a second pair of shoes, specialized for water activities, will come in handy. This type of shoe usually has excellent anti-slip soles. Although not indispensable, they offer an additional level of comfort when hiking in water. Use them with a pair of wool socks or synthetic liners to avoid blisters. For pants, shorts, and shirts, the newer synthetic fibers work very well in the Southwest environment. They breathe well, transferring body moisture away from the skin, and they dry extremely fast (on you or after being washed). Don't forget the indispensable fleece jacket and/or windbreaker, which you should always have handy as temperatures can change radically throughout the day. Don't be fooled by the fact that the land looks like a desert; it can get cold very fast, especially at elevation, during the spring and fall months. When hiking in full sun—a common occurrence in the Southwest—consider a solar cap with a "legionnaire" attachment to protect your ears and neck. Also, frequent application of sunscreen to sun-exposed areas is recommended. Sunburn can hurt like hell and can have potentially life-threatening health consequences later.

There are many good daypacks and photo packs available. Consider one with sufficient capacity to carry not only your photo equipment, but also your additional clothing, safety gear and above all, plenty of water. In summer, dehydration may come easily and without warning. Some of the day-hikes in this book may require a full gallon of water. When hiking in the backcountry, I sometimes encounter photographers carrying "specialized" photo packs for their equipment and only a small hip-bag with just enough space for a couple of energy bars and two pints of water. Not having enough water places you at serious risk in case of unplanned occurrences. Taking the wrong turn or simply extending your visit because every bend of the canyon brings more captivating beauty requires additional resources, especially water. On very long day hikes, I often stash a 2-quart water bladder behind a tree for the return trip. On extended trips, especially in the Escalante area, I carry and use a water filter.

Trekking poles can be helpful on hikes involving lots of ups and downs. They propel you forward going up and relieve pressure on your knees going down. Your poles can also aid in keeping your balance when wading rocky streams.

A word about lodging

I provide no information or advice concerning accommodations, although I do mention campgrounds on occasion. I have found that my readers have very different traveling styles depending on their individual goals, time constraints, and the level of comfort they require. There are many excellent travel guides and web sites available that can assist the reader in finding the specific type of accommodations they desire.

Keep in mind, however, that you'll take many of your best photos during the so-called "golden hour", soon after sunrise and just before sunset. As many of the locations discussed in this book are on dirt roads far away from motels, you may have to camp close to the site to be present during the best light. Doing so, you avoid driving at night on backcountry tracks. What would pass as minor impediments during the day can become very dangerous when you discover them at the last second with your headlights. Depending on the situation, you may be able to opt for organized campgrounds, such as the ones found in many national or state parks (where camping is prohibited outside the official campgrounds). Alternatively, there may be primitive camping where you'll just pick your site in the middle of the backcountry, if this is authorized. This is most often the case on BLM-administered land.

Even if you're sleeping in motels every night, you may want to carry in your car a small tent, a sleeping pad and a sleeping bag, as well as a stash of food and several gallons of water. Should some unforeseen circumstances prevent you from going back to town, you'll be able to improvise a night in the backcountry. You may even become addicted to this approach once you get a taste of it!

When to visit

The Colorado Plateau can be visited year-round. Each season possesses its unique charm and presents various advantages and disadvantages.

Summer monsoon storms make for sublime skies, occasional rainbows, soft lighting due to haze and spectacular sunsets. But there is a high price to pay for that. It's the busiest time of the year on the roads and in the parks. In recent-decades, foreign visitors en masse have also discovered the American West, in organized tour groups or as individuals, crowding the roads and parks, not to mention the motels. In the most popular places, reservations become indispens-able and need to be made in advance to guarantee a place for the night. This can create a serious obstacle to the flexibility of your itinerary by imposing a measure of control on your evening's destination.

The intense heat is not generally a problem in the car or on short walks, but it is a factor on long hikes. Summer sees frequent afternoon downpours with all the risks they entail, especially when visiting the numerous canyons described in this guide. Additionally, dirt roads are sometimes closed by water runoff.

Insects can pose a problem in certain areas, particularly at the beginning of summer when deerflies and biting gnats or "no-see-ums" will attack your skin relentlessly. Unfortunately, it is impossible to predict when and where they will hang out in a particular year.

Finally, the days are at their longest; this allows you to cover a lot of ground and visit many sites. On the other hand, this can considerably limit your photo-graphic opportunities during the day when the sun is high in the sky and your shots will be way too contrasty and without nuance. Bear in mind that the angle of the sun is at its highest in summer. There is no such thing as a "golden hour" at the height of summer, but merely fifteen minutes of very good light after sun-rise and before sunset. As a photographer, I find summer rather exhausting in Southern Utah and I'd recommend concentrating on Colorado and New Mexico at that time of year (see *Volume 3* of *Photographing the Southwest*).

Autumn is the best time to discover the Southwest. It's still warm, but the heat is less ferocious. In the first part of autumn, days are still long but less grueling. Kids and the majority of grown-ups have returned to work and school after Labor Day. The motels empty out. Prices lower to a reasonable level, the parks are less congested and parking near the panoramic vistas no longer requires you to drive around for ½ hour to find a spot. Hazy days become rare and insects no longer make your life miserable.

Fall colors begin in mid-September in the high country and in early November at lower elevations. October and November are absolutely marvelous in Zion or Capitol Reef as the foliage changes and a new, multi-colored palette of yellow, ocher and red appears with a much softer illumination than in summer. Strong rains are relatively rare, although at high altitude locations such as Cedar Breaks or Bryce, snow is possible. Finally, the sun rises and sets at a lower angle and the "golden hour" lasts quite a bit longer than in summer. This is my favorite season for general travel in the Southwest, as well as for photography.

Winter is the off-season and offers exceptional possibilities to enjoy the surrounding tranquility at incredibly low prices. Also, winter's short daylight hours, as well as the low trajectory of the sun on the horizon, are a blessing to the photographer.

With a bit of care to dress warmly, the dry cold is not disagreeable, though it can make camping less attractive. Winter storms often bring rain or heavy snow to the higher elevations and can last several days. However, a snowfall in Bryce can be an absolutely magical experience when, with these alternate periods of beautiful weather, the air attains an unequaled purity and the sky is an intense blue. By the same token, there are few clouds in the sky and it can be tough to come up with spectacular photography including much sky. Nonetheless, unobstructed views such as those one sees in Canyonlands or the Grand Canyon—to give but two examples—reveal extraordinary distances when there is no pollution, as is rarely the case in summer. Large animals descend from the higher elevations and are frequently and easily observed in the valleys.

The main inconvenience is that certain sites become inaccessible, particularly the North Rim of the Grand Canyon, Cedar Breaks, the Narrows of the Virgin and sometimes the trails of Bryce Canyon (at least without adequate equipment, for these last two). Another negative factor is the lack of color in the vegetation. You'll have to be careful not to include bare vegetation in your images; bare branches and bushes don't make very nice foregrounds.

Spring is a magnificent season, although the weather can be very unpredictable. You are as likely to encounter stormy, wet days as you are warm and sunny weather. Precipitation is frequent in March and the rivers and waterfalls are at their highest. High peaks are still snowbound, greenery is sprouting, the trees are leafing out and wildflowers abound in wet years. It's a great time to visit the Canyons of the Escalante, among others, when cottonwood trees explode an intense green and temperatures are still tolerable. However, beware of high water levels, which may make it impossible to wade.

The days are getting longer and prices are still not as expensive as during the height of the season. In late spring, insects can also be a great nuisance. No-see-ums, fond of blood and terribly annoying, as well as aggressive deerflies are to be found along watercourses and in washes.

Archaeological Sites Etiquette

Rock art and ancient dwellings are a most precious heritage of Native American Indians and humanity at large. They are obviously extremely fragile and when not protected, are often the unfortunate subject of vandalism. When photographing rock art and ruins, the first and foremost rule is: Don't touch. Natural oils from human skin can and will affect glyphs and paintings. Even though a slight touch may only remove a minute amount of pigment or sandstone, when you multiply that by many years and many visitors it will eventually lead to irreparable degradation of the art. Even worse than that, is the use of chalk or crayon to enhance or highlight the art for photographs. It compromises the integrity of the art by becoming a permanent part of the design and paves the way for others to add their own mark, thus destroying the precious heritage forever. This is a sad and irresponsible act, which I have observed too many times on otherwise beautiful rock art throughout the Southwest. The Black Dragon (see *Along I-70* chapter) is a prime example of such misguided alteration. Needless to say, you should not cut, chip, or try to remove rock art. The Antiquities Act protects rock art and infractions are subject to very high fines. It is our responsibility as observers and photographers of our era to treat it properly so that it may be preserved as a testimony to those who came before us and for the benefit of future generations.

Please don't blame me as an author for disseminating information about public or lesser-known archaeological sites. Vandals don't read books such as this one, looking for information. Sadly, according to reports, in 90% of cases rock art is defaced by young males—one would have to conclude that the remaining 10% must be immature adults. The best way to prevent this from happening is through education, in schools and at the sites.

Some of the best places to admire and photograph rock art in Southern Utah are Horseshoe Canyon, the Maze, the San Rafael Reef, the San Juan River area, Sego Canyon, Newspaper Rock and surrounding areas. The most outstanding unprotected ruins are located on the Cedar Mesa Plateau. Fortunately, many of the best ancient dwellings are under the protection of some governmental, state, or tribal agency.

To visit hard-to-find panels and significantly increase your enjoyment and understanding of rock art, consider joining the Utah Rock Art Research Association, aka URARA, or one of their local chapters.

Photo Advice & Terminology

If you're looking to improve your photography, visit our web site at www.PhotoTripUSA.com where you'll find a free e-book filled with numerous photographic tips, equipment recommendations, and advice for shooting in the field.

With so many different digital camera formats available today, it can be confusing to talk about lenses in referring to them by the traditional millimeter focal length system. For many years a 50mm lens has been considered a "normal" lens for 35mm photography (now referred to as "full-frame"), but that focal length would be a longish telephoto on a digital point & shoot, a slight telephoto on a DSLR with an APS-C-sized sensor, a slightly wide-angle lens on a medium format camera, and, if it existed, an extremely wide-angle optic for a large format 4x5 camera. However, since most medium and large format photographers are familiar with the 35mm lens equivalents, and camera manufacturers usually list specifications for digital camera lenses by the 35mm format equivalent, I'll use that also as a reference when mentioning a specific focal length.

Most of the time I don't refer to a specific focal length in this book, but talk about lenses in more general terms. Here is a quick guide to my terminology expressed in terms of full-frame (35mm) focal lengths:

Ultra wide angle	14-16mm
Very wide angle	17-20mm
Wide angle	24-28mm
Semi wide angle	~35mm
Normal	~50mm
Short telephoto	85-105mm
Medium range zoom	70-200mm
Long telephoto	300mm and above

Keeping Current

We live in a rapidly-changing world: trails become paved, road numbers change, sites become off-limits while new ones open up, and new rules supersede old ones. The rapid pace of these changes is beyond our ability to keep the information in this book current. But the web is our savior because corrections and updates can be found online at: www.phototripusa.com/updates/

Should you notice an error or change in the information supplied, kindly let us know via email to info@phototripusa.com. The entire community will benefit.

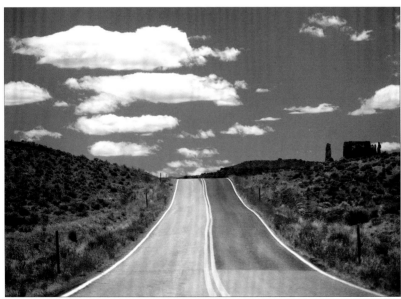

Monsoon clouds are here. Off to the Plateau we go!

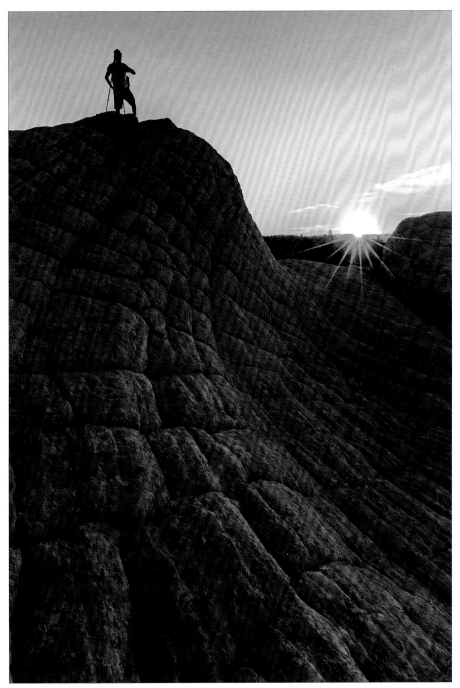

The author at sunrise on Yant Flat © Charles Wood

Chapter 1

AROUND ST. GEORGE

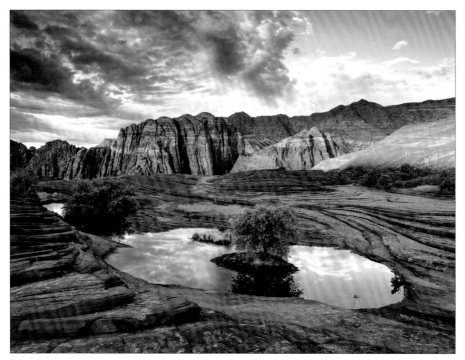

Bonsai Pond

Snow Canyon

Located just a few miles north of St. George, Snow Canyon State Park has seen its visitation skyrocket in recent years due to an influx of population in the St. George area. It has also benefited from the popularity of running, cycling, and rock climbing, and—to a significant extent—the presence of several nearby spa resorts specializing in weight reduction. Despite its relatively small acreage, Snow Canyon packs a tremendous punch of interesting sights along its 4-mile long Scenic Road and numerous trails: intensely colorful sandstone cliffs ranging from white to deep red, lovely pink sand dunes, spectacular cross-bedding alternating with black lava fields, lava caves, and great views from several easily-reached promontories. All this results in excellent photographic opportunities.

Photo advice: The park's diverse colors are best seen in the early morning and from the middle of the afternoon on, but don't go too late or the southern part of the canyon will be in shadow. From the south entrance of the park, begin your visit with short and narrow Jenny's Canyon. Jenny's Canyon is an easy slot canyon, just across the road from the sand dunes. This is a good spot if you've never seen 'Swiss Cheese' style erosion of sandstone. The ½-mile round-trip trail begins at a car park on the east side of the road; just follow the markers on the ground. The trail is closed from March 15 to June 1.

Just across the car park, the sand dunes can be quite nice after a rain or a windy night. Sadly, they are covered by footprints most of the time, which makes taking anything other than detail shots difficult. Next, park just before the campground and hike the picturesque Hidden Pinyon Trail to the overlook, which offers a 360° panorama of the canyon with Red Mountain in the background. You can shoot superb grand scenics from here, or isolate nice perspective shots of the canyon north and south. This walk takes less than 1 hour round-trip.

At the Lava Flow Overlook parking area, about 1½ miles farther north, take the trail leading to the lava beds and tubes and ascend the West Canyon Overlook. From this easily-reached vantage point, you gain another great all-around view. There is some highly photogenic red sandstone cross-bedding all around this overlook. About ¼ mile on the way back to the parking lot, you can take a short side-trip on the White Rocks Trail to your left. Within a few minutes (about ¼ mile), you reach some red and white slickrock making a good foreground for a picture of the park, looking south.

If you are short of time and can do only one walk, my favorite spot in the park is the 1-mile Petrified Dunes Trail, ascending through amazing cross-bedding to ancient petrified dunes peppered with potholes. After a rain, these potholes form pools with nice cloud reflections,—especially scenic at sunrise when the west ridge of the canyon is basked in a warm glow. My favorite view is at 37°12'50" 113°38'45", a spot I like to call Bonsai Pond.

In September, you can observe an extensive Datura bloom along the park road, particularly abundant on the lava fields opposite the campground. Note that Datura are very poisonous.

After exiting the park through the north entrance, drive north for 0.5 mile on UT-18 to a trailhead; the 1-mile round-trip trail leads to an interesting white sandstone amphitheater.

As you drive back toward St. George on UT-18, look for a marked dirt road to the right, about a mile past the park's north entrance. This road leads to the Snow Canyon Overlook, which provides a great bird's eye view of the canyon.

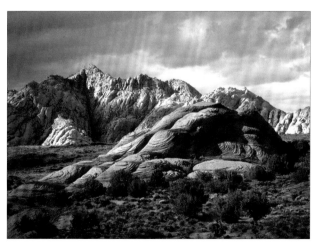

Late summer thunderstorm at sunset © Charles Wood

Getting there: From I-15 northbound, take exit 6 and drive 3.7 miles north on Bluff Street to the intersection with Snow Canyon Parkway. Turn left and drive 4 miles, then turn right onto Snow Canyon Drive, which leads to the south entrance of the park.

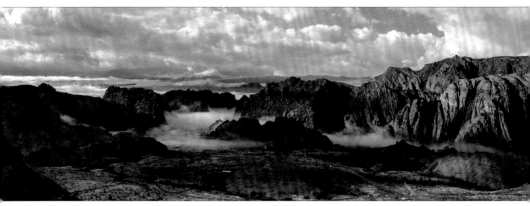

Morning ground fog rolls into Snow Canyon after a heavy rain © *Charles Wood*

From I-15 southbound, take exit 10, turn right off the ramp then left at the light. Follow Red Hills Road for almost 6 miles to UT-18, continuing straight on Snow Canyon Parkway for about 4 miles, then turn right onto Snow Canyon Drive.

Time required: At least 4 hours to drive through the park and do the recommended hikes. There is a very nice campground inside the park for those preferring a starry night over one of the numerous and cheap St. George motels.

Nearby locations: If you think you've seen enough red rock, you may want to immerse yourself for a while in the radically different atmosphere of Pine Valley. There, you'll find a lovely little Mormon community and a pretty alpine valley surrounded by woods. It is a very pleasant location, visited by few other than residents of St. George and surrounding communities. Coming out from Snow Canyon's north entrance, follow UT-18 north for about 15 miles and turn east for another 10 miles until you find Pine Valley Recreation Area. You can also continue past the pretty Pine Valley Reservoir to the campground and hike on the local pack trails.

While in St. George, you are only 30 minutes away from the heart of the spectacular Virgin River Gorge. The gorge has beautiful narrows in its southern part as I-15 crosses the Beaver Dam Mountains southwest of St. George. There is a good rest area and campground about halfway through the gorge, which is the only point where you can take pictures.

Red Mountain

The Red Mountain Trail leads to an overlook with a fantastic bird's-eye view of Snow Canyon and Red Mountain. In many respects, this view is reminiscent of that experienced from Observation Point or the West Rim in Zion National Park and is well worth the moderate effort.

From the trailhead, the first 15-20 minutes are a mild uphill climb on an extremely rocky old Jeep road, fenced-in on both sides, until you reach the Red Mountain Wilderness Area marker. The trail becomes progressively smoother after that and another 15-20 minutes brings you to a junction. The Red Mountain Trail goes on straight ahead; instead, take the left fork with the marker pointing to the Snow Canyon Overlook. Another 10 minutes on this sandy trail brings you to the overlook, with an awesome view of the west arm of Snow Canyon 1400 feet below, and the Arizona Strip in the distance.

Other worthwhile views can also be had from further up on the Red Mountain Trail. Back at the intersection with the Red Mountain Trail, turn left and walk another 15 to 20 minutes (about 0.7 mile) to a series of good vantage points. Continuing south on Red Mountain Trail for another 1½ miles, you arrive at an area of white sandstone with good photographic potential. There is a small pond next to the rim that fills with water after a heavy rain and makes for an interesting photo. Just past the pond, you can climb to a vantage point with some pink slickrock (37°14'16" 113°40'17") overlooking Snow Canyon above West Canyon road.

Photo advice: The best time for photography is in early morning from dawn to sunrise at Snow Canyon Overlook. A wide angle adequately covers the view but makes the end of the canyon too distant; instead I suggest you shoot vertical frames for stitching with a moderate wide angle or a "normal" lens. The very first viewpoint you hit at the end of the trail is the best, but there are other viewpoints to the left you might want to try.

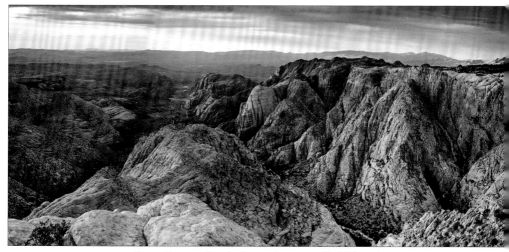

Snow Canyon Overlook, on the way to Red Moutain

For another good vantage point, walk back 150 feet from the rim and ascend the outcrop immediately to the west of the viewpoint (roughly from 37°15'08" 113°39'58"). There is some nicely colored slickrock here that would make a good foreground.

Getting there: From downtown St. George at the intersection of Bluff Blvd. and St. George Blvd., drive north on Bluff St. and set your odometer at the traffic light marking the beginning of UT-18. Drive 11 miles to the marker for the Red Mountain Trailhead. Turn left (west) onto the dirt road leading to the large equestrian car park. The trail starts near the posted map.

Time required: 2½ to 3 hours for the roughly 4.5-mile round-trip to Snow Canyon Overlook, including plenty of time for scouting and photography. Double that if you go as far as the vantage point above the pond.

The Santa Clara River Reserve

The Santa Clara River Reserve is a vast BLM-administered recreational area with an extensive network of well-maintained multiuse trails. At its northern end, the Reserve has a very interesting petroglyph site located at the edge of the Santa Clara Bench, just below the rim. It consists of a classic collection of glyphs: anthropomorphs, bighorn sheep, snakes, etc. carved on large black boulders strewn over about 200 yards. The site's location high above the Santa Clara River makes it even more attractive.

Getting there: From Bluff Street in St. George, turn left onto CR-8 (Sunset

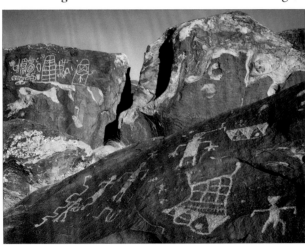

Santa Clara petroglyphs

Blvd.) toward Santa Clara and drive 6.8 miles to the Anasazi Valley Trailhead signpost. Turn left at the gate and continue 0.3 mile to the trailhead. From here, the 1.2-mile Tempi'po'op trail leads gently to the western edge of the site. A number of social trails are clearly visible just below the rim. Pick an easy one and make your way among the dispersed lava boulders in search of photogenic petroglyphs.

Time required: About 2 hours.

Nearby location: Continuing 0.8 mile northwest on CR-8 past the Anasazi Trailhead turnoff, turn right into Kayenta Parkway and follow the signs for the Kayenta Art Village; it has a handful of high-end art galleries including the Earth & Light Photography Gallery whose proprietor, Charles Wood, is one of my main hiking and travel partners as well as a contributor to this book.

Gunlock Mesa

Gunlock Mesa isn't exactly headline material, being as it is in the shadow of Snow Canyon, but it's a little gem well-known to the locals for providing excellent hiking and photography within a dense but spectacular area of sandstone bluffs and canyons. If you are not pressed by time, or if you find Snow Canyon (or Zion) too crowded, you can spend a very nice and productive half-day at Gunlock.

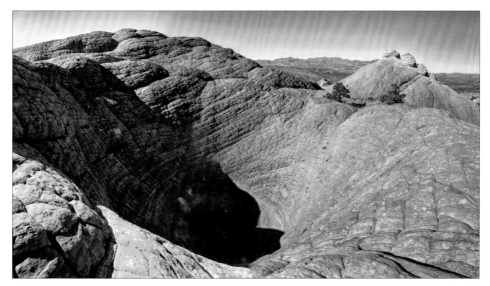

The Vortex, with Camelback in the distance

The mesa is located northeast of Gunlock State Park, which is essentially a large reservoir popular with boaters. In springtime during snowmelt, you'll see waterfalls overflowing from the spillway west of Gunlock Road. In a wet year, these waterfalls can make for very interesting shots. You can park here and walk toward the bottom of the waterfalls or you can park a bit further at the official State Park's car park, pay your fee, and walk along the dam until you reach the spillway.

Heading north on Gunlock Road, take the gravel road to the right just before entering Gunlock. The road ascends steeply to the mesa, soon turning into clay; drive 2.8 miles, make a sharp right just after crossing a small channel and continue for about 0.1 miles to the second car park (use the first one in case it's full). You can see the canyon below and a large photogenic mass of striated sandstone just across it. Follow the trail down, crossing the wash and continuing on the other side. The trail ascends progressively, then more steeply on the sandstone following a photogenic channel. Leave a large mound of sandstone to the right and continue toward 37°16'12" 113°44'50". Find the easy way up and make your way up the ridge following a natural path. You'll encounter

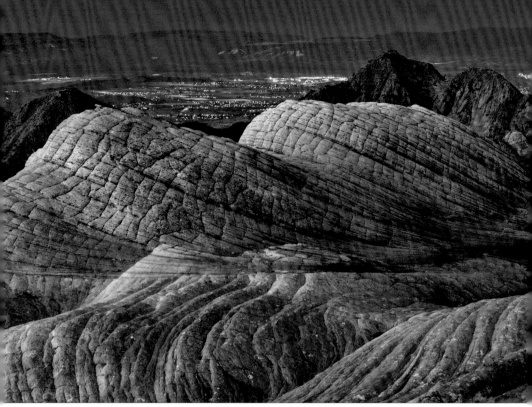

Yant Flat at dawn, looking toward St. George

the Vortex—a peculiar depression thought to have been a sinkhole eons ago—at 37°16'15" 113°44'52 ". Continue past a second, much smaller sinkhole, and stop between the two humps of the Camel's Back for a glorious panoramic view.

Photo advice: Late afternoon is best. An extreme wide angle is needed to take in the entire Vortex. Stitching works but not without some difficulty as you are so close. I partially solved the problem by shooting two rows with a medium-wide focal length to avoid distortion that would have made it difficult to stitch.

Getting there: An alternative is to come from the east on the above-described road. From the north exit of Snow Canyon, continue 7 miles north on UT-18 past Dammeron Valley and turn left on the gravel road at the foot of Veyo Volcano. Drive a little over 5 miles and turn left just before the small channel to the car park.

Time required: About 2½ hours round-trip from the car park with time for enjoyment and photography.

Nearby location: There is an interesting petroglyph panel located at the edge of the Santa Clara Bench, along the road to Gunlock. It consists mainly of a number of anthropomorphs, densely carved on a large boulder perched just above the road. It's a very short walk. Coming from Santa Clara, drive about 3 miles past the junction of Gunlock Road CR-8 and Old Highway 91, aka Beaver Dam Road, and look for a small pullout on the right side, just before mile marker 3. Walk around the corner and look for an old jeep track ascending steeply on the

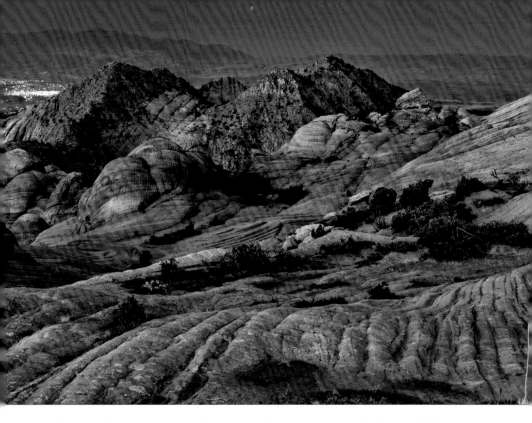

right side. There is more parking space further up on the left side. Walk up the old track for almost 300 yards, then angle steeply right walking back southwest in the direction of the road. You'll find the boulder on the edge of the cliff at 37°13'05" 113°46'35". Its close proximity to the edge of the cliff makes it a challenge to photograph.

Yant Flat

Yant Flat is one of the latest hot spots in the never-ending quest for new icons of the Southwest, and for good reason. It is a spectacular location, easily accessed, with lots of fantastic scenery to shoot.

The Yant Flat area is staggered over several levels. The "Flat" proper is actually the wooded plateau south of the forest road. The area that interests us is actually below the rim of this plateau. The first level down is a vast and incredibly scenic expanse of sandstone, which looks best at dawn and sunrise. The next level consists of sandstone cliffs with intricate patterns and beautiful colors that look best in late afternoon. The next level below is the Cottonwood Wash drainage which is not accessible from here. A day is not sufficient to enjoy Yant Flat thoroughly and photograph the entire site under the best conditions, so you'll have to either spend the night at or near the trailhead, or you'll need to return two or more times, perhaps in different seasons.

Overleaf: Yant Flat at dawn, looking toward Hurricane

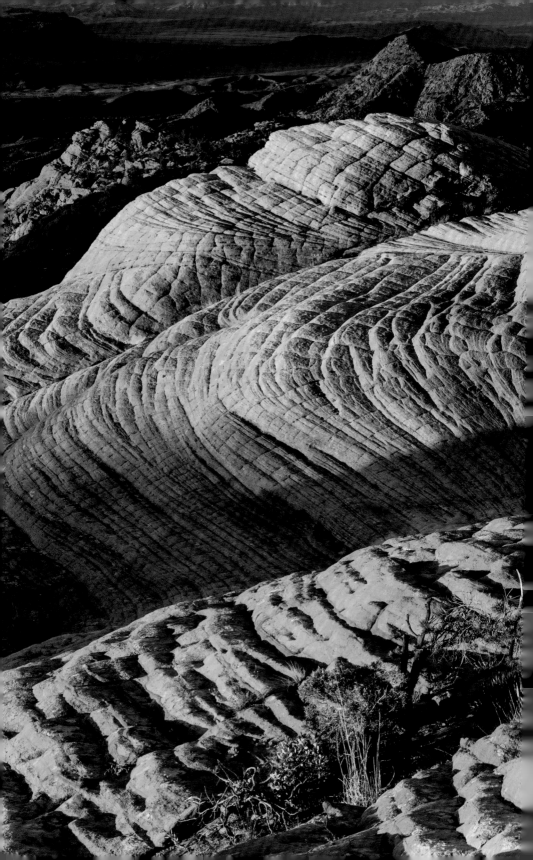

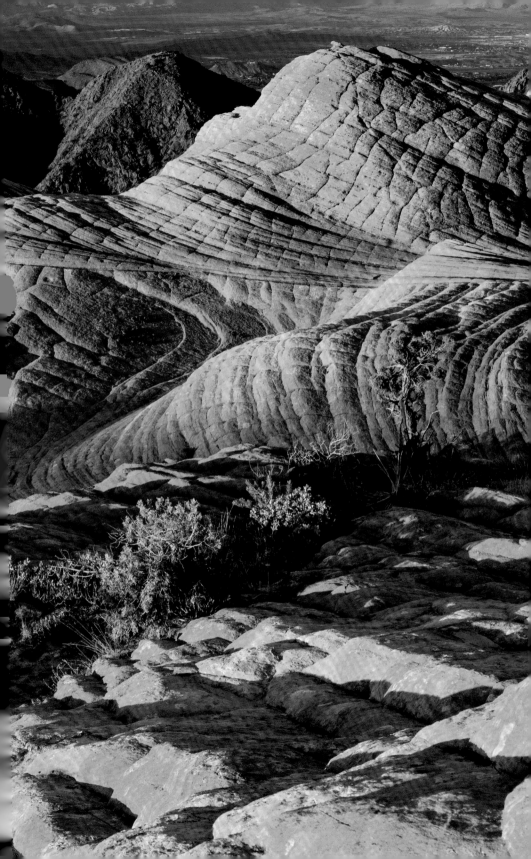

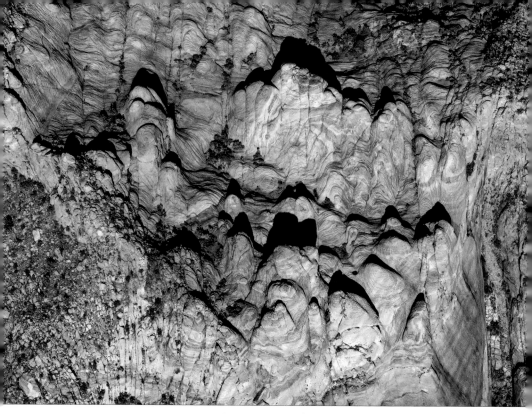

Sunset on Yant Flat

From the trailhead, follow the old Jeep road to the south. Somewhere near 37°13'15" 113°28'21" look for a faint path to the left—this may become a trail by the time you read this. From here, make a beeline to a good entry point to the first level down at 37°13'05" 113°28'08" or another close by at 37°13'06" 113°28'05". Despite the rather thick vegetation, you'll have no problem going in the general direction of these points, and as I said it may have turned into an obvious path. It should take you about 50 minutes (perhaps a little more on a first visit) to cover the roughly 1.5 miles to the rim. You can now contemplate the great potential of the first level and choose where you want to start. Cautiously negotiate the descent on slippery sandy ground and enjoy. For the best light, I recommend that you arrive here at least 35 minutes before sunrise so you can scout a little and be there for the fleeting alpenglow.

For the second level down and the colorful swirls and cliffs—sometimes called Candy Cliffs—just walk down the obvious incline to the southwest, and descend the short narrow crack in front of the big sandstone mound at 37°12'55" 113°28'07". Walk a short distance south past some dinosauresque concretions and follow another crack to a high point where you'll gain a great view westward with lots of beautiful cross-bedding. This view works equally well near sunset. After that, continue less than ten minutes in an easterly direction to a large sandstone mound with yellow and pink swirls. You can circumnavigate the big mound by ascending the sandstone incline from around 37°13'01" 113°27'45" to find interesting shots.

To reach the Rainbow Ridge, continue down-canyon about ¼ mile; the canyon narrows down at a steep angle and you'll have to fend off thick vegetation and possibly some water holes. When you reach the big incline in front of you, continue right for 0.1 mile then ascend steeply to an incredible area of color-ful cross-bedding, swirls, domes, and distant views of Zion. Continue until about

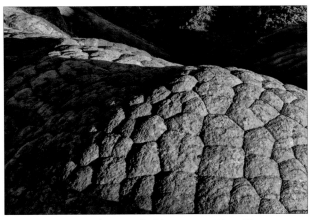

Spectacular cross-bedding in east Yant Flat

37°13'04" 113°27'22" which is as far as you can go, then retrace your steps, looking for more photographic opportunities until sundown in the other direction.

Time permitting or on a future visit, you might also explore the western part of Yant Flat, an area below the rim, south of the end of the Jeep Road. Aim for 37°13'07" 113°28'24" and immediate vicinity. Although less open and not quite as photogenic as a whole, it has some extensive and spectacular cross-bedding and it's a great place to shoot abstracts.

Photo advice: You'll be using many focal lengths, from ultrawide to medium tele-photo. The top level is vast and lends itself well to shooting verticals for stitching in post-processing. The downside is that you will not be able to use your polar-izer, so take single shots too and see later which images you prefer. A polarizer is a must to bring out the color on anything else. Don't forget your headlamp if you go pre-sunrise or return post-sunset.

Getting there: From I-15 northbound, take exit 22. Cross the little town of Leeds for 1.5 miles and turn left under the freeway onto Silver Reef Road just before Exit 23 (reset your odometer). If you're coming from I-15 southbound, take exit 23 and turn right onto Silver Reef Road. Note that exit 23 exists only on the southbound side, so if you're coming from St. George, you must take exit 22 and drive through Leeds. Soon, Silver Reef Road becomes Oak Creek Road. Proceed on Oak Creek Road and at 3.1 miles, bear left onto the Dixie National Forest road toward St. George. Continue on this road until you find the trailhead on the left at about 10.5 miles,

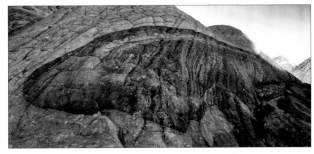

The Candy Cliffs in east Yant Flat

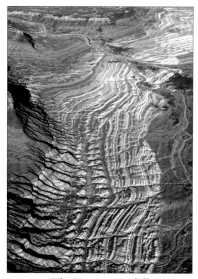

The Hurricane Cliffs

where you can see a dirt road branching to your right, opposite the parking spot. A passenger car will get you there if driven cautiously, although a high clearance vehicle is preferred. The road has steep drop-offs and the last couple of miles are mostly clay, making is impassable after a rain. There are also a couple of sections with sharp stones that could cause some damage to street tires.

I have also used the forest road continuing past the trailhead to St. George. It's in poor condition, making it passable only by high-clearance vehicles or 4WD; it also takes quite a bit longer to drive than the road from Leeds, so don't even bother using this approach.

Time required: A minimum of 3 hours, but you'll likely want to stay 4 to 5 hours or return several times.

Nearby locations: At the base of the Hurricane Cliffs lies a massive display of geologic stratification known as the Hurricane Fault. It is so vast it can only be done justice from the air. Bring out the drone!

Red Cliffs

If you are in the vicinity of St. George and have a couple of hours to spare, consider paying a brief visit to the Red Cliffs Recreation Area. The Red Cliffs are located close to I-15, a few miles northeast of St. George. This small site is heavily patronized by locals on week-ends during spring and fall, due in part to its good campground. It is thus preferable to come during the week so you won't be turned away for lack of available parking (only 33 spots). It will also be easier and more enjoyable to take pictures without the week-end crowds. A 15-minute walk on the Nature Trail leads to a lovely narrow canyon with red slickrock walls and to a small waterfall with some pools and even a swimming hole, depending on water conditions. This particularly photogenic spot has good light without too much contrast from mid-afternoon on. You can easily circumvent

Moki steps © *Philippe Schuler*

the main pool and the waterfall by using the moki steps conveniently carved on the right flank of the canyon; the angle isn't too vertical and a rope is also present to assist you anyway. You can then continue inside the pleasant canyon for a few hundred yards before encountering a dryfall that is too difficult to climb.

Getting there: From St. George and I-15 northbound, take exit 22. At the end of the freeway off-ramp, turn right onto the Old 91 frontage road, travel south 2 miles and turn right after passing the sign for the Red Cliffs R.A. Drive past the two narrow tunnels under I-15 and follow the paved road for 1.3 miles to the campground. If you're coming from I-15 southbound, take exit 23 and turn left onto Silver Reef Road, then right onto Main Street. Travel south for 3.5 miles on Main Street (which turns into Old 91) until the sign for the Red Cliffs R.A.

Time required: 1½ hours with plenty of time for photography.

Kanarra Creek

The hike through the Kanarra Creek Narrows is a fun, easy, and highly rewarding way to experience the typical feeling of a slot canyon with tall red walls, lots of shallow water crossings, nice waterfalls, and lovely reflected light. It can be challenging for some people, however, as they will find two difficult passages with slippery ladders.

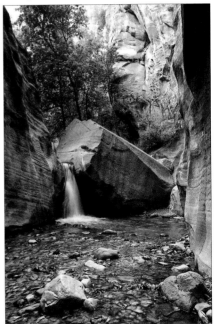

The lower falls

The hike follows the gated dirt road for about a mile from the car park, before joining the creek. From here on, you walk alternatively on the banks and in the stream bed, crossing the creek multiple times before encountering the narrows after about ¾ of a mile. After a short section of narrows you'll come to the first of the lower falls (actually a rock jam) which presents the first obstacle. As of this writing, a new ladder is conveniently wedged on the right side of the falls, with steps for you to climb on and a rope to hang on to. Although there is no guarantee that this ladder will still be there by the time you read this, chances are there will be something in place to help you negotiate the 15-foot drop. This hike is extremely popular with the locals, especially on week-ends and in summer, so you may have to wait in line to climb the ladder. In any case, it's bound to be wet and slippery, so watch your step when climbing up and back down. After passing this obstacle, you'll find the second of the lower falls almost immediately.

These falls are photogenic and you'll want to spend some time here trying various composition/exposure combinations. You can bypass this second set of lower falls by scrambling up on the right side without too much difficulty. However, I found a large pool with chest-deep water during a recent visit. You can continue above for another ¼ mile or so to the photogenic upper falls. In a rainy year, this section may require you to walk in thigh-high, possibly very cold water. It is generally possible to continue past the upper falls, using a ladder that could be in various stages of disrepair, gone altogether after a strong flash flood, or else replaced by some other contraption. Beyond the upper falls, the canyon becomes progressively wider and more verdant, but less rewarding photographically.

Photo advice: At the second lower falls, turn around and in late afternoon, you may catch some nice red light on the wall of the slot just below the falls. At the upper falls, step back to include a small cascade and/or nicely polished round rocks in your shot, depending on the creek's level at the time.

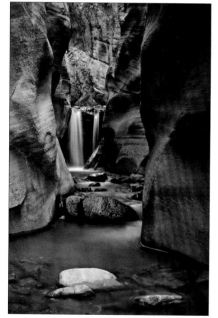

Things can get very wet here, for a variety of reasons. If you carry expensive equipment, I recommend using a dry bag.

Getting there: From Main St. in Kanarraville, turn east on E100 N St. and drive three blocks to the large official parking lot on the left, just below the gated dirt road. There is a $10 parking fee. On hot summer days, the parking could be full and you'd have to use the overflow parking at the town hall (it's free but it adds another mile round-trip to the hike). Don't park anywhere else in town, or you could be ticketed! As of this writing, a small entrance fee is in effect in summer in addition to the parking fee, and the site closes at 7 p.m.

Time required: Allow 4 to 5 hours for the upper falls round-trip, with plenty of time for photography.

Upper falls © Synnatschke Photography

Parowan Gap Petroglyphs

The Parowan Gap is a rather short fault of volcanic origin running across a long sandstone ridge rising out of the desert bed, northwest of the Parowan township. Geologic curiosity aside, it's the large number of petroglyphs lining both walls of the fault that make it attractive to photographers. The Ancestral Puebloans had used the Gap as a form of solar calendar, by noting the position of the sun through the Gap to establish markings of repeated solar and lunar events—a practice that can be observed on several rock art panels throughout the Colorado Plateau. The discovery and established scientific proof of this practice is relatively recent (early 1980s to 1990s) and originated at the Rochester Panel (see *Along I-70* chapter). A pole planted in front of a sandstone face allowed artists and/or shamans to carve the angle of the sun during observable solar events. Such a solar marker also exists at Parowan Gap along with lunar events calendars, but the most striking artwork is the so-called Zipper Glyph, located next to the car park and illustrated in my photograph, which shows 180 tick marks arranged on a V-shaped baseline representing the angle of traverse of the sun between the summer and winter solstices.

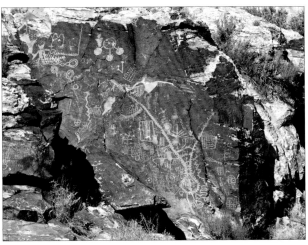

The Zipper panel

Photo advice: Shoot the Zipper glyph whenever the panel is either totally illuminated or in shade. Mid-day should guarantee the former. A polarizing filter will help remove glare and bring out the texture of the glyphs.

Getting there: From Main street in Parowan (accessed from Exit 75 on I-15), turn west onto W400 North St., which turns into Gap Rd. after passing under the freeway. Continue on this road for almost 10 miles to reach the Gap.

Time required: 2 hours round-trip from Parowan should suffice to shoot the Zipper Glyph and a few other panels.

Pine Park

Pine Park is a highly photogenic site tucked in a remote part of Utah, close to the Nevada state line. The best way to describe this site is through analogies to similar looking locations. Think Kasha-Katuwe Tent Rocks National Monument in New Mexico, or Wheeler Geologic Area in Colorado (see *Photographing the Southwest - Vol. 3* for both).

The whitish geologic formations are spread out over several areas and I have not bothered exploring those that were far from the road. Apart from the area near the campground, which I found of little interest, there are two sections that are close to the road and offer great photographic potential.

Photo advice: I suggest you adopt the following strategy for your visit. First off, you should be at the site in mid to late afternoon. Drive all the way to the campground, stopping briefly along the way to observe the different groups of formations and get a feel for the place. The campground is primitive, with a single

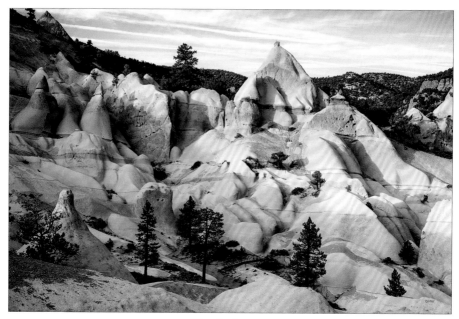

Pine Park sunset

table and no restrooms, but it is pleasant, shaded by pine trees. At this point you can decide whether to stay the night or go elsewhere.

Drive back from the campground—passing the first spectacular site on your right for now—and park off the road at the second site located at 37°31'39" 114°01'51". This site has some interesting "tents" bordering the road, looking like they've been chiseled into a multitude of facets. The main attraction of this site, however, is that you can shoot very interesting abstracts. This can be accomplished by walking around the southern tip of the formations, then locating an obvious channel/ramp beginning about 80 feet east from your car and leading north to a platform. From here, you can shoot the formations shown in the picture to the left in a northwesterly direction.

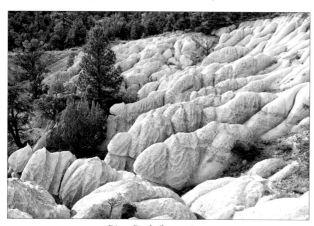

Pine Park formations

No less than thirty minutes before sunset, drive back to the first site and park at the pullout at 37°31'29" 114°01'42" to photograph the domes to the northwest, basking in a warm sunset light.

Getting there: From St. George, take UT-18 for 40 miles to Enterprise, or if coming from Cedar City, take UT-56 for 35 miles, then turn south (left) on UT-18 and drive 11 miles to Enterprise. From Center St. in Enterprise, head west on UT-219 for 15.6 miles. For the last 4.6 miles, UT-219 turns into Crestline Road, becoming a wide, well-graded gravel road. Turn left on the dirt road named Enterprise Road. Drive 0.8 mile, leaving Enterprise Road to the right and drive straight ahead at the sign for Pine Park. Continue on this good dirt road for 9 miles to its dead end at the tiny campsite.

Time required: About a couple of hours on site, not including driving time.

Cathedral Gorge

From St. George, it is easy to make a short foray to this spectacular Nevada State Park located close to the state line. The so-called "gorge" is actually a long, narrow depression flanked by tall eroded spires forming majestic stone cathedrals. The park has two entrances along the highway.

The south entrance, closest to town, provides access to the alluvial floodplain at the bottom end of the gorge. This part of the gorge puts you at eye level with the formations, with several interesting groups along the park road, past the fee station.

Narrow slot canyons carved by erosion twist and turn between the spires, leading deep inside the flanks of the gorge, inviting exploration. All these natural pathways eventually end up in impassable cul-de-sacs, so there is no risk of getting lost. It is great fun—as well as a welcome relief from the brutal sun—to explore these mysterious, shaded corridors. Beware the surprising hardness of the material, however, as it is easy to cut yourself on jagged edges as you scramble around. Parents should also watch their young children, as there are plenty of rises and depressions that could trigger a fall.

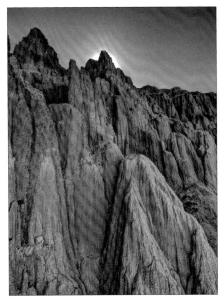

The north entrance leads to Miller Point, at the end of a small mesa. The viewpoint provides a birds eye view of the highly eroded beginning of the gorge. From here you can go down the Miller Point Trail to explore some of the narrow canyons bordering the wash and continue 1 mile to the picnic area.

Photo advice: I recommend the vicinity of the picnic area for most of your photography, both inside and outside the eroded canyons.

For the outside of the formations on the east side, late afternoon is the best time,

Cathedral Gorge spires

although sunrise works well too for formations located on the west flank. Brutal mid-day light should be avoided at all cost. The jagged stone cathedrals tend to look more impressive with some compression, using a standard lens or telephoto. To photograph the slots on the inside, use a very wide angle lens. Detail

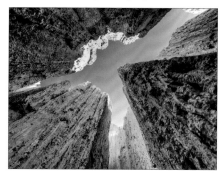

extractions work well in the shade if you avoid including the sky. Mid-morning and mid-afternoon light is best, but even midday light is acceptable.

Cathedral slot canyon

Getting there: Follow the instructions to Pine Park (see previous section), staying on Crestline Road into Nevada until it joins UT-319. Continue to Panaca, then turn north on US-93. The south entrance is 0.9 mile from US-93 junction. The north entrance is 2.1 miles further.

Nearby location: A bit further north, the old mining town of Pioche has some interesting history and is well worth a stop.

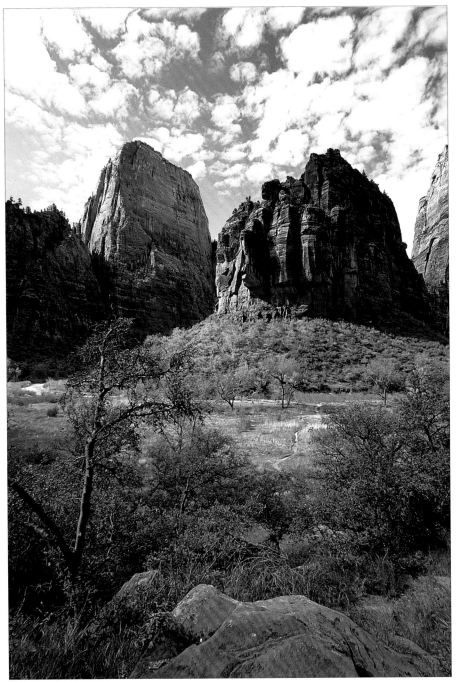

The Organ & the Great White Throne

Chapter 2

INSIDE ZION

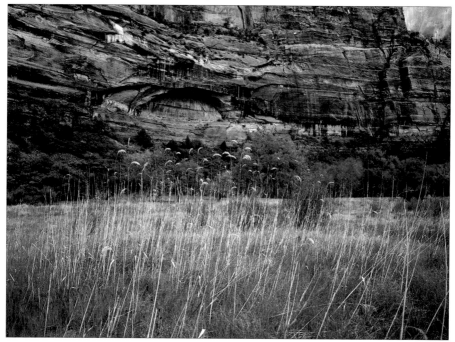

Tallgrass & Alcove in Zion Canyon

Introduction to Zion National Park

Zion is often the first national park visited by travelers making the "Grand Circle" of national parks in Utah and Arizona. It's a spectacular introduction to the discovery of the Colorado Plateau.

For the visitor with little time, the park consists of essentially two parts: the canyon and the plateau.

The canyon is deeply cut (between 2,000 and 2,500 feet), which doesn't make for easy photography because of the great contrast between the sunlit summits and the valley plunged in deep shadow. The NPS has instituted a mandatory shuttle service to reduce the congestion and pollution in the canyon's interior, thus putting an end to everyone's misery trying to find a parking spot at the popular locations. The service is running smoothly and will deliver you and your camera gear to the location of your choice in the canyon in a much healthier frame of mind. From late March to early November as well as week-ends in November, private vehicles are not allowed on the Scenic Drive. Shuttle schedules vary depending on the season and may be subject to change. As of this writing, shuttles run from 6 AM (from the Visitor Center) to 9:15 PM (from the Temple of Sinawava) with an average wait of 15 minutes or less during peak hours.

The shuttle trip to the end of the canyon takes 45 minutes. Note that the Visitor Center's parking area is usually full by mid-morning. In that case, you must first take another shuttle from Springdale to the Visitor Center. While in Springdale, you should make it a point to visit Michael Fatali's gallery for a look at his beautiful and inspiring images.

If you are visiting by car outside the mandatory shuttle season, you can travel with the sun as it crosses the valley and harvest a great crop of photos. If you travel by RV, note that there are parking restrictions in the canyon and you will need an escort to go through the tunnel on Scenic Byway 9.

If possible, the most interesting way to arrive in Zion is by way of the plateau from the east entrance, since the views are particularly spectacular coming from Mt. Carmel. In addition, illumination is best in the morning at the principle viewpoints of the plateau.

If you follow this advice, you have two possibilities: Visit Zion at the end of your "Grand Circle" or make a detour through Kanab. In practice, spending the night at Kanab or Mt. Carmel Junction is very doable if you leave from Los Angeles or Salt Lake City in the morning. If you leave from Las Vegas, you are only three hours from Zion and you'll be hard pressed to resist the attraction of starting from the canyon.

I will begin our visit at the Visitor Center, but the choice is up to you. In any case, the universe of Zion will not disappoint you!

Towers of the Virgin

At sunrise, this is the most beautiful panorama in Zion. If you love beautiful light on rock walls, you won't be disappointed. The sun penetrates the valley through the Pine Canyon fault and bathes the summits of the temples in a warm light. Station yourself directly behind the Zion Museum and mount a semi-wide lens. This will allow a tight framing of the West Temple, the Sundial, the Temple of the Virgin and the Altar of Sacrifice and keep the shadowy zone at the bottom of the photo to a minimum. I prefer the left side of the railing, which shows less of the rather unsightly trail crossing the empty field. A graduated neutral density filter is mandatory in order to maintain detail in the shadowy zone and to conserve the vibrant red and gold color of the high walls. If you don't have one, but are shooting digital, you can bracket a series of shots and later on digitally assemble the best exposed fore-

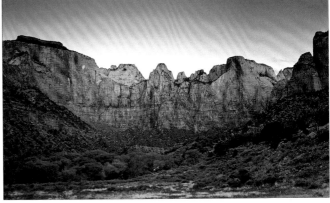

Towers of the Virgin at dawn

ground with a perfectly exposed shot of the golden wall. You can also crop your image into a panoramic format excluding much of the foreground. You'll have about ten minutes before the sun rays irradiate the summits with so much light that the shot gets lost. If you are spending the night close by, in Springdale or in Zion, this sunrise vista is a must. Note that even during shuttle season, you are allowed to drive as far as the Museum and park there.

Another good place to photograph the Towers is from the end of the Canyon Overlook Panorama trail, just above the great alcove.

The Watchman

The Watchman is one of the most photographed icons of Zion National Park—a trophy shot that almost everyone feels obligated to have in their col-

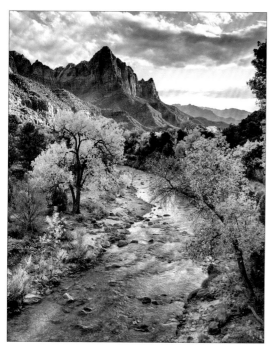

The Watchman & fall colors

lection. The Watchman is a sunset location and there are two good locations for shooting it at that time of day. The closest one is to take the moderate 2-mile round-trip Watchman trail from the Visitor Center, leading to a promontory high above the campgrounds from where it is easy to view and photograph it. Unfortunately, your foreground will be limited to a few bushes, trees and protruding rocks. Not a bad shot, but perhaps not as spectacular as the next one.

The second and most popular location is the bridge near the Canyon Junction shuttle stop. This easy vantage point provides a rather distant view of the glowing mountain face but allows you to include the river and lush vegetation in your vertical framing. I'll grant you that it is a major "cliché" picture,

but it's a classic beauty and there is nothing wrong in having a bit of fun shooting it alongside many other photographers. For a touch of originality, this is a good scene to experiment with in post-processing, if you are so inclined.

Photo advice: A wide to semi-wide angle will allow you to frame the Watchman vertically with some foreground from the promontory at the end of the Watchman trail. A variety of focal lengths can be employed from the bridge.

Nearby location: The Pa'rus Trail is an easy but rewarding 1.7-mile trail between the Canyon Junction shuttle stop and the Visitor Center. The paved trail follows the Virgin River downstream, offering fine views of Bridge Mountain and the Watchman. There is a good photo spot from the river access located behind the South Campground.

Court of the Patriarchs

Zion Canyon reveals its entire splendor slowly as the sun climbs over the surrounding peaks. After sunrise behind the Museum, your first stop on the scenic drive should be to view the Court of the Patriarchs. You'll get the best results between sunrise and mid-morning. At the end of a short trail, you arrive at a viewpoint where you can photograph the Patriarchs with a wide-angle lens. A wide angle is essential to include all three summits. You can also get equally good results with a 28 or even a 35 mm, though you won't be able to fit in more than two of the Patriarchs. Finally, a short telephoto lens will let you isolate them individually.

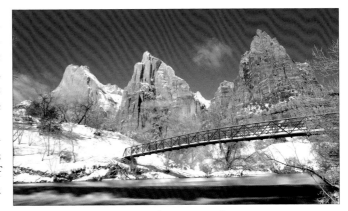

The Three Patriarchs

Although the official viewpoint provides an adequate view of the Patriarchs, it has a rather mundane foreground of tree branches, which will turn completely black on your image when the Patriarchs are best lit in the morning. There is a nicer spot across the road, next to the footbridge leading to the Sand Bench Trail. From here, the Patriarchs assume an interesting triangular shape, looking almost like three symmetrical arrowheads when framed with a very wide angle lens.

Emerald Pools

The Emerald Pools, especially the lower one, are heavily visited and can be reached by a trail of a little over a mile, round-trip, from the Zion Lodge. Or you can take one of about 2 miles, round-trip, from the Grotto parking area. Add another mile, round-trip, if you decide to hike to the upper pools. For most visitors, the attraction of this spot rests in the water droplets raining on you from the main wall of the lower pool—a great source of fun for all. In summer, you'll find it quite pleasant to rest under the maple trees and bask in the fine mist of

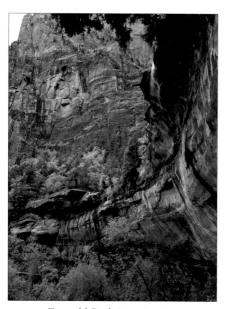

Emerald Pools in springtime

water enveloping you. For the photographer, the main attraction is also the two waterfalls coming out of the Lower Pool, but you'll need a decent flow of water to produce a good photograph. I recommend that you come via the middle trail, by turning left past the footbridge near the Zion Lodge. After having negotiated the switchbacks, you'll gain superb open views of the southern part of the canyon from about halfway up the trail. As you reach the pools, you'll also cross an open area with a nicely polished rock surface, affording a really nice view looking down toward the lodge. Walk down toward the lower trail. There are some very good spots at the edge of the trail leading under the waterfalls, although your back will be against the wall and you'll need a wide-angle lens to frame the entire scene. The waterfalls are best photographed in spring and summer or after a rain. They may be reduced to a trickle if it hasn't rained for a while or may even be non-existent.

The upper pool is another mile round-trip and leads to a waterfall with a year-round flow, cascading down a huge red cliff. It is often in the shade and difficult to photograph, but definitely worth the trip to get a close view of the sheer cliffs of Zion. If your time is very limited, however, you'll be better off staying at the Lower Pools and exploring different compositions rather than going to the Upper Pool. To return to the shuttle or your vehicle, continue under the waterfalls on the short Lower Trail. As the walk to Lower Emerald Pools is easy, consider doing it either before (from the Lodge) or after (from the Grotto) your visit to Angels Landing. The walk to the Upper Pool is a bit harder.

Angels Landing

Because of its central location, this is the most beautiful view of Zion Canyon. To access it requires good physical condition and some exertion, but above all, heights must not make you dizzy. The round-trip from the Grotto parking area is about 5 miles. You'll start your ascent following the steep switchbacks of the West Rim Trail before reaching the welcome shade of Refrigerator Canyon. Scaling another series of switchbacks, you arrive at the first viewpoint, Scout Lookout, where you have an exceptional and very steep view of the upper part of the Canyon's meanders, as well as of the Temple of Sinawava. The next five hundred yards require a lot of effort as you painstakingly move forward up a stunning trail, which is more of a rock flank. Chains are anchored in the rock for use as hand holds. Those who are rebuked by the steep climb to the summit should nonetheless consider tackling the first camel hump past Scout Lookout, known as the Neck, to reach the base of the main climb. This part of the hike is only mildly challenging and the view from the base is spectacular, with the almost vertical narrow spine of Angels Landing close to your lens and a good open view of the canyon.

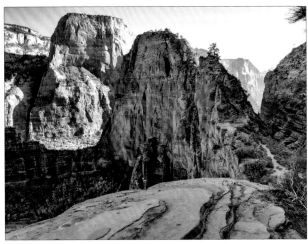

Angels Landing from Scout Lookout

The vista from the top of Angels Landing is sensational and well worth the effort. You can see the entrance to Zion Canyon opening up to the right, while in the center you get a breathtaking view of the Great White Throne. To the left, the canyon meanders toward the Temple of Sinawava.

Photo advice: Angels Landing is always difficult to photograph unless you have a slightly overcast sky or lots of clouds. In the morning, you'll be shooting against the sun and in late afternoon, the western side of the canyon will be in shadow. The best time to shoot is in mid-afternoon. You'll need an ultrawide-angle lens in order to encompass the Great White Throne and part of the canyon. Returning from Angels Landing, you should make it a point to follow the West Rim Trail up for roughly 0.3 mile past Scout Lookout to take advantage of several photogenic viewpoints offering side views of Angels Landing and an open view of the Great White Throne

Time required: 3 hours round-trip. Caution: The end of this trail is not recommended for anyone prone to vertigo. If you have any doubts, skip the end and stay at Scout Lookout, which also offers nice views of the canyon to the north and east. Don't wear sneakers on this hike! You'll need good traction for the end of the trail past Scout Lookout.

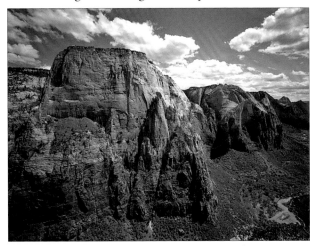

The Great White Throne © *Scott Walton*

Hidden Canyon

Do not let yourself be intimidated by the spectacular switchbacks leading up from the Weeping Rock parking area. The slope may be steep but the trail—about 1-mile long to the entrance of the canyon—is excellent and the going is fairly easy if you pace yourself. You should know, however, that the upper part of the trail just before reaching Hidden Canyon can be very intimidating to people with fear of heights. Soon after the turnoff to Observation Point, you'll find yourself skirting the edge of the canyon on a somewhat precipitous path. Fortunately, there are chains to hang on to at the most exposed spots. You reach the entrance to the canyon after crossing a very short but pretty little slot canyon with beautiful pools of water.

Once inside the canyon, things get cool and quiet in the shadow of a huge wall of sandstone to your right. This is actually the side of the Great White Throne. There are some minor obstructions along the way that can be easily circumvented. However, shortly after the little arch, the canyon becomes obstructed by larger and larger chokestones and you'll have to go back.

Photo advice: The canyon has colorful eroded walls, a nice variety of vegetation, and offers plenty to photograph, even in the middle of day. There is an interesting arch ½ mile to your right. Hidden Canyon is also an excellent location for abstracts.

Time required: At least 2 hours round-trip from the parking area.

Nearby location: From the same Weeping Rock parking area, a short trail leads behind a curtain of water droplets falling from the rock face—the end result of a two-year voyage through the porous rock. Twenty minutes should be enough for a brief visit. I find Weeping Rock particularly interesting in winter when the seeping water forms a long ribbon of icicles reminiscent of fine lace.

Observation Point

This is an exhilarating hike to the highest vantage point in the park. The view of the canyon is stunning, although more distant and less central than the one from Angels Landing. Angels Landing actually looks surprisingly low from here. The view to the left is of the top of Cable Mountain and the Great White Throne.

Most people visit Observation Point by hiking up from the Weeping Rock trailhead in the main canyon. It's a long slog to get there, with over 2100 feet of elevation gain; it feels more like a 10-miler than the actual 8 miles round-trip of the hike. There is a steep 1½ miles of switchbacks past mile 2 (near the junction with the East Rim Trail) before you reach the plateau. This section can be hard under full sun. After another easy half-mile on level ground, you'll experience a distinct feeling of elation when you reach the end of the trail and take in the

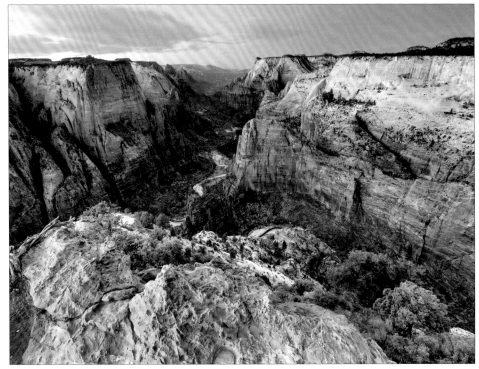

Zion Canyon at dawn from Observation Point

awesome view! For those without the time or interest in going all the way, the section of the trail between mile 1.2 and 2 is particularly scenic, with sheer vertical walls and fine views of the Echo slot canyon. This hike can be combined with the Hidden Canyon hike, with which it shares the first part of the trail (from the junction add about a 1½ hours round-trip).

To really do justice to Observation Point, I recommend a night hike to catch sunrise at the vista point. Leaving Weeping Rock around 4:30 a.m. on the first day after the end of the mandatory shuttle and taking my time, I arrived forty minutes before sunrise. It was a very enjoyable walk thanks to the cool temperature. Hiking at night presents no difficulty on the very well-maintained trail, as long as you have a good headlamp (although you'd still have to go slow and exercise much caution). Your reward will be a much more interesting mood than during daytime, as well as complete solitude to enjoy sunrise.

This sunrise hike from Weeping Rock is not possible during the mandatory shuttle system between late March and early November, as there is no shuttle so early in the morning. An excellent alternative is to come by way of the East Mesa Trail, starting north of Zion Ponderosa Ranch Resort. The trail is well-maintained and easy to follow (a former jeep track for the first mile or so), with very little elevation gain. It brings you to the junction with the Observation Point trail in about 3 miles, only 0.3 mile shy of the viewpoint. On the way back, take a peek at the head of Mystery Canyon, a top destination for canyoneers, which merits a photo if conditions are right. If you'd like to do the thru-hike to Observation Point and down to Weeping Rock in the canyon during the day, you can arrange for the Ponderosa Ranch people to bring you to the trailhead and pick you up at the Zion Canyon Visitor Center. You can also arrange a shuttle with an outfitter in Springdale.

As a third option, and again with a car shuttle, hiking the East Rim trail from Zion's East Entrance to Weeping Rock can include a side trip to Observation Point. Most people do it as a backpack, but the 15-mile day hike including Observation Point is quite doable if you are a strong hiker (see *East Rim* section).

Photo advice: The panoramic view is awesome but a bit distant. A very wide angle is needed to capture the whole scene, but tends to make features such as Angels Landing look even farther. You may want to try shooting for stitching with a standard lens. You'll also get better photos if clouds are present.

Getting there: The trail from the Canyon starts at the Weeping Rock shuttle stop. For the East Mesa Trail, take North Fork Road, located about 2.4 miles east of the East Entrance station on UT-9; drive about 5.2 miles and enter the Ponderosa Ranch Resort entrance. Continue on the unpaved Pine Angle road past the resort for almost 1.5 miles and turn north (right) continuing another 1.5 miles to the Park boundary. The car park is at 37°17'48" 112°54'03", just north of marker 6495 on your USGS topo map. If you're driving a passenger car, you should stop at the resort's desk to check for current road condition, as the last 0.6 mile is a bit treacherous.

Time required: About 4 to 6 hours round-trip from the Weeping Rock parking area. About 3 to 4 hours round-trip from the East Mesa trailhead. About 6 hours for the thru-hike from the East Mesa trailhead to Weeping Rock.

Photo Point

The Great White Throne is without doubt one of the most recognizable symbols of Zion National Park. Unfortunately, it does not allow itself to be photographed as easily as you would like. There are two vantage points: the first one is called Photo Point. It is located just 40 feet down from an unnamed car park, with a spectacular alcove on the other side of the road. A short walk heading northwest along the road from Weeping Rock is required during the mandatory shuttle season to reach this car park. The other viewpoint is Big Bend, which is a regular shuttle stop and a prime spot for fall colors.

Photo advice: Photo Point offers an unobstructed view of the Great White Throne, the Organ, and Angels Landing to the right. Whether you keep to the perfectly satisfactory view from Photo Point, or choose to stroll toward the bank of the Virgin River, the view is always spectacular. The best lighting is still in mid-afternoon, but new sensor technology now allows you to shoot early in the day, when the canyon is shrouded in shadow and later in the evening, when it is backlit. Many years ago, it took me many visits to Zion to finally get the right light and a picture I was satisfied with. Today, it's easy to just open up the shadows and get a perfectly good image. I like to shoot from Photo Point with a very wide angle.

During springtime, tallgrass grows between the viewpoint and the bank of the Virgin, forming a beautiful foreground to shoot the alcove located on the east side of the road, behind the parking spot.

Big Bend Viewpoint is farther up in the direction of the Temple of Sinawava. It allows a rectangular framing of the throne between two walls of the canyon. To the right is the sheer east face of Angels Landing, where you can occasionally spot climbers doing the two-day ascent. This is a great location during fall colors.

Temple of Sinawava

This remarkable area, located at the end of Zion Canyon, is one of those special spots that evokes a mystical and spiritual connection with nature. The happy traveler, intoxicated by the succession and variety of the panoramas of Canyon Overlook, the Towers, the Patriarchs and brief glimpses of the Great White Throne, attains a sort of nirvana when reaching the Temple of Sinawava.

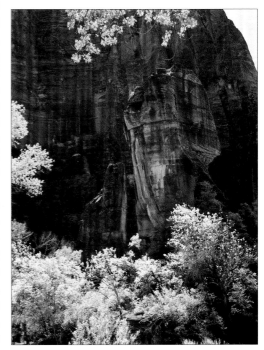

The Pulpit rises in the middle of a cove formed by the river. As a result of the twists and turns of the canyon, its lighting is mediocre in the morning and evening. Try timing your arrival for early afternoon, which is the best time to photograph it. Directly from the parking area, you'll have nice reflected light striking the pulpit on the parking side. I find that a normal lens to very short telephoto works best to photograph the Pulpit from here.

Another good location is from the last bend of the road before the parking area. This is a good place to photograph the Pulpit during fall colors or in springtime when the cottonwoods start to bloom. For the ultimate shot, be there just after a hard rain when the waterfall is active behind the Pulpit. A short telephoto will let you capture the foliage of the cottonwoods, the reddish pulpit and, in the background, the darker walls of the canyon.

The Pulpit at the Temple of Sinawava

Overleaf: Winter view from Photo Point

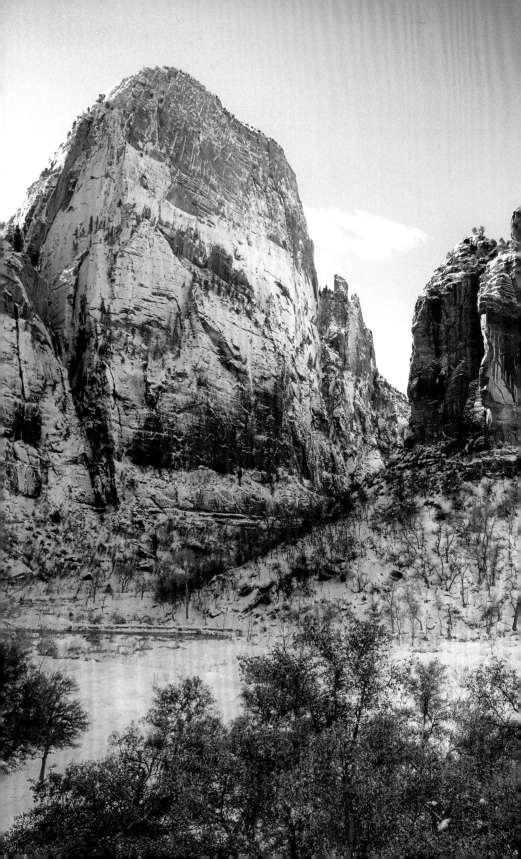

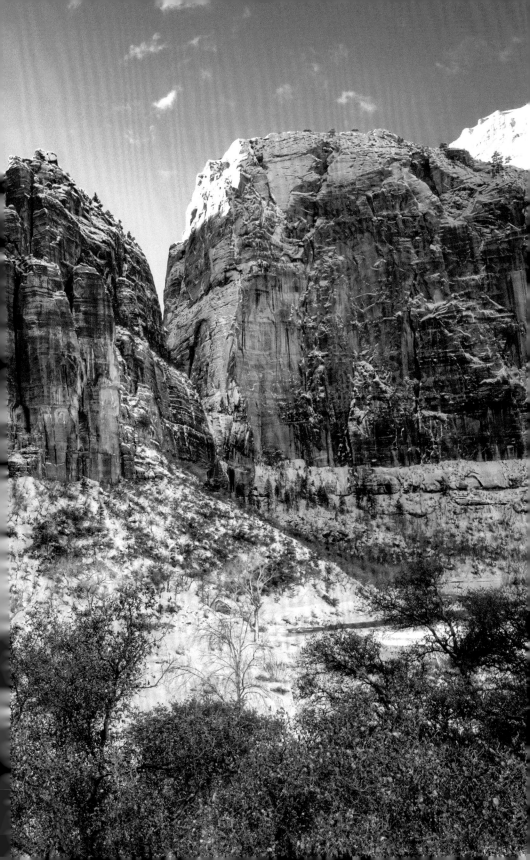

Further on, the 1-mile long surfaced Riverside Walk leads to the Gateway to the Narrows, the entrance to the Virgin River Narrows. The trail, which follows the bank of the Virgin River, offers magnificent views in the spring and early summer, as well as later in autumn when the foliage changes color. At about the halfway point, you'll go past a small cascade worth photographing if it is full.

The Virgin Narrows

It's an indelible experience to go up the Virgin Narrows for 1½ hours or so until you reach the confluence with Orderville Canyon. One of the main draws of the Narrows resides in the fact that you are almost constantly immersed in the Virgin River, often up to your knees and sometimes higher. This contributes immensely to the high fun factor of this great hike, although it may be quite strenuous when the water level is high—especially when walking upstream against the current. Outside of summer, the Virgin River can be very cold or its water level too high, so the vast majority of people hike during summer. If you do not want crowds, summer is not the best time; you will also run the risk of flash flooding in July and August. At the entrance to the Narrows, there is a sign-post warning of the potential risks of flash floods and rating the danger for the day. Permits are not required for day-hikers, but the Park Service strictly forbids walking the narrows on days when a storm is threatening. Keep in mind that the risk of thunderstorms is statistically higher after midday than in the morning. Planning your visit to the Narrows in the morning also allows you to avoid the crowds and to leave time for other sites later in the day.

If you happen to be there off-season, don't let yourself be deterred by air and water temperature. With the proper equipment, you can easily hike the narrows year-round. You can rent a dry suit, as well as neoprene socks and canyoneering shoes, to make the experience safe and enjoyable, although a good pair of hik-ing boots with good ankle support will also do the job. Under a certain water temperature, this equipment becomes absolutely indispensable and several places rent equipment in Springdale. Using a dry suit, I have hiked the narrows in late autumn and early spring and have never felt cold, even in water temperatures below 45°F. You should also consider taking a pair of trekking poles to probe the riverbed for treacherous rocks or holes and to keep your balance if the current is strong. A walking stick is fine but doesn't give anywhere near the stability of two trekking poles. If you carry an expensive camera system, you'll find the trekking poles worthwhile. Two poles will also give you much better speed, an asset if you want to go all the way to Big Springs and take a lot of pictures. Otherwise, there is often a stockpile of pretty rough sticks at the end of Riverside Walk, from which you can borrow.

At the beginning and the end of the mandatory shuttle season, the tim-ing and logistics of a hike in the Narrows can be a bit more complicated.

Opposite page: Early morning inside the Virgin Narrows

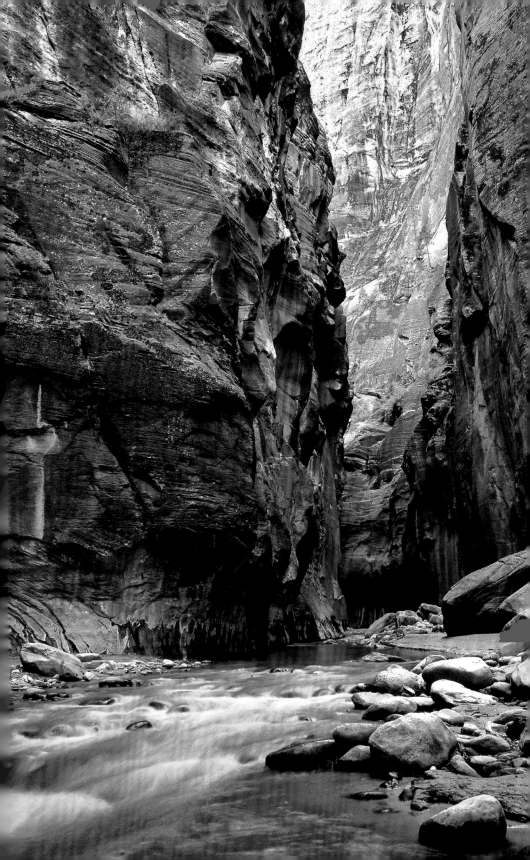

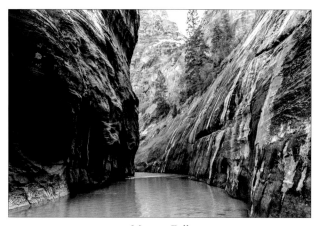

Mystery Falls

The water temperature may be cold enough to require a dry suit. However without the presence of your car you cannot change into canyoneering gear at the Temple of Sinawava parking area, nor can you leave your belongings in your car, then switch back when you come out of the Narrows for other hikes inside the canyon. You'll need to leave properly equipped from the Visitor Center and return there with the shuttle in order to recover the equipment that you didn't take with you into the narrows (clothing, food, perhaps bigger and better photographic equipment) before returning into the canyon for other strolls. If your schedule is flexible, you may want to consider hiking the Narrows at the tail end or just prior to the start of the mandatory shuttle season.

The complete descent of the Virgin Narrows from Chamberlain's Ranch requires two full days as well as preparations and logistics beyond the scope of this book.

Photo advice: I have to admit that it is cumbersome to carry a tripod into the narrows. It is one more heavy item on top of an already loaded backpack and setting it up and packing it away each time you take a photograph requires serious calisthenics. After a few images, however, you'll get the hang of it: dump the trekking poles, remove the backpack, deploy the tripod, attach the camera, compose

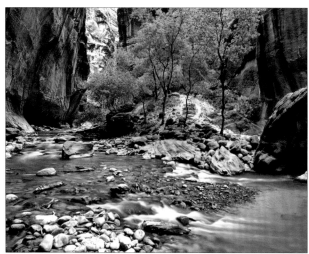

Inside the Narrows © *Momo Vuyisich*

and shoot and then repeat the whole maneuver backwards. It's a chore but that's what you have to do if you want to bring back images with good depth of field, shadow detail and beautiful water action. On the other hand, if you do not intend to enlarge your pictures too much and don't mind black areas with no detail, you can certainly get away with a fast ISO setting and shoot handheld. For less ambitious photography, this is

also a perfect place for a small digital camera. Just remove it from your pocket when
an opportunity presents itself and the zoom
will let you take excellent pictures of people
and scenery. If you are taking an expensive
camera, protect it in an airtight plastic bag.
Should you take an accidental spill, you'll
be glad water didn't get into it.

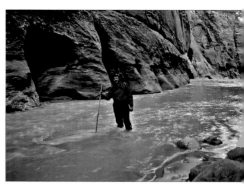

Hiking the Zion Narrows

Reflected light in the Narrows is at
its best in early to mid-morning during summertime and around mid-day in
late autumn and early spring. There is
outstanding photography at almost every
corner. Remember to look back often, you may be surprised at how light forms
a beautiful golden veil over the sandstone from a certain angle. Also, you'll be
surprised how the slightest trace of reflected light on a wall will give you excellent
results using long exposures.

One of the nice features of the Narrows of the Virgin River is also the opportunity to take photos of people wading in the water, fording the narrows.

Time required: If you are short of time, a 1-hour round-trip from the Gateway
to the Narrows will suffice to get a glimpse of the place and take some nice shots
around Mystery Canyon Falls. A 2½ to 4-hour round-trip is necessary to reach
the junction of Orderville Canyon—the final destination for most visitors. If you
choose to explore Orderville Canyon, be aware that after an initial easy walk you
will encounter many obstructions along the way, requiring you to do quite a bit
of scrambling. Instead, I recommend that you continue in the main canyon; its
narrowest section begins soon after passing Orderville Canyon and ends roughly
½ mile before Big Springs. Such a trip, from the Gateway to the edge of the
Narrows and back, takes about 6 to 8 hours with ample time for photography.
If you start at daybreak, this would also put you back at the Temple of Sinawava
at an excellent time for good reflected light on the Pulpit.

Canyon Overlook Panorama

About 5 miles from the east entrance station, you reach this viewpoint from
a parking area located just before the entrance to the tunnel. The pretty trail is
about a mile long round-trip, with interesting views of the beginning twists and
turns of Pine Canyon, a favorite slot for canyoneers. The viewpoint overhangs
the Great Arch, which is in fact an alcove, that you can see and photograph while
descending the switchbacks leading into the valley. From this often windy viewpoint, you'll gain a bird's eye view of the entrance to Zion Canyon. The view is
sometimes hazy, but very pretty on a clear day. Pine Creek and the switchbacks
of the main road are visible below, but they only become sunlit in mid-morning

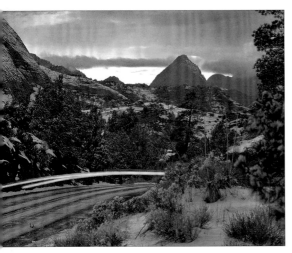

Winter twilight on Zion Plateau

during the summer and the middle of the day in winter. Very early in the morning, you can isolate the West Temple and the Towers of the Virgin with a short telephoto by concentrating on the golden rock face and eliminating the problematic shadow areas. By the end of the morning, the walls are basking in direct sunlight and have lost their relief. Of the park's three high observation points (Angels Landing and Observation Point are the other two) this one is by far the most accessible, but it's also the least grandiose.

The Zion Plateau

All of the southeast area of the park, between the east entrance and the tunnel, is absolutely spectacular and offers numerous photographic possibilities. It is without doubt one of the most fantastic landscapes you'll encounter. The rock walls, some white, some pink, some red, possess extraordinary rounded forms, whereas the summits are ornamented like minarets. A sculptural sensuality emanates from this topography that defies the imagination. The ground switches from polished to checkered within a very short space. Stone tumuli, scorched raw by the wind, burst forth here and there from a ground alternately smooth and

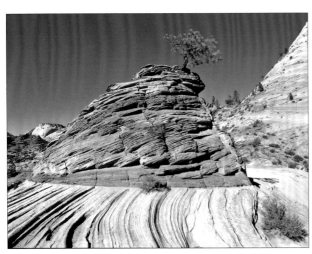

Sandstone tumulus typical of the Zion Plateau

lined. It's an incongruous landscape, kneaded, molded and painted as if by some crazy pastry-chef. Coming from the east entrance, just past Checkerboard Mesa you'll see some really interesting eroded hoodoos on the north side of the road, looking like submarine kiosks. It is well worth stopping there to photograph them with a wide-angle to normal lens. About 2 miles from the entrance, you'll come upon a landmark dear to photographers: a little pinion pine growing on top of one of these eroded sandstone shapes. There are a couple of pullout spots on the south side of the road and the tree is about 150 yards to the south.

Many Pools

This pleasant and easy hike in the center of a drainage leads to a series of large potholes, especially photogenic when they are full of water after recent rains or during spring runoff. There are actually very few potholes and they are encountered early into this popular hike. The best pothole is only 0.3 mile from your car, and getting there is a no-brainer. Just show up with a very wide angle lens. Time permitting, continue north up the wide canyon to about 37°14'12" 112°55'06" as it's a very pleasant hike. The total round-trip to this point is about 2 miles.

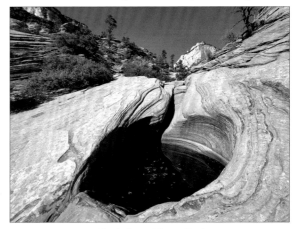

Pothole at Many Pools

Photo advice: Early morning in late spring and early summer, you'll benefit from good reflected light.

Getting there: The closest official pull-out is on the south side of the road, about 0.8 mile past the end of the second tunnel, coming from the canyon on UT-9. Walk north along the road for about 0.1 mile to enter the drainage on the west side of the road.

Time required: If you are only interested in the potholes, 45 minutes should be plenty of time to shoot.

Checkerboard Mesa

A short distance from the east entrance station, you'll find the viewpoint of Checkerboard Mesa, one of the most celebrated views in Zion. The prow of the mesa is inclined at a 60° angle and is striated like a baguette fresh out of the oven. The view of Checkerboard Mesa is a classic and it's difficult to take an original shot even by changing the viewing angle. It is mostly the unusual cross-bedding of the Mesa, more than its own beauty, which makes for the interest in this photo. From the parking between the east entrance station and the mesa, Checkerboard Mesa can be photographed at just about any time of the day, although it looks best from mid-morning until mid-afternoon, with the sun on the left. A medium wide-angle to standard lens will work best. From the pullout right at the base of the mesa, you'll need a wide-angle lens. An ultrawide will allow you to shoot upward while framing pine tree needles. Walking in the direction of the Canyon, you'll find a small hill to your right. This makes an excellent vantage point at sunset to shoot the East Temple silhouetted against the evening sky. A medium zoom will be helpful in fine-tuning your composition.

The East Rim Trail

If you can arrange a car shuttle (privately or through an outfitter), the East Rim Trail makes for a pleasant and leisurely 11-mile thru-hike, for the most part completely away from the crowds. Its scenic interest is good but it doesn't have the same photographic potential as the West Rim, except when you add the side trips to Observation Point or Hidden Canyon and the longer hikes or overnighters to Cable Mountain and Deertrap Mountain. The latter are both interesting alternatives to Angels Landing and Observation Point.

Unless you are hiking as part of a Trans-Zion trek, the natural way to start is from the East Entrance of the park, leaving your other vehicle at the Zion Canyon Visitor Center. About 2/3rds of this hike is an easy gradual ascent on a very good trail. It begins along Clear Creek and Cave Canyon with great, albeit distant, views of Checkerboard Mesa and Crazy Quilt Mountain (the larger mesa west of Checkerboard). The best views are about 2.2 miles from the trailhead.

The next interesting viewpoint is the steep chasm of Jolley Gulch at mile 2.9. Be extremely careful around it. If you want to take a peek at the amazing vertical drop-off just below you, the only way is to crawl on all fours. The trail pursues its gradual incline on the plateau after that, with views of Ponderosa Ranch to the northeast, topping off at mile 5.5 shortly before Stave Spring. Things change drastically at mile 7.3 with a steep descent into the upper part of Echo Canyon. There is a very nice viewpoint at 37°16'38" 112°55'16" where you can rest a bit and catch views of Echo Canyon. The trail remains somewhat difficult until the junction with the Observation Point Trail, where you rejoin civilization. The final portion of the East Rim Trail, along the Echo slot canyon and the spectacular bird's eye views of Zion Canyon is described in the Observation Point section.

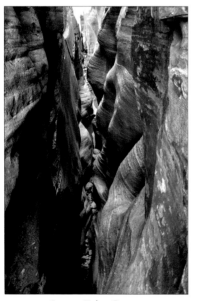

Lower Echo Canyon

Photo advice: I would not burden myself with a heavy dSLR nor a tripod. A small, mirrorless camera, with or without a zoom would be perfectly adequate to bring back quality pictures.

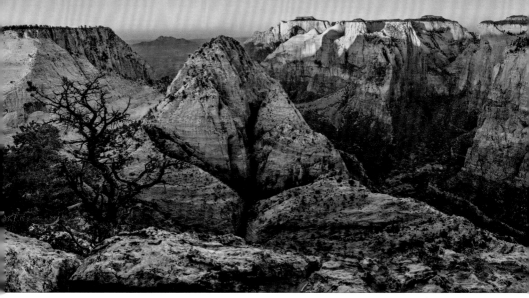

Mountain of the sun & Zion Canyon, from Deertrap Mountain

Getting there: After parking car one at the Zion Canyon Visitor Center (or at Weeping Rock off-shuttle season), drive car two toward the East entrance of the park. Turn left on the spur road located just before the east entrance and drive 0.1 mile to the trailhead.

Time required: About 6 to 7 hours for the thru-hike to Weeping Rock. This hike could be combined with the Hidden Canyon hike, with which it shares the end of the trail (from the junction, add about 1½ hours round-trip). I would definitely leave Observation Point for another day.

Deertrap Mountain

Deertrap Mountain offers an alternative view of the lower main canyon from the East Rim. Although not in the same league as Angels Landing or Observation Point, the view encompasses highlights such as the Towers of the Virgin, the Three Patriarchs, and Mountain of the Sun, that the others don't. It can be an easy hike if you do it right, which means starting from the little used Park entrance near the Ponderosa Ranch.

From the East Boundary trailhead, walk 0.5 mile to the junction with the East Rim Trail, walk south (left) for another 0.3 mile toward Stave Spring and take the right trail at the Y toward Cable Mountain and Deertrap Mountain. About a mile further, leave the Cable Mountain trail to your right, continuing straight toward Deertrap Mountain. All these junctions are signed. A couple more miles brings you to the main Deertrap Mountain viewpoint; this is where you get the best view of the canyon proper. You can continue north for about 0.5 mile, following the rim to closer views of the top of the Great White Throne with its unexpected whimsical hoodoos.

Photo advice: I recommend being at the viewpoint for dawn, which requires hiking with a headlamp or during full moon on the excellent and mostly flat trail. The view is panoramic so you may want to shoot verticals for stitching. The light becomes more contrasty as the day unfolds and by afternoon, you'd be shooting against the sun.

Getting there: From the East Entrance to the park, drive 2.4 miles east on UT-9 and turn north on North Fork Road. Drive about 5.2 miles and enter the Ponderosa Ranch Resort. Continue 0.7 mile past the resort and turn left onto Buck Road. Continue 1.2 miles where there are a couple of junctions but signs guide you to the park boundary. There is space for a few cars by the gate.

Time required: Allow 4 to 5 hours for the 8-mile round-trip to Deertrap Mountain viewpoint and the extra mile for the extension to the north.

Nearby location: The 3.6-mile round-trip detour to Cable Mountain offers a bird's eye view of the mid-canyon and Angels Landing, but the angle is too steep for harmonious images. Instead, the main interest is historical: the remnants of the old cable machinery that used to ferry lumber from a sawmill at Stave Spring to the canyon. This lumber mill was in operation for almost three decades at the beginning of the 20th century. The wooden structure is actually visible to the naked eye from the canyon, to the left of the Great White Throne.

The Kolob Terrace Road

For those with time and a thirst for more grand vistas of the Zion backcountry, it's possible to cross the west part of Zion from north to south by car. You can start either from Cedar City to the north or from Virgin to the south. The road is known as the Kolob Terrace Road and is classified as a Scenic Backway. The road is paved from Virgin to the Kolob reservoir as well as on the last few miles descending toward UT-14 east of Cedar City. The unpaved section can normally

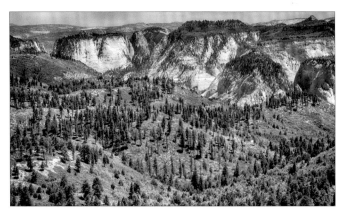

be driven in a passenger car in dry weather; nevertheless, do not leave without checking road condition with the UDOT or the Zion Canyon Visitor Center, as it may be closed due to snow in winter or because of road damage waiting to be fixed.

Most people choose to drive this road from

West Rim from the Kolob Terrace Road

Virgin, but you can start from either Cedar City or Kanarraville. I have been on the Kolob Terrace Road several times and have taken it from each starting point; I have a slight preference for doing it southbound.

After leaving UT-14, the road climbs steadily, providing lofty views of the colorful mountains near Cedar City and extending well beyond I-15. It traverses a semi-alpine ecosystem on its way to Kolob Reservoir—with some nice wildflower fields in early summer—before crossing the boundary of Zion National Park. Take the short detour to Lava Point for a distant bird's eye view of Goose Creek and Kolob Creek canyon and the beginning of the West Rim Trail (See *West Rim* section). Soon after that, the road opens up to a series of superlative vistas, providing a very different view of Zion, before descending toward Virgin and UT-9.

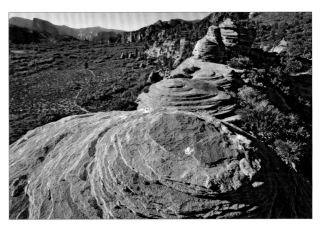

Hoodoo City © Philippe Schuler

Photo advice: Between mile 8 and 16 from Virgin, there are superb views of the back of Zion lit by the afternoon sun, with tall grasses in the foreground. If you are leaving Zion on UT-9 west in mid to late-afternoon, you won't regret spending an extra hour for a quick jaunt on this highly scenic road.

One interesting place to photograph, again from late afternoon until sunset, is Hop Valley Overlook (called Hoodoo City by Joe Braun on his excellent site citrusmilo.com). It is located about 7.2 miles south of Lava Point Road or 13 miles north of Virgin (or 2.6 miles west of Wildcat Canyon trailhead and 4.9 miles north of the Subway trailhead). Park on a pullout at 37°20'26" 113°06'30" on the north side of the road about 0.3 mile east of the Hop Valley trailhead car park. Walk northwest, keeping roughly at rim level. In about fifteen minutes you reach an area of exposed slickrock with colorful hoodoos and good views overlooking Hop Valley.

Getting there: At its south end, Kolob Terrace Road starts on the north side of UT-9 in the town of Virgin. The only clue is the small street name sign. From downtown Cedar City, take UT-14 east for about 5 miles and turn right at the sign for Kolob. From Kanarraville, drive north on Main Street (Old Hwy 81) for 2.8 miles and angle right on the steeply-ascending graded road, joining the main Kolob Terrace road in about 11 miles.

Time required: 3 to 4 hours, depending on how much you stop.

The Subway from the "Bottom"

The Subway is a fantastic location, but reaching it requires a long and difficult hike following the Left Fork of North Creek. The hike itself is not particularly interesting most of the way if you're coming from the bottom trailhead, as most photographers do. However, the surreal sight that awaits you at the end of the journey makes it all worth it.

The Subway proper is a narrow canyon that has been carved in a tunnel-like fashion by the waters of North Creek. In one meander of the creek, it feels like you are in a tunnel, except for a narrow opening at the top. North Creek gently winds its way on the polished red rock under your feet, flowing over pools of azure and green. Small cascades trickle down pour-offs and chokestones further up. The subdued light reinforces the crypt-like feeling of the Subway. It is a very haunting place indeed.

You'll need a permit to visit the Left Fork of North Creek, where the Subway is located. Over the years, the Zion backcountry permit system has evolved to keep up with the growing popularity of the Subway and many other canyo-

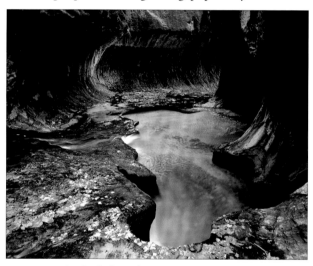

Back of The Subway © Ron Flickinger

neering or wilderness hikes, and it is likely that it will continue to do so. The current system offers a number of options and is quite intricate. Rather than giving you information that may be obsolete by the time you read this book, check the latest details on the NPS website at: http://www.nps.gov/zion/planyourvisit/wildernesspermitinfo.htm.

As of this writing, Subway permits must be reserved in the Canyoneering Day Trips section of the NPS reservation web site at https://zionpermits.nps.gov/wilderness.cfm?. The proper identification is "Left Fork of North Creek". Note that ALL permits (including those with calendar reservations or awarded though the lottery) must be obtained in person the day before, or the day of your trip, at the Zion Canyon or Kolob Canyon Visitor Center.

Photo advice: In late spring and summer, you'll want to arrive either before mid-morning or in mid-afternoon. Otherwise you'll find part of the Subway and the pools in full sun around midday. In the fall, there is no need for a crack-of-dawn departure as you'll want to arrive around midday. It takes at least 2½ hours to get to the Subway from the bottom trailhead.

Opposite page: Magical Pools of The Subway

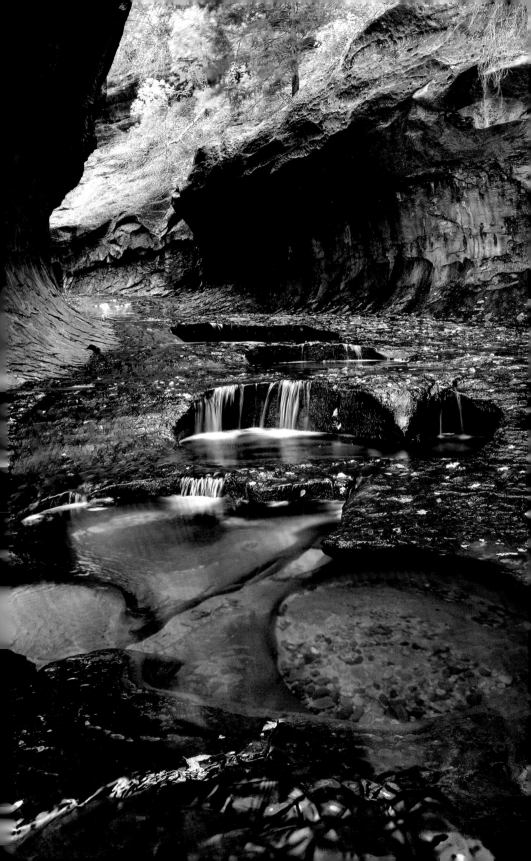

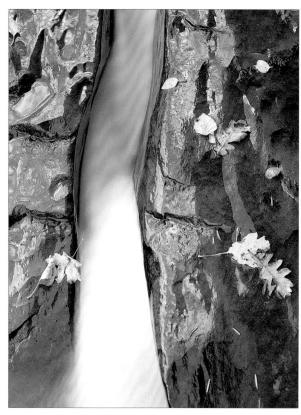

Cobalt Waterflow

At about mile 4 from the bottom trailhead, you'll come to Archangel Falls, a series of small cascades over red slickrock that make a very nice picture. Just a bit further, you'll notice a crack in the bedrock on the right side of the canyon floor. The crack channels water from the creek at very high speed, creating the setting for a terrific picture. In the vicinity, you'll also find a large alcove with mosses and other moisture loving vegetation. Soon after that, you'll arrive at the bend where the Subway and its pools are located.

A wide-angle lens is a must. Regardless of the format you shoot, you'll need a sturdy tripod in the Subway because light is often very dim and you may find yourself working with very long exposures: 1 to 15 seconds if you shoot at low ISO and want maximum depth-of-field. The cold blue-green light creates a very ethereal effect.

Getting there: As previously mentioned, this is a long and tiring hike for many people; it will help to be in shape. If you're thinking of taking heavy photographic equipment, you'd better think twice, because you will feel it all the way and back.

The easiest way is to go from "the bottom", a trailhead marked "Left Fork" located about 8 miles north of the Kolob Terrace Road turnoff in the town of Virgin. To call this entry "the bottom" is a figure of speech because after only ½ mile of flat walking, you must negotiate a difficult descent down a steep route. A walking stick or pair of trekking poles will make this descent as well as the whole day much easier. Once you reach the bottom, follow the creek up the best you can, crossing and re-crossing many times. This involves a lot of boulder-hopping and climbing up steep banks to bypass the larger obstacles. A pair of wading shoes works fairly well for this hike. Sometimes there is a visible trail, at other times it is much less obvious. This "easy" way is a compromise which allows you to see only the lower part of the Subway, albeit the most spectacular one.

A few hundred feet past the entrance to the Subway, you'll find the creek blocked by deep pools followed by a cascade and a rocky escarpment which is impossible to climb without equipment. A rope is sometimes in place along the short wall preceding the deep pools, but don't count on it. Park Rangers routinely remove ropes for obvious liability reasons. A rope exposed to the elements could become

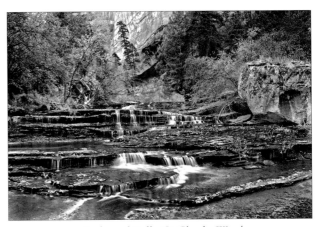

Archangel Falls © Charles Wood

time-worn and break while someone is climbing. If you are a climber with good upper-body strength and are lucky enough to be there when a group of canyoneers happens to come down from the top, you could ask permission to use their rope while it's still in place; chances are they'll be stopping at the Subway for a while and they may agree to wait for you. Be careful not to fall, as you'll need to pull yourself hand over hand up the rope, pushing away from the rock with your feet. Once on top, the obstacles are easily bypassed most of the time and you can continue up-canyon for a couple of hundred yards inside beautiful narrows to photograph the log immortalized by Michael Fatali in his spectacular "North Pole" photograph. I really don't encourage you to do that because this is one of the spots where many accidents happen and coming back down without a harness and belay would be dangerous.

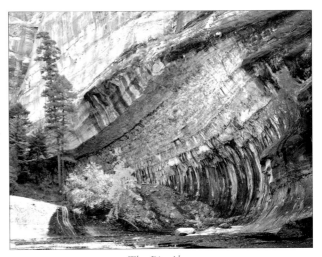

The Big Alcove

Time required: 6 to 7 hours round-trip from the bottom trailhead.

Nearby location: The lower section of the Right Fork of North Creek can be visited as far as Double Falls in one very long 11-mile round-trip slog in full sun. The reward is the very photogenic falls spilling into the green pool below and down a second pool. If you encounter anybody on this tough hike, it will most likely be canyoneers coming from the top.

The Subway from the "Top"

The other way to visit the Subway is to come "from the top down", starting from the Wildcat Canyon trailhead and doing a full traverse to the Left Fork trailhead. This requires a car shuttle, which you can arrange with an outfitter in Springdale.

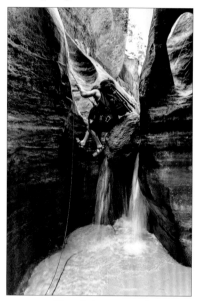

Zion Subway rappel

My personal opinion is that the Subway is much more interesting as a full traverse than the standard round-trip hike from the "bottom". However, this is an entry-level canyoneering route that should not be undertaken by hikers without rappelling skills. The hike requires basic canyoneering equipment in the form of harness, rope, 'biners, and possibly a wet suit if you go outside the summer months. You'll also need a dry bag for your daypack, with food and change of clothes (which will also serve as a flotation device) and a small drybag for your camera. No outfitters are allowed to guide you inside the National Park, so if you have never done canyoneering, you'll need to find an experienced partner or two to make this trip safe. Given the above prerequisites, most people should be able to do this hike as long as they are in good physical condition, have good flexibility, no fear of heights, are willing to do a couple of very short swims in narrow passages, and three short rappels. Even though it is a bit outside of the scope of this book, I thought it wouldn't be too much of a stretch to include it.

Keep in mind, however, that under not so good conditions, the Subway can become extremely dangerous, as illustrated by the National Park Service's log of rescues: an endless litany of people trapped overnight, broken bones, ledged hikers, and hypothermia.

Regardless of ability, if you're going to do the Subway from the top, a specialized guidebook with clear instructions is compulsory reading. I recommend Tom Jones' *Zion: Canyoneering* guide. It has all the information you need for a successful approach and descent of the top part of the narrows, above the Subway.

The 2-mile approach is easy but pay attention to your instructions to find the correct point of descent and avoid getting stuck in Russel Gulch. The first rappel is at a boulder field and it's about 10 feet down to the next level. The creek then becomes deeper, forcing you to swim through a narrow section. The second rappel is very short, but lands you in waist-deep cold water with the creek cascading on your head. This is the most interesting part from a technical standpoint: a 60-foot long swim through a very narrow slot (as in barely-squeezing-your-shoulders-through) called the Bowling Ball Corridor for an almost perfectly-round boulder lodged just above your head. When I was there, small logs obstructed the narrow channel, forcing me to dive under, awkwardly shoving my resisting drybag under the boulder while frenetically treading water. Large individuals may have to negotiate this part sideways. The third rappel is the Keyhole Falls, which is a good spot to take pictures of your party.

You are now in the most beautiful part of the narrows, with only a trickle of water. Within a few minutes, after rounding a couple of bends, you'll come face-to-face with Michael Fatali's iconic "North Pole". I have yet to see a bad photo of the North Pole. As long as the day is not overcast, there is great reflecting light around mid-day, at least enough for your camera to catch a nice photograph using a setting of around ½ second at f/8 at ISO 100. Ironically, the final rappel just above the Subway, which looks (and is) relatively easy to a neophyte, is actually where most accidents happen. Be

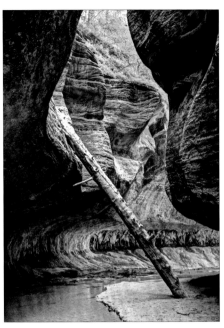

The iconic North Pole

sure to exercise caution and don't try to jump. Alternative points of descent may be available by the time you read this.

For one last swim, you may want to drag yourself through the narrow channel leading to the little grotto behind the falls.

Photo Advice: I use transparent 5-Liter or 10-Liter SealLine bags (depending on which camera I use) whenever things will get wet. SealLine makes very reliable waterproof bags—they have been underwater many times on the Colorado River without any leaks. I carry it attached to the sternum strap of my daypack or hanging from a 'biner on a shoulder strap of my daypack. A small waterproof camera to snap pictures during the swims is also helpful.

Getting there: Parking is at the Wildcat Canyon trailhead, 7.5 miles past the Left Fork car park, where you will leave your second vehicle. You can also arrange for a shuttle to drop you off. This first part of the hike is through pleasant forested land. After 1 mile, the trail joins the Wildcat Canyon Trail for only 0.2 mile until you see the sign for the Subway. After another 0.1 mile the trail splits and you continue to the left. Shortly thereafter you begin your descent to the Russell Gulch drainage on a vast expanse of gently sloping and very scenic crossbedded slickrock. There is no trail on the slickrock but cairns make the route easy to follow. Pay close attention not to follow the bottom of Russell Gulch; instead, cross on the east side (left) and follow the trail until you find the entry point into the Left Fork—a very steep but short scramble on very loose, eroded dirt, landing next to your first water pool of the day.

Time required: A long day, in the 8 to 10-hour range.

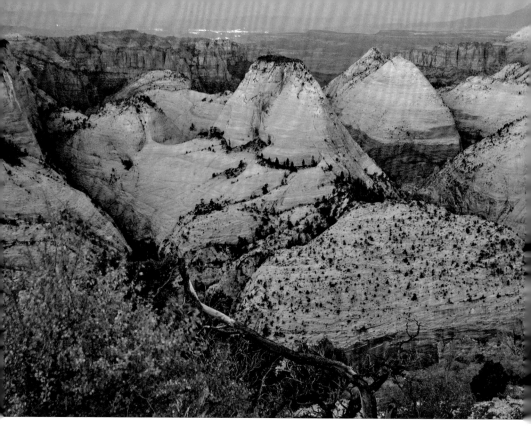

The West Rim Trail

Although this 14.5-mile trail is more often done as a leisurely two-day back-pack, the entire length of the West Rim Trail can be hiked in one long but quite moderate day hike, leaving from the trailhead near Lava Point on the Kolob Terrace Road and ending up at the Grotto picnic area in the main canyon. Except for a short section in Potato Hollow, this hike is essentially flat for the first half and downhill after that. Outfitters in Springdale can drive you to Lava Point for a fee, allowing for an early start without the hassles of a car shuttle. This formula allows you to go light with a mid-size daypack. Just be sure to have plenty of fluids and snacks and avoid the unreliable water sources (water would need to be purified if present). The negative side of this scenario, at least for photographers, is that you hit the most spectacular views around midday when harsh light and/or haze are present.

Hiking up from the Grotto doesn't solve the problem either. You can hike past Campsite #5 and back, but you are still going to hit the best views under mediocre conditions. I have done this too and not everyone would enjoy the 3,000-foot elevation gain.

The overnight backpack is definitely the best solution, although it raises weight and practicality issues if your camera equipment is bulky. You also need a backcountry permit and if weather conditions are bad at the time you've reserved, all the effort could be in vain.

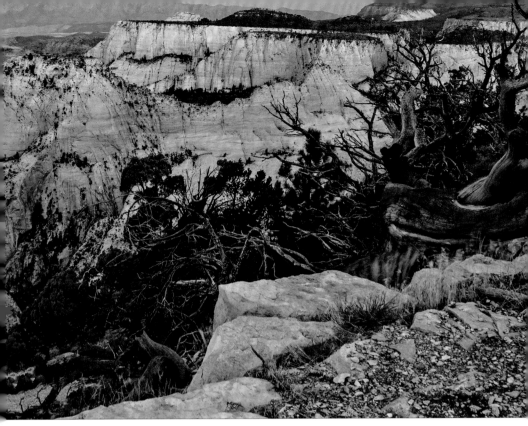

View from Camp 5 at dawn

Having done both the full traverse and the hike from the bottom over the years, I had enjoyed the fabulous views but didn't have a single keeper, not even a passable documentary shot. All were either hazy or totally flat.

I then got the idea of doing a night hike under a full moon. A year before, I had enjoyed hiking Observation Point at night and arriving in time for alpenglow and sunrise. So why not do the same for the West Rim?

I picked a day right after full moon in early October, setting out from the Lava Point trailhead at 3 a.m. Hiking in the night was quite pleasant and my partner and I arrived at Camp 5 with plenty of time to shoot alpenglow and sunrise.

I recommend two great sunrise shooting locations very close to each other. Both are excellent and may be a matter of preference. The most open one is at 37°17'30" 112°59'17", the other one is at 37°17'36" 112°59'17". From these two locations, you have an unobstructed view of some of the most grandiose scenery I've ever seen: mesas, domes, and canyons, Phantom Valley, the Inclined Temple with its funny hoodoos on top, and the Right Fork of North Creek, among others. This is without a doubt a world-class location; it's just not much talked about because of the challenge of reaching it at an appropriate time. The hike from the Lava Point trailhead to Camp 5 is almost 16.5 miles round-trip; 19 miles if the road to the trailhead is impassable and you have to park at the Lava Point Overlook.

On the way back to your car, you will enjoy gorgeous fall colors throughout Potato Hollow in early October, as well as great views of South Guardian

Angel, Great West Canyon, and the Left Fork of North Creek from about 37°20'41" 113°00'17".

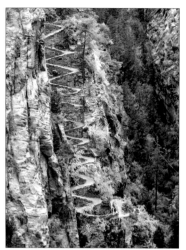

Walter's Wiggles

If you continue toward the Grotto, past Camp 4, the trail turns sharply east and you are presented with awesome views of Heaps and Behunin Canyons to the South. After your reach Cabin Spring, the landscape couldn't be more different. Past the spring, you'll begin your gradual descent on a steep but excellent slickrock trail, skirting around the mouth of Behunin Canyon and the end of Telephone Canyon until you reach the vicinity of Scout Lookout, with its outstanding views of Zion Canyon, the Great White Throne, and Angels Landing. Shortly before reaching Scout Lookout, leave the trail to the right and continue to the end of a promontory; from here you can catch a distant telephoto view of Walter's Wiggles—the switchbacks leading to Scout Lookout.

The West Rim is best done in spring or fall. Summer can be very hot and you'll be in full sun almost all the way; add to this the risk of afternoon thunderstorms during the monsoon. As for winters, days are too short and snow could make the hike dangerous.

Photo advice: I recommend a high-quality mirrorless or a small dSLR with a medium-range zoom for this hike. Most of the views from the rim work well with a normal lens or telephoto. From the two viewpoints I recommend near Camp 5, you'll need to shoot verticals to assemble panoramas in post-processing. A tripod will be needed if you overnight at Camp 6 (the nicest campsite) or Camp 5 (closest to the best views) or if you do the round-trip night hike.

Getting there: From Virgin, take Kolob Terrace Road for about 20 miles to the junction with the Lava Point road. Drive 0.9 mile to the junction with the Lava Point Lookout Trail and take the left fork for 1.4 miles to reach the trailhead. This last portion could be impassable after a rain.

Time required: 8 to 10 hours for either the thru-hike, or the round-trips from Lava Point or the Grotto.

Kolob Canyon Viewpoint

The Kolob section of Zion is rather remote from the main canyon and many travelers pressed for time pass it up. That's a shame because the valley that follows the interstate towards Cedar City is very pretty. Also, the road through the park only runs about 6 miles before reaching the Kolob Canyon Viewpoint, making it a very short trip. All along the route, the view of the impressive red rock walls of the Finger Canyons is remarkable. The detour is worthwhile if you decide to go up to Bryce by way of Cedar Breaks. But don't let it cause you to miss the road from Zion to Mt. Carmel, allowing you to cross the plateau. If you have to choose, the plateau should be the first priority.

Photo advice: The best time is late afternoon.

Getting there: Take Exit 40 from I-15, 32 miles north of St. George and 19 miles south of Cedar City. The Kolob section is frequently closed in winter.

Time required: 1 hour round-trip from Interstate 15.

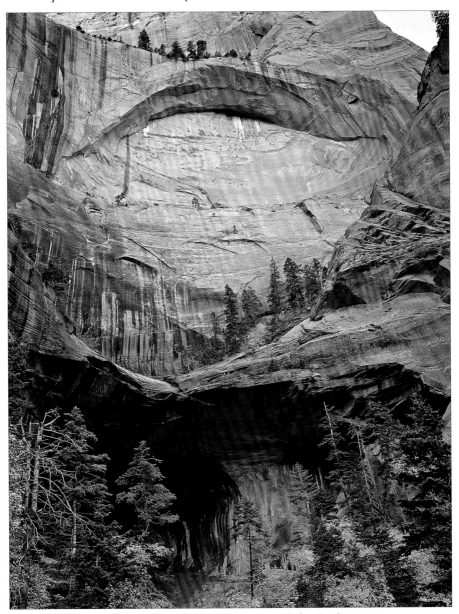

Double Arch Alcove towers over Taylor Creek

Taylor Creek

Located in the Kolob section of the park, the Middle Fork of Taylor Creek is a very scenic and highly recommended hike to a fantastic photographic location: a vast grotto-like alcove, topped by two closed arches carved in a 2000-foot cliff. The trail is easy and suitable for families with children. It is only 2.7 miles one-way to Double Arch Alcove on a mostly flat trail. You will cross Taylor Creek dozens of times, but none of the crossings presents a challenge.

The canyon walls and vegetation are splendid all along the trail and you'll pass two old cabins on your way. There is a patch of lush green grass and mosses at the back of the lower alcove, which contrasts beautifully with the red rock. This is due to the presence of a spring seep.

Continuing along the stream past the alcove, you promptly reach a small cascade which is quite spectacular during the wet season, but almost entirely dry during the drier months, when its beautifully polished patina is revealed.

Photo advice: A wide-angle lens works best to encompass the entire rock wall including some vegetation at the bottom, the alcove and the two arches. It is best photographed around midday under the reflected light from the opposite rock wall, which gives the alcove a fantastic orange and red glow.

In the fall, you'll get the benefit of intense yellows and reds to complement your photos. Some very large pines and spruce trees grow above the first and second alcoves, adding a touch of green to your composition.

Getting there: The Middle Fork of Taylor Creek trailhead is about 2 miles from the Kolob Section entrance on I-15 between St. George and Cedar City. This section of the park is frequently closed in winter.

Time required: 3 hours round-trip from the parking area.

Nearby location: About 1.2 miles past the Middle Fork of the Taylor Creek trailhead, you'll find a large parking area just before a sharp turn. Cross the road and find the unofficial trailhead for the South Fork of Taylor Creek. Heading east into the canyon, the route goes up and down for a while and after one last steep climb, you reach a small hanging valley with nice trees and a lovely meadow. The trail levels off, continuing along the huge, vertical right wall of the canyon until it becomes blocked by chokestones. This is a pleasant hike in a very green, secluded setting, contrasting with the colorful red wall, interestingly eroded in places. There is good reflected light in early afternoon. Count on about 2 hours round-trip from the parking area.

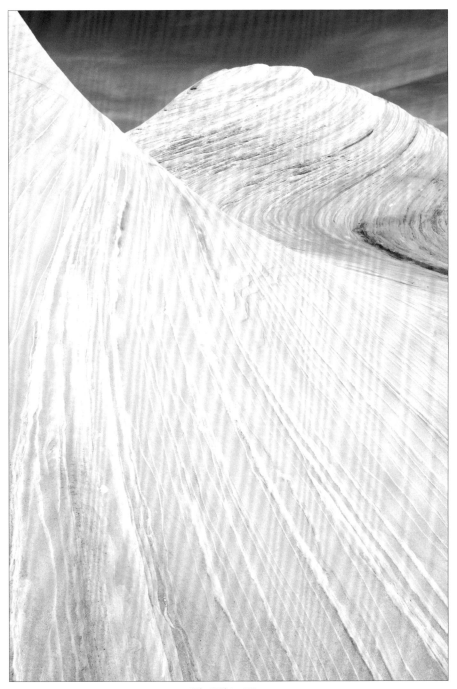

The White Wave

Chapter 3

AROUND ZION

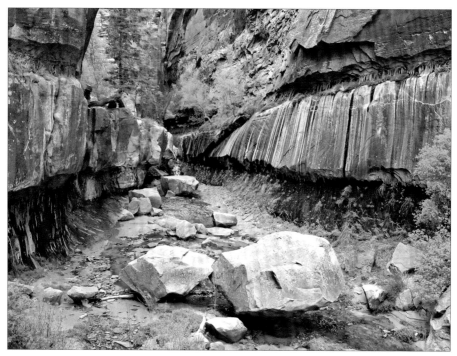

Water Canyon

The Smithsonian Butte

An excellent way to get to Zion is by using the nine mile long Smithsonian Butte Scenic Backway. Seen from UT-59 coming from Fredonia, the scenery is magnificent in all seasons with Canaan Mountain to the east and the tall grass prairie in the foreground. However, it's on the Scenic Backway itself, going toward Rockville, that a surprise awaits you with a spectacular view of the entrance to Zion Canyon. From the mesa, you can clearly see The Watchman to the right of the canyon entrance and the Towers of the Virgin to the left. Just before reaching Rockville, a short detour leads to the old 19th century village of Grafton. Only a couple of structures are still standing today and despite having been renovated in a tasteful manner, Grafton has lost a lot of its old charm.

Photo advice: You'll enjoy the byway much more if you take it from its south entrance on UT-59. Drive about 3.5 miles from the turnoff on 59 and look for an obvious little knoll on the east side with a large juniper at 37°07'33" 113°06'09". There is plenty of room to park your car away from traffic. Walk up the little knoll to gain a nice panoramic view of the entrance to Zion Canyon. If coming from Rockville, drive about 5.8 miles to reach this spot. It is best photographed at sunset.

Getting there: The road begins about 14 miles east of Hurricane or 40 miles west of Fredonia on UT-59 and comes out in Rockville, about 4.7 miles from the west entrance to Zion. It is well signed (also as Goosberry Mesa) on UT-59. The initially excellent clay track deteriorates rapidly as it plunges toward Rockville and you'll have to exercise caution. Do not take this road after a rain, as it can be extremely slippery. If you are coming from Rockville, the road is not signed. Turn south on Bridge Rd., west on Grafton Rd., then south on the Smithsonian Butte Rd.

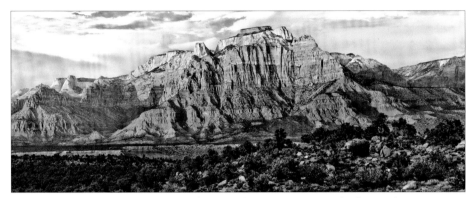

The West Rim of Zion from Smithsonian Butte © Charles Wood

Time required: A 45-minute detour off the main road.

Nearby locations: In recent years, Gooseberry Mesa has become a popular destination for mountain bikers, offering a very good network of trails. The signed Gooseberry Mesa Road starts on your left (west), 2.8 miles from the south entrance of Smithsonian Butte Scenic Byway on UT-59. You reach the pit toilets at 3.6 miles; take the right fork toward the Windmill Trailhead for 1 mile and make a right at the Y at mile 4.6 to park near the rim at mile 5. From here, walk along the narrow road for 0.3 mile to a worthwhile view at 37°09'38" 113°09'49".

Coal Pits Wash, about 2 miles west of Rockville on UT-9, has one of the densest areas of cottonwoods in bloom during fall and spring, offering outstanding photo opportunities.

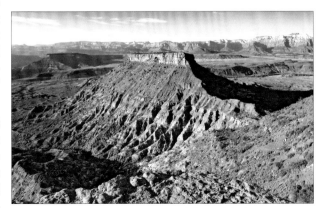

Gooseberry Mesa © Philippe Schuler

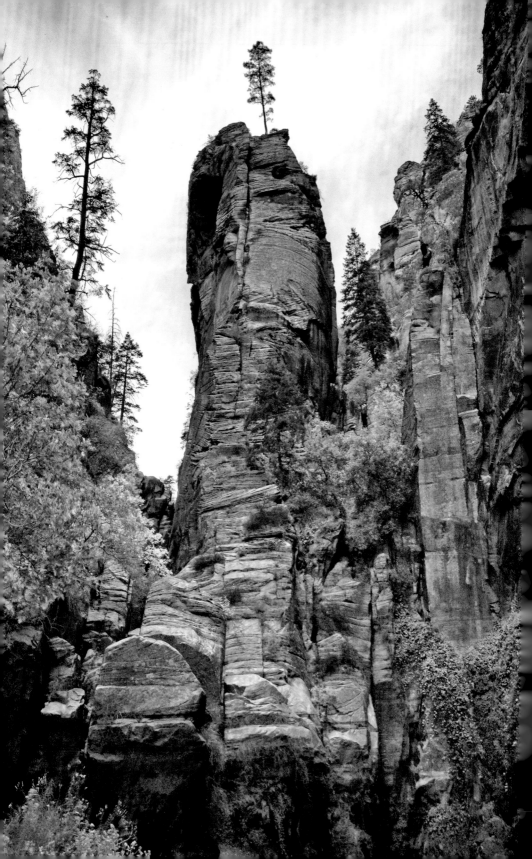

Water Canyon

In the vicinity of Colorado City, lovely Water Canyon is well worth a visit if you're looking for a secluded place. Nested inside the colorful Vermilion Cliffs, its short narrows offer a refreshing atmosphere with their water-weeping cliffs, scattered greenery and tiny cascades. It also provides access to the vast slickrock benches of Canaan Mountain.

The canyon sees a lot of foot traffic on weekends and holidays due to its proximity to the fundamentalist Mormon (FLDS) communities of Colorado City and Hildale. Plan your visit on a weekday if you can. You'll be able to take photographs at your own pace without disturbing the locals, who are not accustomed to see many visitors from outside their community.

From the trailhead, a short 30-minute walk leads to the beginning of the narrows. Along the way, look for an arch on top of the cliff to your right. The first part of the narrows is the most photogenic, but you can go on to an upper level following a slanted ledge to the left. The narrows eventually open up in a slickrock area reminiscent of the Zion Plateau. A steep footpath continues toward Canaan Mountain and the beautiful White Domes (see next section).

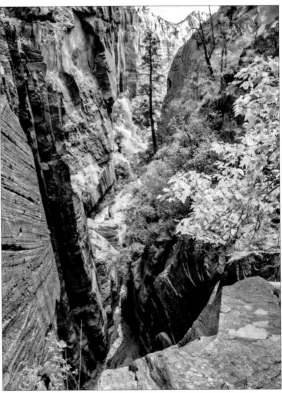

Photo advice: Mid-morning or mid-afternoon work best to avoid sharp contrasts. A tripod and long exposure are necessary to capture the flow of water running through the photogenic cracks in the bedrock.

Getting there: About 22 miles from Hurricane on UT-59, on the west side of Hildale, look for the Fredonia 33 signpost and turn on Utah Avenue, which soon becomes Canyon Street. After 2.9 miles, bear left then make a right on Water Canyon Road, just before the two lanes split to form a loop. Follow the dirt road for 2 miles and park at the end near a reservoir. Even in dry weather, this road may not always be suitable to passenger cars due to some deep ruts.

Time required: About 2 hours r/t to the end of the narrows.

Upper section of Water Canyon

Opposite page: Water Canyon

The White Domes

This hike or backpacking trip is a continuation of the Water Canyon hike described previously. It leads to the top of Canaan Mountain, a vast plateau extending from the Arizona Strip in the South to the Virgin River Valley in the north. From a landscape photography stance, the interest is principally the area called the White Domes: a series of strikingly white sandstone domes rising from the surrounding colorful sandstone. One of the domes has wave-like curves reminiscent of The Wave in the Coyote Buttes (See *Photographing the Southwest Volume 2 – Arizona*) and some have started calling it the White Wave (not to be confused with another place of lesser interest also called the White Wave by a Kanab outfitter).

Photo Advice: If your goal is to photograph the White Wave, you'll get best results in mid to late-afternoon, before the light gives the White Wave too much of a warm cast as well as deep shadows. A wide angle lens is needed to "catch the wave" adequately. There are distant views of Zion from high points around the Domes area. There are also many interesting smaller formations inside the perimeter of the White Wave.

Getting there: From Water Canyon, after climbing the slanted ledge to the left, continue on the well-defined trail above the canyon, then start the long hard ascent on switchbacks following ledges. Minor scrambling is required in a few

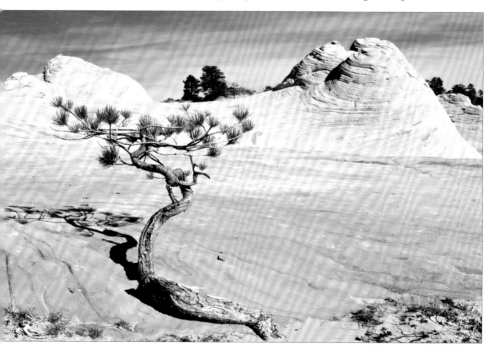

Old domes, Young pine

places and it is one tough hike with a heavy pack and a tripod. Eventually, you reach a flat saddle at 37°03'08" 112°57'54" with a fire ring to the right; a location known locally as Top Rock. Take your bearings here because this is the only spot to get in and out on this side of Canaan Mountain. It is not so easy to find it on your way back, especially in dim light. Locate the trail going down northwest through the forest and finish your descent into the wash below on the steep slick-rock around 37°03'15" 112°58'03". Mark this point as it will be your aim for the climb back when you return from the Domes. Continue west into the wash for roughly ¼ mile to a side wash at 37°03'13" 112°58'18". Follow the wash up for about 0.5 mile and leave it around 37°03'34" 112°58'41", aiming for the Domes a half -mile away at 37°03'47" 112°58'60".

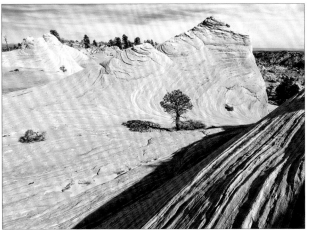

Lone tree on slickrock

Time required: 6 to 7 hours from the Water Canyon car park depending on how long you want to stay at both places. An overnighter would allow you to photograph the Domes at sunrise and sunset.

Pipe Spring

Pipe Spring National Monument, about 19 miles east from the turnoff for Water canyon on UT-59, preserves a collection of buildings erected and used by Mormon pioneers in the last century. Pipe Spring began as a ranch, but was abandoned a few years later after the settlers were killed by Indians. It was subsequently used as a Mormon militia outpost and a fort was built to serve as a refuge for farmers of the surrounding area. The interest is more cultural than photographic, but the site is right along the route and quick to visit. There is a short ½-mile interpretive trail that provides a glimpse into the geology and history of the Arizona Strip. The Monument is located inside the Kaibab Paiute Reservation and the Visitor Center presents many interesting aspects of Paiute Indian culture.

On a side note, the gas station/convenience store run by the Tribe consistently has the cheapest gas around, most likely due to the lack of federal and state tax.

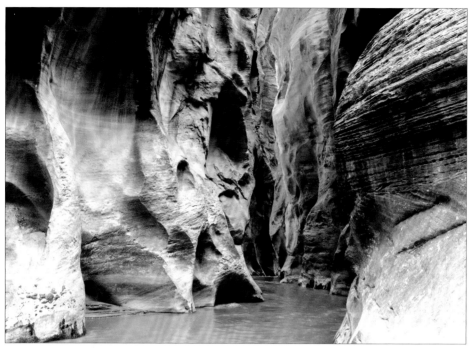

Inside The Barracks

Parunuweap Canyon

Parunuweap Canyon—the East fork of the Virgin River—is an exciting and stunning destination, mostly off the radar for the great majority of visitors to Zion. It is quite similar to its world-famous sibling the (North Fork of the) Virgin Narrows, but it takes considerable effort to get there and back. The reward is a very photogenic canyon that you may well have all to yourself. So what's the point of going through all this effort just to visit a replica of the Narrows, you may ask? Major Powell and Mallory would answer in unison, "Because it's there!" But there are many other good reasons people visit Parunuweap. First and foremost, it is a magnet for canyoneers, who descend to the river via Misery Canyon, (a.k.a. Fat Man Misery). But here is what's in it for us landscape photographers: a truly spectacular approach through vast and extremely rugged country; a beautiful, unspoiled river running between towering sandstone walls; ghoulish narrow passages; great light reflections; and lovely twin waterfalls at the bottom of Fat Man Misery. Now it's up to you to decide if it's worth the 10-hour day, plus driving time to and from the trailhead. Some prerequisites may help you sort it out: you should already have experienced the Virgin Narrows, preferably more than once; you should be a strong, experienced hiker, used to hiking cross-country; you should be able to interpret a topo map or mapping GPS screen and relate it to your surroundings; you should not be afraid of heights, nor of scrambling up and down an extremely steep trail (albeit with good grips).

If you decide to go, get a copy of *Favorite Hikes In & Around Zion National Park* by Bo Beck & Tanya Milligan or look at Tanya's web site www.zionnational-park.com/parunuweap-hike.htm. They have all the details on the route, with a map and waypoints.

Note that after you leave the sandy trail winding its way around the south end of Checkerboard Mesa, the route on the slickrock becomes cairned, but those cairns are sometimes far apart so you need to pay close attention. If you encounter canyoneers along the trail, they are likely headed to Misery Canyon—both destinations sharing part of the trail on the way in, and in totality on the way

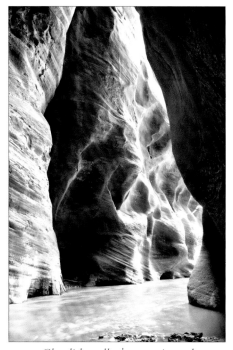

back. Do not follow them into Misery Canyon, but continue south following the cairned trail to the final descent into Parunuweap. The entry/exit point to the river is at 37°10'57" 112°51'52".

Although Parunuweap Canyon is on BLM land (except past Labyrinth Falls), you start at Checkerboard Mesa with a fair portion of the hike on Zion National Park land, so outfitters are not allowed to take you there. You'll be totally on your own, and you will feel the solitude all day. The trail is very taxing, due to its ups and down and the very exposed section as you approach the river. Good route-finding skills are a must and it might be a good idea to have a partner for a first time hike. I suggest you save your route on your GPS so you won't get lost on the return.

If you decide to do an overnighter, there are some good flat campsites at the top of the final descent into the canyon. This means that you'll have to go down and up

Ghoulish walls & recent ice melt

several times. The descent is very steep and requires concentration, as a fall on the sharp rocks could be catastrophic. It is by no means technical, and there are good grips, so just take your time. Once in the river, a pair of hiking poles is a must. I also recommend a drybag for your camera, especially if you intend to visit the falls at the bottom of Fat Man Misery.

Boots are not great for this hike. The river bed has less boulders than the Virgin Narrows and boots will make it harder to extricate yourself from quicksand, if present. A pair of trail runners will work best.

Photo advice: The south end of Checkerboard Mesa is almost an identical replica—albeit steeper—of the north end and is just as striking. The vast slickrock section about halfway into the hike is probably the most dramatic part of the trail. Arriving early to benefit from the best reflected light, I suggest you follow the river eastward toward the section called "The Barracks", about 0.5 mile from the descent. There is a great section of narrows in The Barracks with good reflected light in the morning. Much like its world famous sibling to the north (the Virgin Narrows) Parunuweap Canyon is deep and dark in its most spectacular spots and a tripod is a must to get sharp pictures. You can continue less than 0.5 mile to a boulder obstacle where you have to turn back. This part of the canyon is less photogenic, however.

Return to the mouth of Misery Canyon, which could be partially hidden behind vegetation, walk into the first pool and clamber onto the slide. In summer, the water temperature should be pleasant, while spring and fall will require a dry or wet suit. The twin waterfalls are just a short distance up-canyon. Most of the time, you can just wade to the falls, but in early spring or after a substantial rain there may be small pools to swim. If this is the case, you will definitely need a drybag for your camera and other belongings.

Returning from Fat Man Misery, continue downstream past the entrance/exit point and just around the corner, you will find the Powell Plaque on the right side. It could be hidden behind vegetation, but with increased visitation the plaque is usually in full view. Shortly past the plaque, you'll see the sign marking the national park's boundary. Hiking is allowed as far as the top of Labyrinth Falls, for which you need a rope. Parunuweap Canyon is closed past the falls. The river current is substantially stronger as you get closer to the falls, with waist-high water in places, after a rain. Exercise caution!

Getting there: Park at the pullout west of Checkerboard Mesa on the north side, about 1 mile from Zion's east entrance; there should be room early in the morning. Climb over the small dune and descend toward the string of potholes.

Time required: A 10-hour day, not counting the drive to the trailhead. Start at dawn from the trailhead, if you can. The return hike can be grueling in the afternoon heat and you may have read or heard that some people wait it out until it gets cooler. While this may be OK for people who know the trail well, it's not recommended unless you have a clean route on your GPS. Plan on being back at your car with some daylight left, just in case.

Coral Pink Sand Dunes

This Utah State Park is really worth a detour at dawn or sundown, if you happen to be in the vicinity. As its name indicates, these are sand dunes of a beautiful strong ocher tint. The extremely fine sand, Navajo sandstone ground and sifted by wind over and over again, becomes an extraordinary coral pink in the setting sun. The dunes are formed by hot air currents coming from the south and accelerating as they pass through Moccasin Gap, seen to the southwest of the viewpoint. These currents lose their speed when coming in contact with cold air masses forming above the Grand Staircase region and deposit sand in this area.

The dunes are spread out over a relatively small area, which makes it easy on the hiker or photographer. From the parking area, you can quickly get to the summit of the two main dunes, which are not more than 40 feet tall. The surroundings are not exactly exceptional, but the White Cliffs to the north and the Vermilion Cliffs to the south allow you to add some depth to these superb dunes. This park should not be missed if you are traveling with children.

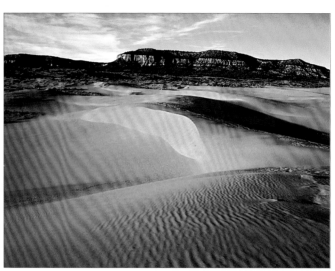

Sunset on the Coral Pink Sand Dunes

Photo advice: The interest here is as much along the order of macro-photography than landscapes. Motifs created by the wind and the vegetation stand out from an interesting pink background. Out of season, you can get fantastic panoramic views of the dunes without any trace of footprints on their summits—something you'll be hard pressed to achieve in Death Valley or Colorado's Great Sand Dunes. Contrary to lighter colored sand dunes, like those of White Sands, it is not necessary to compensate by overexposing. A normal exposure will preserve the shadows and relief of the motifs on the sand as well as the beautiful ocher color. Try to be in position on the dunes at Sunset; you'll be treated to an unbelievably pink glow turning into a dramatic red during a brief but miraculous last minute before the sun disappears behind the horizon. In early summer, there are nice big yellow wildflowers near the boardwalks, making good foregrounds for shots of the dunes.

Getting there: The park is located about 15 miles from Mt. Carmel on the Ponderosa/Coral Pink Sand Dunes Scenic Backway. Coming from Zion or Bryce, leave US-89 about 3½ miles south of Mt. Carmel Junction. If coming from Kanab, exit US-89 about 8 miles north of Kanab. Signs mark the two roads. Watch out for livestock, as they are free to roam along this route.

There is another access from UT-389 southeast of Colorado City via Cane Beds Road. It passes through the Cottonwood Point Wilderness, which has abundant wildlife. The Arizona section of this road is unpaved but normally passable for passenger cars if driven with caution, except after a rain.

Time required: 1½ to 3 hours.

Red Canyon Slot

Red Canyon consists of two short but beautiful sections of twisted narrows, no longer than 200 feet each, with good photographic potential and no water holes or obstructions of any kind. If conditions are right, i.e., if the extremely deep sand along the way has been packed by recent rains, the canyon can be visited almost effortlessly, as you can drive your vehicle right to its entrance.

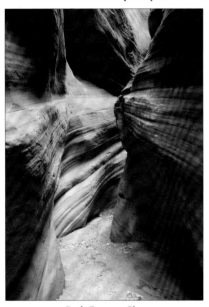

Red Canyon Slot

Getting there: Coming from Mt. Carmel Junction, drive 9.4 miles south and turn east (left) almost 100 yards past the southern route to the Coral Pink Sand Dunes. Coming from Kanab, turn right 2.6 miles past Angel/Kanab Canyon's entrance on US-89. After 0.2 mile on this road, turn left onto signed K2605 and follow it for 1.1 miles, then right on K2672 for 2.2 miles on an extremely sandy track continuing toward the Red Canyon drainage. An easy ¾-mile drive inside the drainage brings you to the mouth of the slot (37°10'46" 112°33'32"). A high-clearance 4WD vehicle is a must and you may have to deflate your tires to gain better traction in the sand. Be sure to carry a shovel for added security.

Time required: About 2½ hours round-trip.

Nearby location: About 5 miles north of Kanab, follow the sign for Kanab Canyon. This good road leads to Angel Canyon, a particularly lovely canyon that can be driven as a short loop. It is the home of Best Friends Animal Sanctuary and Angels Rest pet cemetery who own the property inside the canyon. However, the road through the canyon is public and you're free to wander about. One of the most interesting features is Angels Landing, a spectacular dome-shaped cave of red sandstone with a grassy area and amenities in front. This is a wonderful place to stop and relax if you're passing through the area and are tired. The canyon also contains rock art and some Indian ruins. The loop ends at US-89 and provides an alternate access to the Red Canyon Slot. You'll find the above-mentioned K2605 track to your right, just before reaching US-89.

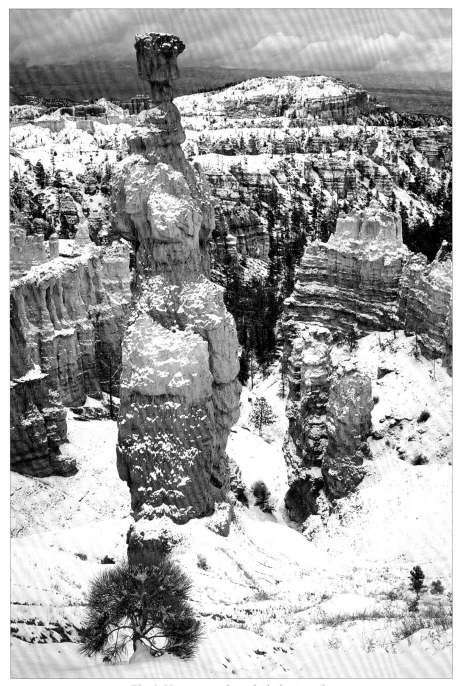

Thor's Hammer under a fresh dusting of snow

Chapter 4

AROUND BRYCE CANYON

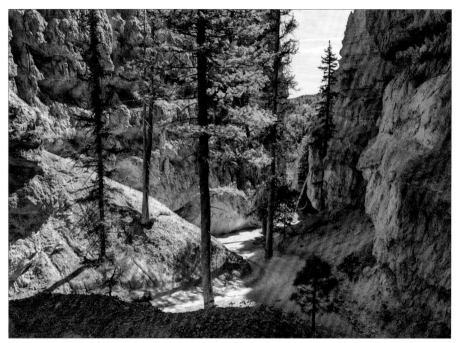

On the Navajo Trail

Introduction to Bryce Canyon National Park

Bryce Canyon, along with Arches, is the park preferred by the majority of visitors to the Southwest, especially foreign visitors, who come from all corners of the globe to admire and photograph it. The whole world, consequently, has seen images of Bryce and the name immediately invokes a geological phenomenon bordering on the supernatural. A case in point: a (now defunct) software application generating 3-D virtual landscapes was named after this national park and its publisher didn't have to explain the choice of name to the public. Happily or unhappily, its proximity to Las Vegas makes access easy. It's unlikely that you'll find solitude or spiritual communion with the environment at Bryce, but you are sure to find a landscape that will hold you in a hypnotic trance the first time you lay eyes on it. It's a landscape filled with weird and incredible formations combined with remarkable nuances of light and saturated with color.

Time required: To get the most out of Bryce, it's advisable to stay at one of the lodges or motels in the area so you can visit the park in the early morning hours and until sunset. It's also recommended that you take at least one hike on the canyon trails —an experience that involves a bit of effort.

Allow 2½ hours by car to visit the Bryce Amphitheater viewpoints and at least 2 hours to hike the canyon. If you don't have much time, go straight to Sunset Viewpoint. The Rim Trail between Sunrise and Sunset Points and Inspiration Point is an easy walk if you don't want to descend into the canyon proper.

Sunrise & Sunset Viewpoints

Sunset Point is arguably the best spot to admire and photograph Bryce Canyon. It's also the most popular and you won't be alone. The view on both sides is excellent, looking towards Sunrise Point on the left or Inspiration Point and Bryce Point on the right. The Silent City is set back from the first viewpoint to the right of the parking area. Despite the name of this viewpoint, mornings and late afternoons are both excellent for photography. If your time is limited, Sunset Point is the best place to catch Bryce in all its glory.

Sunrise Point doesn't offer such a spectacular panorama on both sides and the formations are not as densely packed as those at Sunset Point, but they are just as lovely. It's easier to isolate individual formations from Sunrise Point with a short telephoto lens, however.

Photo advice: You can be sure of one thing, all those magnificent photos of Bryce displayed at the Visitor Center or in the gift shops all around the park were taken either early in the morning or late in the afternoon. If you arrive at Bryce during the middle of the day and only stay a few hours, you can't hope to come away with professional quality photos. The canyon's formations must have a warm light skimming their surface, whether from the back or the side, to bring out the relief and color. For the best light, you should be at one of the Amphitheater viewpoints

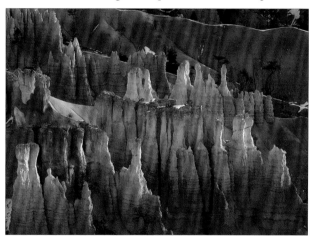

Hoodoos in the early morning

at dawn and use the rest of the morning to descend into the canyon. When shooting, watch out for overexposure, which could wash out the color of the spires.

Inspiration Point & Bryce Point

Inspiration Point offers the best view of the extraordinary conglomeration of spires that make up the Silent City, situated in a recess to the south of Sunset Point. The Rim Trail between Sunset and Inspiration Point displays a constant stream of spectacular views. You can easily stroll it in about twenty minutes. You'll find the crowds much thinner at both Bryce and Inspiration Points, which could make your photography a lot easier in summer.

Navajo & Queen's Garden Trails

To really absorb the magic of Bryce, a descent into the canyon is a must. And by then you'll understand why old Ebenezer Bryce called this canyon "a hell of

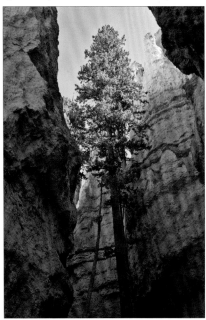

a place to lose a cow" as you take in the views, each more spectacular than the last. Many trails run among the hoodoos and take you right into the middle of these formations. Two of these, Queen's Garden Trail (about 1½ miles) and Navajo Trail (about 2.2 miles) carry most of the foot traffic. This is due not only to their location in the Amphitheater and their beauty, but because they are short and easy to reach. All the trails in the Amphitheater are connected and you can make a loop using the Navajo and the Queen's Garden Trails, which shortens the entire walk to 3 miles. The Navajo Trail descends from Sunset Point, passing by the famous rock chimney called Thor's Hammer and quickly arrives among the spires of Wall Street, which seem immense when viewed from below. The trek is short and not particularly dif-

Wall Street pine © John Stottlemyer

ficult, except for the ascent on the way back. The Queen's Garden Trail begins at Sunrise Viewpoint; it is rather short and not as steep as the Navajo Trail.

Time required: About 2 hours for the entire loop on the Navajo and Queen's Garden connected trails. Begin at Sunset Point, it's both easier and more spectacular. Each trail will take about one hour to complete separately.

Note: These two trails are about 8,000 feet in altitude. It can be extremely hot and dry in summer and it is imperative you carry enough water, a sun hat and sunscreen. You should be able to hike these trails in jogging shoes without problem, but use extreme caution, especially on the steeper parts. These trails are often snow-covered starting in October and continuing until the end of April. At that time, descent can be extremely risky without a pair of shoes with aggressive soles. Once inside the canyon, though, snow and ice are less of a problem and the going is not so steep.

Opposite page: Sunrise on the Amphitheater after a winter storm

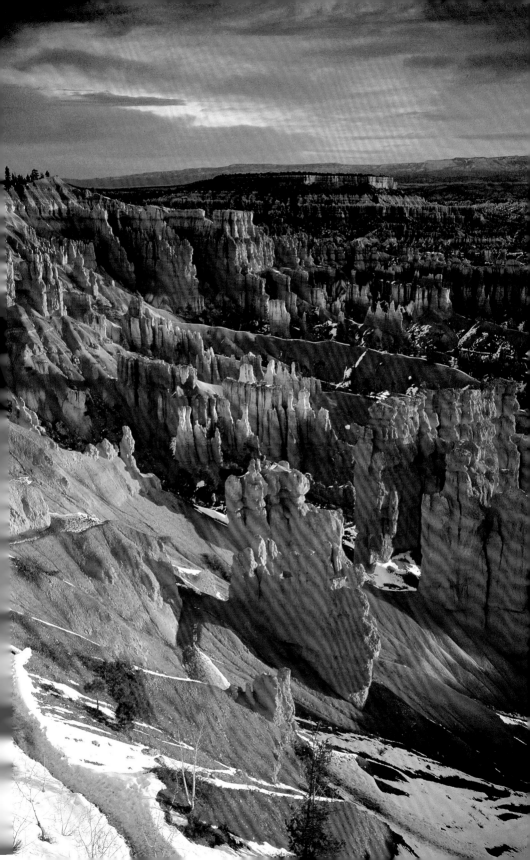

Peek-a-Boo Trail

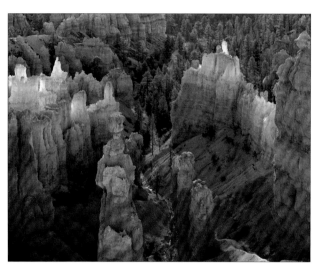

Sunset Point vista © Scott Walton

If you've enjoyed hiking the Navajo and Queen's Garden trails and are craving for more, you'll enjoy the Peek-a-Boo trail. In fact, time permitting, I strongly recommend combining the preceding walks with the Peek-a-Boo Loop. This adds another 4 miles to the walk (including the small connecting trail at the end of the Navajo Trail) for a total of 7 miles and approximately 4 to 5 hours. The Peek-a-Boo Loop offers solitude as well as great opportunities for less cliché photography, particularly at the Wall of Wisdom and The Cathedral. In addition to the beauty of the circuit, its variety makes it interesting, with many small switchbacks, passages close to the edge of the ravine and a couple of very short sections dug into the rock. On the other hand, it is a bit of a roller-coaster and often dusty because of the twice-daily commercial horseback rides. This trail is better hiked clockwise.

If you don't feel like tackling the whole loop on foot, consider a horseback ride. I recommend the A.M. half-day tour, which needs to be reserved at least a day before. Obviously, the odds of getting quality pictures while riding are pretty low, however.

Fairyland Viewpoint & Trail

You'll find Fairyland Point at the end of a 1-mile spur road to your left, between the Park boundary and the Visitor Center. It's easy to miss this road when entering the park for the first time.

Visitors, who tend to congregate around the more famous viewpoints near the Bryce Amphitheater, frequently neglect this one, as well as the trail of the same name. The Fairyland Loop trail is just as lovely and provides a completely different view of the canyon and its formations. The 8-mile trail meanders through Fairyland and Campbell canyons around Boat Mesa, with a short detour to admire the unusual formation of Tower Bridge. This trail has more open views than the classic Bryce Amphitheater's hikes; another bonus for photographers is the many touches of green and wood sprinkled against the red and orange rock chimneys. On the down side, there is a smaller concentration of spires and hoo-doos. The end of the loop follows the rim for 2.7 miles between Sunrise Point and Fairyland Point, but this can be omitted if you've arranged a car shuttle.

If you lack the time to do the entire Fairyland Loop trail or the Navajo/Queen's Garden loop trail, try following the first 1,500 feet of the Fairyland Trail down from Fairyland Point until you reach the promontory visible to the left of the viewpoint. The walk is easy and the views on both sides of the promontory are magnificent.

Time required: About 4 hours for the entire Fairyland Loop trail.

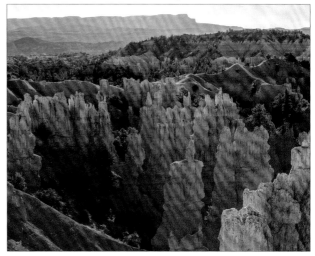

Fairyland Canyon © Tom Till

Mossy Cave

Located in the northern section of the park, this extremely pleasant trail, almost flat three quarters of the way and less frequented, follows a perennial creek meandering among a spectacular landscape of red spires, before reaching a deep alcove with green vegetation. A couple hundred yards before the alcove, a spur trail leads to the right to a pretty little cascade. Water level permitting, you can cross the stream just above the cascade, where an unofficial but well-trodden footpath leads up to openings in the red spires.

Getting there: On the west side of Scenic Byway 12, 4 miles from Tropic or from UT-63, going into Bryce Canyon.

Time required: About 1 hour.

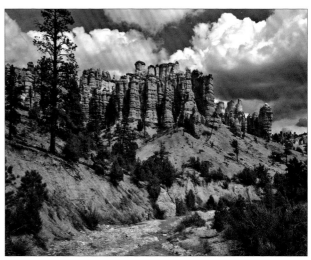

Mossy Cave Castle © John Stottlemyer

Yovimpai Point & Rainbow Point

These two viewpoints, at the southernmost tip of the park, appear very different from the amphitheater. You won't find similar scenery there. This is a superb alpine landscape and an interesting contrast after the Amphitheater, if you have the time. From the Visitor Center, the road climbs southward for 17 miles to the heart of a forest where pines and aspens blend. You'll find lots of wildlife here and an almost total absence of cars, out of season. From Yovimpai Point, the view takes in all the steps of the Grand Staircase to the south. From Rainbow Point, close to 8,500 feet in elevation, you have a sensational, unobstructed panorama of the Pink Cliffs, the highest tread on the Grand Staircase. The 1-mile round-trip Bristlecone Loop Trail gives you the opportunity to view some ancient bristlecone pines and take spectacular photos of the tortuous forms of these members of the world's oldest living plant species. Some of their cousins in California's White Mountains are 5,000 years old and still growing. On the way back to the main area of the park, you can stop at several viewpoints along the road. However, these are not as spectacular as those from the rim of the amphitheater, arguably with the exception of the Natural Bridge viewpoint.

Time required: At least 2 hours round-trip from the Visitor Center. If you're short on time, concentrate on the main amphitheater close to the Visitor Center.

Red Canyon

Red Canyon, under the jurisdiction of the Dixie National Forest, is an excellent prelude to Bryce if you are coming from Zion. For the majority of visitors, Red Canyon usually means a quick stop along the side of the road to snap a few shots before continuing on to Bryce. That's too bad, since Red Canyon has a personality all its own. Its formations are definitely different from those of Bryce and some colors—reds in particular—are even more intense. For off-season visitors, arriving in greater numbers all the time, it's a first-rate alternative to the icy, snowbound trails of Bryce.

Among the variety of available trails, the easiest and most pleasant is without doubt Pink Ledges, a 1-mile loop of less than 30

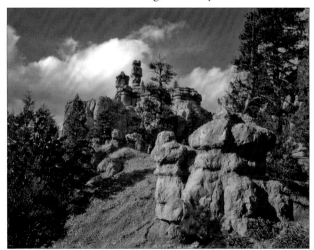
Red Canyon vista

minutes, starting from the Visitor Center and passing several extremely aesthetic viewpoints. The trail is very easy and a perfect alternative for those who don't want to tackle the Navajo/Queen's Garden loop trail in Bryce Canyon.

Much more difficult is the Photo Trail, located ¾ mile west of the Visitor Center. This short trail climbs steeply to the heights and offers some nice vistas. The contrast between the abrupt halt of the angular formations and the peaceful valley of the Sevier River below is interesting to observe.

For longer hiking, the Cassidy Trail, about 1 mile east of the Visitor Center, offers solitude and a pleasant stroll far from the crowd in a lovely, steeply-banked canyon bordered with trees. Nothing too photogenic, however.

For an even longer hike (about 4.5 miles with 700 feet of elevation gain) also away from the crowds, you can do a nice loop around the colorful mountain south of Scenic Byway 12. Starting across from the Visitor Center, take the Red Canyon bicycle trail to site #23 of the campground, where the Buckhorn Trail begins. Walk up this trail until its juncture with the Golden Wall Trail where

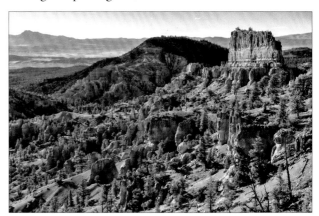

Golden Wall Trail © *Philippe Schuler*

you'll be rewarded with photogenic slickrock hoodoos, huge walls that turn golden in late afternoon, as well as spectacular views of the red rock country and the Sevier Valley in the background. An easy descent brings you back just west of the Visitor Center. Count on about 3 hours for the entire loop with time for photography.

If you enjoyed Red Canyon and would like to add a little variety to your photography, I highly recommend a short hike along the Casto Canyon Trail in the western part of the park. To get there, drive about 1½ miles west of the Visitor Center and take Casto Canyon Road for 3.2 miles, heading north. This dirt road is normally passable by passenger cars. The Casto trail is shared with ATVs and equestrians, but a brief jaunt along the first ½ mile brings beautiful views of formations similar to Red Canyon, yet different. The northwest side (to your left) offers the most attractive shots, but the east side makes a great panoramic shot at sunset just a couple hundred yards from the trailhead.

About a mile south, Losee Canyon offers a good hike, but is less interesting photographically. The exception is the Arches trail, an easy 0.7-mile hike that leads to a photogenic red wall with several windows, hence the trail's name. Along the trail you'll pass a stone structure alleged to have served as a food storage for Butch Cassidy and his gang.

Photo advice: In adapting to the angles of the sun, the light is as good in the morning as in the afternoon. If the sun is very strong, be careful not to under-expose the red rock if you use a matrix-type meter. Conversely, take care not to overexpose the rock. A setting of ½ f/stop on either side should be enough to assure a perfect exposure. The east side of the Pink Ledges Trail is highly recommended for photography.

Getting there: Either follow SB-12 west from Bryce Canyon or from US-89, go east on SB-12 toward Bryce.

Time required: About a half hour for a brief tour of the Pink Ledges. Up to one entire day if you hike the Buckhorn-Golden Wall loop and trails in the Casto road area.

Cedar Breaks National Monument

This National Monument resembles Bryce, though it presents some original formations. Cedar Breaks is laid out in the form of a vast, uninterrupted semi-circular amphitheater, deeper than Bryce is and equally as colorful. Does it merit a detour? Without hesitation, yes, for enthusiasts desiring complete insight into the national parks of the Southwest, but no, for visitors who only have a week to ten days to do the Grand Circle.

Cedar Breaks' location is close to 10,000 feet high and the summit is often subjected to extremely violent winds. Be sure to take a windbreaker on all hikes, even in summer. The Monument closes around mid-October because of heavy snowfalls and remains closed until late May. The plateau is less obstructed than that of Bryce, with some good-size prairies interspersed among the forest pines. Scenic Byway 14 between the valley of the Sevier River and Cedar City is absolutely lovely. In winter, the snowfields of Duck Creek are invaded by snowmobiles, a very tempting sight if you do not mind the noise.

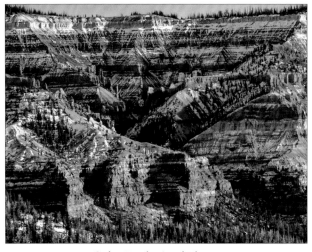

Cedar Breaks Amphitheater

Photo advice: Four viewpoints allow you to photograph the amphitheater along the 5-mile long Scenic Drive; each one is a bit different from the other. If you are pressed for time, Point Supreme is probably the best, as well as the most crowded. The Wasatch Ramparts trail is a nice walk with excellent late afternoon and evening views and allows you to photograph a rare group of ancient Bristlecone pines at Spectra Point. If you can be there in July, you'll have great wildflowers in the meadows on the east side of the road.

Getting there: On UT-148 from Scenic Byway 14 connecting with US-89 to Cedar City or from Scenic Byway 143 connecting Panguitch with I-15. Coming from the north,

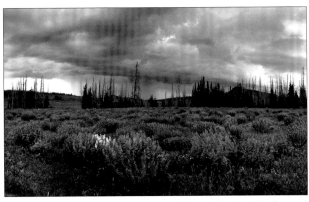

Thunderstorm at Cedar Breaks © Charles Wood

you'll pass the ski resort at Brian Head.

Time required: 1 to 1½ hours to cross the park and take pictures from the viewpoints. Add a couple of hours for a leisurely stroll on the Wasatch Ramparts trail.

The Twisted Forest

Close to Cedar Breaks is one of the best sites in the Southwest to photograph Bristlecone Pines. The site is part of the Ashdown Gorge Wilderness but the area where the trees are located is known as the Twisted Forest. The ancient trees are numerous, quite big, and more photogenic than at Cedar Breaks. From the car park, the trail goes down briefly before ascending extremely steeply—at this high elevation I guarantee you'll be gasping for air—passing through the first spectacular open grove. There are some really good compositions to be found here, so you may want to spend some time at this grove. The trail continues up for a short while until it reaches a ridge, where you are greeted by an awesome 1,300-foot drop-off. Using caution, continue to the right along the ridge in search of interesting bristlecone specimens below. While there is no real danger if you pay attention, this is not a place to take young children. Continuing just a couple hundred yards on the ridge brings out distant views of the Cedar Breaks amphitheater—within reach of a medium telephoto.

Keep an eye on the weather in late afternoon. The ridge is at 10,000 feet and temperatures can drop tremendously in a matter of minutes.

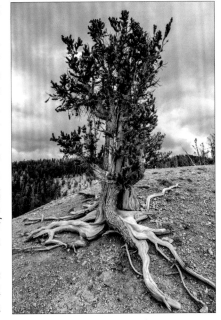

A gnarly old Bristlecone

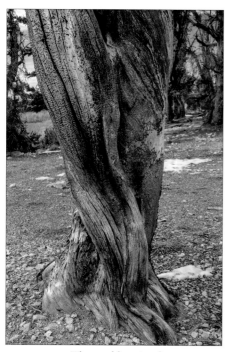

Thoroughly twisted

Photo advice: A wide or very wide angle lens works best for Bristlecone pines, including detail shots.

Getting there: From Cedar Breaks on UT-143, turn left on Sugarloaf Mountain Rd., located just past the big curve when approaching Brian Head village (2.8 miles from the junction between UT-143 and UT-148). Continue 2.5 miles, then make a left on Summit Canyon Rd. and drive another mile until you see the sign for the car park, which is on a short spur to the left. From downtown Parowan, take UT-143 for about 7.5 miles, turn right on Dry Lakes Road and follow it for 7 miles until you see the sign for the car park. Watch out for ice or mud in late spring and early fall. After an early October storm, I slid on a large patch of ice on a downhill curve (while in 4WD), and ended up with my two left wheels in a ditch before I could stop my truck.

Time required: 2½ to 3 hours including travel time.

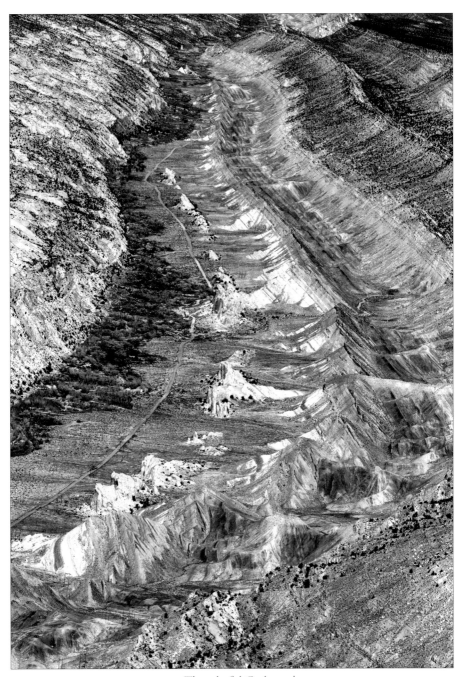

The colorful Cockscomb

Chapter 5

ALONG THE PARIA

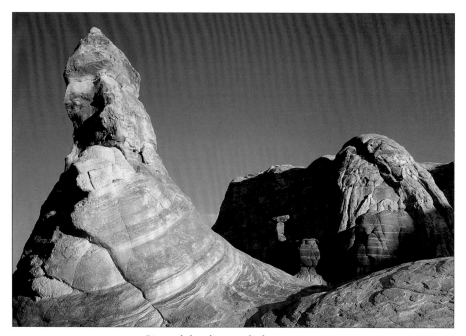

Rimrock hoodoos catch the morning sun

The Cockscomb

The fantastic Cockscomb is a 50-mile long fault crossing the Grand Staircase and the Vermilion Cliffs National Monuments from north to south, roughly following Cottonwood Canyon Road (BLM-400) and House Rock Valley Road (BLM-700). From the sky, the Cockscomb appears like a giant wound on the earth's crust; it is arguably one of the most remarkable geologic formations of the Colorado Plateau, especially in the section north of US-89 following Cottonwood Canyon Road.

After visiting the principal sites along the Cockscomb, we'll explore other spectacular geologic formations located on both sides of US-89 in the vicinity of the Paria River drainage.

Cottonwood Canyon Road

Driving the 40 miles of narrow and unpaved Cottonwood Canyon Road is truly enchanting if road conditions are favorable, which is most of the time. There is outstanding scenery all along, or accessible from, this popular route: a high plateau to the north including a narrow canyon and an impressive arch, a splendid valley lined with spectacular geologic formations and cottonwood trees in the center, and colorful badlands to the south. In the following sections, I'll describe landmarks and side trips along the road in a north to south direction.

Cottonwood Canyon Road is often passable by passenger cars, with some caution. However, you should always stop to check the weather forecast at the visitor centers in Cannonville, Kanab, Escalante, Big Water or the Paria Contact Station before embarking, as rain can make the road impassable even for 4WD vehicles. Under no circumstances should this road be driven if rain is threatening. After a heavy thunderstorm, the route can become a muddy morass in just a few minutes and trap any vehicle for hours or even days. Practically every year, some motorists get stranded in the mud for a couple of nights before being pulled out at great cost once the tow truck gets through. The BLM closes the road for extended periods of time when it is deemed too muddy to be passable. If it hasn't rained much during summer, it can also be very sandy in places, especially south of the confluence of Cottonwood Wash and the Paria River.

Exercise caution on Cottonwood Canyon road, as many people have a tendency to drive it a bit too fast.

Getting there: Cottonwood Canyon Road officially starts at the end of the paved road leading south from Cannonville on Scenic Byway 12 to Kodachrome Basin State Park. If you are coming from US-89, you'll find Cottonwood Canyon Road near milepost 18, about 4 miles past Church Wells when coming from Page and about 2 miles past the Paria Contact Station turnoff when coming from Kanab.

Time required: Don't count on using Cottonwood Road as a shortcut, it is a place where you should take your time. Many interesting spots border Cottonwood Canyon Road and you'll want to stop often to explore and photograph, easily stretching the 1½ hours it takes to hurriedly drive it into a much longer time. You'll need at least 1½ days to visit all the sites described below with sufficient time for photography. It's possible to camp anywhere along the road since Grand Staircase-Escalante National Monument is jointly administered by the BLM, and their policy concerning camping in the wild is very liberal.

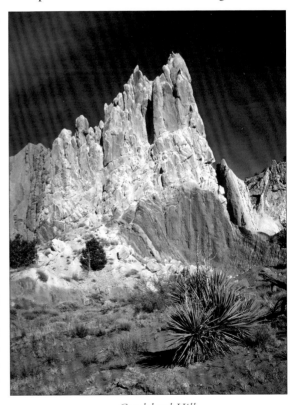

Candyland Hill

Round Valley Draw

Located close to Cottonwood Canyon Road, this is an interesting canyon with a good section of meandering narrows that can be hiked in a relatively short time. The wall color is rather pale but there is good texture to the sandstone.

After signing the trail register, hike for about ¾ mile inside the wash, which is quite open at this point. Some people have driven their 4WD inside the wash right to the beginning of the narrows. Please, don't follow their example; it is illegal to drive off the Monument's existing roadways.

It is easier to enter the narrows right at their onset, a very obvious spot looking from above like a corkscrew. The slot immediately starts with a mildly challenging 12 foot drop-off that can be negotiated without help and without any chimneying by most agile persons. A short sling will come in handy to drop your bag to the bottom and, later on, to get past the bigger obstacles. Although it's not really deep, the initial part of the slot feels quite narrow and closed in. After a while, the canyon opens up a bit and you reach a first chokestone that is easily circumvented. Soon after that, there is a second chokestone that is much larger and deeper, requiring some careful hand and foot placement to descend to the lower level on the right side. It is best to have a partner for this obstacle.

Once you've cleared the second chokestone, the narrows become very tall, but after another 10 minutes they open up and the canyon becomes much wider. The point where the narrows end is quite photogenic when you look back. From then on, it is less than ½-hour to the junction with Hackberry Canyon, about 2½ miles from the start, where you can retrace your steps to return.

Getting there: About 6.7 miles south of the beginning of Cottonwood Canyon Road at the Kodachrome Basin State Park junction, just after a steep descent, you'll see a marker on the north side of the road announcing the crossing of Round Valley Draw. A dirt road leaves to the south with a small sign pointing to the Rush Beds. This is your road. Although it is usually in good condition, this road is infrequently maintained and high-clearance is recommended due to deep ruts in places. You may be out of luck after a bad flood and there is a narrow passage over a wash after about 1 mile that can be problematic in some years. I have been there after a flash flood collapsed both sides of the road, leaving only inches on each side of the tires, forcing me to retreat. You'll reach the car park on the right side after about 1.6 miles.

You may also choose to enter Round Valley Draw from the bottom of the narrows, via Hackberry Canyon, by descending a steep trail from the Upper Slickrock Bench Road. You'll find this road 5.8 miles from the beginning of Cottonwood Canyon Road. Be sure to bear left at the Y after you've crossed and closed the fence line behind you and you'll reach the recommended trailhead for people backpacking Hackberry Canyon. The higher car park at the end of the right spur requires a considerably longer descent through very loose scree.

Time required: 1½ to 3 hours, depending on how long you wish to stay in the narrows and how far you want to go.

Grosvenor Arch

About 10 miles from the northern end of Cottonwood Canyon Road, or 2.8 miles past the junction with Round Valley Draw's access road, you'll find the turnoff for Grosvenor Arch. From here, it is only a mile to the spectacular double arch spanning almost 90 feet and towering 152 feet above the ground. The area around the arch is developed, with amenities and a paved trail to the bottom of the arch. It is possible to climb to the back of the arch using a steep path on the east side.

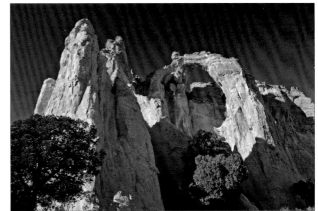

Photo advice: There is a great angle from the very bottom of the arch, shooting straight up with a very wide-angle lens. The light color of the Dakota Sandstone bestows a warm golden hue to the arch in the late afternoon sun. Early morning works well too, with the roofs of the two spans basked in golden backlight.

Grosvenor Arch © John Stottlemyer

Candyland & The Cottonwood Narrows

About 3½ miles south of the Grosvenor Arch turnoff, you'll come to a saddle dominating some extremely colorful badlands on the east side of the road with another saddle less than 0.3 mile further south. Some BLM Rangers like to refer to it as Candyland due to its white and red rocks and pinnacles. This is arguably the most spectacular photographic spot on Cottonwood Canyon Road and you can easily spend an hour walking and photographing between the two saddles. This spot has an even better perspective from the south and is best lit in the second part of the afternoon.

On the west side of the road and about halfway between the two saddles, you'll find the upper entrance to the Cottonwood Wash Narrows, which run somewhat parallel to the road. Take one of the footpaths going down and go left for the main narrows. These narrows are only moderately spectacular but they present the advantage of being short, with no obstacles, and close to the road.

You can also enter from the south, about 1 mile downstream, from a car park on the west side of the road. From here, follow the footpath crossing the wash and leading to the lower entrance. About 0.2 mile from this lower trailhead, to the left, is an interesting sandstone wall with many intricate patterns.

Heart of the Cockscomb

Right at the heart of the Cockscomb, there is an excellent undeveloped camp-site about 5 miles south of the lower entrance to the Cottonwood Narrows (it is less than 10 miles south of the Grosvenor Arch turnoff). This makes a good base for exploring the sights along Cottonwood Canyon Road and allows you to experience good light after sunrise and before sunset.

Continuing south on Cottonwood Canyon Road about 0.8 mile from the campsite, you'll notice near the west side of the road a group of white limestone bluffs sticking out at an impossible angle with shades of purple-colored clay on their backside. This fascinating hogback is a great spot for photography. You can reach a good vantage point (37°18'58" 111°53'07") painlessly by walking in a broad circle from the south without having to traverse any gullies. This spot is best photographed just before sunset.

About 1¼ miles south of the campsite, you will cross a low pass over some badlands with an incredible view of the serrated ridges of the Cockscomb mono-cline. Park at the pullout for a great mid-telephoto shot compressing the perspective of the monocline. This is best photographed in the morning.

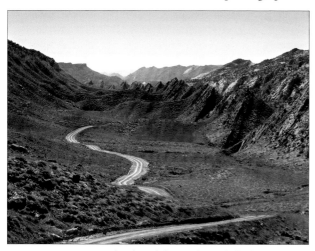

Serrated ridge of the Cockscomb fault

As you near the towering shape of Castle Rock, dominating the ridge to your right, the road now levels off inside the fault. One major problem you'll soon notice as you search for photo opportunities, is the almost constant presence of electrical lines marring the landscape.

About 15 miles south from the Grosvenor Arch turnoff, you can drive up the Brigham Plains Road (BLM 430) to the top of the Cockscomb if you have an SUV with good clearance. From here, you'll have a fantastic bird's eye view of the fault. It makes a great photograph looking north, preferably in late afternoon. Looking west across the fault, you'll see the unusual cross-bedding of Yellow Rock and, in the distance, you will catch a glimpse of Mollie's Nipple and No Man's Mesa. The beginning of Brigham Plains Road is extremely steep and a bit intimidating, but it is not difficult to drive as far as the crest, which is less than a mile away from Cottonwood Canyon Road. Go back the same way and don't expect to make a loop continuing on the Brigham Plains Road, as it becomes really bad further up and most people turn back when things get nasty.

Lower Hackberry Narrows

If you feel you've been in your car too long and are in need of a good hike to stretch your legs. Lower Hackberry Canyon is just the place for you: an easy, refreshing jaunt inside a spectacular setting. There is, however, one minor caveat: Hackberry Canyon has a perennial stream and requires frequent wading in ankle-deep water, so you must be willing to get your feet wet. I must add that there is some quicksand—nothing dangerous but your legs can sink to your knees into the soft watery sand. Take a pair of wading shoes or some boots you're not afraid to waste. There is no scrambling involved, so an old pair of running shoes would do just fine.

After parking, cross Cottonwood Wash and enter the deep, vertical walls of Hackberry Canyon. The narrows are immediately very deep but large enough at the top to be well lit. The sandstone walls, already beautiful from the get-go, turn a very dark red after 1 mile. A tall sandstone needle called Finger Rock appears on your right. Around mile 1.7, the canyon becomes suddenly wider for about 2 miles and loses part of its appeal, so this can be a good place to backtrack. If you continue on, look for some cairns and a faint footpath to your left at about mile 4.3. A short walk leads to the well-preserved remains of the Frank Watson cabin.

Getting there: Drive back north ¼ mile on Cottonwood Canyon Road from the Brigham Plains Road junction, about 15 miles south of the Grosvenor Arch turnoff, and find the car park on the east side of the road.

Time required: About 2 hours to see the best part of the narrows; at least 4 hours to see the Watson Cabin.

Yellow Rock

Near the junction of Cottonwood Canyon Road and Brigham Plains Road, you can also climb to Yellow Rock, a vast expanse of colorful slickrock with a large amount of yellow—as the name implies. There are also many patches of beautiful reddish and pastel sandstone as well as some spectacular cross-bedding, somewhat reminiscent of the Coyote Buttes. The 360° view from the top of Yellow Rock is simply awesome. This is an outstanding photographic destination and one of my favorite spots in the Paria area. I have visited it numerous times and each trip has led to new discoveries and interesting photography. I have no doubt that you'll feel the same way. Be forewarned, however, the beginning of the trail is a very steep hill with a 45° incline and very loose rocks. Be extremely cautious if you decide to attempt it. Although it is not physically hard per se and there is no danger of falling a long way, the potential is there to hurt yourself or twist an ankle, especially during the descent. It is preferable to do this hike with a partner.

The hill takes less than 20 minutes to climb until you reach a saddle. From there, you can see into the mouth of Hackberry Canyon to the north. The trail then turns into a well-trod path, cairned at regular intervals. It climbs steadily for a short while until the enormous humpback of Yellow Rock comes into full view. It is an impressive mass of colorful, cross-bedded sandstone. Although appearing very distant at first glance, due to the lack of perspective, you'll be

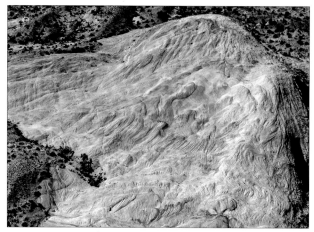

The massive scale of Yellow Rock

surprised later on at how quickly you reach the first slab of sandstones.

Look behind you and note the tall sandstone outcrop looking like horns, close to where you emerged from the hill. Remember to aim just to the left of this outcrop when you return.

There are now several ways to reach Yellow Rock itself and it's up to you to decide. You cannot see everything under the best light in a single outing, so pick one direction and go; you can't go wrong anyway.

If you decide to leave the main footpath and go north, you'll come to a patch of serrated dark rocks eroded into Gothic shapes. Continuing in the same direction while descending toward the sea of slickrock, you'll notice some remarkable rocks resembling petrified wood. A bit further yet, you'll find yourself looking once again into Hackberry Canyon. At this point you can start hiking west, making a gradual ascent on some truly amazing slickrock slabs.

If you continue on the main footpath from the spot where I suggested that you look back at the horned outcrop earlier on, you'll soon reach the base of the sea of slickrock. You can choose to climb directly to the top of Yellow Rock, where you'll find the largest patches of yellow and orange, or you can follow some distantly spaced cairns on the slickrock, circumnavigating the base of Yellow Rock to the left, which is the south side. Once again, you'll be treated to some lovely, multicolored slabs of slickrock. A small outcrop in the form of a Tibetan stupa will come into view on the south side of Yellow Rock. This is a good place to aim for, as you'll be following long slabs of slickrock looking like scales of giant snakes along the way.

Climbing to the top of Yellow Rock from its eastern side is much easier than it seems and provides a breathtaking 360° panoramic view. To the north, you'll see Castle Rock; to the west, the Paria drainage with No Man's Mesa and Mollie's Nipple in the background; to the southwest the badlands of Old Paria and in the distance the reflection of cars on US-89. To the south you'll see Yellow Rock Valley and the Box, a deep canyon cutting through the Cockscomb fault, linking the Paria to Cottonwood Wash. To the northeast, you get an awesome view of Cottonwood Canyon Road and the stegosaurus-like fins of the monocline stretching in the distance at the center of the fault.

Time permitting, you can rejoin the trail cir-
cling Yellow Rock to the south and hike to a rock
garden in a valley to the west. Better yet, you can
aim toward the impossibly colorful area which you
can see to the south and explore it to your heart's
content. With a car shuttle, an outstanding cross-
country traverse can also be undertaken in the
direction of the Box via the very reddish formation
of Red Top that you can spot from Yellow Rock.

Photo advice: The best light is in late afternoon
and until sunset. Most of the sea of slickrock in
front of Yellow Rock is in the shade ½ hour before
sunset. Watching sunset from the top of Yellow
Rock is an exhilarating experience, so it's best to
do your photography on the sea of slickrock prior
to that. All kinds of focal lengths can be used on

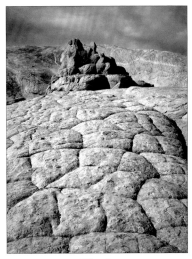

The Stupa

Yellow Rock, from a super-wide angle to accentuate the unreal look of this site
to a telephoto compressing the cross-bedding's perspective. You may want to
consider a slight amount of underexposure to further accentuate the colors.

Getting there: Park at the junction of Cottonwood Canyon Road and Brigham
Plains Road (BLM-430). If you're coming from the south, this car park is located
about 14 miles from US-89. To find the Yellow Rock Trail, aim southwest toward
an opening in the Cockscomb in the first drainage about 300 yards south of the
mouth of Hackberry Canyon. There is no footpath and you have to cross a couple hundred yards of thick brush and trees separating the road from Cottonwood
Wash, where you may have to wade a bit if the creek is running.

Time required: Plan on a minimum of 2½ hours, but this area can be explored
for hours on end.

Nearby location: The Box of the Paria is a short but pretty 1-mile canyon cutting
through a portion of the Cockscomb fault and linking Cottonwood Wash to the
Paria River near the Old Paria town site. You'll find an access road to your right

about 2.3 miles south of the junction of
Cottonwood Canyon Road and Brigham
Plains Road. In dry circumstances, it is
possible to walk the entire length of The
Box, fording the rocky bed of the Paria
River several times in shallow water.
This is a fun hike, leading to some large
eroded windows and sheer walls with
good reddish color. The Box also pro-
vides access to the aforementioned Red
Top and Yellow Rock Valley.

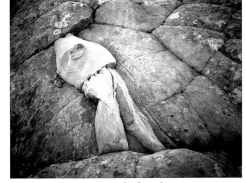

Body found

Hackberry Heights

Close to Yellow Rock and just north of Hackberry Canyon lies another vast field of sandstone, but this one's dominant hue is more in the pink tones, with accents of yellow.

The approach is similar to that of better-known Yellow Rock: A convenient car park just across the dry wash, followed by an extremely steep climb, then an easy incline to the top once you reach the plateau.

The climb has about the same angle as Yellow Rock, but it is longer and requires a sustained effort that may be too much for some—the total elevation gain is almost 900 feet. On the plus side, it is easy to follow and there is almost no scree underfoot so you get good traction. The rocks are very sharp however, so take your time and watch your foot placement. Regardless of the shape you're in, it's bound to give you a pretty good workout, so be sure to have plenty of water and to pace yourself.

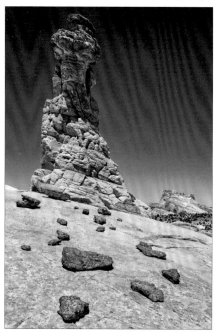

Big Cottonwood Hoodoo & The Castle

Start the climb on the right side of the wide gully and you'll see some cairns almost immediately. You'll reach the beginning of the plateau after approximately 20 to 30 minutes. From here, it's easy to follow the cairns to the ridge, which takes another 20 to 30 minutes. At the ridge, you'll discover the colorful hanging valley, with a round-ish sandstone dome in front of you and a vast expanse of sandstone bordered by a brownish slickrock wall to the left that turns golden at sunset. Note how the wall leads to a canyon to the far left. Eventually, you will exit the valley through this canyon to make a loop back to your car. Now look to the right end of the wall and the distant sandstone ridge and notice a tiny-looking hoodoo in the distance. This hoodoo is your goal. To reach it, begin by switchbacking down to the base of the aforementioned sandstone dome, then continue walking down on a mild incline to a depression in the sandstone leading toward the canyon. Cross this depression close to its beginning, where it's almost flat, and begin a gradual climb toward the hoodoo. It will take no more than fifteen minutes to reach it. It's a wonderful feeling to be crossing this colorful and isolated sea of sandstone. As you get closer, you'll realize that the hoodoo is actually very tall. From the hoodoo, you can see the rim of Hackberry Canyon and Yellow Rock to the south, part of the Cockscomb to the east, the sandstone dome, and the Castle in the distance to the north.

After taking photos, retrace your steps to the point where you crossed the depression, then follow the latter down toward the mouth of the canyon. Continue for about twenty minutes on an easy gradual descent inside the sandy canyon until you reach the other side of the wide gully you ascended at the beginning of the hike. Follow the slickrock to your left to rejoin the initial trail and return to your car.

Photo advice: Avoid the brutal mid-morning and early-afternoon sun on this remote and exposed plateau. The best light will be in the first hour after sunrise, when the hoodoo is lit on its best side. The initial climb will be much easier in the cooler temperature, but don't start until there is enough light to see the cairns after you reach the first ridge. Late afternoon light is also very good, but don't linger because the descent would be extremely dangerous in the dark.

Getting there: From Cottonwood Canyon Road, take the short spur leading to a small car park at 37°16'18" 111°54'16". The initial climb tops out near 37°16'36" 111°54'24". The depression I mention is roughly at 37°16'36" 111°54'47" and the big hoodoo is at 37°16'22" 111°55'01".

Time required: 3½ to 5 hours.

The Wahweap Hoodoos

The Wahweap Hoodoos are some of the most beautiful white pedestal rocks in the area and are becoming more frequently photographed by visitors from all over the world.

From the trailhead, walk in Wahweap Creek for almost 4 miles until you find the first hoodoos—including a very tall one—at the foot of the left cliffs. The walking is easy and it will take about 1¼ hours to get there at a normal pace. There are three groups of hoodoos along the cliff to your left. Each group is separated from the others by a couple hundred yards. The first group is the least interesting, despite the presence of a very tall hoodoo, and your time will be much better spent at the second group—which I like to call 'Hoodoo Central'. Better yet is the last group, the 'Towers of Silence', which is the most interesting photographically, at around 37°09'45" 111°42'45".

Photo advice: All the Wahweap Wash hoodoos are best photographed from sunrise to early morning regardless of

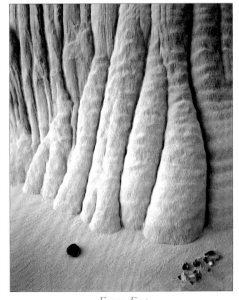

Furry Feet

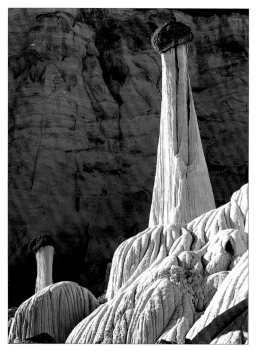

Towers of Silence in Wahweap Wash

season. During the winter months, however, there is no direct light on the Towers of Silence but a very nice soft light instead. In summer, the Towers are directly illuminated from sunrise on while the tall silt-stone cliff in the background remains in shadow. This allows for nice contrasty shots making the Towers stand out, although the background will tend to have a slight bluish cast.

Under direct light conditions, be sure to apply at least +½ stop to +1 full stop of exposure compensation to your shots or they'll turn slightly greyish. Jpeg shooters can experiment with different white balance settings to get several variations in tonality. The Wahweap Wash hoodoos area is all silt-stone and offers many possibilities to turn small details into fascinating abstracts.

Be sure to tread lightly and not to bump any formations with your feet or tripod. Leave this amazing and delicate area as pristine as possible, so those who come after you can enjoy it just as much!

Getting there: As of this writing, there is only one authorized access to the Wahweap Hoodoos, starting from the little community of Big Water. Leave US-89 at Big Water, drive through town and at the Y with Smoky Mountain Road, bear left on Nipple Creek Road (BLM-327) heading northwest. Follow it along the ponds of the Fish Hatchery for 3.8 miles to the Wahweap Creek cross-

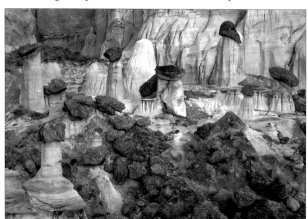

Hoodoo Central

ing. Continue ¼ mile past the creek to a car park on the right side of the road. Walk in the wash, straight past the big fence. Wahweap Creek is the main wash heading north to the right of Coyote Creek. The latter, which is heading west, is narrower and has redder cliffs.

Note: The old access road via BLM-431 is now fenced

at the junction with BLM-430, and the bench is now a Wilderness Study Area. Access is closed to all mechanized travel, including mountain bikes.

Time required: You'll need half a day to explore and photograph the two most interesting groups of hoodoos.

The White Rocks

The White Rocks are located in a seldom-visited area north of Church Wells and west of the Upper Wahweap Creek drainage. It consists of outstanding badlands, white hoodoos and red-capped towers. The soft white shale, remnant of an ancient seabed, has been twisted into remarkable shapes by forces of erosion. It is a fascinating area to explore and photograph, often with the striking silhouette of Chimney Rock in the background.

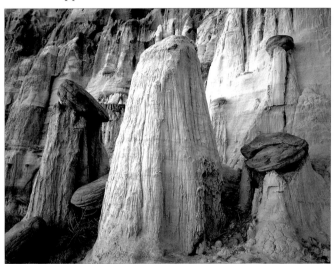

From the trailhead past the locked gate, walk due north for almost 2 miles to reach the end of a broad canyon near 37°09'38" 111°45'47". You'll find tall hoodoos jutting out

The Great White Ghost

from the bench, an area I call lower White Rocks. Exploring the upper White Rocks, located further to the east, is more difficult. It involves hiking on rough terrain, with steep slopes and no trail, and requires good routefinding skills. There is no shade and the heat reflection from the whitish eroded terrain is brutal. This is not a hike you'd want to do on a hot day. To get to the upper White Rocks, backtrack about 0.4 mile from the end of lower White Rocks to a broad side-canyon to the east. Take this canyon, passing some massive hoodoos, and continue 0.6 mile over a sandy plateau to reach a vast eroded depression with many hoodoos. A good waypoint to aim for is a huge 40-foot tall hoodoo at 37°09'22" 111°45'11". It is surrounded by many smaller ones peppered along the cliffs of a large white amphitheater, with striking touches of purple in places. Another group can be found ¼ mile to the east. Aim up for a striking twisted-shaped hoodoo at 37°09'23" 111°44'57". From here, walk (cautiously) east, staying right below the rim, to another group of impressive, colorful hoodoos. After taking it in, continue walking east, still just below the rim. The going gets easier as you

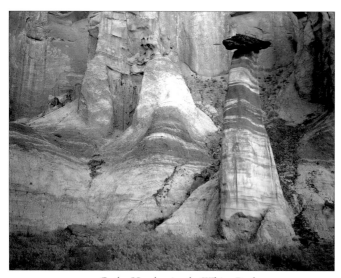

Cocky Hoodoo in the White Rocks

reach a slickrock area in a rather flat canyon with strikingly beautiful reds and pinks, and other subtle nuances. You can now exit to the rim at 37°09'16" 111°44'22". This spot is where you'd park if BLM-431 (and the side road leading to this point), were to reopen to vehicles one day—a long shot at the time of this writing. Cross the old Jeep road and walk east a few hundred yards, along a fence, to the edge of Sidestep Canyon, a vast amphitheater with more hoodoos. Going down into and hiking inside this canyon are both difficult, but you can get good shots from the rim with a medium-range zoom. The easiest and shortest way to return to your car from the former car park on the rim is to walk down the old Jeep road and hike cross-country, aiming for 37°08'27" 111°44'49" where you can cross the wash. Continue close to the rim (as the wash turns into a canyon) to where you parked earlier, close to the reservoir.

Photo advice: There are many different groups of hoodoos with varying orientation inside this wide area and it is impossible to recommend a perfect time of day, except to say that early morning before sunrise is always a good time for the White Rocks, as the ground can turn dreadfully hot later in the day. I find that white hoodoos photograph well in the shade under a bright blue sky, when they acquire an interesting bluish cast.

Getting there: With the closure of BLM-431 past the junction with BLM-430, a.k.a. Brigham Plains Road, the upper White Rocks are no longer accessible from the top (Jack Riggs Bench), making visiting them a lot more strenuous. Access to both the lower and upper White Rocks is now strictly from the little community of Church Wells. Coming from Page on US-89, turn right at a red dirt road located 0.5 mile before Church Wells. It is BLM-435 and it's easy to miss! Follow it north for about 3.2 miles until you come to a cow fence with a gauntlet and a reservoir to your right. The track beyond this point is now closed shortly past the reservoir, so this is your trailhead.

Time required: 4 hours or more, from Church Wells, to explore the lower and upper White Rocks from the bottom.

The Rimrocks Hoodoos

The Rimrocks is an outstanding area of badlands and hoodoos, located just north of US-89 between the southern end of Cottonwood Canyon Road and the Cockscomb fault. It contains a large number of fascinating hoodoos, mushroom rocks and rock towers. The most prominent and accessible landmark of the Rimrocks is Toadstool Hoodoo (see page 1 of this book), a spectacular sandstone spire, shaped a bit like the Seattle Needle with a larger rotunda at the top. The area around Toadstool Hoodoo offers endless photographic opportunities, at different times of the day. About 30 feet from Toadstool Hoodoo is another prominent hoodoo, shorter and rounder. They are close enough to each other to make an oft-photographed duo. About 200 feet behind Toadstool Hoodoo, near the cliff, is a series of striking rock-capped sandstone towers, perfect for a late afternoon shot. Once you're done photographing Toadstool Hoodoo, follow the cairns on the rim to the west for about 300 yards until you come to a somewhat hidden recessed area to your right. It contains several large white towers, capped with brown slabs of hard rock. This area is in deep shadow until late morning and is best photographed in late afternoon.

Back on US-89, about a mile further to the west of the car park, lies another recessed canyon full of spectacular white towers coiffed with cap rocks. You can see this area with the naked eye from the Paria Contact Station across the road, but it is best observed with binoculars.

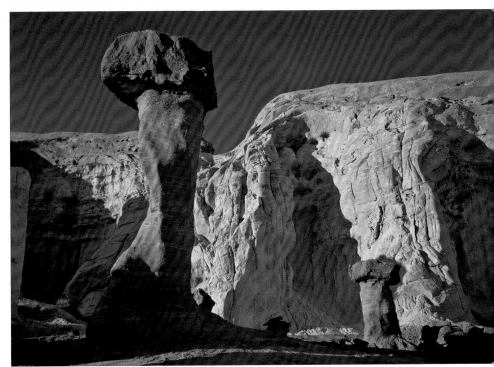

Rimrock hoodoos in late afternoon sun

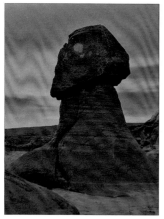
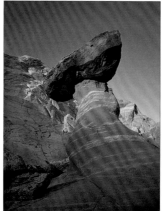
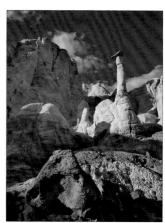

Hoodoos come in all shapes and sizes

Photo advice: Early morning and late afternoon both work well, with a preference for the afternoon. There are plenty of formations so you're guaranteed to find some that will be correctly exposed. Toadstool Hoodoo itself can be photographed successfully from different angles, with a variety of focal lengths and under various light conditions.

Getting there: On US-89 near milepost 20, about a mile east of the turnoff for the Paria Contact Station, there is a signed car park on the north side of the road. Cross the opening in the fence, sign the register, and follow the wash to the north for about 15 to 20 minutes. There is also a footpath running along the wash with cairns laid out in the second half to indicate the best way. Climb the low badlands at the end and the hoodoos will come into view. Despite the fact that the area north of the Paria Contact Station is fenced, it is all public land and can be explored on foot, at your own risk. This area is very fragile, so tread lightly.

It takes quite a bit of effort and route finding to climb to the other ledge, where the white hoodoos visible from the Paria Contact Station are located. Few people visit this area, so it's best to go with a companion. Cross the fence north of US-89 opposite the Paria Contact Station's road and walk northeast to the mouth of the canyon. You'll notice that the canyon ends in three arms; follow the right arm though a slot canyon, then scramble up carefully to the ledge, where the hoodoos will come into view.

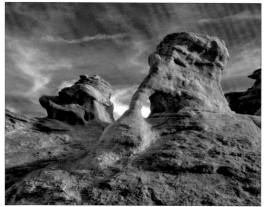

Oliphant

Time required: At least 1½ hours round-trip from US-89 for the Toadstool Hoodoo area alone.

Old Paria

Old Paria (also known as Old Pahreah) is an easy side trip off US-89 between Kanab and Page, accessible to all passenger cars except during or after a rain. It is an area where history meets breathtaking Chinle formation badlands for a highly rewarding photographic journey. The good dirt road starts innocuously enough but soon becomes roller-coaster like as it straddles a narrow ridge dominating colorful badlands on the right side. As the road dives down into the Paria valley it can become washboard-like, requiring some caution. You'll soon arrive at the site of the former Paria movie set. Originally erected in 1963 for the filming of Western movies, it was destroyed by a flash flood in 1999, rebuilt by the BLM with help of local funding, only to fall victim to arson in 2006. With such a tragic past, it comes as no surprise that there are no further plans to rebuild the set. Still, a set of interpretive panels, a picnic area, and restrooms are present. The stars of the show are now the exquisite, colorful badlands surrounding the old site!

A few hundred yards down the road, you'll find the Old Pahreah cemetery, the only remaining testimonial to human presence in the area. Take a short walk around the cemetery; it is a very moving reminder of the hard life of the early settlers who tried to eke out a living in this desolate area. About ½ mile further, you end up on the banks of the Paria. Across the river is the actual location of Old Pahreah, but nothing remains standing. Following the river to your right, you'll soon enter a pretty 1-mile long canyon known as the Box of the Paria; it leads through part of the Cockscomb fault to Cottonwood Wash (see *Nearby location* under the *Yellow Rock* section).

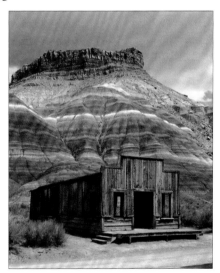

Old Paria 1999 © *Philippe Schuler*

Photo advice: In the vicinity of the picnic area or the cemetery, take some time to explore and photograph the amazing badlands, some of the most colorful you'll ever see in the Southwest, especially in the warm late afternoon light. If you are lucky enough to have a dark stormy sky, with streaks of light falling on the badlands, you'll be rewarded with amazing contrast and beautiful hues. If rain seems imminent, be sure not to linger in this area; you may not be able to climb the steep ramp leaving the picnic area. On your way back, take your pictures from the pull-out on the flat ridge, immediately after the ramp. It has a splendid view looking down into the badlands.

Getting there: At the Historical Marker, about 40 miles northwest of Page or 10 miles northwest of the Paria Contact Station turnoff on US-89, take the good

BLM-585 dirt road heading north and follow it for 5 miles to the movie set.
Time required: About 1 hour round-trip from US-89.

Wire Pass – Buckskin Gulch

This foray inside Wire Pass and a short stretch of Buckskin Gulch will give you a quick, but spectacular insight into the narrows of the Paria River area. Many people consider Buckskin Gulch as having the most interesting narrows on the Colorado Plateau.

Do not venture into Wire Pass and Buckskin Gulch if bad weather is threatening. Once in the canyon, you won't be able to get out in case of flash floods. The enormous tree trunks lodged in the walls several feet above you testify to the force and height of the flash floods that can hit any time of the year, but particularly in summer.

The marked trail begins across the Wire Pass parking area. Buy your self-permit (no quota) and follow the dry bed of the wash for about 1 mile before reaching the entrance to the first narrows. These narrows, a few dozen yards long, will give you a little preview of what awaits further on. Soon, you enter the true narrows of Wire Pass and move along between very dark walls, over a hundred feet high. Depending on how the last flash flood affected the canyon, you may have to scramble above choke stones as high as 8 feet at the first and/or second narrows; in some years, this may present a challenge to some. You'll eventually reach the junction with Buckskin Gulch at 1.7 miles from the trailhead. Look for some faint petroglyphs at the base of the right wall, just at the junction. Follow Buckskin Gulch downstream as long as you like or time permits, the walls are higher and even more impressive than in Wire Pass. You'll likely encounter pools and mud-holes that will give you an inkling of what it looks like further down Buckskin Gulch and deep inside Paria Canyon.

Photo advice: The narrows are generally around 10 feet wide, with some narrower passages about 3 feet wide. They are also very high and therefore quite dark, except around mid-day, but you will find nice reflected light in mid-morning. A wide-angle lens will let you maintain the depth-of-field and show the canyon's dimensions despite the wide aperture you'll be forced to rely on. With a firm grip and in good light, it's perfectly possible to photograph with a hand-held camera using a high ISO.

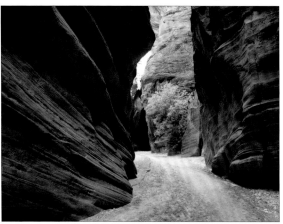

A wider passage in Buckskin Gulch

Getting there: From the Paria Contact Station turnoff, head west on US-89 toward Kanab for about 4.8 miles (just past milepost 26). You'll come to a hard-packed dirt road branching off to the left when the highway makes a wide curve to the right, immediately past the Cockscomb. This is House Rock Valley Road (BLM-700). Be careful not to miss it, as it is not clearly visible when coming from Page because of the angle and the fact it is slightly downwards from the highway. Using this well-maintained track, usually passable to passenger cars with some caution, pass Buckskin Trailhead at 4.4 miles and continue for another 4.2 miles to the Wire Pass parking area. House Rock Valley Road is slippery when wet and can be closed for a while after a particularly strong storm.

Time required: 1 hour round-trip to get to the Wire Pass trailhead from US-89; up to 3 hours in the narrows to really enjoy them.

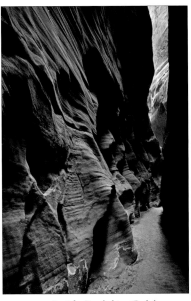

Inside Buckskin Gulch

Edmaier's Secret

Few people use the Buckskin trailhead to access the Gulch and the Paria, so this entry concentrates exclusively on an interesting feature located close to the Buckskin Trailhead. Most people know it as Edmaier's Secret, for German photographer Bernhard Edmaier, who published an aerial photograph of it. While Edmaier's Secret is an interesting destination in its own right, it's also and primarily a great spot to visit if you're looking for something to do while waiting for a permit to the Wave. In fact, several factors contribute to make it a no-brainer as a prep trip to the Big W: Proximity to the BLM Visitor Center in Kanab, opportunity to check conditions on House Rock Valley Road, a chance to hone your skills ascending and descending

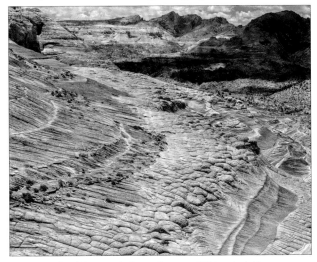

Looking south from the top of Edmaier's Secret

steep slickrock slopes—in case you're planning on exploring the back of Top Rock (see *Photographing the Southwest Vol. 2 - Arizona)*—and last but not least, it combines well with a morning/midday jaunt inside Wire Pass.

Seen from a distance, the mound of fractured sandstone that forms Edmaier's Secret is not particularly noticeable, but it gets more appealing as you get closer. The interest lies essentially in the spectacular humps of brainrocks forming the sides of the mound, which rises a hundred feet above the wash. However there are also some neat formations at the bottom on the northeast side and nice lace and striations on top on the southeast side.

After crossing the large sandy wash in front of the main mound, I suggest you don't start climbing it immediately; instead ascend southeastwardly following a gentle slope starting around 37°02'46" 111°59'43". This leads in a couple of minutes to an area of teepees and brainrocks from where you gain an excellent view of the main mound of Edmaier's Secret to the southwest. After shooting from here and getting your bearings, you're ready to go to the main mound. Before you leave, though, look back northeast below and notice a long row of fins. These fins, at 37°02'52" 111°59'31", photograph well in the late afternoon light; it's a good spot to finish the day.

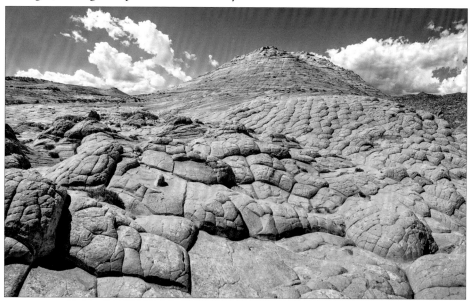

Edmaier's Secret

Now walk southwest and start climbing the fractured slickrock slope of the main mound, following a natural approach on the slickrock. If members in your party find it difficult to climb straight up, you can do a gradual ascent by switch-backing. Once on top, there are few obstacles. Walk south toward the end of the mound and explore at your leisure. This is where you'll find the most interesting formations, shapes, and views. The view directly south over a very long band of slickrock humps is quite unique.

Return the way you came or you can cautiously descend the eastern slope, where you'll find some beautiful lace formations.

Photo Advice: Either early morning or late afternoon works well. Returning to the trailhead is fast and easy, so you can stay until sunset.

Getting there: Park at the Buckskin Gulch Trailhead, off House Rock Valley Road, pay your fee, sign the register, and go. The trail basi-

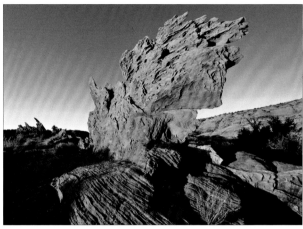

Lace rock below Edmaier's Secret © Philippe Schuler

cally follows the wash, with occasional shortcuts, for a little under 2 miles. You'll know you're there when you reach the wide sandy wash to your left.

Time required: 3 to 4 hours from the trailhead with plenty of time for exploration and photography.

Nearby location: If you can arrange a car shuttle, leaving car #1 at the Buckskin Gulch Trailhead and continuing to the Wire Pass Trailhead where you leave car #2, you could spend the first part of the day exploring Wire Pass and a bit of Buckskin Gulch downstream, then return via Buckskin Gulch upstream to Edmaier's Secret and to car #1.

Paria Canyon

Paria Canyon is arguably the most famous classic backpacking trip of the Southwest. Most backpackers take four to six days to hike the 38 miles from the White House trailhead near US-89 to Lee's Ferry on the Colorado River; I personally think that this awesome trek is best enjoyed over six days. The full Paria Canyon thru-hike is described in the third edition of *Photographing the Southwest Vol. 2 - Arizona.*

If you do not have that much time or are not inclined to backpack, you can get a good idea of what Paria Canyon looks like by day-hiking down from the White House trailhead. You can walk to the confluence of the Paria and Buckskin Gulch and back in a moderately difficult 15-mile round-trip, taking the better part of a day. The first few miles are usually dry most of the year, but you should expect numerous water crossings, muddy areas or water holes further down, and even some knee-deep wading before the confluence. There are some outstanding features to see in this upper part of Paria Canyon, even on a day hike. At mile 2, you reach the Windows, an area of deep holes—small and large—carved by water and wind and spread in three groups separated by several hundred yards on both

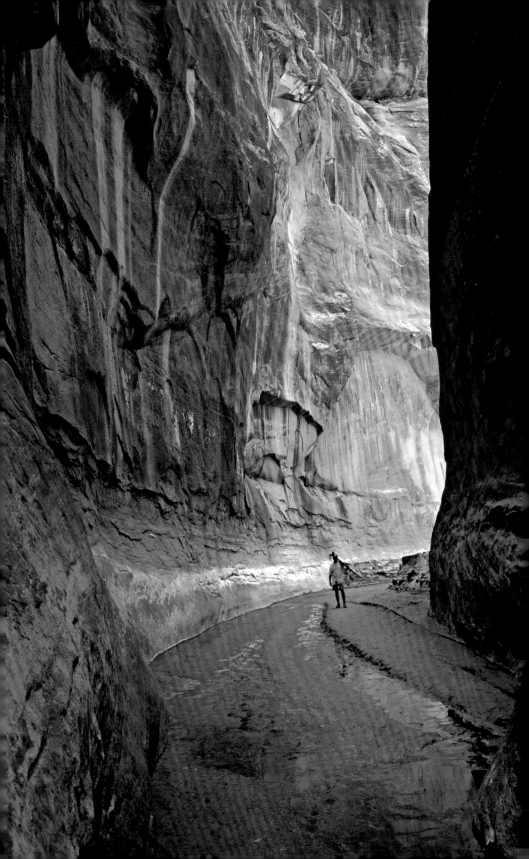

sides of the canyon. The real narrows begin at mile 4, becoming narrower and more spectacular as you progress. At mile 6.7, powerful Sliderock Arch makes a great picture. The confluence with Buckskin Gulch, at mile 7.3, is truly majestic. You can then follow Buckskin Gulch for a little over a mile and explore narrows even darker and narrower than those of Paria Canyon.

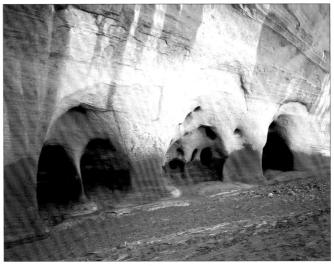

The Windows in Paria Canyon

Photo advice: As usual in narrows, it's best to be there in mid- to late-morning to take advantage of reflected light. The area around the confluence of the Paria and the Buckskin offers truly spectacular shots.

Getting there: Take US-89 from Page (30 miles) or Kanab (43 miles) and turn off at the sign indicating the "Ranger Station" (aka Paria Contact Station) near milepost 21. There, get the latest weather and trail information (also posted on the registration board when the station is closed), and, if chances of rain are slim, proceed to self-register and pay your day-use fee. Unlike the nearby Coyote Buttes, there is no quota on the number of day hikers into Paria Canyon and nearby Buckskin Gulch. There is a limit of 20 permits a day for backpackers, regardless of which trailhead is used. The Paria Contact Station sells an excellent map called *the Hikers Guide to Paria Canyon*, which is very helpful for backpacking the Paria to Lee's Ferry.

The White House trailhead and campground are at the end of a 2.2-mile well-graded dirt road going south from the Ranger Station.

Time required: At least 8 hours including a short foray into Buckskin Gulch. Before embarking on such a long day-hike, however, you should consider the much easier and shorter trip into Buckskin Gulch from Wire Pass, described in the following section.

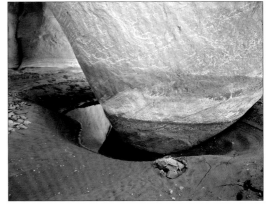

Sandstone & mud

Opposite page: Paria & Buckskin Gulch Confluence

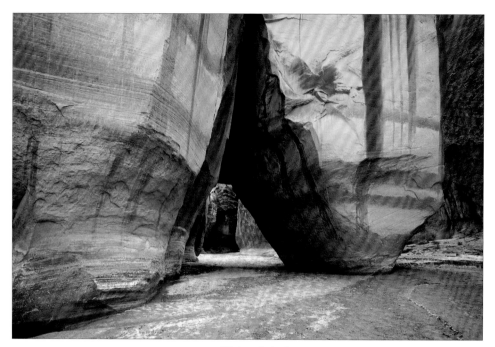

Sliderock Arch

Cobra Arch

Cobra Arch is a remarkable arch, in the shape of the lithe body of the snake of the same name, complete with checkerboard striations reminiscent of the serpent's scales. Its span is about 60 feet long. It is often visited by backpackers coming off Buckskin Gulch by the difficult Middle Trail. Photographers will want to take the more conservative approach of coming via Long Canyon Road (BLM-750), but even that is not an easy affair. After driving on this dirt road, it's a cross-country hike over rough terrain with no trail, requiring a topo map and good navigation skills. It's one location where a GPS will prove really useful. Still the result is worth it, as Cobra Arch is truly unique.

Getting there. Take Long Canyon Road (BLM-750), which leaves from the Paria Outpost on the south side of US-89, 0.5 mile west of the Paria Contact Station turnoff. It is worth noting that the friendly owners of the Paria Outpost provide a 4x4 shuttle service for destinations such as Wire Pass, Buckskin Gulch, the White House trailhead, and Lee's Ferry. They also offer guided tours to remote locations in the area, such as Coyote Buttes South and White Pocket, featured in *Photographing the Southwest Vol. 2 - Arizona.* The unmarked dirt road takes you to the Middle Trail trailhead in about 8 miles. The first 4½ miles follow a canyon to the right in a southwesterly direction and are usually well graded. After turning left at a Y, turn left again 0.3 mile further onto the West Clark Bench, heading southeast. The track becomes quite sandy, which may be a challenge in dry years. Inquire about current conditions first and don't attempt it in a passenger car. Park just past the fence, about 3.2 miles from the last junction (or 8 miles from US-89).

Ponder the trail marker warning you about the potential hazards of this hike, decide whether you are fit to go, sign the register and

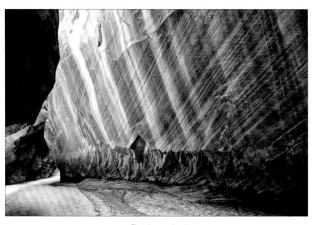

Paria striations

follow the fence line south to the ledge overlooking the sandy plain. The view from here is expansive, taking in the Coyote Buttes to the west, the so-called Dive, the Buckskin gorge, and Steamboat Rock to the distant south. To the southeast, you'll notice two promontories: an obvious one less than a mile away and a very large one about 2 miles away. The first one is the one just above the word Dive on your topo map. The larger promontory, in the distance, is the one to concentrate on. Just below it is a straight plateau and another smaller, lower promontory. This is your goal. Check your topo map to reference that point.

Now, walk about a hundred yards east along the ledge until you see the cairn marking the descent (37°02'32" 111°55'10"). Before going down the slickrock ledge, look in front of you and locate the reddish footpath skirting the right side of a small rise, close to the edge of a drop. It's behind this rise that you'll descend

to the next step, the sandy plain below the Dive. Descend on the fragile slickrock and follow that footpath, then find the easiest way to descend to the plain. Once you are in the plain, take a minute to get your bearings and take a waypoint if you have a GPS. You'll thus be able to easily locate this spot on the way back and it will make it a lot easier to climb the cliff at the right spot

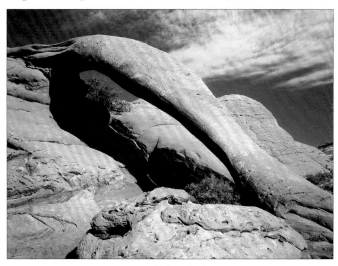

Cobra Arch

and return to your car. The route to the arch now becomes non-existent and you're on your own. Just make a beeline through the very sandy terrain, crossing a few washes and aiming for the aforementioned promontories. If you follow that straight line, it is only 2½ miles to the arch, taking approximately 1½ hours from the car park. Be sure to look back at regular intervals and get your bearings. When you reach the large promontory, climb through the sand until you reach the slickrock hump, then continue in the same southeasterly direction, dropping down on the other side. You can now see a jumble of rocks in front of you; the arch is hidden behind it. Continue in the same direction and you'll find it (37°01'15" 111°53'44"). Note that the arch is not located at the foot of the main cliff to the left, but a little bit more to the south. I do not recommend this hike in summer, when there is no shade. Trudging back up in the sand would not be pleasant.

Photo advice: Cobra Arch is best photographed in mid-afternoon, from its west side, to bring out the snake-like shape and texture. A wide-angle works well for that shot.

Time required: About 5 hours round-trip from the BLM-750 turnoff on US-89, next to the Paria Outpost.

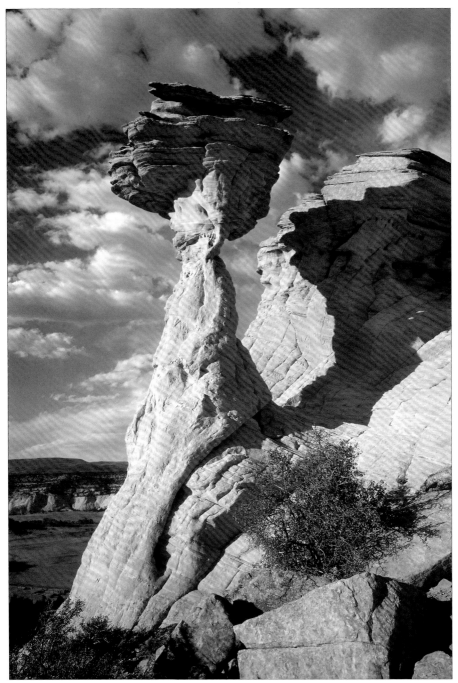

Hoodoo near Boulder Township

Chapter 6

ALONG SCENIC BYWAY 12

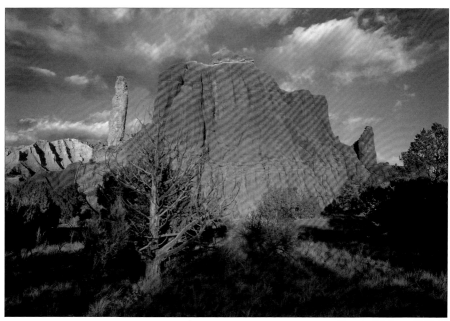

Kodachrome Basin at sunset

Introduction to Scenic Byway 12

Scenic Byway 12 easily ranks among the top scenic roads in America, with the section between Escalante and Boulder considered by some to be the most beautiful paved road in Utah! Scenic Byway 12 (or SB-12 for short) passes through some of the most grandiose scenery, winding through spectacular slickrock ridges and canyons, red rock cliffs, pine and aspen forests, alpine scenery, and quaint rural towns. This amazing diversity makes it a unique route, and a joy to drive, no matter which way you approach it. Be sure to allocate plenty of time to driving SB-12; not only does this beautiful route have plenty of curves and ups and downs, but it has also numerous pullouts providing great opportunities to appreciate and photograph the awesome scenery.

For the purpose of this book, we will travel SB-12 from west to east. The road begins at US-89, 7 miles south of the town of Panguitch and 8 miles north of the town of Hatch. It ends at the junction with UT-24 in Torrey.

Kodachrome Basin State Park

This small park has some large Entrada sandstone monoliths, but it is the sand pipes—spectacular rock columns forming surreal fingers pointing to the sky—that give esthetic and geologic originality to the place. The columns are formed of a beige colored rock. Lots of easy trails ranging from ½ mile to over 3 miles will take you among the formations. Do not miss the short drive to Chimney Rock, the biggest sand pipe anywhere, and to Shakespeare Arch Nature Trail, a short ½-mile trail leading to a lovely little arch discovered in 1976.

Campsites and cabins are available, but the park is extremely popular and you must make reservations for summer or holiday camping.

Photo advice: Leave the car at the small parking area before the campground and follow the trails. The main paved Nature Trail is marked with several information signs and takes only a quarter of an hour to walk. It's full of interesting views of the finger-like formations mentioned above. For a better view of the park, from the same parking area but on the other side of the road, follow the 1½-mile long Angels Palace Trail and its side spur on the plateau, offering good bird's eye views of this area. A few hundred yards south, you can also follow the 1½-mile long Grand Parade Trail, which passes by other spectacular monoliths.

The park is magnificent at sunset when the ocher sandstone walls become blood red. It certainly deserves its name. A 15-minute walk up the beginning of the Panorama Trail leads to the Ballerina Slipper, which is still lit when darkness already engulfs the rest of the park.

Getting there: Leave SB-12 in Cannonville, heading south toward Cottonwood Canyon Road for 7 miles to the park entrance.

Time required: 3 hours round-trip from SB-12, including about 2½ hours to tour the park if you're doing all the described hikes.

Skutumpah Road & Willis Creek

Starting south of Cannonville, Skutumpah Road (BLM-500) crosses the western section of the Grand Staircase-Escalante National Monument following a north-south direction and continues south as Johnson Canyon Road (BLM-501) to meet US-89 about 9 miles east of Kanab. A high-clearance vehicle is recommended. This road rarely experiences closure and is often the best alternative to reach the southern section of the Monument when Cottonwood Canyon Road is closed due to inclement weather. Note that you must cross Yellow Creek—a tributary to the Paria—just after entering Skutumpah Road. This crossing could be difficult after a rain.

Although not as photographically rewarding as Cottonwood Canyon Road overall, it nonetheless provides access to a few interesting narrows, among which are Willis Creek and Bull Valley Gorge.

To find Skutumpah Road, drive almost 3 miles from SB-12 toward Kodachrome Basin State Park. There is a sign at the beginning of Skutumpah Road indicating Kanab is 61 miles. After ascending a steep grade about 1 mile up Skutumpah Road, there is a very nice panoramic view of the valley with Powell Point and The Blues visible in the distance. In late afternoon and with some dramatic clouds, this view lends itself extremely well to a panoramic shot. It shouldn't be missed if you find yourself driving near Cannonville or Kodachrome Basin.

A few miles further—about 6.3 miles from the beginning of Skutumpah Road—you'll find a large and obvious car park to the right with a trail register for Willis Creek. Willis Creek is a lovely little canyon with a year round flow and several short sections of narrows. The creek, which is accessed on the other side of the road, is extremely easy to explore, having none of the usual chokestones and drop-offs of most narrows in the Grand Staircase and elsewhere.

There are several groups of narrows over the short 1.3-mile stretch leading to the confluence with Averett Canyon. The best group is the very first one, located only 0.2 mile from the trailhead. The canyon walls are less than a hundred feet high and a fair amount of light penetrates inside. The best time of

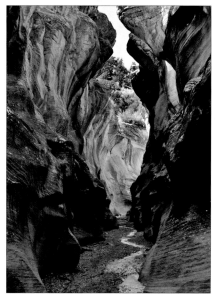

Willis Creek Narrows

the day is in mid to late morning and again mid-afternoon to avoid direct light on the walls. Rather than being straight on top, the walls present some unique and fascinating protrusions, making them quite interesting to photograph. The second most attractive group of narrows is the last one, located just before Averett Canyon. Although it sounds tempting to return to the road via Averett Canyon, there is a large chokestone close to the confluence of Averett and Willis Creek, preventing you from doing so.

About 1.6 miles further south along Skutumpah Road, Bull Valley Gorge has much deeper and darker narrows, as well as a more challenging exploration. It does not offer, however, the same photographic potential as Willis Creek.

Johnson Canyon

Continuing southwest, Skutumpah Road joins paved Johnson Canyon Road 25 miles past Bull Valley Gorge and almost immediately enters a spectacular 4-mile section through the predominantly white walls of Johnson Canyon. I recommend driving this section in both directions to enjoy different views and prolong the experience. About 3.2 miles from the junction, (13 miles from UT-89) look east for a large patch of whitish slickrock with two small conical mounds and a tall pine tree at the base of a bright cliff. Although it can be photographed from the road with a long telephoto, it's worth bushwacking the 0.8 mile round-trip to the patch to photograph the colorful striations at close range. Park on the west side of the road around 37°12'53" 112°22'28", walk southeast on the rim of

Johnson Wash and find a slope that is not too steep to descend to 37°12'49" 112°22'25". Walk northeast to cross the wash and look around for a suitable cow trail climbing southeast around 37°12'50" 112°22'21". Cross an old fence and continue on a cow trail around the rim, aiming for the sandstone patch near 37°12'54" 112°22'10". A wide to ultrawide lens is all you need. The best light is in late afternoon.

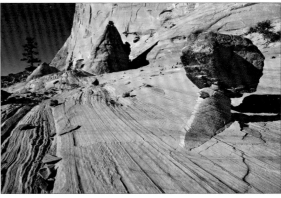

Johnson Canyon slickrock © *Philippe Schuler*

Escalante Petrified Forest

As the name indicates, this Utah State Park was once an ancient forest engulfed millions of years ago by an inland sea. You'll find many multicolored pieces of petrified tree trunks as the trail reaches the plateau. Because of its close proximity to the town of Escalante, a quick visit is easy to include in your plans and should not be missed if you've never been to Petrified National Park in Arizona–although the latter is on a much larger scale.

The moderately difficult Wide Hollow Trail winds about a mile through juniper and pinyon pines before reaching the petrified trees and a viewpoint overlooking Escalante. The Sleeping Rainbow Trail spur adds about ¾ mile to your visit. It's a bit of an up and down climb and footing can be tricky in places, but it's a worthwhile detour to take for close-ups of the most beautiful and colorful petrified trunks.

Photo advice: To get good color, it's best to photograph the petrified wood away from direct sunlight. If the sun shines brightly, look for pieces of wood shaded by junipers or improvise some kind of reflector. In addition to the large quantity of petrified trees, you'll find a forest of pygmy junipers and ancient dwarf pines that make for interesting photos.

Getting there: Located next to the Wide Hollow Reservoir and campground, on a side road about 1 mile west of Escalante.

Time required: You'll need 1½ hours for a comfortable visit. There is not much to see near the parking area, except for some sample trunks for display. If you don't have time or don't care to walk, don't bother with this detour.

Nearby location: A short distance from this State Park, you can see a lovely little pictograph with a unique design representing people holding hands in a circle. Unfortunately, this isolated petroglyph has been vandalized and its location, which is unmarked, is a bit hard to find. About 4½ miles west of the town of Escalante, take the graded Main Canyon Road, leaving SB-12 northwest. Reset your odometer and drive exactly 1.6 miles from the junction with SB-12. Look for a faint path on the right side of the road, just before a tiny hill covered with boulders. The path gently climbs to the right for about a hundred yards toward a tall rock with the pictograph on its south face (37°45'56" 111°42'42"). It is best photographed in early to mid-morning or on an overcast day.

Smoky Mountain Road

The Kaiparowits Plateau is crossed north to south by Smoky Mountain Road (BLM-300), a 77-mile dirt road connecting Escalante on UT-12 to Big Water on US-89. The Kaiparowits Plateau forms the central section of the Grand Staircase-Escalante National Monument. It is a vast, untamed area—one of the most remote in the continental U.S. Below the surface lie immense reserves of coal, which have attracted intense interest from the energy industry. Attempts to mine the coal were initially thwarted by the costly logistics of transporting it from such a remote location and were temporarily put to rest by the creation of the Monument, but the fight is probably not over.

Smoky Mountain Road is seldom graded and is sometimes in such poor condition that it is too risky to take. Each year several visitors have to be rescued at great cost, so inquire about conditions at the Escalante or Big Water Visitor Center beforehand. The difficulty rating assigned to this road is for normal conditions, when its surface is dry and graded. Do not consider it a shortcut to Page; it will take you at least five to six hours to get from Escalante to Page, possibly without seeing a single soul. Cottonwood Canyon Road is a shorter and considerably more scenic alternative.

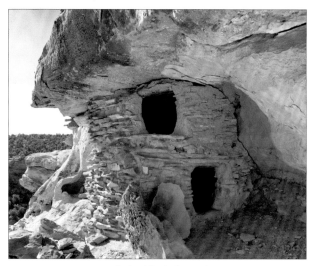
A double-decker ruin

Smoky Mountain Road leaves SB-12 from the west side of the Escalante township. Initially paved, the road becomes graded as it enters Alvey Wash, a broad and pleasant canyon lined with cottonwood trees. There are several pictograph panels in this part of the wash. The most easily spotted panel is on the west side of the road just before Coal Bed Canyon, about 4½ miles from SB-12. More pictographs can be found on the east side of the road,

½ mile south of Coal Bed Canyon. There are also a few granaries (storehouses of the Ancestral Puebloans) tucked here and there under ledges. Arch hunters will want to take Coal Bed Canyon to look for Horizon Arch (see next section).

Alvey Wash eventually turns into a wide drainage with sagebrush as it approaches the two hands of Collet Canyon. The left hand of Collet Canyon is passable by high-clearance 4WD vehicles (as of this writing), leading to Hole in the Rock Road near Twenty Mile Wash.

Overall, the rest of the trip on Smoky Mountain Road feels long and at times rather tedious. There are some interesting ruins on the plateau, but rangers are not allowed to disclose their location and they are hard to find.

From a purely esthetic standpoint, the most interesting part of the road is its southern section, from Kelly Grade to Nipple Bench.

Horizon Arch

Horizon Arch is a superb little arch located high on a flat mesa, less than 4 miles from Escalante, as the crow flies. It is unfortunately rather difficult to access, as the route is off-trail all the way from where you park your vehicle and requires good routefinding skills. The arch's good photographic potential, however, warrants a presence in this book. If you think you'd like to see and pho-

tograph it, you should be in good condition and able to climb or descend at a steep angle over slippery talus and/ or large boulders. The hike requires rugged shoes with good support, a topo map and preferably a GPS. Do not attempt this hike alone and notify someone of your where-abouts. If something happens to you and you can't walk back, it may be a long time before someone finds you.

After leaving your vehicle in Coal Bed Canyon near the

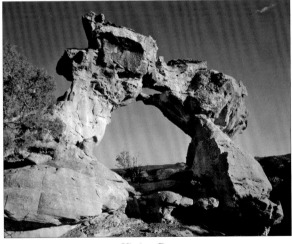

Kissing Dragons

mouth of Mitchell Canyon, walk upstream in the latter wash toward the north-west for about 1.1 miles. Look to your right for a pile of boulders masking the entrance to a smaller wash (37°43'39" 111°39'27"). After scrambling over the boulders, enter the small wash and follow it northeast for 0.4 mile. The wash eventually splits into two arms at a point normally marked by a large cairn (37°44'00" 111°39'33"). Now comes the hard part; although it's only about ½ mile to the arch, it will feel longer than that. Be sure to take your bearings from this spot, because it will be harder to find the right way coming back from the arch. Instead of continuing in either of the two arms of the small wash, start climbing straight up toward the northeast, ascending the steep slope on a combination of talus, dirt and slippery red rocks. After reaching the mesa, continue northeast, making sure you're staying close to the east rim.

As you make slow progress through the dense vegetation of the mesa, it comes as a jolt when the silhouette of the distant arch first comes into view. One final effort brings you just below the arch (37°44'24" 111°39'48"). It is befuddling that the forces of erosion have left such an amazing formation standing, although the arch appears quite fragile; it is hoped that it will resist for a long time for the enjoyment of future generations.

Photo advice: Horizon Arch is best photographed from the back in late afternoon, but don't linger too much to avoid descending in the dark. There are several good compositions, all within a wide to semi-wide angle range. Photos taken from the bottom front will be more of a documentary nature.

Getting there: From Escalante, follow Smoky Mountain Road for 4½ miles through Alvey Wash. Turn northwest into Coal Bed Canyon, paying attention not to miss the track, which is just past the wash bed, and makes a sharp angle. From here on, a high-clearance vehicle, preferably 4WD, is a necessity. Follow the wash, which becomes progressively narrower, alternating between a sandy and rocky bottom, for a little over a mile. Park near the mouth of Mitchell Canyon to your right. Occasionally, there are ponds dug near the entrance to Mitchell Canyon which will stop vehicular travel and add about a mile to your round-trip hike.

Time required: About 4 hours round-trip from Escalante.

Hell's Backbone Road

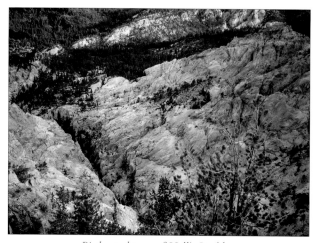

Scenic Hell's Backbone Road provides access to one of the most outstanding wilderness areas in the Southwest: the Box-Death Hollow Wilderness. The road was built in the 1930s by the Civilian Conservation Corps. It is about 40 miles from Escalante to its junction with SB-12 near Boulder, taking almost three hours to drive, including short stops. Despite a brief hair-

Pink sandstone of Hell's Backbone

raising section around the Hell's Backbone Bridge, this dirt road is easily driven by passenger car in dry weather and before snow sets in.

Starting from the east side of the Escalante township, you'll enjoy an outstanding display of checkerboard sandstone stretching several miles on the east side of the road (this section of the road is also known as Pine Creek Road). Along the way, the Lower Box trailhead provides access to The Box of Pine Creek, a beautiful canyon tucked in between high sandstone cliffs. About 14 miles from town, take the signed road leading to lovely Posey Lake. Here a short but steep trail leads to a nice overlook with a distant view of The Box. Back at the junction, Hell's Backbone Road continues its ascent, winding through a forested area to reach Hell's Backbone Bridge. The section just before and after the bridge has dramatic views of the Death Hollow Wilderness, its sheer pink Navajo sandstone cliffs contrasting with the green alpine environment (you are at over 9,000 feet elevation). This is an outstanding photo spot, one hour before sunset and in the early morning. The road continues on and meets SB-12 about 3 miles southwest of Boulder. If you are based in Boulder and do not want to do the whole loop, the round-trip to the Hell's Backbone Bridge is only 34 miles.

Death Hollow

So you're tired of crowds and want to have a little canyon paradise all to yourself? Try Death Hollow. Contrary to its ominous-sounding name, it is one of the most verdant canyons in southern Utah, thanks to its widely spaced white and pink Navajo sandstone walls and pure mountain water. Wildlife and vegetation are remarkably abundant and people are few.

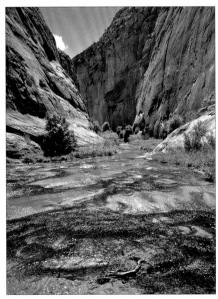

You may find it strange that I'm touting this area, at the risk of attracting the very crowds that would mar the feeling of solitude of Death Hollow. Not a chance, because Death Hollow is hard to get in and out of, requiring a very long hiking day or a multi-day backpack for many people, as well as almost constant wading. It is one of the least visited narrows in the Colorado plateau and is likely to remain so.

Before planning a trip to Death Hollow via the Escalante River, inquire about the water level at the Ranger Station or you may find yourself wading in frigid water up to your waist. When walking along the banks of Death Hollow, watch for poison ivy. It is advisable to wear long pants.

Death Hollow Narrows

Getting there: Death Hollow is a small tributary of the Escalante, located northeast of the town of Escalante in the Box-Death Hollow Wilderness. It can be hiked from the top by starting from the Hell's Backbone Road as a multi-day canyoneering adventure or it can be reached more leisurely from one of the two trailheads on the Escalante River, by walking to the confluence with Death Hollow. The confluence is located about halfway between the two trailheads with a distance of 14 miles between them. The Escalante Town trailhead is located just east of town, only ½ mile from the marked turnoff on SB-12. The Escalante River trailhead is located just past the bridge on the Escalante River, 15 miles east of the town of Escalante.

Time required: 2 to 3 days for a relaxing trip. You'll need several hours just to get to the confluence of the Escalante and Mamie Creek. You can then wade your way through the canyon for several miles or until you encounter drop-offs that require technical equipment. In one very long day, strong hikers can do a short one-day incursion from the Escalante Town trailhead into Death Hollow. With a light daypack you'll need about 2½ hours to reach the confluence, which leaves a few hours to explore Death Hollow before returning the way you came. Avoid doing this lengthy walk on a hot summer day, as the temperature can rise tremendously inside these canyons.

If you are physically very fit, there is yet another way to do a short incursion from the town of Escalante into Death Hollow via a sneak route, requiring that you scramble down, and then up, in excess of 1000 feet of fairly vertical canyon walls. Having done this route myself, I don't recommend doing it without the help of a knowledgeable guide. My advice is to take the leisurely route; you'll be able to carry more photographic equipment and come back with better images.

Escalante to Boulder

This amazing section of SB-12 between Escalante and Boulder is the highlight of this road trip and should not be missed. There are not enough superlatives to describe its spectacular beauty. The road traverses the most outstanding slickrock scenery, rugged and colorful, with delicate hues ranging from white to dark pink.

Coming from Escalante, SB-12 successively passes the Head of Rocks and Boynton Overlook viewpoints before descending toward the beautiful canyon of the Escalante River. There it crosses the Escalante River, providing access to several sites (see *Escalante Natural Bridge, Hundred Handprints* and *Phipps Arch* sections) before entering the highly photogenic Calf Creek area.

Past Calf Creek, SB-12 steeply ascends to the unique and spectacular Hogback Ridge. It is so narrow in places that you can see the landscape on both sides of the road, a thousand feet below. This impressive view stretches for miles but is difficult to photograph.

After the descent and just before entering Boulder, look for a big hoodoo high on the hill to your left. You need to cross private property to get to it, so ask for the landowner at the store to obtain permission.

Old Sheffield Road Hoodoos

Very nice hoodoos on top of a ridge, a minute walk from the road: talk about a no-brainer opportunity for hoodoo lovers! There is little more to say, except for the following strong words of caution.

Getting there: Park your car safely off the beginning of Old Sheffield Road (a.k.a. Spencer Flats Road). Do not, under any circumstances, park along the highway, stop, or linger on the road looking for Sheffield Road. Coming from Escalante, you'll find yourself downhill in a blind spot and traffic tends to come barreling down the road. If

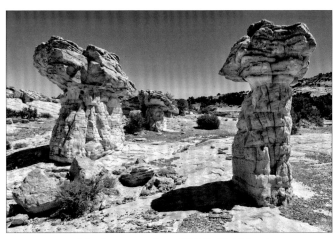

Hoodoos across from Old Sheffield Road

you're driving at a slow speed or worse, stopped on the road, you could easily cause a collision.

Once safely parked on Old Sheffield Road way past the cattle guard, walk down to the road, listen for possible oncoming traffic, and cross the road quickly when you're absolutely sure it's safe. Parents with kids should be in red alert mode.

Once you've crossed, simply walk down directly opposite Sheffield road and you'll almost immediately come to several nicely eroded hoodoos with big caprocks. Enjoy the moment and repeat the safety precautions on the way back!

The Boulder Mail Trail

Established in 1902, the Boulder Mail Trail was used to transport mail and supplies from Escalante to the isolated town of Boulder (and vice versa). Mules and packhorses were employed for the occasionally treacherous route, especially at the crossing of Death Hollow, which forms a deep sandstone gorge. In 1910, a telephone line was strung, basically from tree to tree, and provided Boulder with communication to the outside world. When SB-12 was finished in 1940, the trail lost its usefulness. Repurposed today, the trail is remarkably well cairned and very easy to follow from the trailhead near Boulder as far as Death Hollow. For a good part of the way, you will be following the old phone lines, so even if cairns are missing you can use the phone wire as a guide. Some literature tends to paint a picture of the Boulder Mail Trail as crossing vast expanses of slickrock. This is only partially true, as a major part of the hike is on sand. The view down into Death Hollow as you reach the edge of the plateau is phenomenal and you'll wonder how you can possibly descend to the river from this elevation in such a short space. Although very steep, the trail is actually rather easy

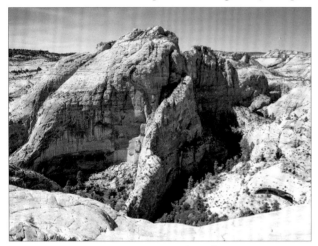

Arriving at Death Hollow

to walk down and doesn't have any exposed portions to fall off the edge. Still, it is very rocky and requires caution and concentration as tripping on the rocks, especially while descending, could result in significant physical harm. This portion of the trail could also become very slippery in rainy weather.

There is a lovely, shaded campsite to your right just as you reach Death Hollow. You can rest there in the early afternoon hours or spend the night to make the trip easier. Photo opportunities of reflections in the creek are very good close to this spot and it is easy to explore upstream or downstream just by wading in Death Hollow. Return the way you came. Hiking the Boulder Mail Trail in its entirety is outside the scope of this book.

Photo advice: There are good views along most of the slickrock portions of the trail, much less so on the sandy portions. The most interesting photography is on the approach to the final descent. You'll find a sandstone wall to the right with some nice striations as well as little trees rising out of the stark sandstone landscape. The view down Death Hollow proper is the highlight of the trip and is absolutely stunning. It requires a very wide-angle lens to capture on one shot, but stitching a few images will produce an excellent panorama encompassing the full view of the meander.

Getting there: From Boulder town at Burr Trail, drive 3.1 miles southwest on SB-12 and turn right on Hell's Backbone Road. Take the unmarked jeep road almost immediately to the left. Continue for 0.5 miles, crossing the Boulder airfield's runway. Passenger cars might want to stop here, while high-clearance vehicles must pick their way carefully through the rocky moguls on the last 100 yards to the trailhead. Trail length is 11.4 miles round-trip and moderately strenuous, with a 2000' elevation gain. Spring or fall are best since it is very hot in summer with no water between the creeks, so bring lots of it. Death Hollow runs year-round but must be filtered. If you do this hike as an overnighter, you will need a free permit obtainable from the BLM office in Escalante.

Time required: 8 to 10 hours, unless you are camping overnight. An early departure will allow you to enjoy the cool hours. You can then explore Death Hollow downstream to Mamie Creek in late morning and rest by the river during the midday heat. It would be best to return in late afternoon to avoid the heat and enjoy better light.

Escalante Natural Bridge

This is a pleasant hike along an easy section of the Escalante River. If you have limited time or are not inclined to walk a long way from your car, this hike is for you. It will give you some experience of what it is to hike in one of the Escalante canyons and, as an added bonus, you'll see an impressive natural bridge, a nice arch, Indian granaries, and rock art. One caveat, though: you'll have to get your feet wet repeatedly, so use a pair of wading shoes if you have them.

From the Escalante River trailhead, walk about a hundred feet to the river and cross it. There could be stones conveniently laid out or a tree trunk for crossing. However, things change constantly and it may not be the case when you're there. Some trekking poles or an improvised staff will make it easier to cross. The trail follows the gently moving river, cutting a direct line in the middle of the canyon and forcing you to cross the river several times. In about 45 minutes, a brisk pace on the flat terrain will get you from the trailhead to the Escalante Natural Bridge. You can't see the bridge from a distance, as it is somewhat hidden in a side canyon to the left. The best viewpoint is from the river's bank with a few cottonwoods in the foreground. However, it's worth crossing the river one more time and following the short footpath to see the end of the side canyon from under the bridge.

Back on the main trail, continue another few minutes upstream and look for a shallow alcove in the cliff to the left; follow the obvious footpath climbing toward it. In the alcove, you can observe and photograph a couple of interesting granaries perched like an eagle's nest. To the left of the alcove, you can also see a few interesting petroglyphs, unfortunately vandalized. In the fall, this is a great viewpoint to photograph the golden cottonwoods bordering the Escalante.

Return to the river, continue upstream for a few

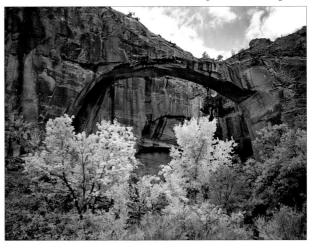

Escalante Natural Bridge

more minutes and the Escalante Arch will come into view on top of the same side cliff. The arch is small and not spectacular by itself, but you may want to photograph the entire cliff, with cottonwoods in the foreground.

Getting there: The Escalante River trailhead is about 15 miles east of the town of Escalante on SB-12. Slow down as you approach the bridge crossing the Escalante River and turn left into the parking area, immediately after the bridge.

Time required: About 2½ hours round-trip.

Nearby location: If you're interested in a longer hike and can arrange a car shuttle, follow the Escalante River upstream between the Escalante River trailhead and the Escalante Town trailhead. This 14-mile long hike is almost flat with numerous easy river crossings and can also be done the other way around. Most people prefer doing it as a two- or three-day backpack, exploring Death Hollow along the way (see *Death Hollow* section in this chapter), but it can also be done in one day. Avoid hot days if possible and do not undertake this hike if there is a risk of flash flooding. In late spring and early summer, you may want to wear long pants and long sleeves to ward off nasty deerfly bites.

Although the canyon has spectacular cliffs in the section close to the Escalante Town trailhead, the sandstone is less colorful and the vegetation less interesting. The above-described section near the Escalante River trailhead is the most esthetically and photographically rewarding.

The Hundred Handprints

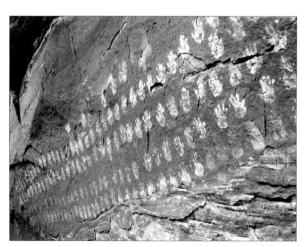

Hundred Handprints © Philippe Schuler

The Hundred Handprints panel, perhaps one of the largest pictograph panels in the Monument, is located just above the Escalante River trailhead. This unique panel is very close but not necessarily easy to find the first time around.

Starting from the parking area, follow the trail heading northwest to the back of the house for 300 feet. Note that the land behind the house is private and fenced; please do not trespass. The following description takes you to the panel outside the private property. Leave the trail and take the well-trod footpath to the right for another 150 feet to a first rock ledge. Scramble up a few feet to reach the ledge ascending gently to your right and follow it for about 100 feet. Look up to your left and locate a faint path going up steeply. A couple of cairns may be present, but if you don't see the cairns, the footpath is located just past a small cactus bush on the ground. Follow this faint path up. It soon angles to the left to reach the plateau. Once there, look at the sandstone outcrop 600 feet in front of you and notice the deep depression in the middle. To the left of this depression, halfway to the top, you'll see a large flat panel with the hundred handprints. You can walk to the bottom of the slickrock below the panel but don't try climbing to the ledge where the panel is located. It is much harder than it looks and it would be very hazardous! From here, you'll need a mid-size telephoto to capture the handprints.

Follow the bottom of the cliff to the left on the slickrock ledge and in a few minutes you'll reach a group of interesting petroglyphs overlooking the Escalante Canyon. If instead you follow the footpath to the right under the cliff, you'll find other petroglyphs that vandals attempted to saw off the wall.

Once you know where the Hundred Handprints panel is, you can easily observe it with a pair of binoculars from the Boynton Overlook on SB-12.

Phipps Arch

A short trip to Phipps Wash is another good hike from the Escalante River trailhead, although if your time is limited, I'd give the preference to the Escalante Natural Bridge hike. After crossing SB-12 under the bridge, a good trail follows the left bank of the Escalante River, eventually crossing the river about ¾ mile from the trailhead. You then follow the Escalante on the right side, close to the cliff. If the river level is high, there is a bit of shallow wading involved from time to time. Another easy ¾ mile brings you to the mouth of Phipps Wash, to your right and under a dense canopy of cottonwoods. The easy footpath continues up the pretty wash. Maverick Natural Bridge is located in the first side canyon to the west, but fails to impress. Access to Phipps Arch is another few minutes up canyon, but it is high on the cliff and not visible from the bottom. When a broad side canyon appears to the left, look for cairns indicating the beginning of the ascent, and although there is a path, it's not always easy to follow. As you get closer to the arch, you'll need to do a bit of Class 4 scrambling for about 12 feet. This may be a bit intimidating for some but just take your time, look for holds and you should be fine. After passing this obstacle, the trail remains steep but presents no other challenge and soon the massive arch (37°45'23" 111°24'37") comes into view.

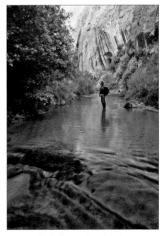

Photo advice: Cross under the arch and go to the other side near the circular sandstone dome. A moderate wide-angle or normal focal lens works best.

Time required: About 2½ to 3 hours round-trip.

Wading the Escalante

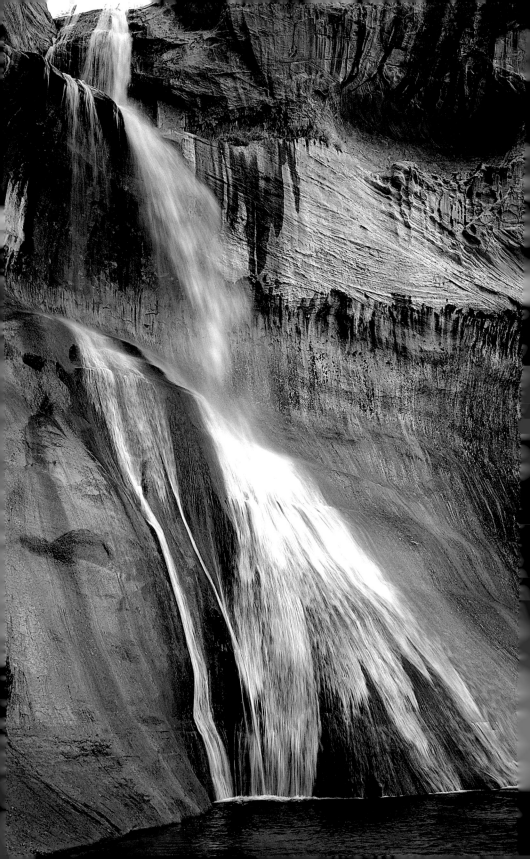

Lower Calf Creek Falls

This delightful 6-mile round-trip walk follows Calf Creek upstream, inside a wide but beautiful red rock canyon, to where the trail ends at the 126-foot high falls. In my opinion, this is one of the most rewarding short hikes in Utah. The self-guided, interpretive nature trail is sandy, but mostly level and easy to follow, making it a perfect family hike. A leaflet with descriptions for the numbered stakes along the trail should be available at the start of the hike. About ½ hour into the hike, stop at number 9 for some interesting rock art. Looking north across the canyon, you can spot in the distance three large painted figures near the bottom of the cliff wall. As you near the falls, the

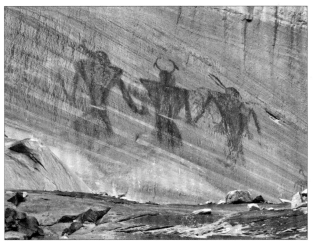

Three shamans

canyon narrows and the trail offers more shade. The desert varnish on the canyon walls becomes more noticeable and offers a pleasing contrast to the tall grasses and cottonwood trees trailside. At the base of the falls is a good size pool, which could tempt the summer hiker to indulge in a refreshing dip.

Photo advice: A wide-angle lens is necessary to capture the entire falls, while a moderate telephoto will capture some interesting details. The morning will find the falls in shade while full or dappled sunlight may be present in early afternoon. The subtle and varied color of the rock and moss behind the falls is best captured without direct sunlight. In the fall, yellow leaves can grace the rock, adding a nice contrast to the scene. Watch out for wind-blown spray from the falls and protect your gear. While the falls are the main subject, don't neglect the grasses, trees, canyon walls and rock art along the way. Beaver dams along Calf Creek can create clear pools reflecting the cliffs and the sky. Avoid weekends in the high season, when the place is swarming with locals looking for a cool spot.

Getting there: About 16 miles east of Escalante and 11 miles west of Boulder on SB-12, turn off at the sign for the Calf Creek Campground. Fee required.

Time required: 3 hours for a comfortable pace and time for photography.

Opposite page: Lower Calf Creek Falls

Upper Calf Creek Falls

Although not as tall and spectacular as the Lower Falls, the Upper Calf Creek Falls are easily reached and provide a nice opportunity to relax in the coolness of the water on a hot day. The walk is also quite pretty and not as difficult as it may seem, when looking down from the top. Also, chances are that you'll be alone at the falls, at least outside of the main holidays.

The 2.2-mile round-trip trail is almost entirely on slickrock but is well cairned. Despite a 500-foot loss in elevation, it is an easy descent and the walk back up doesn't feel strenuous if you pace yourself. About a third of the way down, you'll pass through an impressive field of black lava boulders strewn all over the place, in stark contrast with the pale sandstone. These boulders are remnants of volcanic activity from nearby Boulder Mountain. As you approach the falls, the trail splits; take the upper path to the right, leading on top of the falls and some deep pools upstream. Retracing your steps, continue on the lower trail to reach the bottom of the falls. The 86-foot falls drop into a large pool under a photogenic shady alcove. The green mosses and ferns, the pool and the misty veil of the falls are extremely inviting and you'll want to sit here and relax for a while.

Getting there: Access to the trailhead is by a short but rough spur road located on the west side of SB-12, about 5½ miles north of the Calf Creek campground, while almost halfway between mileposts 81 and 82.

Time required: 1½ hours.

Around Boulder Mountain

Boulder is one of the last communities of the West to have been linked to civilization with a road. SB-12 opened in 1940 but remained partially unpaved until the mid-eighties and the section crossing the forested area around Boulder Mountain was the last to be paved.

In the hamlet of Boulder, the Anasazi State Park provides an interesting glimpse into the life and culture of the Fremont Basketmakers, who originally settled this region. The museum has many interesting interactive exhibits. Behind the museum, there is a replica of a typical Puebloan-type

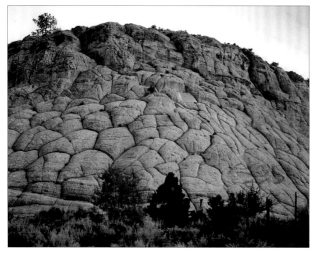

Spectacular cross-bedding outside Boulder

ancestral dwelling and the excavated ruins of the Coombs site with a partially reconstructed pit-house. Even if you do not visit the Museum, the State Park rangers are an excellent source of information for local hikes and the latest weather forecast. This is helpful if you want to explore the area without driving all the way to the Escalante Visitor Center.

To the north of Boulder, SB-12 turns into a true mountain road while crossing Boulder Mountain—an ancient volcano over 50 million years old. Near the highest point on the road, you can photograph large groves of aspens. Fall colors are usually at their peak during the second week in October. Of the three viewpoints on the road to Torrey, Homestead (11 miles north of Boulder) is the most spectacular. From here, your eye embraces hundreds of miles, including the Waterpocket Fold, the Circle Cliffs, and the Burr Trail. SB-12 offers other superb panoramic views of Capitol Reef and the Henry Mountains from the viewpoints at Steep Creek (12 miles north of Boulder) and Larb Hollow (8 miles farther). For photography, the viewpoints on Boulder Mountain are best in the afternoon with a medium to long telephoto. Watch for deer on the road, especially in early morning and evening.

The Burr Trail

The Burr Trail (BLM-100) is an old track used by the Mormon pioneers when moving their livestock from the high-altitude pastures of Boulder Mountain to the warmer grazing areas of the Waterpocket Fold. The trail, paved in the 1980's up to the boundary of Capitol Reef National Park, crosses beautiful country that is still wild and remote. Just outside Boulder, the Burr Trail passes through a series of beautifully cross-bedded Navajo sandstone petrified dunes. These domes are heavily striated and very photogenic. Then comes Deer Creek and its delightful little campground and soon after that you'll reach

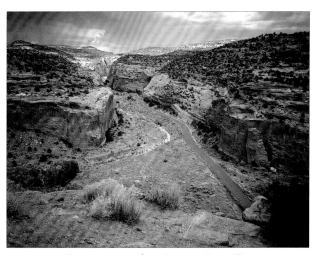

Summer storm brewing over Long Canyon

the 7-mile long gorge of Long Canyon. There is a pull out on the left side of the road allowing you to contemplate and photograph a superb view of the first ½ mile of the canyon. After that, the road drops down to canyon level and you reach the trailhead to the Lower Gulch Outstanding Natural Area. The road through Long Canyon is pure pleasure, passing through sheer sandstone cliffs

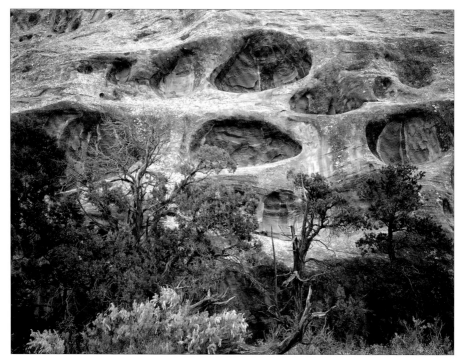

Swiss Cheese in Red

with fantastic desert varnish and finely eroded areas. Don't miss the surprising little slot canyon, partially hidden behind tall trees on the left side of the road, about 0.8 mile past the bridge over The Gulch. It's a great spot for a break on a hot day with good photo potential when reflected light is present.

As you exit Long Canyon, a large pullout offers a superb panoramic view of the Circle Cliffs, Waterpocket Fold, and the Henry Mountains, with some highly colorful badlands to your right. 10 miles later, as the Burr Trail becomes a dirt road, the west face of the Waterpocket Fold and Strike Valley come into view very nicely. Soon, you'll be crossing the Fold and reaching the steep switchbacks leading down into Strike Valley. You can drive down the spectacular switchbacks and continue south toward Bullfrog Marina or north toward UT-24 via Notom Road.

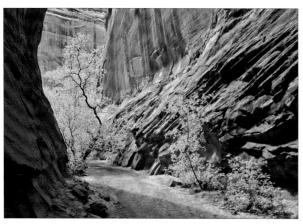

Long Canyon slot © John Stottlemyer

Photo advice: The road traverses Long Canyon from about mile 10 through 17 coming from Boulder; its walls are eroded in the form of highly concentrated deep holes dug into the deep-red Wingate sandstone. This phenomenon—known as "Swiss cheese"—makes for great photography, producing highly saturated reds when photographed under reflected light. Scenery along the Burr Trail is best photographed in the early morning and in afternoon.

Time required: At least 1½ hours for a short drive from Boulder to the end of Long Canyon and back. Half a day is needed to drive to the boundary of Capitol Reef and visit Strike Valley Overlook (refer to the *Capitol Reef* chapter).

Little Death Hollow

Little Death Hollow is one of the most exciting slot canyons in the Escalante drainage, with just the right amount of technical challenge to spice things up, but not make it too difficult. Although not quite as spectacular as others photographically, this 7 mile long slot canyon can nonetheless yield some great action shots and its beautiful red walls of Wingate sandstone, often pock-marked with spectacular Swiss cheese, are definitely worth shooting.

To visit Little Death Hollow without suffering 8 miles round-trip of nondescript wash-walking from the main trailhead on the Wolverine Loop Road, driving inside Horse Canyon provides an excellent 4WD alternative. This is assuming weather is cooperating and the road is in good condition. Horse Canyon Road is usually graded once a year for the benefit of local ranchers and it is suitable for high-clearance vehicles when conditions are right. Horse Canyon is a wide but beautiful Wingate sandstone canyon with some absolutely outstanding desert varnish in places—arguably some of the best desert varnish in the Southwest. There are very pleasant primitive camping spots at the end of the road, both near the mouth of Wolverine Canyon and, a few hundred yards further, near the mouth of Little Death Hollow.

From the end of Horse Canyon, Little Death Hollow can be followed on foot for approximately 1½ miles before encountering the first truly technical obstacle. All the choke stones before that can be easily scaled or skirted and present no real challenge to a fit person.

At the confluence of Horse Canyon and Little Death Hollow, a 20-minute walk south brings you to the Escalante River where you can rest a while before returning to your vehicle.

As you walk back to your car from the mouth of Little Death Hollow, look for a striking Native American profile formed in the distant sandstone to the left, as the wash opens up.

Photo advice: Little Death Hollow is neither very deep nor narrow and becomes very bright around midday. It is best photographed until mid-morning and from mid-afternoon on.

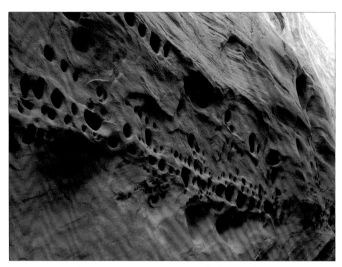

Fine "Swiss Cheese" in Little Death Hollow

Getting there: Take the Burr Trail (BLM-100) for 18 miles from Boulder and make a right on the marked Wolverine Loop Road (BLM-110). After about 5 miles, turn right to enter Horse Canyon Road (BLM-112) and follow this dirt road for about 13 miles until it ends. Before embarking on the Wolverine Loop and Horse Canyon, always check road conditions and weather forecast. There are many patches of clay on the former and some very deep sand ¾ of the way on the latter. It will be a long walk back if you get caught there during or after a rain.

Nearby location: There is an interesting petrified forest area within colorful badlands further up on the Wolverine Loop Road, about 5 miles past the junction with Horse Canyon.

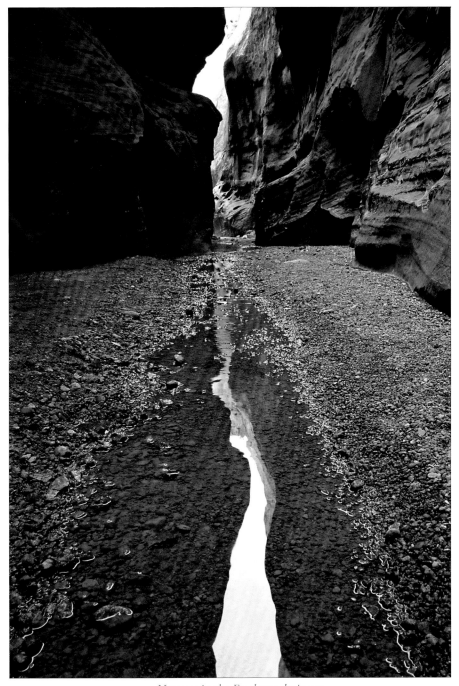

Narrows in the Escalante drainage

Chapter 7

CANYONS OF THE ESCALANTE

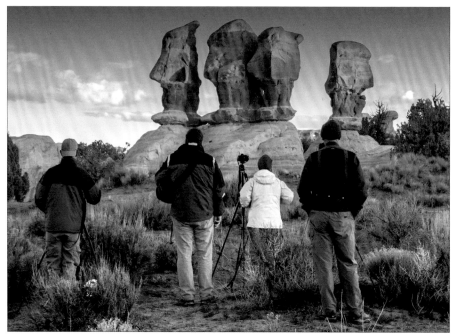

Early morning shoot at the Devil's Garden

The Escalante River drainage is a huge area of colorful sandstone canyons interspersed with plateaus. It includes some of the most remote country in the Southwest. The Escalante, last river in the continental U.S. to be named, meanders slowly in its midst before joining Lake Powell. Its many tributaries form a maze of deep sandstone canyons containing arches, natural bridges, slot canyons, waterfalls, as well as abundant vegetation and wildlife. These canyons, reminiscent of Glen Canyon before Lake Powell, offer well-prepared visitors some of the finest desert hiking in the world. The few highlights I describe in this book are just a small portion of what lays there, waiting to be explored.

This chapter concentrates on canyons accessible from Hole-in-the-Rock Road and its spur roads. The Visitor Center in the town of Escalante can help you plan your trip and discover for yourself this incredible backcountry. Escalante is also the site of several motels, B&Bs, restaurants, and outfitters, making it an excellent base for exploration.

Hole-in-the-Rock Road

Hole-in-the-Rock Road owes its name to the Mormon pioneer expedition which created it in 1879 to establish a presence in Bluff. In order to cross the Colorado River, they had to cut a primitive route in the cliff. Hole in the Rock Road (BLM-200) starts from SB-12 about 5 miles east of Escalante township and heads southwest for about 55 miles until it dead-ends at Lake Powell. Except for some short sections and the last few miles of the road, the landscape along Hole-in-the-Rock Road is not especially interesting. The Escalante is far to the east and not visible while the aptly named Straight Cliffs, to the west, are exactly that: straight and barely changing for dozens of miles. However, as you'll find out in the next sections, there is an incredible amount of great scenery to be enjoyed and photographed from trailheads along Hole-in-the-Rock Road.

Except during or immediately after a violent storm, the gravel-covered Hole-in-the-Rock Road should not present any difficulties for the ordinary passenger car until you get to Devil's Garden, about 12 miles from the start. Past that point, the road is generally suitable for passenger cars in good weather, using caution, up to Dance Hall Rock about 25 miles further. An SUV is advised past that point, as the road becomes progressively narrower and more tortuous, with some rocky slopes, and potentially delicate passages appearing without warning: mostly treacherous deep ruts and gullies created by recent rains. The same goes for the side roads leading to the trailheads mentioned in this chapter, taking into consideration the fact that they are even less frequently maintained and generally require a high-clearance vehicle, or 4x4 for the sandy ones. In any circumstance, it is advisable to stop at the Visitor Center in Escalante to check on weather and road conditions.

The highlights of this area are described from north to south along Hole-in-the-Rock Road, but this is merely to help locating them. Exploring them cannot be done just following this order due to the great driving and hiking distance. To see them all requires several forays on Hole-in-the-Rock Road over a period of several days. At-large camping is allowed along the road, but prohibited at the trailheads.

Cedar Wash Arch

Anxious to discover the popular highlights of Hole-in-the-Rock Road, few visitors bother taking the time to visit Cedar Wash Arch. That's sad because they'll miss a nicely shaped, soft colored arch that can be seen with almost no walking. Time permitting, try beginning or concluding one of your days on the road by paying it a visit.

From the car park, find the well-trod path straight ahead and follow it for 300 yards until you reach the rim. Turn left and follow the rim (overlooking a lovely valley with almost white sandstone) for another 200 yards until you get a good but distant view of the arch. The arch can be found about halfway from the valley bottom.

Photo advice: You can continue as much as you like along the rim of the very pleasant canyon, but the arch actually looks best from a distance with a mid-range telephoto. It is best photographed in mid-morning with some sidelight defining edges around its span.

Getting there: Almost 3.5 miles south of the SB-12 and Hole-in-the-Rock Road junction, take Cedar Wash Road (BLM-210) heading southwest. Although the road isn't marked, there is a sign indicating the wash. Drive about 3.6 miles to the pullout just where the road turns sharply northwest in the direction of the Escalante township. Alternately, you can come directly from Escalante by heading south on Center street and following the dirt road for about 10 miles.

Time required: Less than 1 hour round-trip from the Hole-in-the-Rock Road turnoff.

Zebra & Tunnel Slots

The short but superb Zebra Slot is the latest craze among photographers now that Peek-a-boo and Spooky have become so popular. Still, you're bound to meet few souls on the 2-mile one-way trip down Halfway Hollow from the car park to Harris Wash. Arriving at Harris Wash, take your bearings so you can easily locate the trail to Halfway Hollow upon your return. Your first goal should be the Zebra Slot, so bear left, following the broad wash to the north for about ½ mile until you catch a glimpse of the Zebra drainage to the right. Follow it as it progressively becomes a narrow canyon and then the slot itself (37°39'39" 111°25'02").

Zebra Slot is sandy at the beginning and often filled with deep muddy pools, especially in wet years, but it can also be totally dry. To avoid disappointment, be sure to stop by the Visitor Center to check on the condition of the slot. Navigating through the slot is easy at first, but gets tricky toward the end when the slot narrows drastically. You'll have to do a bit of easy chimneying in order to get to the best spot, where you can photograph the beautifully-striated and colorful narrow walls with moqui marbles encrusted in the delicate sandstone. At the end of this spot, you can also scramble up a slightly more difficult dryfall to gain an interesting downward view. Beyond this point, the slot canyon is blocked by a deep pool.

Even with a fast ISO, a tripod is a must. This is a very tight place and you'll need all the depth of field you can get from your lens so the nearest walls are not blurred. The best time to photograph the slot is in mid-morning before the sun strikes the walls directly.

Your next destination is Tunnel Slot. The tunnel, which is about 80 feet long and ends as abruptly as it begins, gets its name from the fact that it is almost closed on top. There is plenty of room to move standing up and no obstructions, except for possible water pools. The slot makes for interesting pictures around midday even though its walls are not as colorful or striated as Zebra's. The normal way to get there calls for retracing your steps to the spot where you came in from Halfway Hollow. Continue east for another 1 mile inside Harris Wash until you find the wide entrance to the Tunnel drainage to your left

Opposite page: The Zebra Slot

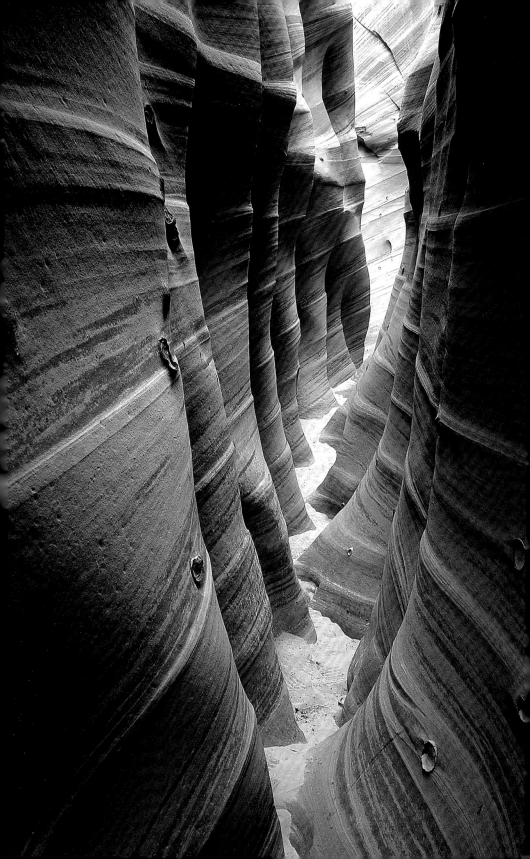

(37°39'08" 111°24'23"). From there, it is less than 0.3 mile to the slot. If you do it this way, you are pretty much guaranteed to find your way to Tunnel Slot, but you are looking at almost one hour of walking in Harris Wash with not much to see. An alternate solution is to go cross-country from Zebra Slot over what I call the "Sea of Slickrock" to reach Tunnel Slot directly at its narrow back entrance. Although this is a short cross-country walk, a topo map, a GPS if you have one, and some route-finding skills are essential. For this shortcut, turn left in the first wide opening as you exit Zebra Slot, climbing a gentle slope until you reach a vast expanse of slickrock where you'll find several interesting subjects to photograph. Bear east, leaving a small sandstone hill to your left and skirting a little sand dune. After cresting a low notch, you'll notice a narrow canyon to the east. Aim in that direction, gradually descending on the sandstone until you reach the sandy bottom leading you to the back entrance of Tunnel Slot. Return to Halfway Hollow the normal way in Harris Wash to go back to your car.

Getting there: Take Hole-in-the-Rock Road for 8 miles until you find a place to park on your right, at the cattle guard. The trail begins just across the road and follows Halfway Hollow northeast, with some shortcuts, for less than an hour until Harris Wash, where you'll bear left for Zebra or right for Tunnel. If needed, a couple of hundred yards past the cattle guard, a tiny spur road to your right leads to a corral and has plenty of space to park on the side.

Time required: About 5 hours round-trip from the car park for both canyons. Trying to combine this hike with a visit to Peek-a-Boo and Spooky slot canyons (see *Dry Fork* section) would be too much. However, you can combine it with a visit to Cedar Wash Arch and the Devil's Garden.

Red Breaks

Red Breaks is known by most as a slot canyon, but I consider it more as a vast area contributing to the greater Escalante River drainage through Harris Wash and encompassing not only the large twin drainage of the canyon proper, but also all the surrounding slickrock, buttes, and gullies that lie between the end of Old Sheffield Road to the North and Harris Wash to the south. The Red Breaks slots, however, are in a gray area when it comes to visitation: experienced canyoneers will find it an easy challenge, but it's a tad beyond the comfort zone of most photographers carrying a dSLR and a tripod, with

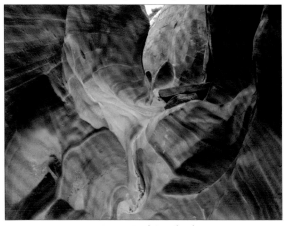
Lower Red Breaks slot

its numerous chokestones, narrow passages, quasi-permanent pools, and exposed sandstone contours allowing little margin of error. This is still not technical canyoneering and agile people will have no real problem climbing over or squeezing under chokestones and other obstacles using basic chimneying, including one chokestone (if it's still there by the time you read this) under which you have to heave yourself up through a very narrow opening. Furthermore, there is one 15-foot 5.3-rated slab to ascend that might be too much for some.

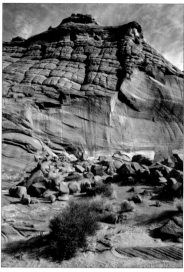

Wide section of Upper Red Breaks

Don't do this hike alone and let someone know where you're going. Accidents happen, even to experienced hikers. The slot is narrow and a Spot tracker or personal beacon might not be able to find the satellites. You and your partner(s) should have good wilderness navigation skills, good preparation, and a modicum of canyoneering skills. If not, there are two excellent guides in town to help you enjoy Red Breaks safely: Mark Saunto at Utah Canyons and Rick Green (and staff) at Excursions of Escalante.

I almost exactly followed the loop described by Steve Allen in hike #10 of his excellent *Canyoneering 3* guidebook, so rather than repeating the route's description, I'm giving a plug to Steve, adding a few remarks of my own below.

Most people venturing into Red Breaks do so from the Harris Wash trailhead as it takes only thirty minutes to get totally immersed into great slot canyon action. If you come from the Old Sheffield Road trailhead, follow the route I describe for the Volcano in the next section, but turn south and ascend the slickrock between dome 6015 and the dome to the south with the 5800 contour line aiming for 37°41'42" 111°19'24". Continue climbing, then cross east below dome 5887 to drop down into the east fork of Red Breaks. If you are on your way to the Volcano and your time is limited, I recommend that you visit the East Fork, which is more spectacular. If you are continuing south towards Harris Wash, the end of the East Fork where it meets the main canyon has some very large pools and it's better to climb on top of the mesa separating the two forks. Likewise if you want to return to Harris Wash avoiding the main fork, walk east far enough on the ridge between Red Breaks Canyon and the old road (mentioned in the Volcano section) in order to avoid the numerous

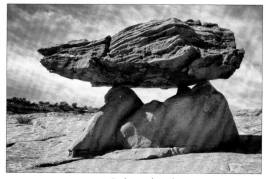

Balanced rock

drainages leading to the main fork. Eventually, you will meet the old road going to the wash and the trailhead.

Photo advice: There are some beautiful walls with reflected light in the early morning as soon as the slot narrows down. Leave that big tripod in the car or at the motel or it will seriously hamper your movement and your balance.

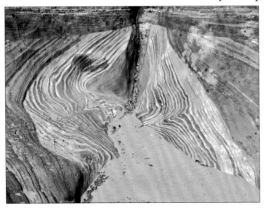

Striations in Upper Red Breaks

And it will get bashed, especially if it's hanging outside a photo back-pack. You should have no difficulty getting sharp pictures, using a com-bination of high ISO, internal stabi-lization, and resting your camera on a rock or against a wall. Depending on when you do the hike, you might need more room than your photo backpack can accommodate. In the fall and spring, which are the best times to visit Red Breaks, you'll need extra clothing, water, and food. You will also need a sling to lift your packs and possibly a 40-foot rope to help the less agile members of your party (you're not doing this one on your own, remember). Note that the probability of getting wet up to your knees and possibly higher is very high, unless it's an uncommonly dry year.

Getting there: From Hole in the Rock Road at SB-12, drive about 10.5 miles and turn left for 6 miles on the signed and well maintained road to Harris Wash Trailhead. Cross the river, and continue north toward Red Breaks Canyon. See the *Volcano section* for access to the Old Sheffield Road trailhead.

Time required: 2 hours for a quick trip up to the chokestones from Harris Wash. A very long day to do the full loop up the west fork and down the east fork.

The Volcano

This is a longish cross-country hike to a spectacular formation in the shape of a volcanic crater, although there is nothing volcanic to it but the name. Locals have known it for quite some time under the name of Cosmic Ashtray and it used to receive plenty of visitation until the northern part of the road was closed above the Harris Wash trailhead. I'll stick with the name I first heard from German author Peter Felix Schäfer, who himself had heard it from Michael Kelsey.

You'll need plenty of water, sunscreen, the 'ten essentials', and the usual items you would need for a cross-country hike in the middle of nowhere. Include a GPS with spare batteries, plus the Red Breaks 7.5' USGS map, and a compass just in case. I also carry a personal tracking device and a tablet with built-in GPS and the appropriate Red Breaks digital topo map loaded in. This makes

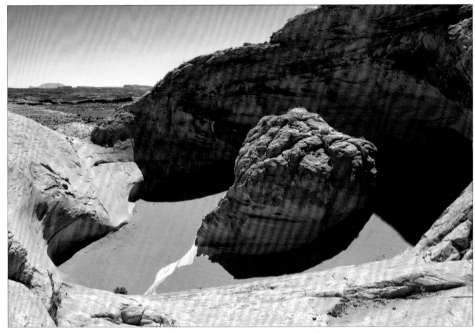

The Volcano from the west side

monitoring progress and following elevation lines considerably easier and goes a long way toward not getting lost. Also, it would be a very good idea not to hike this one alone.

The hike starts at the Harris Wash Trailhead. After crossing the wash (closed to all vehicles), follow the old road for about of 3.5 miles. After leaving the road, walk north following an obvious path and ascend the ridge that will eventually lead you to the Volcano in another ¾ mile.

It is also possible to hike to the Volcano from Big Spencer Flats, at the current end of the Old Sheffield Road. This is a more interesting alternative in my opinion, albeit requiring some routefinding. After leaving the road, I suggest you keep walking high enough to avoid sand patches as much as possible. Hiking on sandstone is a breeze, trudging in sand is a bear. You'll be traveling east/southeast for about 2.5 miles, aiming roughly for 37°41'46" 111°19'04", then due south for another mile, aiming for elevation marker 5847 on your topo. The Volcano is located southeast of this summit, at 37°40'59" 111°18'57". With all the detours to avoid gullies and sand, you'll end up walking about 4 miles one way. Study the approach on Google Earth/Maps beforehand to get a good idea of the terrain.

Once you're done photographing from the west side, descend to a safe contour line and follow it northeast for a tenth of a mile until you see a natural path going up to the north side of the Volcano; a small gully starting near 37°40'60" 111°18'54" leads you to the edge. This is also where intrepid souls use moki steps to descend to the sandy bottom. If you're going to do it, be sure that one experienced person in your party can help those needing assistance going back up.

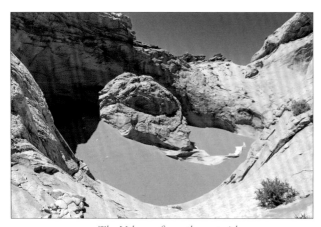

The Volcano from the east side

Photo advice: You'll need a wide-angle or ultra-wide angle lens to capture the entire basin; you might also consider stitching three or four vertical shots. I prefer the view from the west side, but both are interesting anyway. The Volcano is basked in sunshine all day, including early morning and late afternoon, as it sits so high up. Its deep basin has strong shadows at any time of the day on its southern and eastern flanks, so your photographs will benefit from some kind of high dynamic range processing.

Getting there: About 10.5 miles from Escalante on SB-12, turn right on Spencer Flat Road (a.k.a. Old Sheffield Road) and continue for 5.8 miles. At 37°42'47" 111°22'25" you'll come to a sign welcoming hikers; continue straight for another 0.9 mile to a good car park on the left at 37°42'37" 111°21'27".

Time required: From either trailhead, count on 6 hours at a leisurely pace, with plenty of time for rest and photos.

Nearby location: The Old Sheffield Road trailhead is also the access point for Spencer Canyon *(not covered in this book)*, leading to the Escalante River at its confluence with The Gulch.

Little Valley

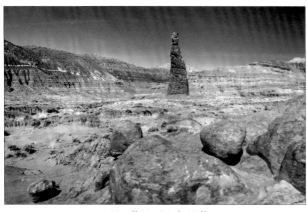

Needle in Little Valley

Little Valley is a rarely visited area south of Harris Wash with a great number of eroded goblins and other interesting rock formations with weird shapes. You can easily observe those, less than a mile away from the suggested car park below. Look north and you will notice a tall needle-like formation in the distance. If you begin with this impressive needle, simply aim for it at 37°35'57" 111°20'35. I suggest you stay on top of the wash as long as you can to keep it in view. Returning to your car, it will be easier and faster to simply walk inside the wash. The most interesting goblins are just a few hundred yards east of the Needle.

Photo advice: The light is good at dawn and sunrise. Late afternoon also works.

Getting there: Leaving Hole-in-the-Rock Road about 10.5 miles from SB-12, drive 2.7 miles on Harris Wash Road and take the right fork, continuing another 3.4 miles. There is a good parking spot around 37°34'58" 111°20'50".

Devil's Garden

Don't confuse this site with another of the same name located in the northern part of Arches National Park. Escalante Devil's Garden is a small site consisting of petrified sand dunes, weirdly shaped monoliths, small arches and colorful hoodoos. Almost by the side of the Hole-in-the-Rock Road, Devil's Garden is a must, due to its proximity to SB-12 and the considerable photographic potential it offers. If you are spending the night in Escalante, it's possible to make a quick visit at sunrise or sunset, even though more time would definitely be warranted. Consider using the nice picnic area for breakfast or dinner after shooting.

There are no marked trails from the parking area and you can immediately wander as you please in the Devil's Garden. However, your natural tendency will be to make a loop around these curiosities following the traces of previous visitors to the top. The spectacular rock formations are among the most beautiful on the Colorado Plateau and are found less than 1,500 feet from the parking area. Some have very strange shapes, reminiscent of Easter Island statues. The elegant Metate Arch is the most recognizable landmark of the Garden, thanks to its remarkable double span.

Photo advice: The Golden Hour light is preferred with these types of spectacular formations, but the terrain and the angles vary so it's possible to get some interest-

ing shots even during the day. The nicest photos are taken after sunrise when the Straight Cliffs are well lit in the background or just before sunset when the monoliths take on superb golden hues. If you're going to explore other sites along Hole-in-the-Rock Road, my advice is to stop at Devil's Garden first in order to thoroughly check the area and previsualize

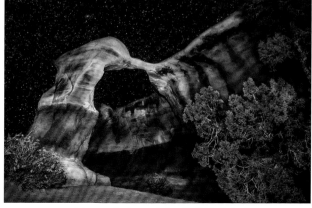

Metate Arch at night © *Rich Schafer*

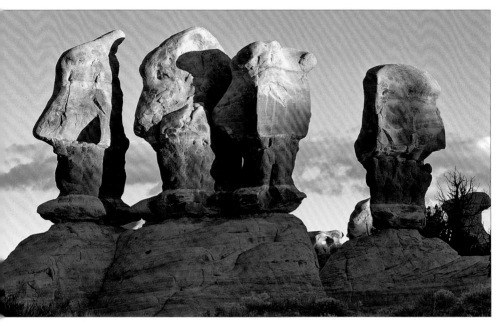

Whimsical figures of the Devil's Garden

what you'll want to photograph. This will optimize the short time you'll have later on when you stop to take photographs before sunset on your way back to Escalante. Try some low shots, isolating the formations against the sky to bring out their relief as it's difficult to convey any sense of scale. A wide angle lens is necessary to frame Metate Arch entirely.

Getting there: Take Hole-in-the-Rock Road for about 12.2 easy miles from where it branches off SB-12 and turn right on BLM-225 for another 0.3 mile to the parking area.

Time required: At least 1 hour on-site if you take photos. If combining this visit with the Dry Fork of Coyote Gulch and its slot canyons, a classic circuit, you'll need at least 6 hours round-trip from Escalante.

Nearby location: The Twentymile Wash Dinosaur Megatrackway has a huge amount of documented dino tracks spread out over a long bench of whitish sandstone. It's easy to locate and photograph the tracks. From the Devil's Garden junction, continue south for about 1.6 miles to the signed Collet Top Road and take the latter for 2.4 miles. The site is on your right.

Out of Egypt

The Egypt Bench serves as the entry point to some of the most remote and beautiful tributary canyons of the Escalante River, among which are Fence, Choprock, Neon, Ringtail, the lower part of Twenty Five Mile Wash, and Egypt-3 Slot.

Except for the trailhead area which is known for its Carmel formation, the canyons are mostly Navajo and Wingate sandstone, which makes them particularly colorful.

Each canyon can be visited individually in the course of a day-hike, but a backpacking trip of at least 3 days, combining several canyons, will allow you to visit at a relaxed pace with lots of time to photograph during the right light. Note that all the canyons along the banks of the Escalante are located inside Glen Canyon National Recreation Area and therefore require a backcountry permit if you stay overnight. If you do not want to backpack or if you prefer a little more comfort, several outfitters offer multi-day guided adventures in the area, leading you to the best spots with most of your gear carried by mules, llamas, or goats.

If you choose to explore this area on your own, you'll need a good topo map, such as *Trails Illustrated's Canyons of the Escalante*; you'll also benefit from reading additional guidebooks specializing in this area. If you wish to bench-walk between two canyons for fun or to save time, you'll need some route finding skills, a compass and possibly a GPS with spare batteries. You'll also need a hat, sunscreen, insect repellent during deer fly season, and plenty of water. Fresh water can usually be found on the ground in many of the canyons, but it needs to be filtered and treated. Some springs also exist but are not always reliable, especially in summer or during a dry year.

Walking these canyons is generally done mostly on slickrock and sandy ground but count on occasional wading to cross the Escalante River and its tributaries or traversing pools in narrow sections of side canyons. Prior to your trip, inquire about the water level by calling the Escalante Visitor Center. During springtime or a rainy year, you may find yourself wading into frigid water up to your chest. Unless the water is abnormally cold, you'll find this a relaxing experience. Any kind of shoes will work for wading. I recommend using a pair of woolen socks to avoid blisters and ward off hypothermia if the water is cold. A pair of polarized sunglasses will help spot treacherous rocks under water, as well as deep pools.

Photo advice: In late spring and throughout summer, cottonwoods explode with green foliage, creating extraordinary contrast with the red canyon walls and wonderful photographic opportunities. There are endless ways to play with reflections in water holes. Outside of Neon Canyon, which is described in the following section, my favorite canyon is Choprock for its numerous photographic possibilities and its many nice narrows waiting to be explored. There is a huge and spectacular alcove located a few hundred yards from the confluence with the Escalante, that makes a great base camp for the leisurely exploration of the entire area.

Getting there: To reach the Egypt Bench trailhead, follow Hole-in-the-Rock Road almost 17 miles from SB-12. Turn left on BLM-240 and follow it for about 9.5 miles; bear right at the Y and park ½ mile further on a large car park near the edge of the ridge. A high-clearance vehicle is a must, as the second half of BLM-240 is too rough for passenger cars, crossing several washes and rocky sections.

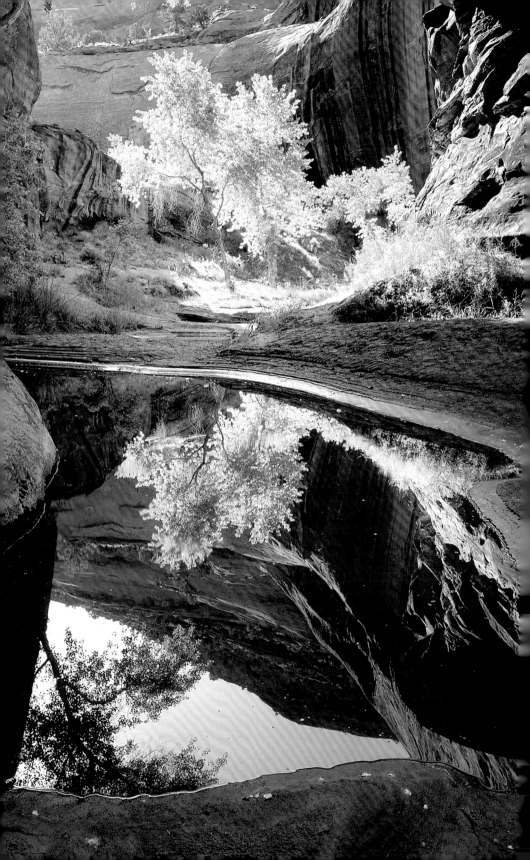

Neon Canyon

Neon Canyon and the so-called Golden Cathedral are part of the Escalante drainage and are accessible from the Egypt Bench trailhead. They merit their own special mention, however, in view of their great beauty and interest to the photographer.

Located inside the lower section of lovely Neon Canyon, the Golden Cathedral is a tall grotto of Wingate sandstone, with two large collapsed potholes on its roof and a substantial pool of water at the bottom. Wingate is a glorious reddish variety of sandstone often striated with desert varnish, giving it an almost animal fur-like appearance. The superb light-reflecting properties of the Wingate confer a fantastic red glow to the grotto. Around mid-day, beams of light cast whimsical spotlights on the dark-green water at the bottom of the grotto. They also create magical animations on the walls if the wind agitates the water surface or if you skip a stone intentionally. This is without a doubt one of the most spectacular sights of the Southwest.

Photo advice: You may want to pare down the amount of photographic equipment you'll take into the canyons if you backpack without an outfitter's assistance. The best time to photograph the Golden Cathedral is between 11 AM and 2 PM, depending on the season. You'll want the entire grotto to be in the shade before photographing it. The reflected light from the canyon walls upstream from the grotto is what bestows the glorious golden glow to your images.

In recent years, this spot has become renowned for rappelling and you stand a good chance to bring pictures of canyoneers hanging from their ropes below the potholes. Enthused as you'll be by the Golden Cathedral, don't neglect the wonderful opportunity of photographing cottonwoods alongside Neon Canyon's glorious red walls.

Getting there: Follow Hole-in-the-Rock Road almost 17 miles and turn left on BLM-240 toward the Egypt Bench trailhead, as described in the *Out of Egypt* section. There are a couple of alternatives to reach Neon Canyon from the trailhead: the most scenic, but longer way, is via Fence Canyon, or you can make a faster beeline across the plateau. I recommend the latter to photographers only doing a day hike, in order to maximize available time inside Neon Canyon. From the rim near the parking area, locate the prominent mound of sandstone known as Round Dome, about 3 miles to the east-northeast. This landmark is located just behind the entrance to Neon Canyon. Noting the direction of Round Mountain is important—a compass could be useful here—because this natural beacon will often be out of sight as you progress on the plateau below. Descend the sandstone slope following a cairned path, noting the marks of horseshoes on this old horse trail. Once on the sandy plateau, leave the Fence Canyon trail to your left and continue cross-country for about 2 miles toward Round Dome on relatively flat ground, alternating between sand and slickrock. Along the way,

Opposite page: Cottonwood reflection in Choprock Canyon

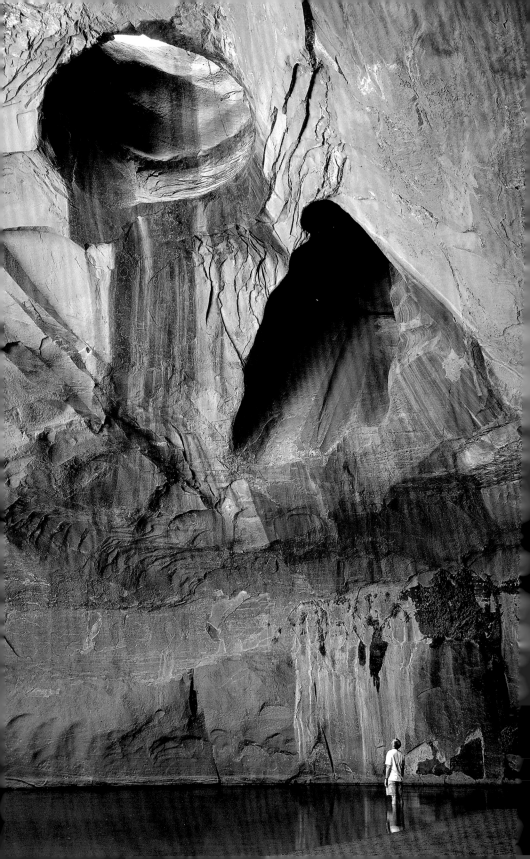

look back frequently to memorize the spot where you started your descent; it can be hard to find when the light has changed on the way back. When you reach the end of the plateau, you'll be overlooking the Escalante River canyon just across from the entrance to Neon Canyon with Round Dome in the background. Follow the rim to the right and locate the sand dune that allows an easy descent to the Escalante River. Find a path through the dense vegetation just across from the sandstone wall to the right of the mouth of Neon Canyon, then cross the river at this relatively shallow spot. Continue inside Neon Canyon for a little under a mile until you reach the fabulous Golden Cathedral. Return to your car the way you came.

Time permitting, you could try exploring the top of Neon Canyon, above and beyond the Golden Cathedral. To do so, backtrack to the confluence with the Escalante. A couple of hundred yards before you reach the confluence, you'll notice to the right a slickrock slope with a forgiving angle. Climb it and you'll find a good trail on top. Follow it to the right until you get past the potholes of the Golden Cathedral. You'll have a magnificent view of the top of the Cathedral and the verdant streambed of upper Neon Canyon.

Time required: At least 6 hours round-trip from the parking area, or as part of a multi-day backpack combined with Choprock and nearby canyons. If possible, allow more time to relax on the soft sand at the edge of the Golden Cathedral and to take pictures at different intervals for best results.

Dry Fork of Coyote Gulch & Slot Canyons

Located about 33 miles outside Escalante township, the Dry Fork of Coyote Gulch is a great opportunity to explore a couple of spectacular slot canyons and have a lot of fun, without major crowds and commercial trappings. The Dry Fork of Coyote Gulch combines several canyons: the narrows of Dry Fork proper and three slot canyons located in side drainages. These are Peek-a-Boo, Spooky, and Brimstone.

When you reach the dry riverbed at the bottom of the cairned trail coming from the car park, the narrows of Dry Fork are located immediately to the left. Though not in the same league as the more famous Buckskin Gulch narrows, they are nonetheless quite spectacular. The walls, a lovely ocher color of Navajo sandstone, are about 10 to 15 feet apart and around 70 feet high. A few minutes walking in the narrows gives those who don't want to venture into the slot canyons a chance to shoot some nice pictures.

Peek-a-Boo is an absolute must for slot canyon devotees. It's an extremely narrow and twisted passage about ½ mile long, with beautiful shapes, striations and a unique double bridge. It is blessed with excellent lighting due to the low height of its Navajo sandstone walls. The slot is easy to find, only a couple hundred yards downstream from the narrows of Dry Fork. Follow the dry creek

Opposite page: Contemplating the Golden Cathedral

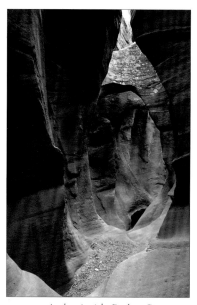

Arches inside Peek-a-Boo

bed of Coyote Gulch eastward until you see the crack in the wall that marks the entrance of Peek-a-boo, to your left (37°28'54" 111°13'00"). You must get into it by climbing up the wall, but toeholds cut in the rock will help and no special equipment is needed. At times, a shallow pool of water near the entrance to Peek-a-Boo can make things quite slippery. Once you've overcome this part, your progress will be easier. You'll have to wriggle through a narrow hole located about 150 feet from the entrance to be able to explore the upper part of the canyon, where you can only advance one step at a time scraping the bottom of your pants. The most spectacular twists and turns are found barely 600 feet from the entrance of the canyon. Alternately, Peek-a-Boo can also be accessed by climbing a sandy hill to the left of it, and dropping in near its eastern end.

Spooky is the next slot canyon, about ½ mile downstream to your left, north of a big sand dune (37°28'54" 111°12'33"). It's incredibly narrow, with interesting textured walls in places and, as its name indicates, spooky. You can easily enter it from the riverbed of Coyote Gulch and a few steps are enough to give you a good idea of its appearance.

Here, I'll describe a loop including both Peek-a-Boo and Spooky. It requires some scrambling and route finding, and you should not attempt it if you are

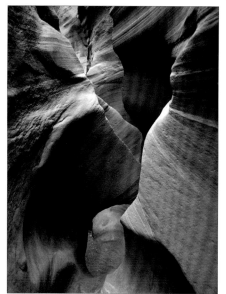

Twisted passage

alone or claustrophobic! Large people should also make sure they won't get stuck at the end of the loop, which is the narrowest section. This section is near the riverbed entrance of Spooky, so it's easy to check before embarking on the loop. Start with Peek-a-Boo, as it is easier to come back from the top of Spooky. Peek-a-Boo's slot ends up in a shallow wash; locate the cairns going up to your right and follow them and the faint route eastward for about ½ mile until you meet Spooky's sandy wash. Follow it to the right, then proceed cautiously into the slot. This exciting little adventure requires a bit of chimneying or potential crawling on the ground, so large photo backpacks are out of the question.

Brimstone, the third slot canyon, is only for experienced teams of canyoneers and should be avoided by casual photographers. It is located further downstream from Spooky in Coyote Gulch, with a 10-foot drop-off which will be difficult to negotiate on the way back. Once at the mouth of the canyon, you'll still need to walk another mile in the sand before reaching the narrows. The slot itself is extremely narrow, deep, dark and tortuous. In 1996, a photographer got stuck in Brimstone for eight days, before being miraculously rescued! The story doesn't say whether he got any good images, but it should be enough to discourage anyone who doesn't know exactly what they're doing.

All these slot canyons harbor a dwarf species of rattlesnake. Although it's not known to be aggressive, be careful where you step and put your hands. Given the always present risk of flash flood, be sure to check the weather forecast at the Visitor Center in Escalante before heading for the canyons.

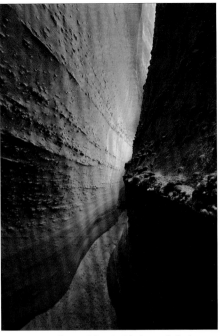

Spooky Gulch © Philippe Schuler

May and June may be the best months to visit, as there are fewer pools of water and mud and the risk of thunderstorms is statistically much lower.

Photo advice: Peek-a-Boo is better photographed in mid-morning or afternoon to avoid contrast problems. Spooky is best lit around mid-day and it is way

too dark at other times. A wide angle is indispensable in these narrow slot canyons to capture as much as possible of the rock walls, as well as to maximize the depth-of-field and avoid blurring the rock walls in the foreground. A tripod is necessary to work with a small aperture if you shoot low ISO. With ISO 100, you'll find yourself exposing for ¼ of a second to several seconds depending on sunlight. Peek-a-Boo's good overall lighting makes it possible to work hand-held, using ISO 800 or more, but you may pay the price in lack of depth-of-field unless you use a point-&-shoot with a small sensor. Pay attention not to scrape your lens against the walls and watch for footprints in the foreground of your compositions.

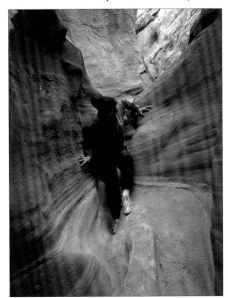

Crawling inside Peek-a-Boo

Getting there: To reach the trailhead, follow Hole-in-the-Rock Road about 14 miles past Devil's Garden (this is about 26 miles from the intersection with SB-12) until you see a sign for Dry Fork Coyote Gulch to your left. Follow the track (BLM-252) for almost 2 miles to the parking area. Be sure to bear left at the spot where the track forks. The second part of this track can be too rough for passenger cars. Leaving the parking area, keep your eyes on the cairns to follow the ½-mile long trail descending from the ridge to the dry riverbed of Coyote Gulch.

Time required: About 3 hours round-trip, excluding Brimstone, from the car park. If combining this visit with Devil's Garden, as many people do, you'll need at least 6 hours round-trip from Escalante.

Coyote Gulch

I have had the good fortune to visit over eighty countries and to trek to the far corners of the world and I rank Coyote Gulch up there with the greatest hikes of all. To me, Coyote Gulch epitomizes the best that Southwest's Canyon Country has to offer: huge, colorful canyon walls, beautiful desert varnish, remarkable geologic features such as bridges and arches, a perennial stream, hanging gardens of ferns, cottonwoods, great little waterfalls, lots of birds and wildlife, and wonderful campsites everywhere. Add to that no bandits, no need for pack animals, no high-altitude sickness, no need to pack gallons of water, shade almost everywhere, and no freezing your bones at night. Above all, it has an unmatched ratio of beauty and enjoyment versus physical exertion and risk. This is a must-see location in one's lifetime, well worth a little advance planning and preparation.

The entire hike is only 12 to 13 miles long one-way, with several possible entry and exit points, thus offering multiple options.

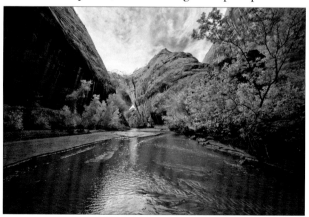

The best way to visit Coyote Gulch is as a thru-backpack with a car shuttle. I have hiked Coyote Gulch in both directions and my favorite scenario is to start at the Fortymile Ridge trailhead, ending up at Redwell. I have to say that it's a bit more dramatic the other way around because you'll finish with the most outstanding features. In each case, it's a leisurely two-day backpack, but three days will give you more flexibility to kick back and enjoy this amazing canyon and take better photographs. You should consider this option even if you do not have

Approaching Jacob Hamblin Arch © Charles Wood

two cars ; it is easy and relatively inexpensive (for a small group) to hire a shuttle in Escalante. An advantage of this solution is that the 4WD shuttle will deliver you to the Fortymile Ridge trailhead that is a little bit harder to drive to, in some years, because of the deep sand. In contrast, driving to the Redwell trailhead is not particularly challenging.

There is a third entry/exit point into Coyote Gulch at Hurricane Wash, right on Hole-in-the-Rock Road. However, it involves a long, fatiguing trek in soft sand that is a blemish on the rest of the experience. There is a shortcut out of Hurricane Wash with a relatively short cross-country hike to Chimney Rock for a car shuttle. However the road to Chimney Rock is the sandiest of all and there is always the possibility to get bogged down if you don't have a pair of shovels. The Redwell entry/exit is a more preferable option, both scenery-wise and for your legs and your vehicle.

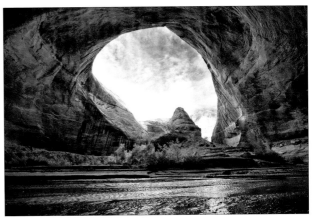

Jacob Hamblin Alcove © Charles Wood

If you don't want to backpack and you are very fit and used to long day hikes, it is possible to hike the entire canyon from end to end in one very long day, using a car shuttle. Once in the canyon, the hike is almost entirely flat, the ground is soft and you don't need to carry any water if you take a filtration device. In the absence of a car shuttle, all other options require either more time and more effort or less time and less to see. If you want to backpack the entire length of Coyote Gulch without a car shuttle, you'll need to hike a total of about 25 miles in 3 or 4 days. This is of course a great trip if you can afford the time. You can also visit Coyote Gulch over time, splitting your visit into segments. This is a nice incentive to return to this magnificent place.

Note that there is a sneak route in and out of Coyote Gulch at about the halfway point, near Jacob Hamblin Arch. Using this sneak route as an exit is tempting because it allows you to do Coyote Gulch from the Fortymile Ridge trailhead as a day hike with plenty of time inside the canyon. It should not be undertaken by backpackers, unless they have a rope and are experienced climbers. Agile day hikers with good scrambling skills and no fear of heights can negotiate the climb, but extreme caution is required. You undertake this climb at your own risk, knowing that if you slip or fall you can get badly hurt. Using this route to descend into Coyote Gulch is even more scary and I discourage it. Exposure is tremendous and if you panic and freeze while looking down, you'll be in serious trouble.

Now let's get started and discover this fabulous place together!

I suggest an early start from Fortymile Ridge. It's best to find a spot to spend the night not too far from the trailhead. Start at daybreak, following the cairns to the northeast, in the direction of the Escalante and Coyote Gulch confluence.

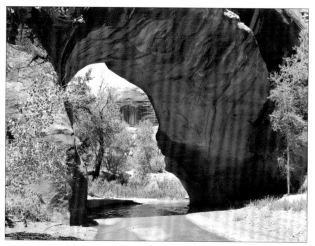

Coyote Bridge

This 2-mile long cross-country traverse is mostly on slickrock but is cairned and you should have no difficulty locating the fissure called Crack-in-the-Wall (37°25'09" 110°59'06"). The panorama is spectacular from this point. It is a great pre-dawn shot, but it gets totally lost in bright light shortly after sunrise.

Crack-in-the-Wall does not represent any technical challenge. An initial 10 foot drop to get into the narrow crack is easily negotiated by the assistance of well-placed stones. After that, you'll need to walk sideways and downward for a few dozen feet, pushing your pack ahead of you. It's a bit awkward but everybody manages. Individuals with a substantial girth may think twice before attempting this.

Just below Crack-in-the-Wall, you begin your 600 foot descent in almost 1 mile on a huge sand dune toward Coyote Gulch. It is a well-marked trail. The main rationale for doing this hike in an easterly direction is to avoid hauling yourself up the dune with a heavy load and in full sun at the end of a day, unless you make your last camp near the bottom of the dune and ascend it in the early morning.

Just before arriving in the gulch, you'll see some trail markers; follow a path to the right to hike downstream into the Gulch until you reach the confluence with the Escalante. River level, current, and temperature permitting, a short hike upstream in the Escalante reveals views of Stevens Arch, high above the canyon.

For a high view of Stevens Arch, hike back into Coyote Gulch and look for a faint path out of the canyon to the right. It is hard to locate from inside the canyon so it pays off to see its precise location during the last stages of your descent on the dune. Coming from the Escalante, it is about 100 feet before the spot where you first crossed the gulch earlier on. After a couple of minutes of hiking up this path, you'll need to scramble up a 10-foot slickrock wall. There are good holds and if you are agile, it shouldn't be a problem. This is the only obstacle on this path. The rest is easy and in about 0.6 mile you'll arrive at the viewpoint after skirting a large mesa on its right side. The view of the massive opening of

Stevens Arch is outstanding. Retrace your steps back to the bed of Coyote Gulch and use the same trail you came in to avoid some obstacles in the gulch. In a couple of minutes, you'll be back at the trail markers where you'll go down again into the streambed and begin your journey upstream into Coyote Gulch.

From then on, the hike is pure enchantment. You'll be mostly walking in ankle- to calf-deep water and occasionally climbing out of the streambed to shortcut a meander or circumvent some obstacle. Just take it easy, splashing happily in the shallow waters and stopping often for photography. There is beautiful reflected light and every meander of the river brings a new surprise. The canyon is incredibly riparian and you walk to the constant sound of birds. Lizards and all kinds of insects abound and you may need some protection against gnats in early summer. There are colorful lithe snakes along the banks or in the water and presumably, also the odd rattlesnake, but they'll most likely hear you and get out of your way. Springtime and autumn are equally as good. With a mild temperature, this is a dream walk. In summer, be sure to drink a lot, you may forget that your body is thirsty; just scoop and filter water from the riverbed.

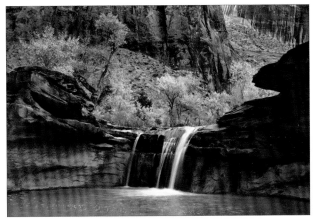

Lower Waterfalls © Charles Wood

You'll pass several beautiful waterfalls during the first quarter of the hike over a 1½-mile or so stretch of the canyon. The first one can be easily negotiated to the left. One presents a bit of an obstacle and you must scramble up 10 feet of slickrock on the right side.

These are the last obstacles. After that, it's miles of easy walking inside the canyon, successively encountering geological features such as Cliff Arch, Coyote Natural Bridge and Jacob Hamblin Arch. If you want to exit the canyon at the Jacob Hamblin Arch, the unmarked sneak route starts near the burnt pit toilets (too expensive to be rebuilt, for now), a couple of hundred feet downstream from the arch.

Continuing inside Coyote Gulch, the canyon starts widening quite a bit after the confluence with Hurricane Wash. At some point, you'll climb on the slickrock and pass a very nice little slot canyon from above before going back into the streambed. There is dense vegetation up to the last mile before Redwell, but the last couple miles offer no shade.

Photo advice: Arguably the most outstanding feature of the hike is Coyote Natural Bridge, best photographed from the east side in early to late afternoon. The bridge is then in the shade on that side but receives beautiful reflected light on its well-exposed bottom part. Close to the bank, downstream, it's up to you to frame the bridge including some of the riverbed and vegetation if its not basked in direct light. You need to avoid direct lighting at all cost; anything else goes.

I also prefer Jacob Hamblin Arch from the east side, shortly into the afternoon in autumn or spring. There is good reflected light on the arch then and the sun is not low enough to over-irradiate the northern arm of the arch which can be seen through the eastern opening. With a little haze it will shine just right on the cottonwoods below.

All the waterfalls should be photographed in the shade with long exposures to get the best results. A polarizing filter will attenuate the burn of the highlights and bring out the colors. Use a neutral density filter if the light is too strong.

Getting there: To reach the Fortymile Ridge trailhead, follow Hole-in-the-Rock Road for about 36 miles and turn left on Fortymile Ridge Road (BLM-270). Follow this dirt road heading northwest for about 6.8 miles until its end. The last couple of miles can be very sandy, although I've driven it several times with a 4WD SUV without any difficulty.

The trail leaving from the water tank at mile 4.3 of the Fortymile Ridge Road is used by people wanting a quick in and out into Coyote Gulch, using the Jacob Hamblin Arch sneak route both ways. The main benefit of this trailhead, generally accessible by passenger car, is to avoid driving in deep sand to the official trailhead. The time to hike from each trailhead to Jacob Hamblin Arch is about the same, as the shorter distance from the water tank trailhead is offset by the more sandy terrain. A GPS, or at least a compass, is very useful to return to your car from the Jacob Hamblin Arch to either trailhead.

The Hurricane Wash trailhead is located almost 34 miles down Hole-in-the-Rock Road, right by the road.

The Redwell trailhead is located at the end of a 1½-mile spur road (BLM-254), normally in good condition. The turnoff is marked at about 30 miles down Hole-in-the-Rock Road.

Time required: 8 hours or more for the day-hike loop from Fortymile Ridge trailhead via Crack-in-the-Wall and the Jacob Hamblin Arch exit. A two to three-day backpacking trip allows a longer and more leisurely discovery as far as Redwell or Hurricane Wash and is photographically more rewarding.

Nearby location: You can also pay a visit to the tall spire of Chimney Rock, standing out defiantly to the north in the middle of the arid bench–a monkey wrench in the erosion process. As Chimney Rock stands out unobstructed, it is easily photographed during either the morning or evening golden hour. The marked Chimney Rock access road (BLM-255) is located on the east side of Hole-in-the-Rock Road shortly past mile 32. Inquire about its condition at the Escalante Visitor Center, where you'll most likely be warned that this 3-mile road is the sandiest in the area, with only sporadic maintenance. I have personally experienced no difficulty in reaching Chimney Rock in a high-clearance 4WD SUV with lowered tire pressure, but this is definitely not the place for a passenger car.

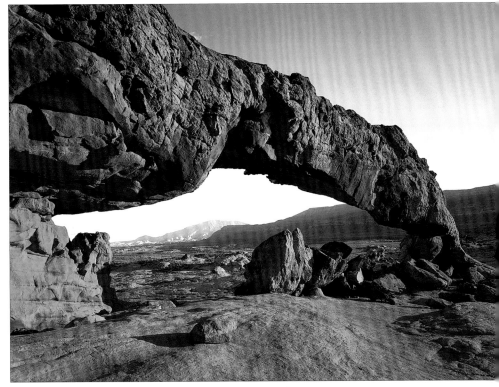

Sunset Arch

Sunset Arch

Sunset Arch is a beautiful, if somewhat tortured, arch set on a backdrop of slickrock dunes with the whale-like bulk of Navajo Mountain on the horizon. Your initial reaction when seeing the arch is likely to be one of surprise: how can such an arch have formed here, in the middle of this vast sandy bench land, with only a few flat slickrock outcrops and lacking all the usual cliffs, canyons and creeks providing the usual geological context for its siblings? By contrast, Sunset Arch appears to have been deposited here almost artificially, or by some kind of accident of nature, for the sole benefit of photographers and amateur geologists.

In any case, it is easy to explain its success with photographers, thanks to its elegant slender span and compact bulk, sweeping surroundings and ideal orientation for catching the warm golden hour light. Only the long driving time and lack of a graded trail stand between its current isolation and an onslaught of visitors. Let's hope it stays that way, as it would spoil much of the charm of this very special arch.

A short distance to the south of the arch lies another arch, referred to by some as Sunrise Arch. This arch is flatter, more closely wedged into the slickrock bed and less photogenic.

Photo advice: As its name implies, Sunset Arch is at its best right before sunset from October to April. You should arrive at least ½ hour before sunset or you'll miss the show, as the sun effectively disappears behind the Straight Cliffs when it's still a little bit high. In contrast to its rather dull appearance during the day, the arch takes on a beautiful brownish-orange color in late afternoon. The late afternoon sidelight also exposes a great deal of detail in the arch and its slickrock base. Set up your tripod in the northeast corner of the sandstone platform and frame Sunset Arch with Navajo Mountain under its span. A wide angle lens works best for this.

At sunrise, you can also shoot a tightly framed shot of the pink light illuminating the underside of the arch and the Straight Cliffs.

Getting there: Follow Hole-in-the-Rock Road for about 36 miles and turn left on Fortymile Ridge Road (BLM-270). Follow this track for about 4.3 miles and stop at the car park near the water tank. From about mile 3 on, one can distinguish the faint, isolated silhouette of Sunset Arch, about a mile to the southeast. Look close to the horizon or you will miss it as it is impossible to make out the opening beneath its span. If you manage to spot the arch, you can park at a pullout exactly 3½ miles from the beginning of the track (37°23'12" 111°03'36") and walk south-southeast.

At the water tank car park, get your bearings before starting the 1.2-mile cross-country hike traversing the sandy plateau due south. This is the easiest access with the least amount of gullies to cross. Count on ½ hour to reach the arch. Be sure not to drift eastward toward a group of rocks that could pass for the arch, nor to leave the arch behind you if you're not paying close attention. Sunset Arch is located on the upper part of the slickrock area (37°22'33" 111°02'54"). You'll find a compass or GPS very useful to return to your car, especially after sunset.

Time required: About 2 hours round-trip from the car park, with time for photography and a brief side trip to the smaller arch close by. Sunset Arch fits well at the end of a full-day outing on Hole-in-the-Rock Road that would also include a visit to Devil's Garden and the Dry Fork slot canyons or Broken Bow Arch.

Dance Hall Rock

Dance Hall Rock is a large mound of Navajo sandstone with an overhang in its center forming a mini-amphitheater. It provided convenient shelter for weary members of the original Mormon Hole-in-the-Rock expedition and the large flat platform in front of the rock was used for music and dances, hence the name. One can easily imagine on the walls the long shadows of Mormon pioneers dancing at night around wood fires to the sound of fiddles.

Photo Advice: While the amphitheater proper makes for interesting photos using a very wide angle and a few boulders to the right as a foreground, the most interesting feature is actually located on top of the rock. There, you'll find some unusually deep potholes, including some with trees growing inside. The golden light is of course best to enjoy the extensive and very dramatic 360° view from above Dance Hall Rock, but it is not necessarily the best time to photograph the potholes. The latter would photograph best on a cloudy day to eliminate deep, blocky shadows. Your next best bet is pre-dawn or post-sunset light with a long exposure and perhaps some exposure blending.

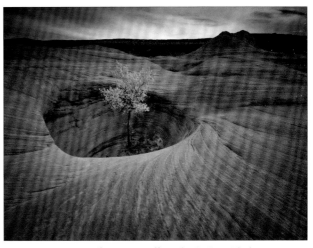

On top of Dance Hall Rock © Ron Flickinger

I strongly recommend a tripod and a very wide angle lens.

Getting There: Follow Hole-in-the-Rock Road about 37 miles south. Dance Hall Rock is on the east (left) side of the road, about 0.8 mile past Fortymile Ridge Road and the track is signed. A BLM interpretive sign greets you at the cul-de-sac parking. To get to the top, follow the sandy wash to the left of Dance Hall Rock for about 200 yards and find an easy slope on the slickrock to reach the top without any difficulty.

Time required: 30 minutes for a snapshot; 1 hour for the potholes; but photographers in search of more than a documentary picture should allow 2 hours to try different angles and compositions and fully enjoy the marvelous view.

Broken Bow Arch

The hike down Willow Gulch to Broken Bow Arch passes through some beautiful and varied scenery typical of the wet canyons in the Escalante drainage. This easy but rewarding hike has it all: Lots of slickrock, a perennial stream flowing through a scenic canyon, beautiful vegetation and a chance to see some wildlife. The highlight of the hike, however, is the massive Broken Bow Arch, so named by Escalante schoolteacher Edison Alvey in 1930 when he found a broken Indian bow beneath it.

The 4-mile round-trip hike begins on a well-worn path behind the trail register at Sooner Bench. As you descend, look for a formation shaped like a graduation cap. Upon reaching the wash, head down canyon. The first set of narrows are bypassed by staying high, on the right side of the canyon. The wash quickly broadens but soon constricts into passable narrows. Shortly, a side canyon crosses your path; consider saving its exploration for the return trip if time permits and continue straight ahead in the main wash.

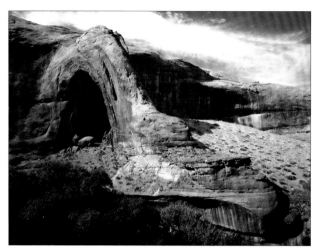

Broken Bow Arch

The second canyon encountered is Willow Gulch. As you approach the confluence, you'll notice that the scenery begins to change. Willows and cottonwood appear as the water starts to flow. Take your bearings at this junction for the return trip, bear to the left and follow Willow Gulch down the canyon; it soon widens into a lovely area for camping or picnicking on the large benches, particularly on the left side of the stream. As you proceed down canyon you may either follow the streambed or the well-worn bypass trails which crisscross it. After a few more twists and turns and a prominent bend in the canyon, Broken Bow Arch comes into view. Caution: there are occasional patches of quicksand along the water's edge about halfway to the arch.

Photo advice: Depending on the time of day and on the light, climb the hills to the east or west of the arch to get the right angle. Distant shots yield the best results as tightly framed shots fail to represent the scale of the arch in its environment. While the arch is the main attraction, the willow, cottonwood and beautifully streaked canyon walls along the way also make good subject matter.

Getting there: To reach the Willow Gulch trailhead, follow Hole-in-the-Rock road almost 42 miles from SB-12. About 1 mile past Sooner Wash, in the flat area of Sooner Bench, BLM-276 goes diagonally to the left, leading to the parking area in 1.4 miles. From Sooner Wash on, the road is too rough for most passenger cars and you'll need an SUV.

Time required: From the car park, plan on about 3 hours; more if exploring side canyons and photographing extensively. Including the round-trip to Escalante, you'll need a full day if you want to combine this hike with a visit to Devil's Garden and Sunset Arch.

Reflection Canyon

The Reflection Canyon rim offers a spectacular view of Lake Powell, meandering snake-like around island rocks. Michael Melford's iconic photo for the National Geographic was highly instrumental in creating awareness for this very scenic location. Getting there requires a demanding 16-mile round-trip trek on rough, unmarked terrain, constantly in full sun, with no water other than what you're are carrying, and minimalist camera equipment. For safety reasons, the hike is best done as an overnighter, preferably with a partner or as a group. You'll need a lot of water: one gallon per person, per day, in mild weather; more if you tend to sweat a lot or if temperatures are in the 80's. Doing this hike in higher temperatures would be exposing yourself to exhaustion and dehydration and is strongly discouraged. Fortunately, Reflection Canyon looks its best in early spring, especially mid-April, when the weather is not too hot and the lake level is at its lowest, revealing the island rocks even more.

Also needed is a GPS device capable of displaying your progress on a topographic map (and a paper version as a backup), with key waypoints entered as a reference. A Personal Locator Beacon or Spot tracking device is also advisable.

It is quite possible to do this trip as a day-hike if you are a strong hiker with backcountry experience and routefinding skills, as well as highly motivated by the view which is the main point of the hike. Readers considering a solo trip should be well prepared, as it's unlikely you'll encounter anyone. Also, keep in mind that you will be missing the best light in late afternoon and early morning.

Photo advice: The view from the rim is fantastic and arguably better than from the water or from the air. If you are rebuked by the difficulty and/or the logistics of the hike to the rim, I am discussing aerial and nautical alternatives in the *Out of Bullfrog* section of *Chapter 10 - Around Hanksville.*

Getting there: Trip reports, along with route and GPS waypoints, can be found on the internet. The following is a brief overview of the location, the hike, and what it entails. The starting point is the Llewellyn Gulch trailhead (car park at 37°15'18" 110°58'53") just south of the Hole-in-the-Rock Road, about 6 miles before it dead-ends at Hole-in-the-Rock proper. At first, you'll follow a small trail

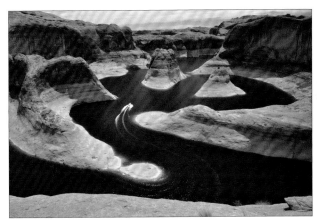

Reflection Canyon from the rim © Philippe Schuler

that vanishes shortly after crossing Llewellyn Gulch; from then on it's all cross-country. Stay as close as possible to the Straight Cliffs to minimize going up and down ravines and washes, or worse, being unable to cross one. Around 37°11'36" 110°56'50", aim east using your GPS to stay on course over the slickrock for the last two miles to the long-awaited viewpoint, which only reveals itself at the last moment (37°11'15" 110°55'08").

Time required: Allow 4 hours each way not counting any stops, more for the return if you're tired. An overnighter will make the trip more pleasant, while almost certainly guaranteeing better pictures.

Hole-in-the-Rock

Hole-in-the-Rock—which lends its name to the road we've followed in the course of this chapter—was constructed by Mormon pioneers intent on crossing the Colorado River to establish a settlement near Bluff. You have to see this place for yourself to comprehend the incredible engineering feat it was to blast and cut through the rock flanks to reach the Colorado River. Although the place of the crossing is covered by the waters of Lake Powell, most of the trail leading to the ford is still very much like it was.

The descent to the lakeshore is not particularly rewarding from a photographic standpoint, but it is a moderate scramble taking about 1 hour round-trip and is well worth doing, considering the historic value and fun factor. As you descend the steep path, you'll wonder how the pioneers managed to lower 80 wagons down and across the Colorado River through this narrow gully. The elevation loss is about 600 to 800 feet depending on the lake's level at the time you read this. The vast majority of people doing this hike are actually boaters coming up from the lake. Refer to *Chapter 10 - Around Hanksville* to access Hole-in-the-Rock by boat from Lake Powell.

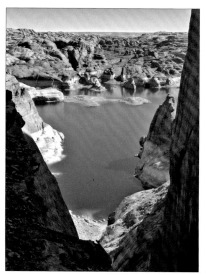

Lake Powell from the trail

Photo advice: There are two good spots. My preferred one is on a flat ledge located on the left side of the gully, a couple of minutes down from the top. This ledge is hard to miss. It is wide at first but ends up being just a few feet wide with a sheer drop, so be very careful!

Another good spot is from the rim on the left side of the car park. Just walk up the rim for about 5 to 10 minutes to find a suitable location.

Of course, if you've never been close to the lake except at a marina, this is your chance to take a swim in the lake and/or snap a few shots.

Time required: To visit Hole-in-the-Rock is not exactly an easy matter. The one-way trip involves driving close to 55 miles of unpaved road. Depending on road condition, it takes 2 to 2½ hours to reach the very end of the road, where Hole-in-the-Rock is located. The last 5 miles of Hole-in-the-Rock Road have been improved; they are no longer difficult and definitely within the capabilities of standard SUVs. Count on 1½ hours on location, with time for photography and to descend to the lake.

❖ ❖ ❖

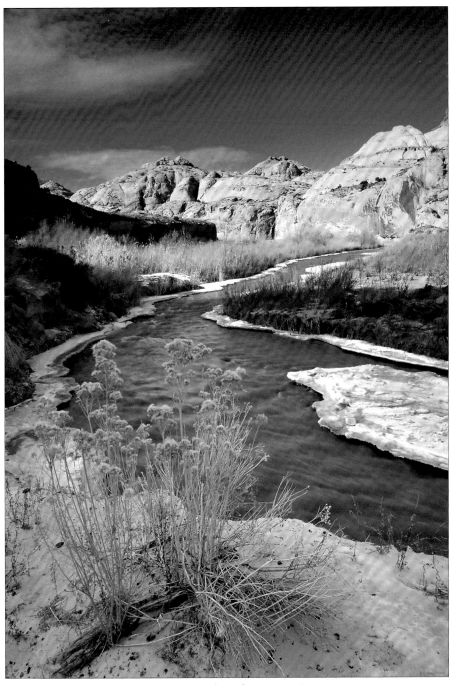

Wintertime along the Fremont River

Chapter 8

CAPITOL REEF

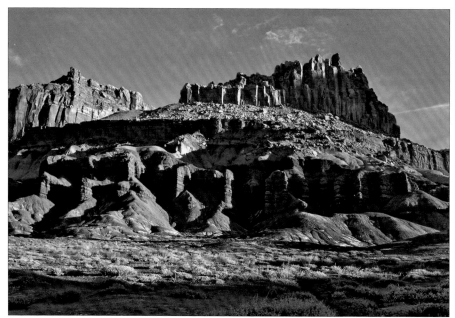

The Castle at dawn

Introduction to Capitol Reef National Park

This extraordinary park is often overlooked by visitors to the Southwest and isn't heavily frequented outside of summer and holidays. This may be due to its geographic location, which makes it less accessible than its better-known neighbors of Bryce and Arches; the fact that there are no well-known icons that would-be visitors can readily identify may also be a factor.

This trend is gradually being reversed due in part to the added presence of Grand Staircase-Escalante National Monument to the south and a surge of new motels built just outside the park, in Torrey.

Nevertheless, Capitol Reef is one of the jewels of Utah, thanks to its unmatched geological variety, fantastic scenery, surprisingly rich vegetation and lack of crowds. But be forewarned! This park only reveals a small part of itself to the casual visitor. Sure, you can cross it in the course of a few hours, including a short incursion on the famous Scenic Drive, but there is plenty more great scenery awaiting off the beaten track. Plan on at least two days in the park because you need to hike its many trails and explore remote areas with a 4WD vehicle to fully appreciate it.

One of the principal attractions of Capitol Reef is the great geological diversity of its landscape and sedimentary layers. This translates into an extraordinary palette of hues and textures, great for visitor and photographer alike: cliffs, ridges, domes, canyons, monoliths, and badlands come in a huge diversity of colors. These become even more striking during the golden hour. You can better appreciate this exceptional relief with a bit of knowledge of the paleo-environment of

Capitol Reef and the forces of erosion which are constantly at work exposing them. Free brochures are available for travelers at the Visitor Center. Don't miss this opportunity as Capitol Reef, more than any other park, gives you tremendous insight into the geologic history of the Colorado Plateau—the essential ingredient behind these landscapes that we so much admire today.

Torrey, a small town at the west entrance of the park, makes a perfect base for your explorations. Over the course of the last few years, Torrey has seen a great deal of expansion. Where in the 1980's there wasn't a single motel, now there are almost a dozen vying for your business. The beautiful oasis of Fruita, inside the park, is especially nice if you are car camping or want to pitch a tent. During autumn and springtime, it is one of the most pleasant campgrounds anywhere.

Around Panorama Point

Coming from Torrey on UT-24, you discover a superlative road, bordered to the north by impressive cliffs that become even more spectacular during the golden hour, mornings and evenings. Among the formations at the base of the cliffs are Chimney Rock and the Castle. Chimney Rock isn't really awesome in itself, but it photographs nicely in the afternoon from the parking area, when the dark red Moenkopi formation capped by the white Shinarump sandstone really stands out. As for the Castle, it offers a remarkable collection of sedimentary layers that can be enjoyed right by the side of the road. For an in-depth immersion in this area, try the 3½-mile Chimney Rock trail. It begins at the parking area 3.1 miles past the west entrance of the park (and an identical distance from the Visitor Center). After some steep but short switchbacks, the trail becomes much easier and almost flat along the loop on top of the mesa. You will enjoy dramatic views above Chimney Rock, the Reef, and the entire area. This is best photographed in late afternoon.

One of the best spots to photograph this area is Panorama Point, located on a spur road to your right, 0.6 mile east of the Chimney Rock trailhead. From this promontory, you get a splendid panoramic view of the western part of the park with Capitol Dome, the Castle and the Henry Mountains in the distance. A sign claims that this spot is the least polluted in the United States and that, on a clear day, you can see over 130 miles!

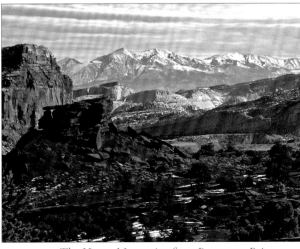

The Henry Mountains from Panorama Point

Even though the validity of this claim is questionable in this day and age, you'll certainly rejoice in the fact that you can see at least 60 miles on most days.

In the morning, Panorama Point affords an excellent view to the west in the direction of Torrey. Toward the east, a medium range zoom works great for capturing Capitol Dome and the Henry Mountains in the afternoon.

Continuing almost another mile on the dirt road south of Panorama Point, you can take the short 1-mile round-trip foot trail to aptly named Sunset Point, which offers a fantastic view in late afternoon. You can use either a normal lens to photograph the various geological strata of the reef or a medium telephoto to capture the shadows of the formations on the red cliffs. From the same parking area, a very short trail leads to the Goosenecks of Sulphur Creek, a promontory above a deep canyon that is unfortunately difficult to photograph because of the shadows, although mornings are better.

With a car shuttle, you can enjoy a refreshing hike in Sulphur Creek. The hike is a little over 6 miles, but is easy. You are usually wading in ankle deep water, with three waterfalls easily bypassed. It's a good place to photograph family or friends, but don't expect slot canyon 'keepers'. The hike begins across the highway from the Chimney Rock trailhead parking area and ends just behind the Visitor Center. This hike must not be done if there is a risk of flash flood or if the creek is knee deep or more behind the Visitor Center. Check with the rangers.

Fruita Oasis

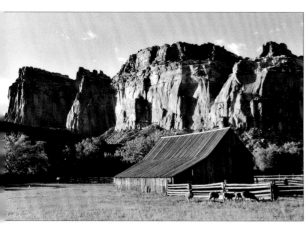

Fruita Oasis © Philippe Schuler

In all seasons, Fruita is an oasis where it's nice to relax between two rocky landscapes. This old Mormon colony is located on the banks of the Fremont River and has abundant vegetation, contrasting heavily with the surrounding desert. Near the Visitor Center, a cabin containing pioneer-era artifacts is visible from the road and warrants a brief stop.

The historic orchards are open from June through October for public harvesting. Inside the designated orchards, you can eat as much as you want; however, you pay for the fruits you take outside. The vast grassy area adjoining the pleasant picnic grounds with its peaches, wisteria and jacarandas allows you to get some great shots when they're in flower in March

Opposite page: Scenic Drive near Grand Wash

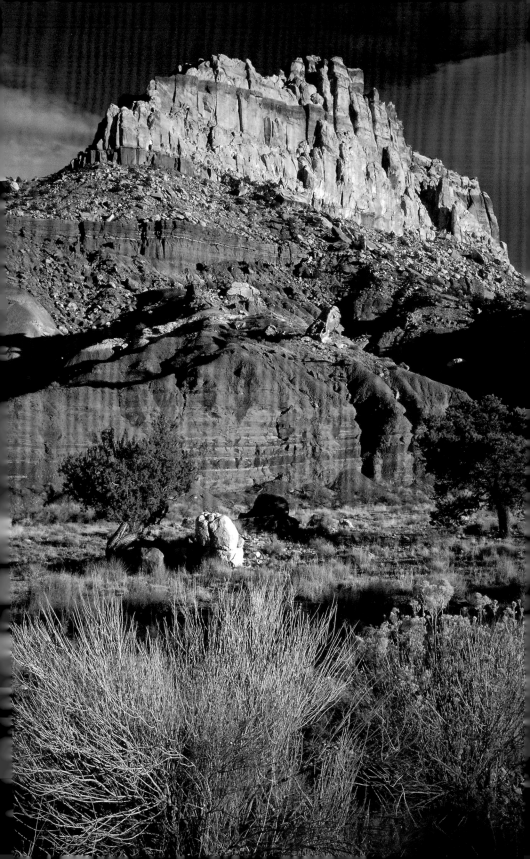

and April. The cottonwoods bordering the Fremont River around Fruita are magnificent in spring and fall.

If you don't feel like doing the full 6-mile hike in Sulphur Creek (see previous section) you may be tempted by the mini version. Just behind the Visitor Center, a short footpath quickly brings you to a shallow crossing and a series of lovely pools. You can follow the creek upstream for less than a mile to a small waterfall emptying into a pool.

The Fremont Gorge Overlook trailhead is located near the Blacksmith Shop. This little-known walk provides a great view of the Castle from atop a high mesa. A mid-range telephoto is perfect to frame the castle and surroundings. After a mile or so, the Castle really opens up and, at about 1½ miles, you'll get an optimum view in mid-morning or mid-afternoon.

Just before the campground's main entrance (almost opposite Gifford House) look for a sign indicating the Cohab Canyon trailhead. After a 0.3-mile ascent on steep switchbacks, you'll come to the entrance of this small hidden canyon with colorful Wingate sandstone walls peppered with photogenic "Swiss cheese". After about ½ mile on flat ground from the canyon's entrance, you'll come to a sign pointing to a spur trail going up to your left; a short walk on this trail leads to two nice overlooks. The North Overlook towers above the Fremont River while the South Overlook offers a photogenic view of Fruita. The round-trip to the overlooks takes about 2 hours from the trailhead. Time permitting, you can continue inside Cohab Canyon, ending up on UT-24 near the Hickman Bridge trailhead. With a car shuttle, you can also take the longer Frying Pan trail, leading south to join the Cassidy Arch trail and ending up in Grand Wash.

The Scenic Drive

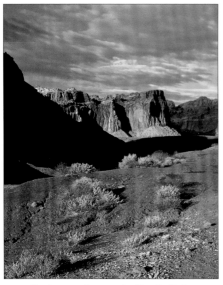

The Scenic Drive, which begins after passing the Fruita campground, offers some spectacular views of geological features such as Grand Wash, Fern's Nipple, the Slickrock Divide and the Egyptian Temple—all this along a 7-mile stretch of paved road. Get yourself one of the mini-guides to the Scenic Drive at the Visitor Center and stop at the various landmarks, following the interesting explanations on the sedimentary origins of the park.

After making sure that no flash flood danger is in the forecast, continue your drive on a good dirt road winding down 2.2 miles between the tall cliffs of beautiful Capitol Gorge. This short but spectacular road is passable by any passenger car in good

Early morning on the Scenic Drive

weather. Where the road dead-ends, a 2-mile round-trip foot trail leads toward the end of the canyon, passing by the Pioneer Register and the Waterpocket Tanks (the latter are more interesting when water is present). The 4-mile round-trip hike to the Golden Throne is more strenuous but you'll have good views all along. If you time your arrival at the foot of the Golden Throne toward the end of the afternoon or sunset, you'll really understand how it got its name.

The entire Scenic Road is especially photogenic while driving back from Capitol Gorge in late afternoon. That's when you get the best light on the sensuous, multicolored sandstone walls and layers of Capitol Ridge. Less than a mile past the spur to Grand Wash, locate the last little hill before the road starts its descent toward Fruita, park on the right and enjoy one of the most photogenic views in the park. You'll be looking at badlands topped by pillars and cliffs to the right, with the narrow road winding down spectacularly toward the Oasis and the Castle in the background. You can use a wide range of lenses to capture either grand scenics or small details of this beautiful landscape.

Hickman Bridge & the Navajo Knobs

Following UT-24 from the Visitor Center in the direction of Hanksville, the Fremont corridor presents a festival of colors with a number of orchards. The ubiquitous tamarisk lining the riverbed is particularly photogenic in autumn.

Shortly before reaching the Hickman Bridge trailhead, stop at the Fremont petroglyphs pullout, as well as at the very moving Mormon schoolhouse. A boardwalk makes it easy to observe and photograph the ancient Fremont glyphs, preferably when they are in the shade.

The self-guided nature trail to Hickman Bridge is a short and easy 2½ miles round-trip. The bridge is somewhat ensconced below a ridge and you'll need a wide or very wide angle to photograph it, framing a part of the canyon below. Press on toward the Rim Overlook Trail, branching from the previous trail after a few hundreds yards from the trailhead, for a series of interesting sights. Soon after the branching sign, the unique shape of Pectol's Pyramid comes into view across the Fremont River. About 0.6 mile from the sign, just past a small reddish butte, look to your left for an outcrop of light-colored sandstone with photogenic black lava boulders. These boulders make an excellent foreground to

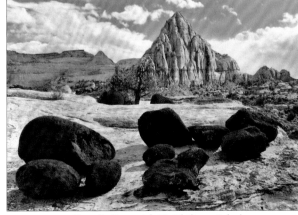

Pectol's Pyramid © Philippe Schuler

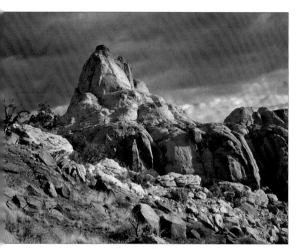

Navajo Dome

shoot Pectol's Pyramid from the best perspective. A wide angle lens will yield the best results, but you can also use a short telephoto to concentrate on the Pyramid. The Pyramid can be photographed in the early morning, however, only its left face will be well lit. Mid-to-late afternoon offers better light. A few hundreds yards further up on the trail, you'll be able to catch excellent views of Navajo Dome to the right with a standard lens to short telephoto.

At 2½ miles from the car park, the Rim Overlook provides a nice bird's eye view of Fruita and the Fremont Valley. Continuing toward the Navajo Knobs for another 2.2 miles until the top of a knob, you'll be rewarded with an awesome 360° vista of the valley and surrounding canyons. Unfortunately, unless you have exceptionally beautiful clouds, this panoramic view is too expansive to yield a compelling picture.

Introduction to Cathedral Valley

Cathedral Valley with its huge monoliths and panoramic vistas is, in my view, one of the most remarkable spots on the planet. An incomparable majesty emanates from the place. Its remoteness and the rare presence of other members of our species make you feel deeply privileged to find yourself in such an untrammeled natural sanctuary. This feeling is even more prevalent if you get a chance to camp at the remote campground in Upper Cathedral Valley. From there you can have the whole valley to yourself during the golden hour. Note that dispersed low-impact backcountry camping is permitted on BLM land just outside the park for even more solitude. Although I have yet to encounter another visitor at the remote campground within the park in several trips to this valley.

Happily or unhappily, it's not easy to visit and many visitors to the park abstain from venturing there. Few people choose to drive the 57-mile Cathedral Valley Loop crossing many distinctive parts of the valley; the drive requires a minimum of six hours to be thoroughly enjoyed. The Cathedral Valley road is a perfect example of a "feasible" road that's nevertheless risky because of its fragility and isolation. Don't try to drive this road in a regular car, even less so in a camper! Road conditions can vary a lot, depending on whether you are traveling before or after a rain or whether the bulldozer resurfaced the road, usually once a year.

Never set out before asking the rangers about the condition of the road and how deep is the river ford. The rangers will systematically discourage visitors from adventuring down this and other Cathedral Valley roads in ordinary cars and they do so with good reason: each year, visitors get stuck in the mud or a rut that suddenly appeared from nowhere. The rescue could easily set you back $1,500 or more.

Always check the weather forecast, as some clay-based parts of the road can be impassable to any vehicle when wet. Fill up your fuel tank and take a lot of water and some food, just in case. Don't forget to buy the cheap, but excellent booklet entitled *Self-guided Auto Tour of Cathedral Valley* at the Visitor Center in Fruita. When used in combination with the park map, it is sufficient to do the main loop road. As the mileage of each stop and intersection is precisely recorded, you should encounter no surprises if you stay on the road and check your odometer regularly. However, if you want to drive other roads branching from the main loop road, you'll definitely need to get a topographic map before setting out. This is true of all the roads described below, outside of the main loop road. All these roads include many branching secondary roads that don't show on the large-scale maps and it's easy to set off down the wrong path.

Once all these precautions are taken, you can start the loop from the River Ford, located a dozen miles east of the Visitor Center on UT-24. The reason I suggest starting from River Ford is that it's better to cross the ford at the beginning of the loop rather than having to backtrack if, for some reason, you find out that you can't make it or the gate is locked.

If there is no risk of rain later in the day, you could also start before dawn from Caineville, about 18.6 miles east of the Visitor Center on UT-24. This allows you to reach Lower Cathedral Valley at sunrise and continue up the valley with the sun behind you. Coming from Torrey, you can stop at the ford first to check it and make sure that you'll be able to cross it later, before beginning the loop counterclockwise at Caineville.

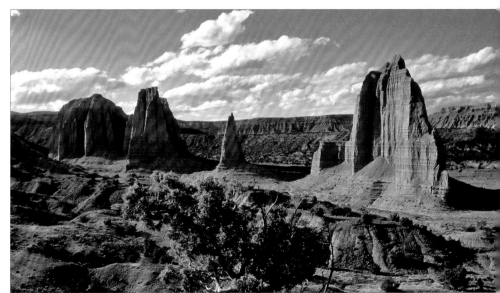

Upper Cathedral Valley monoliths

Instead of doing the whole classic loop, it's also possible to reach several parts of the valley from various side roads. Not only will you be able to discover different landscapes, but by combining different approaches, you'll see and photograph the most interesting spots during the golden hour. This assumes you can devote a couple of days to the area.

For clarity's sake, the valley's main attractions and their respective access are described separately below.

The South Desert & the Bentonite Hills

The road on top of the South Desert and the Bentonite Hills, called the Hartnet Road, begins at River Ford and follows a dry riverbed between the extreme northern end of Waterpocket Fold and the depression of Cathedral Valley. The Bentonite Hills, about 9 miles from River Ford, are remarkable for their rounded forms and strange checkerboard appearance colored by the Morrison formation. Under the right light, all the colors of the rainbow can be seen. Several exceptional viewpoints are accessible from the road, as you follow it to the northwest from River Ford.

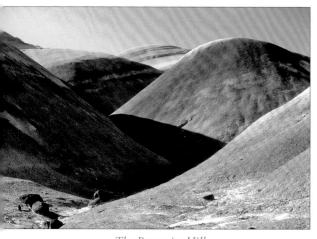

The Bentonite Hills

At about 14 miles from River Ford, a side road leads to the Lower South Desert Overlook. The South Desert is a large valley running parallel to the Waterpocket Fold. The viewpoint yields a splendid view of Jailhouse Rock, with Temple Rock and the Fishlake Mountains in the background.

About 3 miles from the intersection with Lower South Desert Overlook, a 1-mile trail leads eastward cross-country to a saddle with a good view of the great monoliths of Lower Cathedral Valley: Temple of the Sun and Temple of the Moon. If you think this view is beautiful, wait until you're in the valley proper.

About 10 miles further along the road, a short track to your left leads to the Upper South Desert Overlook. This overlook is very impressive and gives a good idea of the depth of the South Desert depression if you include a bit of the plateau in the foreground. From the edge of the knoll, those suffering from fear of heights could get weak in the knees.

During the next mile or so, you'll encounter spur roads leading successively to Upper Cathedral Valley Overlook, Hartnet Junction with Polk Creek

Road (a.k.a. Thousand Lakes Mountain Rd.)—allowing access to UT-72 over Thousand Lakes Mountain—and the Cathedral Valley remote campground. The campground is located just before the switchbacks leading down into Upper Cathedral Valley (all these individual stops are covered in the next section).

Getting there: Take the Hartnet road, located 11.7 miles from the Visitor Center on UT-24. The biggest problem will be the fording of the Fremont River, 0.6 mile past the beginning of the road. You ford the river on a rocky bed, which is usually not too deep, but watch out for potential engine flooding in a low clearance car. The River Ford is passable most of the time. However, the gate is locked during spring runoff and after rains, when even a 4WD can get stuck. Check at the Visitor Center, where rangers will let you know if it's passable or not. Beyond River Ford, the track is sometimes passable in a passenger car if you pay close attention and drive slowly, and depending on whether the bulldozer has been through recently or not.

Time required: 2 to 3 hours to Upper Cathedral Valley.

Upper Cathedral Valley

Located at the far north end of both the park and the Middle Desert, Upper Cathedral Valley is one of the highlights of Utah. The majesty that emanates from the powerful monoliths and the encircling mountains is reinforced by the isolation and the effort it takes to get here.

If you came from the River Ford via the Hartnet road, as described in the previous section, you'll catch your first glimpse of Upper Cathedral Valley from the spectacular Upper Cathedral Valley Overlook. The latter is located at the end of a short spur road to the right, past the Upper South Desert Overlook. From the edge of the plateau you can admire the entire Upper Cathedral Valley in all its splendor and capture excellent shots in the second part of the afternoon.

Soon after that, you'll reach the junction with Thousand Lakes Road, coming down from the mountain in front of you. Bear right and ½ mile later you'll come to the primitive Cathedral Campground, with its six campsites. If you've come equipped, spending the night here will allow you to catch some fabulous evening shots of the extraordinary Entrada sandstone walls as they turn bright red against the darkening sky. Canyon country at its very best!

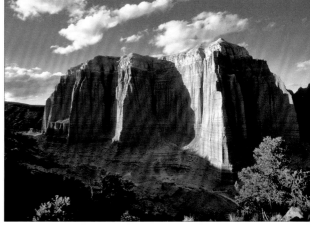

The uppermost giant monolith at Cathedral Valley

From the campground, descend the switchbacks to enter the valley. About 2 miles past the campground turnoff, you'll come to a "Viewpoint" sign on the north side of the road. There, you'll find a narrow footpath leading up to a low plateau with a spectacular close-up view of the two main groups of 500-foot high monoliths and the Walls of Jericho in the background. This easy hike is 2 miles long round-trip, and offers different angles for photographing the monoliths, which are best lit in the second part of the afternoon.

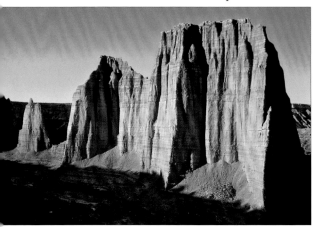

Upper Cathedral Valley

Less than 3 miles farther, heading north-east, you'll come to the Cathedral Valley junction. Immediately to your right, you'll see a sign pointing to the Gypsum Sinkhole—a gigantic, sunken artesian well almost 200 feet deep and over 50 feet in diameter. It is well worth the mile-long detour on a good spur road, although it's practically impossible to photograph because of its size.

Next, following Caineville Wash Road on the way to Lower Cathedral Valley (see next section) you'll be crossing the Middle Desert with its many different geological features.

Getting there: There are four possible ways to reach Upper Cathedral Valley. The easiest way for passenger cars and small-size campers to get to this distant spot in good weather conditions, is from the north, by way of a dirt road leaving from I-70 at Exit 91. The road goes straight south, leaving UT-72 to the right. This wide dirt road is 27 miles long and crosses the forebodingly-named Last Chance Desert. It is usually well maintained for the use of local miners and ranchers, and doesn't present any major difficulties, except for a few wash crossings that could be flooded during and after a rain. The road ends up at Cathedral Valley Junction, close to Gypsum Sinkhole. It's also possible to reach Cathedral Valley Junction by following the Caineville Wash Road from UT-24 (see next section). The other access point to Upper Cathedral Valley is the previously described Hartnet Road from River Ford, near UT-24. Perhaps the most scenic access is by way of Thousand Lakes Mountain Road (aka Polk Creek Road) coming west from UT-72. About 12 miles north of Loa on UT-72, take the dirt road to the right for almost 5 miles in the general direction of Elkhorn Campground. This road is usually in excellent condition until you reach a high altitude pass (at about 10,000 feet) in the Fishlake National Forest. At the fork in the road, do not take the Elkhorn Campground spur to the right; instead, continue straight ahead for about 7 miles, following the signpost indicating Cathedral Valley. Here the descent becomes quite tricky and it is out of the question to take an ordinary passenger car over this portion of the road. Only a high-clearance vehicle can make it, preferably 4WD during winter or spring runoff. This route is especially remarkable as it makes a spectacular transition between two radically different ecosystems, one a high-altitude alpine environment and the other the exceptional desert of Cathedral Valley. There are exceptional photographic opportunities, especially in autumn, when you'll pass through strands of yellow aspen mingling with green conifers before reaching the ocher color of the desert. These mountains are the habitat of a great variety of wild animals. In the course of one trip, I counted almost a hundred mule deer coming down the side of the mountain in great leaps and bounds.

Time required: You can reach Cathedral Valley Junction in approximately 1 hour from the I-70 off-ramp, provided you don't stray off the path. A topo map will help you sort out the many side roads. You should also be able to reach Hartnet Junction from UT-72 in about 1 hour. Count on 2 to 3 hours for the other routes. Getting there is one thing, but it's a shame if you can't devote at least a couple of hours to exploring this exceptional spot.

Lower Cathedral Valley

Lower Cathedral Valley is better known by the name of the two fantastic monoliths that it harbors. The Temple of the Sun and the Temple of the Moon illustrate many coffee-table books and well-deserve their names. Reaching up 400 feet from the desert ground as if trying to grasp the heavens, these two solitary temples cut an imposing profile against a rich blue sky of unmatched purity. At sunrise, these "high priests" of the mineral universe don their incandescent garments for a brief, fleeting moment, to celebrate the miracle of nature.

Both monoliths can be photographed individually at close range or you can shoot them together from nearby Glass Mountain, using a short telephoto to collapse the perspective of the two Temples and the cliff behind them. The hoodoos at the foot of the cliff are also quite nice. Glass Mountain itself, a small mound consisting of selenite crystals, is an interesting geological curiosity, but doesn't make for a compelling photograph.

Getting there: To get to Lower Cathedral Valley and the famous Temples of the Sun and the Moon, it's best to come from the Caineville Wash road described below.

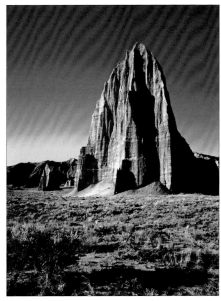

Temple of the Sun & Moon

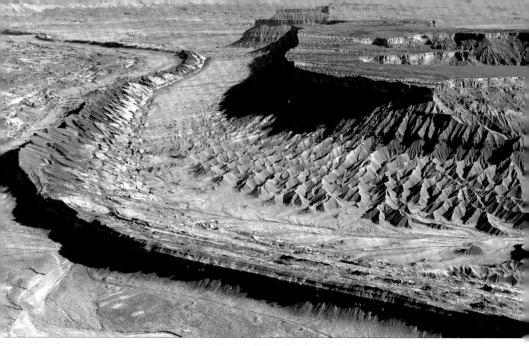

Caineville Badlands aerial

It is the easiest and fastest way to get there for sunrise and, under good conditions, you can make it in a passenger car, if you don't mind the bumps. Coming from I-70 via Cathedral Valley Junction, you'll pass numerous washes between the two valleys about a dozen miles apart and the state of the road can be extremely variable.

The junction for the Temples is located about 16 miles from the Caineville entrance on UT-24. A 1-mile spur leads from the main loop road to the foot of the Temples and to Glass Mountain.

Time required: 3 hours round-trip from Caineville; 2 hours one-way from either I-70 or UT-72.

The Caineville Badlands

The Caineville Badlands is a vast isolated expanse of dark gray hills of Mancos shale striped with interesting colors. Traveling through the heart of these badlands on the Caineville Wash road, you'll encounter from time to time round blocks of basalt tossed out by the explosion of Boulder Mountain about 50 million years ago and then later deposited here by glacial action. These badlands are actually very deep, forming a bed of sedimentary rock between 2,000 to almost 3,000 feet thick. While contemplating this extreme desert universe, it's easy to imagine the inland sea that once covered this part of the valley.

You can also observe a long stretch of badlands directly from UT-24 just east of the turnoff to Caineville Wash Road. There are a couple of spots on the north

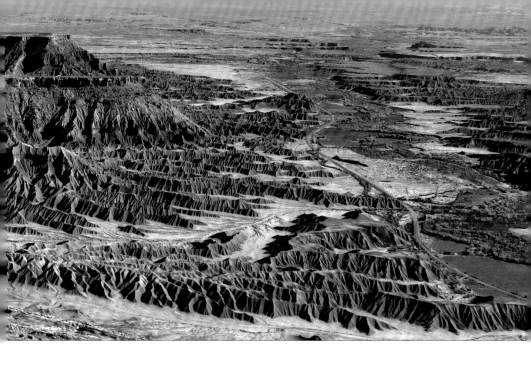

side where you can drive on BLM land and get close to the badlands for further exploration. These badlands are best photographed in late afternoon. You'll also notice the imposing presence of Factory Butte rising on the horizon like a tall ship to the northeast (see *Around Hanksville* chapter).

If you find these badlands attractive and don't mind a tough hike to the top of North Caineville Mesa, you can almost replicate my aerial shot (see below) by following, very cautiously, the route described here: www.capitolreef.org/trails.html?trail=27.

Getting there: You'll find the Caineville Wash road 18.6 miles east of the Visitor Center on UT-24. A sign by the side of the road indicates the distance to Lower and Upper Cathedral Valley. This road will take you right into a fantastic universe of badlands in just 2 or 3 miles, passing the northern edge of the Bentonite Hills. If you want to continue on to Lower Cathedral Valley, this road can usually be negotiated with a passenger car by driving carefully if the weather conditions are right. It's a long drive, though (about 34 miles round-trip) and you'll be bounced and jolted the whole way.

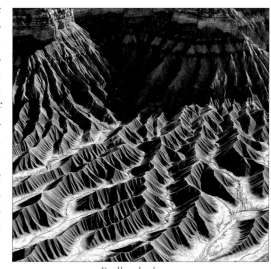

Badlands close-up

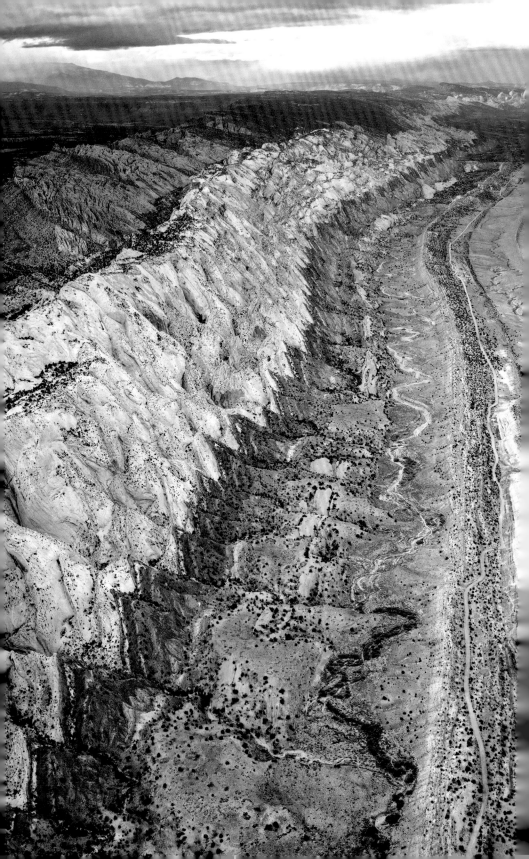

Time required: Less than an hour for a quick excursion into the heart of the badlands; 3 hours round-trip for the drive alone if you continue on until Lower Cathedral Valley.

Waterpocket Fold

Located in the southern part of the park, this strange and spectacular geologic formation is unfortunately less spectacular when seen from the ground than in the aerial photograph adorning the NPS brochure. But it still warrants a detour if you can afford the nearly full day that it will take to drive the 125-mile loop described below. Note that this tour—one third of it on dirt roads—encompasses the superb Burr Trail, described in *Chapter 6 - Along Scenic Byway 12.*

You can get to the Waterpocket Fold by way of the Notom-Bullfrog Road, which starts from UT-24, 9 miles east of the Visitor Center. This road is paved along the first 10 miles and well maintained thereafter, so it's suitable to passenger cars in dry weather.

You get a very good view of the Henry Mountains to the east and the strange nipples of Capitol Dome to the west from the top of the hill, about 6 miles from UT-24. The Waterpocket Fold doesn't really become visible until after you pass the spur leading to Cedar Mesa Campground, about 22 miles from the junction with UT-24. Even there, this extraordinary geological phenomenon remains a bit disappointing when seen from the Notom-Bullfrog road, especially in comparison to aerial photos.

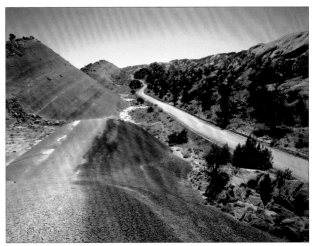

Badlands along the Notom-Bullfrog Road

Instead you may want to concentrate on details in the landscape. This area contains amazingly colorful stripes of tufa, lining the badlands on the east side of the road. They are best photographed in early morning, when still in the shade, or in late afternoon. However, to really bring out the color, nothing beats an overcast or rainy day; just remember to eliminate the sky from your image.

Less than a dozen miles further, you'll come to the well-marked junction leading west to the Burr Trail. As you reach the base of the fold, the dirt road climbs toward the Circle Cliffs in a series of steep and spectacular twists and turns carved

Opposite page: Waterpocket Fold looking north above Strike Valley Overlook

in the flank of the hill. Unless the road has been weather-damaged, these switch-backs are usually passable in a passenger car in dry weather.

Less than a mile after the switchbacks, you'll encounter on your right the road leading to Strike Valley Overlook and Upper Muley Twist (see next section). These are the only points from which you can capture the true expanse of Waterpocket fold. After a couple of miles, the Burr Trail becomes paved and leads to Boulder, where it joins UT-12. You can then drive north on UT-12 and west on UT-24 to complete the loop.

Instead of turning on the Burr Trail, you could continue on the Notom-Bullfrog Road all the way to the Bullfrog Marina, where you can cross Lake Powell by ferry to Hall's Crossing and either descend towards Monument Valley or climb back up towards Moab (see *Chapter 10 - Around Hanksville*).

Strike Valley Overlook & Upper Muley Twist

Strike Valley Overlook is a remarkable vista point, accessible via a short hike, from where you can photograph the wide expanse of the Waterpocket Fold. It is a must if you are entering or exiting Capitol Reef from the Burr Trail.

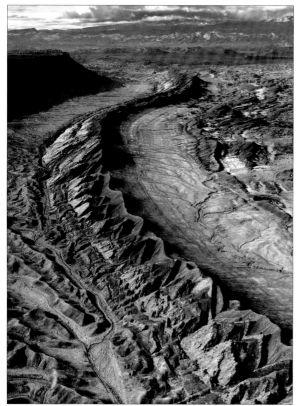

From the same trailhead, Upper Muley Twist offers a rewarding, albeit strenuous, hike and yields more panoramic views of Waterpocket Fold, but it is harder to photograph successfully.

Getting there: Via the Burr Trail from Boulder, or via Notom-Bullfrog Road (from UT-24 or from Bullfrog). The junction with the dirt road to Upper Muley Twist Canyon is less than 1 mile west from the top of the Burr Trail switch-backs. This 3-mile dirt road has been recently improved. At the time of this writing, it was suitable to any SUV up to the trailhead in dry weather. Things can change quickly, so be sure to check with the rangers. Note that you can spot several arches along this road.

Waterpocket Fold looking south

Strike Valley Overlook is about ½ mile east from the trailhead parking and offers a fantastic panoramic view of Waterpocket Fold. At the edge of the rim, follow it to your right to the very end of the cairns for the best photographic location. Here, you'll find a rock outcrop that makes a good foreground to add depth to this otherwise huge panorama. Use your wide angle in moderation, otherwise you'll end up with an image that doesn't carry enough visual impact. A moderate wide angle will work well, allowing you to include enough of the valley while emphasizing the gentle curve made by the Waterpocket Fold to the south.

If you prefer to explore Upper Muley Twist, just follow the wash at the trailhead until you reach Saddle Arch on your left, at a little under two miles. This nice arch is not easy to spot at first, but it is almost opposite the small sign to the right of the wash indicating the Rim Trail. It is a very rough climb up the Rim Trail. You'll reach the top in less than 30 minutes and the rim of the plateau in another 10 minutes on flat ground. From there, the trail follows the rim north for another two miles, offering good views of the Waterpocket Fold. There are also nice views of a large red slickrock ridge, to the west.

You can either retrace your steps or do the full loop coming back through the Upper Muley Twist Narrows, which are not particularly spectacular. Upper Muley Twist gets awfully hot in summer, so take plenty of water if you want to do the full loop. You'll need minor route finding skills, following widely spaced cairns. Some easy scrambling over slickrock is also required.

Time required: For Strike Valley Overlook, at least 1½ hours from the junction with the Burr Trail if you reach the trailhead by car. 6 hours for the Upper Muley Twist loop.

Halls Creek

Halls Creek Overlook is one of the least visited viewpoints in Capitol Reef, as it is a very long way from the Visitor Center and town amenities, and requires a high-clearance vehicle. It does, however, offer an outstanding view of the lower west side of Waterpocket Fold as well as the back of Circle Cliffs and is well worth the detour if you are traveling on Notom-Bullfrog Road.

From Halls Creek Overlook, the view of Waterpocket Fold to the north is expansive and well lit from early to mid-morning. Looking straight across the valley, you can distinguish the outline of Brimhall Bridge, with its double span tucked inside an imposing canyon carved out deep inside the cliff.

The overlook serves as a trailhead for Brimhall Bridge, as well as for a hike to Hamburger Rocks to the north and for the long trek to the Halls Creek Narrows, far to the south. For these three hikes, you'll first need to descend 800 feet on a steep trail leading in 1.2 miles to the bottom of Halls Creek. Going up during the return trip can be strenuous on a hot summer day.

Once in the valley, you'll find the entrance to Brimhall Canyon about 0.2 mile south across the stream. Don't be fooled by the easy hike inside the

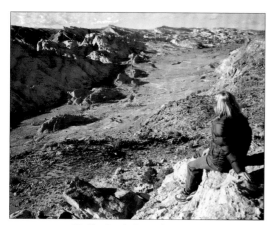

Halls Creek from the Overlook

initial part of the canyon. Although Brimhall Bridge is less than a mile from this point, it is quite an adventure which should not be undertaken alone. Soon after climbing the slippery slope of a dryfall, you reach a 100-foot long narrow passage, usually filled with dark water, which you must wade deep into or even swim. Exiting at the end of this pool requires a hard scramble on large boulders—difficult to do when you're wet. You must then climb a steep slope on loose rocks to reach a ridge, where you gain your first close view of Brimhall Bridge. For the best angle, follow the ridge to the south and, with caution, find your way down to the creek. I don't recommend Brimhall Bridge as a photographic location, unless you are specifically prepared or sure that the narrows are dry. Otherwise, you may not even be able to carry your camera across and out of the deep pool and it may not be worth the effort.

From the bottom of Halls Creek, you can also choose to hike north in the main wash to the photogenic Hamburger Rocks, a small group of dark red dwarf hoodoos with oval shapes, set on a bed of light-colored sandstone. You can sight them west of Halls Creek after about 2 miles. Continue walking until you're below the hoodoos and climb up a short distance to reach them. The hoodoos are just south of the Muley Tanks on your topo map.

Continuing 7½ miles south along the wash from the foot of the switchbacks below Halls Creek Overlook is the only way to reach the serpentine 3-mile long Halls Creek Narrows, with their tall colored walls and perennial water flow. This 22-mile round-trip cross-country trek is usually done as a 3-day backpack.

Getting there: From the partly paved/partly graded Notom-Bullfrog Road, about 44 miles south of UT-24 or 23 miles northwest of Bullfrog Marina, take the signed track heading southwest to Halls Creek Overlook. Follow it for about 3 miles until the spur to the overlook. This track is very rocky in places and requires high clearance. Although not technical, it is not suitable for passenger cars due to sharp rocks that could easily puncture a tire.

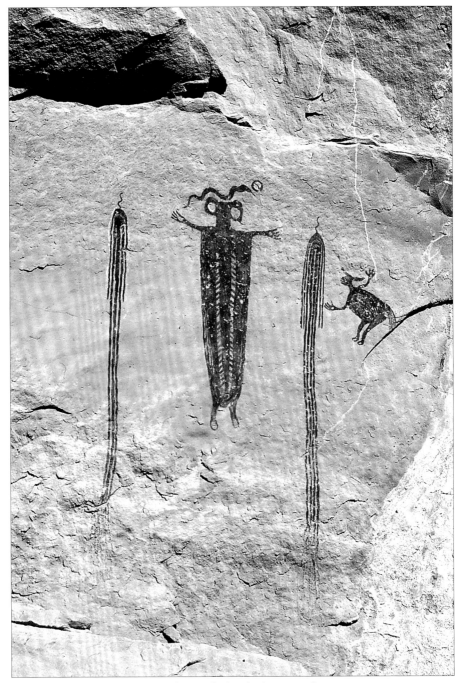

The Head of Sinbad pictograph

Chapter 9
ALONG INTERSTATE 70

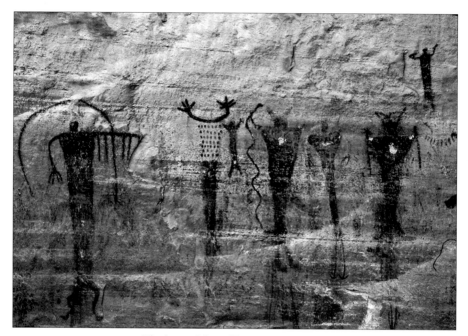

The beautiful Buckhorn Wash pictographs

Interstate 70 Corridor & San Rafael Swell

As it crosses the San Rafael Swell between Fremont Junction and Green River, I-70 is without contest one of the most scenic interstates in the Southwest. This freeway was the last portion of the east-west interstate system to be finished, opening up an extremely remote part of rural Utah to visitor traffic. A series of rest areas line the freeway, allowing you to photograph spectacular views of the San Rafael area. All merit a stop, but with a bit more time you'll find a lot to explore and photograph on short road trips from the freeway.

The San Rafael Swell is one of the last great wilderness areas of the Southwest without National Park or Monument status. Although this area has been under consideration for more robust federal protection at various times in the past, it is unlikely that the current status quo will change. If this were to happen, it would undoubtedly attract a much larger number of visitors. For now, not too many people are aware of its expansive panoramas, monoclines, buttes, deep canyons, and rock art and even fewer are venturing on its confusing network of dirt roads. And indeed many people representing a wide spectrum of interests and political sensibilities would rather keep it this way.

In the course of this chapter, we will discover a number of remarkable natural landmarks and rock art sites, starting out from I-15 and heading east.

Fremont Indian State Park

Visitors coming from I-15 and driving east on I-70 can get a great introduction to the Fremont Culture at this State Park. The Fremont Culture was centered essentially around the northern part of the fertile and beautiful Sevier River Valley, which you may have followed if you came from the south on US-89. This part of I-70 crosses the very scenic Clear Creek Canyon, making it very appealing to stop, stretch your legs, and learn something new. This is also a good overnight camping spot as the temperature is always brisk and skies are usually clear.

The visitor center has excellent exhibits of the Fremont culture, including a reproduction of a pit house. There is a large quantity of petroglyphs, accessible from numbered pullouts along the frontage road, with interpretive trails (fee required). They are generally hard to locate. Be sure to ask for the various trail fliers to make your visit more instructive and enjoyable.

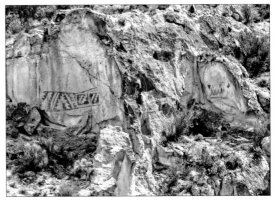

Indian Blanket

Photo advice: While most of the panels are classic Fremont petroglyphs, there is one striking exception: a 250-year old Paiute pictograph called the Indian Blanket. This huge reddish/orange drawing (as well as a smaller one to the right) is located high on the cliff on the other side of the freeway so it looks very small to the naked eye. Locate it first through the metal sight installed on the viewing platform located about 1.5 miles east of the visitor center, then pull out that big boy telephoto you've been carrying. You'll need to use it at the long end, so stabilization or a tripod are a must to capture this very original design.

Getting there: Fremont Indian State Park is at Exit 17 on I-70, 17 miles east of the junction of I-15 and about 21 miles southwest of Richfield.

Time required: 2 hours for a short visit; up to a day if you hike most of the trails in the park.

Rochester Rock Art Panel

The Rochester panel is a large petroglyph panel consisting of a mix of animal figures, anthropomorphs and a kind of rainbow carved on smooth rock. It's easily accessible, via a good dirt road and an easy trail, and makes a good picture if you are looking for rock art. The location, on a rocky promontory overlooking the Muddy River 200 feet below, is also quite nice. If you are going toward the Wedge Overlook or Nine Mile Canyon from Fremont Junction on I-70, you should consider this short but interesting detour.

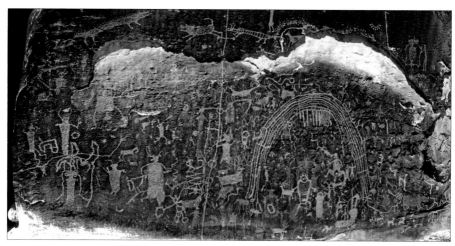

The Rochester panel

Getting there: From Exit 91 on I-70, take UT-10 north and drive 12 miles to the town of Emery. About 3½ miles past Emery, near milepost 18, turn right in the direction of Moore for ½ mile, then south at the first gravel road to your right; this road has a small sign indicating the panel. Follow it for about 3.8 miles to the parking area. The easy ½-mile foot trail leads southward to several scattered groups of glyphs but the main panel, facing east, steals the show.

Time required: About 2 hours round-trip from I-70.

Moore Cutoff Road's Snake panel

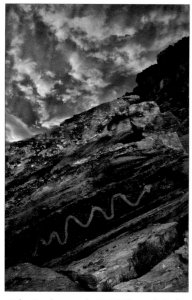

From Exit 116 on I-70 drive northwest on CR-803 (a.k.a. Moore Cutoff Road). At around mile 13.1, as the road begins a sharp turn north, look for a small paved car park, just below a tall knoll. Coming from Moore, make a right turn onto CR-803 and head east for 4 miles. After making a sharp turn to the left on this road, you'll arrive at the above-mentioned car park. From here, walk toward the boulders to the west. You will easily locate two Snake petroglyph panels on large boulders in close proximity to each other. The longest snake glyph is about 8 feet long and by itself. A smaller squarish boulder features a number of smaller snakes. To the east of the car park, you can also see faint dinosaur footprints on a huge sloping boulder.

Time required: About 1 hour r/t from I-70.

The Snake panel © Philippe Schuler

Nine Mile Canyon

Don't let the name fool you. Nine Mile Canyon is 40 miles long and takes at least half a day to thoroughly enjoy. The canyon got its name from a nine-mile triangulation done by one of J.W. Powell's topographers during the mapping of the area. Nevertheless, the 100-mile round-trip from Wellington to the gate which ends public access to the canyon provides an exquisite foray deep into the Book Cliffs Wilderness. The road leaves from Wellington, southeast of Price, and takes you through one of the largest concentrations of rock art in North America. The road goes through a remote area offering an interesting variety of landscapes, from semi-alpine to fertile cultivated land to dry canyons. Despite the heavy presence of trucks using the road, an abundance of wildlife can be seen at dawn or dusk.

Most photographers will want to visit the canyon to photograph rock art, and in particular the famous Hunting Scene panel, located near the end of the canyon.

Photo advice: Petroglyphs and pictographs, mostly of the Fremont era, can be found by the hundreds on the canyon cliffs, but unless you use a detailed booklet and drive very slowly, you will miss most of them. Stop at the Chevron gas station in Wellington and ask for the *Guide to Rock Art in Nine Mile Canyon* This useful booklet provides milepost information for many of the panels. If possible, bring binoculars to spot items high on the canyon walls. You will need a telephoto to photograph many of the rock art panels; others are at eye level or slightly above and call for a normal lens.

Getting there: From I-70, take Exit 91 for UT-10 N and drive about 64.5 miles, turning right on Ridge Rd. toward Wellington. Bypassing Wellington, you'll reach US-191 in 7.3 miles. Take it east (right) for 0.3 mile and turn left at the sign for Nine Mile Canyon. This is Soldier Creek Road, named after the Buffalo Soldiers, the famed troop of black caval-rymen who actually built it

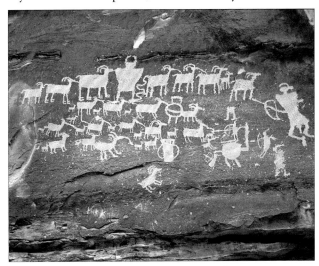

The Hunting Scene in Nine Mile Canyon

in 1882. A marker at the truck stop retraces the history of the road and points out the location of some of the more prominent panels. The road is entirely paved, but watch out for huge trucks traveling back and forth at high speed for oil and gas exploitation. After 21.5 miles, you reach the bridge over Minnie Maude

Creek which marks the official entry into Nine Mile Canyon. The Hunting Scene Panel is located about 1.2 miles from the entrance of Cottonwood Canyon Road, which begins to your right about 23.6 miles from Minnie Maude Creek.

Time required: At least half a day from Wellington, but a full day will be more suitable for serious rock art hunters.

Wedge Overlook

To the northeast of Fremont Junction on I-70, UT-10 to Price offers the easiest access to this two popular site located in the heart of the Swell, although

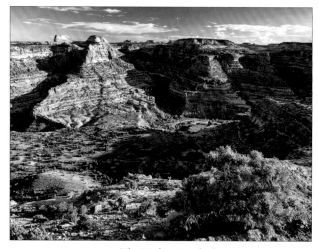

The Wedge Overlook

it's possible to come from Exit 131 off I-70. From exit 91, drive 38 miles to Castle Dale and about 1 mile north of town, take the signed and well-graded gravel road (CR-401), suitable to passenger cars in dry weather. Follow it east for 12.8 miles and, at the fork, turn south for about 6.7 miles on an equally good road leading to a breathtaking view of the San Rafael River at the Wedge Overlook. The viewpoint is 600 feet above the gorge—a great destination to photograph "Utah's Little Grand Canyon". Early morning light and late afternoon light are best but you'll have to deal with shadows in the canyon. There are maintained tracks following the canyon east and west leading to additional viewpoints.

Buckhorn Draw

About 15 miles east from UT-10 on CR-401 beginning north of Castle Dale, or 2.4 miles east from the turnoff to Wedge Overlook, turn right at the sign on well-maintained BLM-332 to visit the Buckhorn Draw area. About 2½ miles from the junction, park past a cattle guard and follow a short trail heading east to a petroglyph panel. Almost 3½ miles farther, park at the sign for the highlight of the road: the Buckhorn Wash Panel, which has been repeatedly vandalized and restored. The panel, in the Barrier Canyon style, is right by the side of the road; it is fenced off but easily photographed with a normal lens to medium telephoto. These are, in my opinion, some of the finest pictographs in the Southwest. Road 332 continues for 23 miles toward I-70, which it meets at Exit 131. Along the

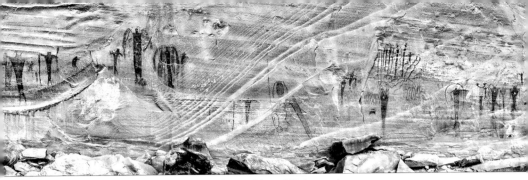

The Buckhorn Wash panel

way, it traverses beautiful Buckhorn Canyon, followed by grassy open areas. This is a remote area of magnificent scenery, although easily accessible, yet few people know about it. A great place for relaxing and camping.

Head of Sinbad

Sinbad Country is a vast region extending on both sides of I-70 and bordered on its north side by a long butte known as Locomotive Point. Locomotive Point harbors a number of pictograph panels, which until now have been spared by vandals. The most beautiful of these panels is referred to as the Head of Sinbad pictograph.

The Head of Sinbad panel is exquisite in its simplicity: a single shamanistic anthropomorph with an interesting hairdo, surrounded by two elegant and simply ornamented stick-like motifs and a curiously waving buck, revealing the artist's sense of humor. On another panel, a bit to the left, you can photograph an anthropomorph holding a snake; his neighbor is a dead ringer for E.T. There are more panels to the east along Locomotive Point.

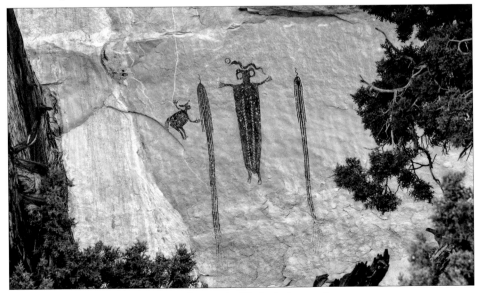

The Head of Sinbad pictograph

Photo advice: Personally, I love this beautiful artwork so much, I'm content to contemplate it alone against its background of golden sandstone. You may also want to frame the panel between the trunks of the obvious junipers facing it.

Getting there: With the former access near milepost 124 now blocked by boulders, the only access as of this writing is from Exit 131 on I-70. From the south side of I-70, take the frontage road west then head south. About 4 miles from I-70, go right for 1 mile then right again. Continue northwest for 3½ miles and turn right at the Dutchman Arch sign, taking the narrow concrete tunnel under I-70. In general, the dirt road to the Head of Sinbad panels is passable by passenger cars as far as the underpass; however, I have also seen it with nasty ruts requiring a high clearance vehicle. I have also encountered a high level of muddy water insider the underpass proper. North of the underpass, go right for ¼ mile, then right again at the next fork for about 0.5 mile, then left for 0.3 mile to the car park and its wooden fence. This last segment has deep sand and is impassable for passenger cars.

Time required: About an hour from I-70 including photography.

Dutchman Arch

Dutchman Arch is sometimes called Dutchman's Arch, which is at least grammatically correct. Strangely the BLM sign pointing to it nearby has it as 'Dutchmens Arch'. The arch can be photographed from both sides; it is best seen in late afternoon.

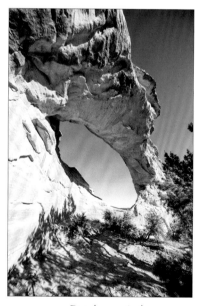

Dutchman Arch

Getting there: Just north of the aforementioned concrete tunnel in the Head of Sinbad section, turn left and drive 0.3 mile on a dirt road heading west, then north. At the junction, turn left due west for ¼ mile until you reach the car park for Dutchman Arch.

Nearby locations: Further west on I-70, there are two view areas in close proximity to Exit 116. Devil's Canyon Viewpoint can only be accessed from the eastbound side of the Interstate; it is the least interesting photographically but still warrants a stop. Eagle Canyon Viewpoint, on the westbound side, can be accessed from both directions and offers striking views of the domes surrounding Eagle Canyon. Most of us see this panorama in full daylight as we travel between locations on I-70, and every time I stop here I'm telling myself that I should return at sunrise or sunset.

Lone Warrior

Hardcore rock art aficionados may want to pay a visit to the Lone Warrior pictograph. The Lone Warrior is an interesting, although somewhat faded, pictograph consisting of a lone cat-like anthropomorph wielding a shield.

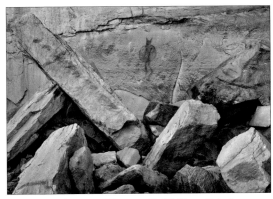

The Lone Warrior © Philippe Schuler

Getting there: Returning from the Head of Sinbad panel or Dutchman Arch, drive past the tunnel and turn southwest (right) for 1.6 miles, then right on a spur track for ½ mile to the car park. The panel is located behind the second fence at 38°51'12" 110°48'13".

Photo advice: Try including foreground rocks in your composition. A polarizer will help bring out detail from the very faded silhouette.

Time required: 30 minutes from the beginning of the spur and back.

Swasey Cabin

Swasey Cabin was built in 1921 by the notorious Swasey bothers (no less than four of them) who herded cattle in the area. They picked a very photogenic place as the cabin is erected in close proximity to an interesting pinnacle called the Broken Cross, which can be conveniently included in your picture. Sunrise is a good time to shoot the cabin if you are car-camping.

About 0.2 mile west from the cabin is the so-called "Icebox", where the broth-ers used to stash their perishables. While interesting from an histori-cal point of view, there is nothing really photogenic here.

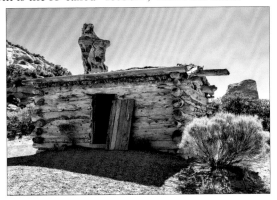

Getting there: Back at the junc-tion of the Lone Warrior spur, continue south on the main track for 0.8 mile and turn west for another 0.7 mile to the large car park next to some restrooms and Swasey Cabin.

Time required: 30 minutes.

Swasey Cabin

Eagle Canyon Arch

Eagle Canyon Arch is a spectacular jughandle arch (taller than it is wide), attractively located in a meander of the canyon whose name it bears, a short distance south of the twin bridges crossing over the canyon on I-70. Although this 90-foot arch is featured on the 7.5' USGS topo map as "Natural Arch", it has been largely ignored by the mainstream until now, mostly because of the

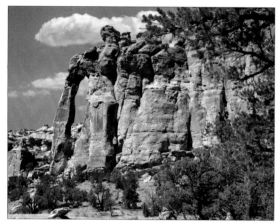

Eagle Canyon Arch

long drive required to get there. Visiting the arch requires a 4.8-mile round-trip hike along the old Jeep track that descends westward into the canyon from Swasey Cabin and continues north past the double-span bridge of I-70. The first mile of the track is in very poor condition, with many tall sandstone steps and is not passable by standard SUVs, so park at Swasey Cabin, make sure you have plenty of water, and hike.

Photo advice: The arch is facing south and looks best in late afternoon, before shadows from the opposite canyon wall interfere.

Time required: 2½ hours from Swasey Cabin, including time for photography.

Family Butte

Family Butte is a seldom visited but quite striking formation deep in the heart of the Swell. It consists of several tall spires that actually make me think of the decals you see on the rear windows of large grocery-getter SUVs; only the dog is missing.

Photo advice: The best and easiest way to view and photograph the Butte is from the south side of the dirt road when it comes fully into view without obstacles to interfere, shortly past a side spur at 38°45'45" 110°49'52". Just climb the slope next to the road to get a bit of elevation. A long telephoto is a must as the butte is still quite distant at this point. To get a closer view, albeit at a less attractive angle, take the side spur north, angle left at the first opportunity and park at the end of the track at a well-used unofficial campsite. Walk north to get some elevation and an unobstructed view. There are no views from the west side of the butte.

Getting there: From the Swasey Cabin junction, continue south about 6 miles then turn west (right) for 0.7 mile. Turn right and drive 2 miles (passing a road on your left) to a dirt road on your right. Take it for 0.2 mile, then a spur to the left leading to a car park. Accessing Family Butte from UT-24 via Temple Mountain Road is also fairly easy and safe. Count on 45 minutes drive time from Exit 131 on I-70 or almost 1 hour from UT-24.

Nearby locations: Heading further west on the main dirt road for about 15 miles (this is the most scenic part of the Reds Canyon Loop),

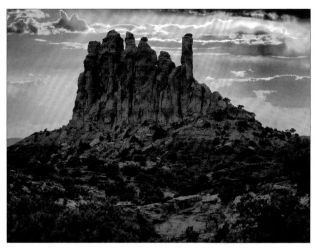

Family Butte

you reach Tomsich Butte trailhead, the starting point for further explorations of the remotest parts of the Swell. You can catch a distant shot of Hondoo Arch before exploring Muddy Creek. The Upper Chute of Muddy Creek starts about 3.8 miles from the car park.

Spotted Wolf Canyon

As it crosses the Reef forming the eastern side of the Swell, I-70 arguably becomes one of the most scenic highways in the Southwest. Whether traveling eastward from the San Rafael Swell or westward from Green River, crossing the impressive barrier of the San Rafael Reef is a truly memorable experience.

Heading eastward, the Spotted Wolf Canyon viewpoint is located on the west side of the Reef, about 11 miles past Exit 131 and 6 miles before Exit 149 for UT-24. It offers a superlative view of the freeway meandering its way down the Reef with the Book Cliffs on the horizon. It's a great wide-angle shot if you don't mind including the gently curving freeway in the foreground.

Coming from Green River, the fantastic presence of the Reef is best experienced from a little hill above the last rest stop before the ascent.

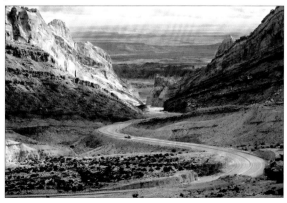

The Reef through Spotted Wolf Canyon

Black Dragon Wash

The highlight of this popular canyon, located off I-70, is a striking pictograph of a strange bird-like figure reminiscent of a pterodactyl or dragon.

To visit Black Dragon Wash, you must be coming from Green River, as there is no exit from the south side of the freeway. You can't use one of the occasional median crossings, as these are for emergency use only and the highway patrol would likely ticket you. Technically, there is no exit either on the north side, just an unmarked pull off area ¼ mile past milepost 147, which you'll find approximately ¾ mile beyond the bridge over the San Rafael river or about 2.5 miles west of Exit 149 for UT-24 (where you can make a U-turn if you're coming from the west on I-70). There is a marked BLM dirt road and a cattle gate, which you have to open and close behind you. Follow the road north for about a mile in open country, then turn left for

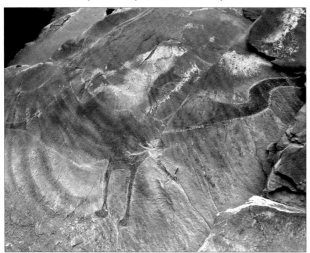

The amazing Black Dragon

another ¼ mile inside the reef. The road is in decent shape and passable to a passenger car. With high clearance, you'll be able to drive the next ½ mile to a parking area located right below the panel. Passenger cars should stop before that, when things become rough.

The panel is on the north side of the canyon. It is at least 30 feet up on the cliff and appears rather small to the naked eye. Someone apparently decided one day that the red pigment had become too faint and drew a white outline with chalk around the dragon to make it easier to see. This exemplifies too well the risk of leaving prominent rock art unprotected. Outlining Indian rock art with chalk or drawing over it or around it is no different from painting over Michaelangelo's work in the Sistine chapel.

Once you have located the dragon, make your way up the rocky path that leads to the base of the ledge where it's drawn. Be extremely cautious as the path is slippery and the ledge is very narrow. There are several other pictographs with anthropomorphic as well as abstract shapes near the Black Dragon.

Photo advice: You'll need a wide angle lens to fit the dragon into your frame; it's about 7 feet wide from wing tip to wing tip. Bracket your exposure to obtain the best tonality. Some oblique mini-ledges to the right of the Dragon could be included in your composition.

Time required: 1 hour round-trip from I-70.

Nearby location: About halfway back from the Black Dragon parking area to I-70, you can turn west on a short ¼-mile spur road leading to the Petroglyph Canyon trailhead. Walk southwest along the reef for about ten minutes until you reach the mouth of Arch Canyon. Head inside the canyon and soon after its entrance take a short spur southwest and look for a small but undamaged panel on the north wall. The hike is about 1.5 miles round-trip.

The Crystal Geyser

Near Green River is a little-known but interesting natural phenomenon: a geyser—inadvertently "revealed" by someone drilling for oil! The trouble is, it isn't exactly Old Faithful! The geyser erupts only once or twice every 24 hours, so you'll need either luck, to be there at the right time, or patience. As of this writing, eruptions are only a few feet high and much less impressive than they used to be, due to rocks stupidly dropped into the geyser's blowhole by idiots hoping to trigger an eruption. Even if you don't see the geyser erupt, you can still photograph the colorful travertine deposits cascading down to the river. They are created by the lime-saturated water flowing out of the pipe

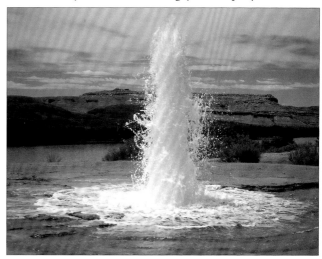

The Crystal Geyser

Photo advice: Anytime in the day is fine to photograph the geyser if it's erupting. Be sure to protect your equipment if you're shooting at close range or some nasty whitish paste will blanket it and it will be hard to remove. The geyser is not hot so there doesn't seem to be a danger of getting burns, but you should be cautious of where you step as there are a couple of hot bubbling mud holes next to it. Overexpose ½ stop to accurately convey the color of the column of water. The colorful travertine deposits around the geyser make good subjects for abstracts.

Getting there: From Exit 164 on I-70 just east of Green River, follow the dirt road heading southeast for about 2½ miles. At the junction, turn right and continue south, then west, for another 4 miles in a desolate landscape until you reach the geyser near the riverbank.

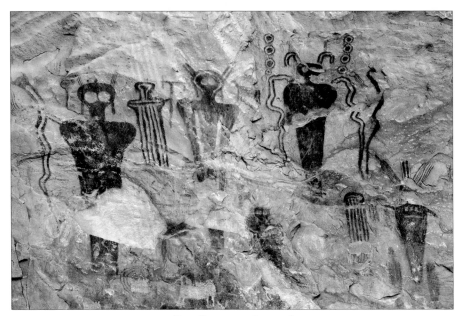

Sego Canyon main panel

Sego Canyon

Sego Canyon is as good as it gets for motorists who would like to see some prime rock art without sweating it out. If you are traveling on I-70 between Green River and Grand Junction, all you need to do is take Exit 187, about 25 miles east of Green River, drive north past Thompson Springs and continue for about 3½ miles on a paved road. Just follow the sign over the tracks and up canyon to an obvious parking area on the left side. It doesn't get any easier than that!

A short trail leads to a large and beautiful Barrier style pictograph panel. This panel is best photographed with a normal lens or a short telephoto. There are a couple of interpretive markers providing an overview of the various periods and styles of rock art.

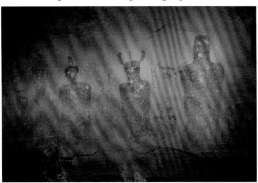

If you walk a little bit along the road past the parking area, you'll see some large anthropomorphic figures painted on the sandstone just 60 feet from the fence. These impressive pictographs are badly faded and partially vandalized, but still worth the brief detour.

Fun with light painting © Jerry Day

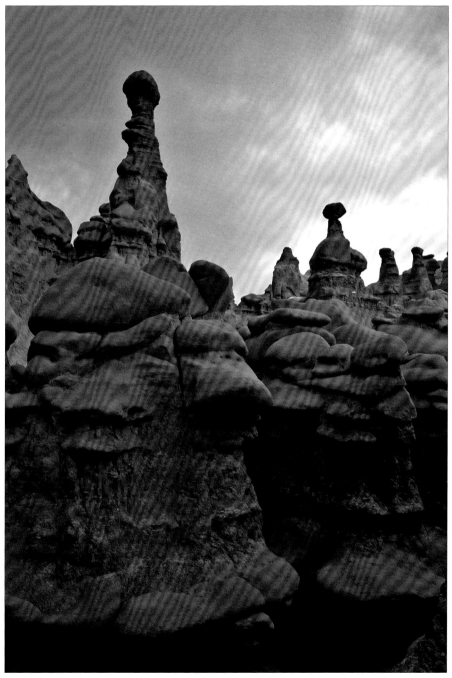

Goblin Generals

Chapter 10

AROUND HANKSVILLE

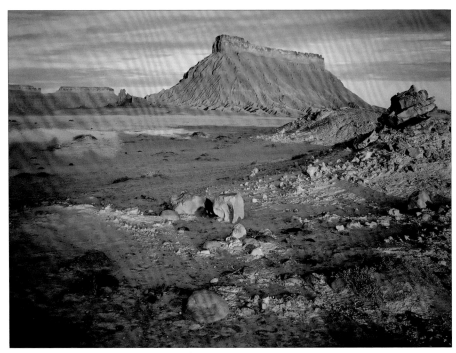

Red Planet (Factory Butte)

Hanksville will serve as our gateway to discover the area covered in this chapter. There isn't much to see in this tiny town (with the exception of the Wolverton Historic Mill near the BLM office), but it provides a very convenient base of exploration and all the basic services: gas, food, lodging, a landing strip, and of course, the BLM visitor center for up-to-date information on road conditions.

Factory Butte

I have to admit that I have a particular fondness for Factory Butte, despite the fact that it generally elicits a big yawn from other photographers. I don't exactly know why I'm so fond of it; I suppose it's simply because of its awesome shape and sheer volume—a cross between a gigantic nuclear power plant and the Titanic. Every time I drive along the Fremont River, on my way in or out of Capitol Reef, I feel a pinch of excitement when the majestic butte comes into view. It took me several tries to capture a satisfactory photograph of Factory Butte, however. Once, for lack of adequate scouting and preparation, I missed the sunrise by a few minutes despite getting up at the crack of dawn. Finally, I decided on a more systematic approach. I scouted various locations in the evening, alongside Coal Mine Road, photographing until nighttime before returning to Hanksville. The next morning, I made sure I arrived at the chosen location with a few minutes to spare. I firmly planted my tripod, waited and was finally rewarded with a fantastic sunrise shot—the warm light illuminating the Martian foreground and bringing up nice shadows on the lovely badlands at the base of the butte.

Photo advice: Excellent views of the butte start opening up on the eastern side at about 4 miles from UT-24 on Coal Mine Road (a.k.a. Muddy Creek Road). Factory Butte is best photographed at sunrise from a spot about 5.6 miles along Coal Mine Road. There are also lovely badlands on the southern end of the butte that can also be photographed in late afternoon. For a special experience, treat yourself to an aerial shoot from a small plane or drone. There is a good campsite at Mile 7.

Getting there: Drive about 11 miles from Hanksville toward Capitol Reef on UT-24 and turn right on Coal Mine Road, a good dirt road leading toward the butte. An information panel located soon after the beginning of the road will reassure you that you are on the right track. A word of warning: further up on Coal Mine Road, do not try to cross Muddy Creek as a shortcut to Goblin Valley unless you've talked to a BLM ranger in Hanksville and confirmed the creek is passable. The creek often has quicksand and you can easily get stuck, even with a 4x4. A tow from Hanksville would be costly, and your engine could be ruined.

Goblin Valley State Park

In Goblin Valley, erosion has carved an extremely pliable variety of Entrada sandstone into extravagant shapes, offering your astonished eyes a spectacle of goblins, ghosts, and other fantastic creatures. They are seemingly awaiting a magic wand to awaken them to start walking as if in an animated motion picture. If you are on a family vacation, it's almost guaranteed that your imagination will be as stimulated as that of your children.

A formation called the Three Judges greets you on the left as you enter the park; it is worthy of a photo in late afternoon. But it's at the covered viewpoint at road's end that the most compelling sight awaits you—a vast army of goblins, camped in the depression below the parking area, mineral creatures looking like something out of a Tolkien story.

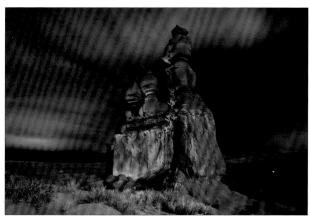

The Three Judges © Jerry Day

Overleaf: Factory Butte badlands aerial

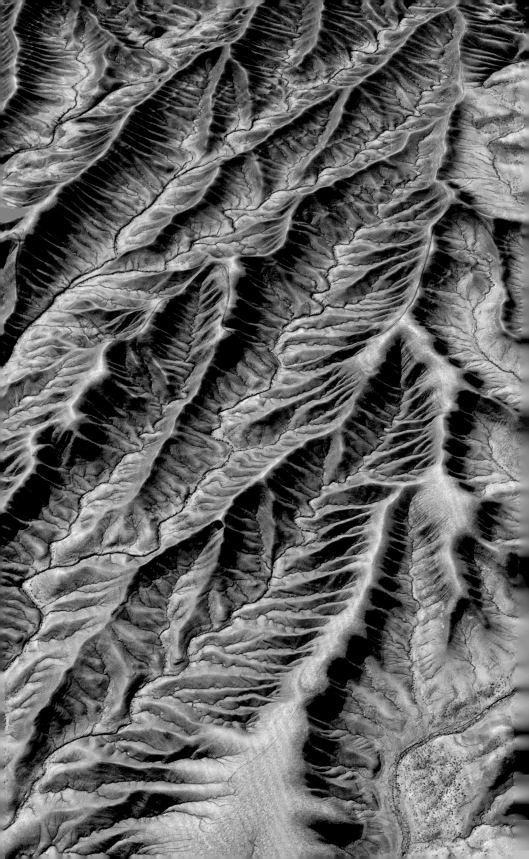

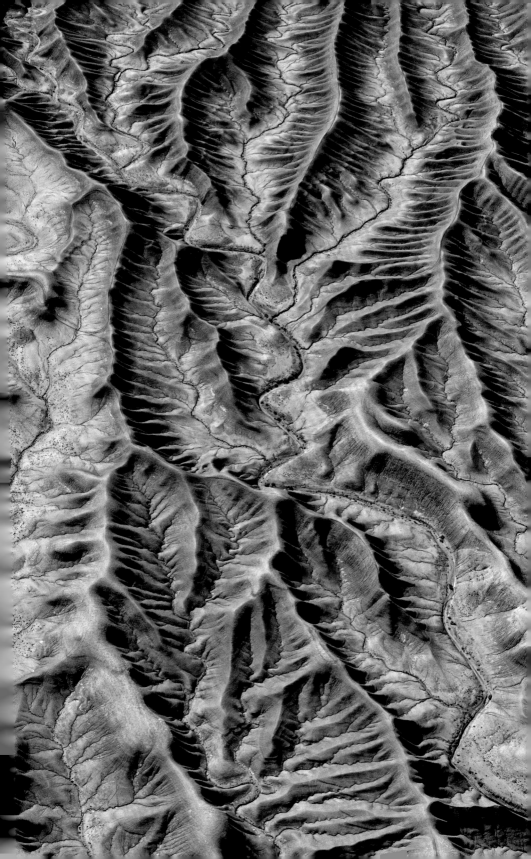

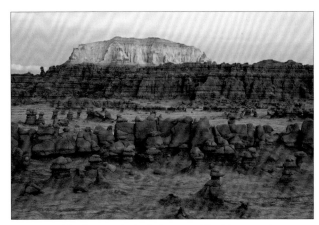

Hoodoos at dusk © Synnatschke Photography

Start your visit by enjoying and photographing this panorama right from the observation point, as it is truly superb. In summer, you risk catching in your viewfinder lots of Lilliputian-sized humans photographing these ferocious goblins.

Goblin Valley has three official foot trails: the 1½-mile Carmel Canyon Trail, leading to views of Molly's Castle as well as providing access to Goblin's Lair; the 1.3 mile Entrada Canyon Trail; and the 2.1-mile Curtis Bench Trail, offering a superb view of the Henry Mountains from the trail's highest point.

However, the most rewarding walk, from a photographic standpoint, is a descent into the depression from the covered viewpoint and walking among the goblins where you can let your imagination run wild.

Photo advice: Avoid visiting Goblin Valley when the sun is high in the sky as your pictures will have too much contrast and will look flat under a uniform sky. Ideally, early morning or evening is best, as the main view of the depression is oriented to the south. You can take excellent shots from the covered vista point

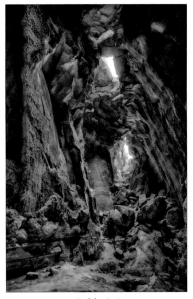

Goblin's Lair

using a variety of lenses. A telephoto will work well to compress the perspective and make the goblins very dense in your picture. Walking among the goblins, the formations located on the left side of the basin generally offer the best photographic opportunities. There is a particularly remarkable spot that you should photograph: crossing the basin at 1 o'clock in the direction of the cliffs, look for a large copper green dome. It may look quite far from the observation point, but it's really only a short 10-minute walk. Climbing up, you'll find a passage leading behind a group of very high formations. You'll come out into a true fantasyland of spires and chimneys.

The Goblin's Lair is a 70' tall cavern with several skylights and is a fun place to visit and photograph. It is located on the east side of the park and accessed via a 1.4-mile round-trip trail from Molly's Castle Overlook. It requires climbing a short but steep rise at the end of the trail, as well as some scrambling to reach the floor.

Getting there: The turnoff from UT-24 is located 24 miles south of I-70 and about 20 miles north of Hanksville, at milepost 137. Drive west for 5.2 miles then turn left toward the south and drive 6.4 miles to reach the entrance of the park. Herds of antelope are sometimes visible along the road.

Time required: At least 1½ hours if you want to photograph extensively and wander around among the goblins. Add another 1½ hours to visit Goblin's Lair. A night walk can be a magical experience during full moon.

Nearby Location: Molly's Castle is a fortress-like rise located 1½ miles east on a signed 4WD track starting about 0.4 mile before the park's entrance. Gilson Butte, a bit further east, is similar but closer to UT-24. More remarkable are the lovely formations located on both sides of UT-24, about 5 miles south of the Goblin Valley turnoff. These beautiful groups of goblins and mushroom rocks are very photogenic in the morning or evening sun, coming from Hanksville.

Little Wild Horse Slot Canyon

This highly rewarding hike, both very visual and tactile, lets you penetrate right into the heart of the San Rafael Reef. You're guaranteed to bring back some nice memories and shots from a trip inside Little Wild Horse Canyon. Access is easy and the walk through the slot canyon is not difficult. This explains why Little Wild Horse Canyon has become a classic hike and one of the most visited locations in San Rafael Reef, especially in season and during legal holidays.

After parking your car, take the trail leading to the dry wash bed and follow it for a few hundred yards. As the riverbed narrows, about 10 minutes after leaving the trailhead, you'll come to a sort of dry waterfall about 8 feet high. The best way to get around this obstacle is to ascend the inclined plane on the left side, just a few yards before, and return to the wash just after the dry fall.

Continue about 200 yards past the dry fall and turn right at the easily missed fork into Little Wild Horse Canyon. The other fork leads to Bell Canyon.

A popular loop hike is to follow Little Wild Horse Canyon for about 2 miles to its end, then follow a jeep trail west, then south, to the entrance of

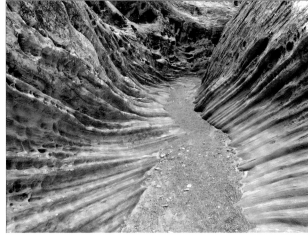

Little Wild Horse Canyon © Synnatschke Photography

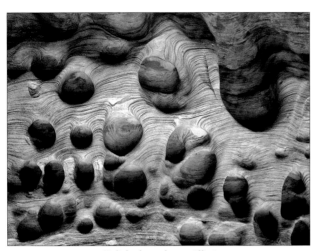

Polished sandstone illusion
(Turn upside down to see the actual eroded niches)

Bell Canyon. You can then descend this shorter slot canyon until it meets with Little Wild Horse. It takes about four hours to do this loop, but the best photographic opportunities are in Little Wild Horse Canyon, so we'll concentrate on a round-trip inside this canyon.

Little Wild Horse Canyon starts revealing its strange splendor a few hundred feet further on. It begins with a series of very interesting holes and niches carved out by water action on the walls. At a height of about 200 feet, the latter are tightly constricted in some places, no more than a couple of feet wide at shoulder height. In some places, you'll need to place both hands on the rock wall and perform a series of push-up motions so you can move forward inside the highly slanted, shallow corridor. But, generally speaking, the walk is never difficult. However, be careful you don't get stuck and twist an ankle when the fault contracts down to a few inches under your feet.

Follow your exploration up-canyon for as long as your heart desires but go at least ½ mile to really take in the atmosphere of the place. After the first hundred yards or so, the slot canyon widens, but a second section, even narrower than the first and also much more interesting, awaits you a bit further on. Keep walking until you reach a sort of wide section, with some trees, about 50 minutes from the fork with Bell Canyon. The canyon continues on even higher, but by now you have seen the most interesting part.

Photo advice: Little Wild Horse Canyon consists of a very brown type of Wingate and Kayenta sandstone near the ground with light colored Navajo sandstone on the very high walls. Mid-morning and mid-afternoon are best for reflected light, but it's generally quite dark in the narrower portions of the canyon. There are some wider spots where the sandstone takes on soft pinkish hues.

Getting there: Leaving Goblin Valley State Park (see previous section), turn left about 0.4 mile past the park exit; a sign points to Little Wild Horse Canyon. Drive 5.4 miles on this paved road to a parking area. In case of flash flooding, your car will be protected here as it is above the riverbed. A sign tells about such a flash flood experienced by a visiting couple, with a photo showing their Landcruiser washed away by the high water. Take this very seriously, particularly on a summer's afternoon. Flash floods are generated by rain falling on the Reef far above the entrance of the canyon and you won't necessarily see it. If you are caught by a flash flood while you are in the canyon, you'll be in great danger. Never forget that it's storms such as these that are responsible for the creation of the beautiful walls of this slot canyon.

Time required: About 2½ hours round-trip from the parking area.

Wild Horse Canyon

On the way to Goblin Valley and Little Wild Horse Canyon, you can look into nearby Wild Horse Canyon for a little known but interesting pictograph panel. Although quite small, the anthropomorphs depicted on the panel are finely drawn and very well preserved, despite some graffiti on the left side. As a bonus, you may want to visit Wild Horse Window (see next section).

After parking, descend into the wash and head west toward the reef for about ¼ mile to the canyon's mouth, where you'll see 'Wilderness Area' markers. Enter the small light-colored narrows to the left and continue up-canyon. The walls become progressively taller and about ½ mile northwest past the markers, the canyon widens, assuming a wide circular shape. From here on, look up to the right for a raw of small

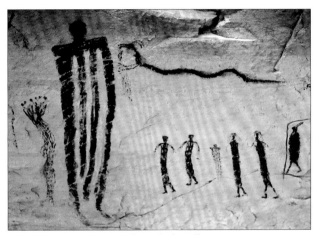

Thou Shalt Follow

alcoves where the panel is hidden. You can access the alcoves via a slickrock ramp beginning close to some big boulders to your right. To visit similar hard-to-find panels and to significantly increase your enjoyment and understanding of rock art, you might consider joining a field trip of the Utah Rock Art Research Association, a.k.a. URARA.

Photo advice: A wide angle lens works best to capture the entire panel, which can later be cropped in panoramic format; you can also isolate some groups of anthropomorphs with a normal lens to fill the entire frame.

Getting there: On UT-24, take the turnoff for Goblin Valley State Park and drive 5.2 miles to Temple Mountain Junction. Turn left on Goblin Valley Road for about 0.3 mile and right on the third spur road. Go another 0.3 mile from the paved road and stop at a wide car park (38°38'51" 110°39'46"), just before the road descends into the wash.

Time required: About 1½ hours round-trip to photograph the panel.

Wild Horse Window

Wild Horse Window, a.k.a. Eyes of the San Rafael and Eyes of Sinbad, is a huge and spectacular alcove lit by a hole in its roof. Note that the pictographs you may see inside are fake and appeared in the last decade.

From the Wild Horse Canyon car park (see previous section), scan the cliff to the northwest for the Window. From here it looks like a big dark cave and it's quite obvious. But if you're not entirely sure, continue a couple of hundred feet on the spur road until it becomes more visible. Memorizing the topography around the Window, which is not located in Wild Horse Canyon proper, but farther north, will help you find your way later on, especially if you want to get there directly after photographing the Wild Horse Canyon panel.

Follow the good hiker's trail crossing the sandy bottom of Wild Horse Wash to where it hits the slickrock around 38°38'55"110°39'55". (Note: I'm providing this intermediate waypoint in case the trail gets wiped out by a flash flood.) Start your ascent on the slickrock, following occasional cairns to a small hanging valley at 38°39'04" 110°40'13". The hikers's trail resumes on the left side (south) of the valley and you can now make a beeline following the natural channel in a northwest direction until you reach the window at 38°39'11"110°40'35".

Less flexible individuals might have trouble with the last little ledge that you need to descend just before reaching the window. This minor obstacle is easily

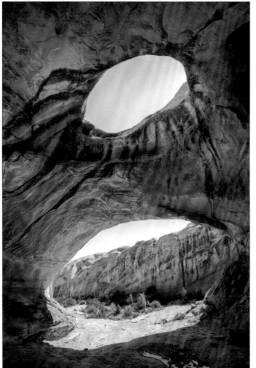

bypassed by following the potholes to the right. They are usually filled with water, but are very shallow.

If you came from the Wild Horse pictograph panel, Wild Horse Window is less than 0.2 mile north of the main canyon, as the crow flies. Reaching the Window from here calls for a modicum of routefinding skills. If you feel up for it after seeing the panel, retrace your steps from the panel toward your car and shortly before the canyon narrows you'll see a slickrock slope to the left, allowing you to easily climb out to the plateau. Continue on the slickrock for a short while until you meet a little canyon leading northwest to the Window.

Photo advice: There are many possible compositions; however, an ultra-wide angle is a must to capture more than just a hole in the roof of the alcove. The deep alcove receives indirect light

Wild Horse Window

from both openings and should look good most of the day, but the huge contrast between the inside of the alcove and the outside makes it very challenging.

Getting there: Wild Horse Window shares the same car park with Wild Horse Canyon (see previous section).

Temple Mountain Pictographs

If you continue northwest on Temple Mountain Road (coming from UT-24) past the intersection with the Goblin Valley road for about 0.9 mile, you'll see a large pullout to the right (northeast). Looking up at the overhang, you'll see a row of nice Barrier-style pictographs. Unfortunately, the top of the figures has been lost to erosion and, to make matters worse, the pictographs have been repeatedly vandalized. Still, it's a very nice panel, definitely worth the detour. In the accompanying photograph, I have taken the liberty to remove the most obvious traces of vandalism to show it partially as it once was. An isolated horned figure from the more recent Fremont period can be seen a few feet to the left. A medium telephoto is necessary to photograph the panel.

Nearby location: If you follow Temple Mountain Road further north, you'll enter Sinbad Country, an attractive combination of vast desert expanse, small hills, buttes and grassland, with lots of interesting canyons and rock art wait-ing to be explored away from crowds. Temple Mountain Road is usually passable by passenger car, with caution, but may require a high-clearance vehicle at times. It goes all the way to I-70, offering an interesting alternative to reach Little Wild Horse Canyon or Goblin Valley State Park from the Interstate (taking Exit 131 south).

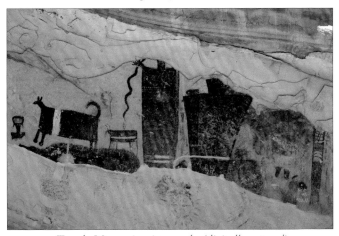

Temple Mountain pictographs (digitally restored)

Crack Canyon

Crack Canyon consists of several sections of narrows, extending about 2.5 miles though the San Rafael Reef. For the purpose of this book, I will only dis-cuss the first narrows, which present the most interest to photographers. From the new trailhead, it takes almost a mile of nondescript wash-walking from the

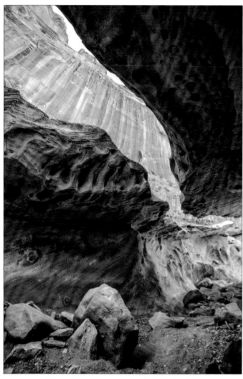

The subway section of Crack Canyon

car park to reach the first narrows. While there is no sign prohibiting you to drive past the trailhead (as of this writing), my advice is don't do it. You'll save at most 15 minutes and you may incur serious damage to your stock 4WD vehicle if you take a wrong turn.

Photo advice: Soon after you enter the canyon, you are wowed by the most amazing displays of giant "Swiss cheese". The gnarled sandstone provides plenty of intimate landscapes and abstract texture compositions, but it's the incredible split level "subway" and its twists and turns that I find most interesting. A tripod is of course required if you want fine detail with no noise, as well as adequate depth-of-field. The best time to photograph the first part of the slot is in early to mid-morning, and then again in mid-afternoon after the sun has passed behind the tall walls. It's worth waiting for the sun to pass to eliminate any hot spots.

Getting there: Coming from UT-24 and continuing past the turnoff to Goblin Valley State Park on Temple Mountain Road, drive 2.2 miles until the road forks off to the left (southwest). This stretch of road, known as the Behind the Reef Road, is a fairly well-maintained dirt road and most cars should have little trouble under normal conditions. Drive 4.1 miles to the car park, BLM register, and trailhead.

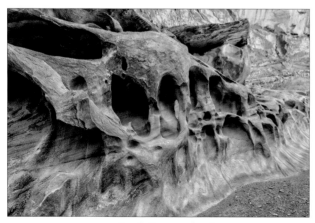

Crack Canyon detail

Time required: Allow 2 to 3 hours to visit the first section of the narrows where the best "Swiss cheese" is located.

Nearby locations: Going on southwest past Crack Canyon on the Behind the Reef Road, you'll come to trailheads for Chute Canyon, and the upper narrows of Little Wild Horse and Bell canyons.

Burr Point

While traveling on UT-95 from Hanksville to Hite or vice versa, you may want to take a quick side trip across the Burr Desert to the Dirty Devil

River Overlook, also known as Burr Point. It offers a remarkably expansive panorama of the canyon area formed by the Dirty Devil River, which is fed by the waters of Muddy Creek and the Fremont River.

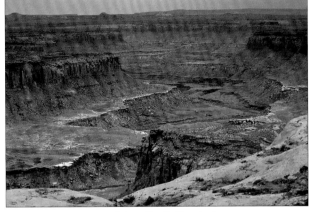

Photo advice: The view is spectacular and lends itself well to shooting verticals for stitching a panorama. This is a great late afternoon location.

Dirty Devil Overlook

Getting there: Drive about 15.5 miles south of Hanksville on UT-95 or 10.5 miles north of the UT-276 junction and turn east at the Burr Point sign. Using caution, the 10.5-mile dirt road is generally suitable for passenger cars, except during and after a rain.

Arsenic Arch

Little known Arsenic Arch is a gem of an arch, well-hidden inside a tributary of Poison Spring Canyon. Lying isolated in the midst of a slickrock hill perched above the canyon, the small but elegant arch will delight dedicated arch hunters and photographers alike.

From where you park, walk north for almost ½ mile toward the canyon. Follow the rim until you spot the arch, located at 38°06'20" 110°32'21", about 60 feet below the rim. The safest spot to descend from the rim is about 0.3 mile southwest (left) of the arch at 38°06'09" 110°32'29". You have to skirt to the

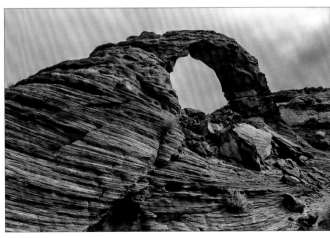

Arsenic Arch

right around a deep canyon before you can reach the slickrock hill where the arch is located.

Photo advice: A moderate wide angle captures the entire arch perfectly. The best time to photograph the arch is at sunset, although early morning will work too.

Getting there: On UT-95, about 20 south of Hanksville or 5.7 miles north of the junction with UT-276 (just opposite the Little Egypt access road), turn east onto a sandy track normally in good condition in dry weather. There is a rocky wash to traverse after ½ mile, but the track becomes good after that. If you look carefully, you can briefly spot the arch on the left hand side from a hill located at about mile 4.6, just before the signpost for the Sahara Sands. There are a few pullouts near mile 5.2 (38°05'51" 110°32'26").

Time Required: About 2 hours from UT-95.

Little Egypt

If you've enjoyed Goblin Valley, consider a brief stop at the Little Egypt Geological Site. Little Egypt is a free access site offering its share of goblins and hoodoos whose eroded shapes apparently evoked Ancient Egyptian temples for those who named it. Despite being more colorful—deep red with white stria-

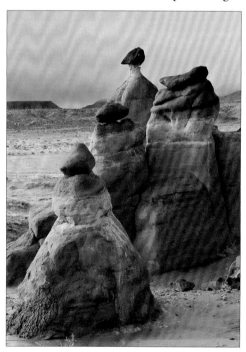

Egyptian Hoodoos

tions—than their Goblin Valley counterparts, the formations fall a bit short in terms of photographic potential; their shapes offer less variety and they are too densely grouped together. Do not hesitate to explore each end of the site; you'll discover interesting hoodoos that are not visible from the car park.

Photo advice: Mostly oriented to the east, Little Egypt's formations look their best in the early morning sun. A wide-angle lens works very well here.

Getting there: On UT-95, about 20 miles south of Hanksville or 5.7 miles north of the junction with UT-276, look for the North Wash/Eagle Creek sign and take the good track leading west. After roughly 1½ miles, a spur track appears on the right, leading to a large car park overlooking the site at the foot of the cliff.

Time required: About 1 hour.

Leprechaun Canyon

Leprechaun is a short, yet impressive and photogenic little canyon, part of a larger system called the Irish Canyons—hence the whimsical name. As it requires so little effort and relatively little time, I recommend a stop to enjoy and photograph its wide narrows and golden walls. Awareness and visitation seem to have increased a lot after it became public knowledge that a scene in the movie "127 Hours" had been filmed inside Leprechaun Canyon. There is an established car park and many social trails going in and out of the thick brush that stills covers the sandy wash. This abundance of trails has the benefit of making the approach quick and easy.

From the car park, follow the wash for ½ mile to a fork. Continue in the right fork, bypassing a very tight slot canyon by climbing a little bit to the right. Soon you'll find yourself inside the wide, spectacular narrows of Leprechaun. The lower walls of the canyon, as well as the canyon floor itself, are chock-full of interesting details, but the best is yet to come. After about 0.2 mile from the fork, the narrows make an abrupt turn to the right and the next 500 feet provide the best photo ops, especially looking back toward the subway-like turn. The narrows now turn into a slot, ending for hikers at the junction of the Main fork and the bottom of East (or right) fork at 38° 01'46" 110°31'45", where you turn back. The East fork is a popular technical canyoneering route beyond the scope of this book.

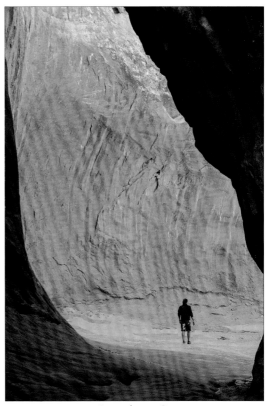

Photo advice: Early to mid-morning is the best time to enjoy and photograph the canyon.

Getting there: Driving about 28 miles southeast from Hanksville on UT-95 or 2 miles southeast from the junction with UT-276, look for a short spur on the north side (left) of the road. Drive 0.1 mile to the obvious car park on the left.

Time required: 1½ to 2 hours, with plenty of time for photography.

Leprechaun Canyon

Hog Springs

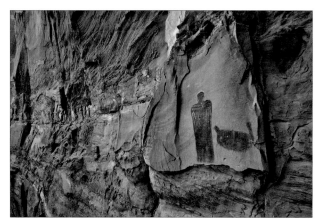

Hog Spring's Cleopatra pictograph © *Philippe Schuler*

About 33 miles southeast from Hanksville on UT-95 or 7.2 miles southeast from the junction with UT-276, the Hog Springs picnic area, on the west side of the road, gives you the rare opportunity of photographing a very nice specimen of Barrier-style pictographs, known as the Cleopatra panel, with no effort at all. From the parking area, walk along the right side of the road toward the south for about 400 feet. At the third post, find the path descending from the road, cross the small stream and head toward the big alcove. To the left of the alcove, you'll find a well-preserved Barrier Canyon anthropomorph looking like it was just plucked out of Horseshoe Canyon's Great Gallery (see *Canyonlands–The Maze* chapter). You'll achieve a more dynamic image by including some of the surrounding cliff in your shot.

From the picnic area, a pleasant trail follows the Hog Canyon drainage to a small intermittent waterfall flowing into a pool; an easy 1-hour round-trip walk.

Crossing Lake Powell

There are two routes crossing Lake Powell; one using a couple of bridges, the other a ferry. The first option is by continuing southward on UT-95. From Hog Springs the highway winds its way down toward the lake through a spectacular Entrada sandstone canyon, pock-marked by "Swiss cheese", before entering Glen Canyon N.R.A. Eight miles past Hog Springs and 4 miles before reaching the first bridge, a short road leads to an elevated

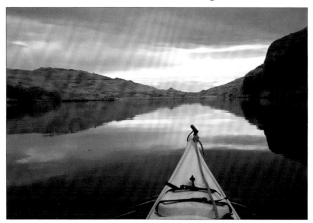

Quiet morning near Moki Canyon © *Gene Mezereny*

viewpoint providing an awesome bird's eye view of the north end of Lake Powell. The Hite Marina is just across from the Colorado River, offering only land facilities at the time of this writing, due to the low lake level. The confluence of the Dirty Devil River and the Colorado is visible to the left, surrounded by an alien landscape of petrified dunes. A set of two bridges spans the two rivers as UT-95 continues east following White Canyon toward the Cedar Mesa plateau.

If you'd like to try the ferry route, UT-276 branches out toward Bullfrog from UT-95, about 7.2 miles north of Hog Springs. The section between the Henry Mountains and the Little Rockies is very scenic.

From Bullfrog one can catch the "Charles Halls" ferry to Hall's Crossing. The 3-mile crossing takes about ½ hour to connect the northern and southern portions of UT-276 across Lake Powell. The ferry runs seasonally (typically four round-trip crossings daily), roughly between Memorial and Labor Day, although dates vary year-to-year. As the schedule is subject to change and there are occasional service interruptions, verify it beforehand by calling (435) 684-3088.

Nearby location: About 4.3 miles north of the Bullfrog Visitor Center, the Burr Trail (a.k.a. Notom-Bullfrog Road) leaves UT-276, angling northwest toward Waterpocket Fold and Capitol Reef. It is alternately paved and graded but generally passable for passenger cars in dry weather. Another 4.8 miles after leaving UT-276, a small car park on the south (left) side of the road serves as the Pedestal Alley trailhead. A 3-mile round-trip cairned trail leads through a stark desert landscape to a bunch of interesting reddish hoodoos.

Out of Bullfrog on Lake Powell

According to most experts, the severe drought the Southwest has been experiencing during the last decade is unlikely to abate; there might be some better years, but the general trend is for less rainfall overall. This, of course, affects Lake Powell and the entire ecosystem downstream. Even though we haven't seen a repeat (as of this writing in 2014) of the record low of 145 ft. below full pool in April 2005, the lake has remained consistently low. With the Hite Marina now too distant from shore, Bullfrog and Halls Crossing are the two marinas still operating in the northern part of Lake Powell, with Bullfrog supplying most of the rental traffic. Houseboats and small craft are aplenty and provide access to some photogenic locations that would otherwise be hard to reach. I will concentrate on four easy-to-reach locations that are of interest to photographers.

The closest and probably most popular is Defiance House, about 14 miles upstream from Bullfrog, then 2.5 miles up Forgotten Canyon. A "refurbished" cliff dwelling built high on a cliff, with a nice kiva and pictographs of three warriors, provides a good introduction to Ancestral Puebloan culture. A wide angle lens is recommended. The popular expression "your mileage may vary" applies perfectly to Defiance House. Based on water level you may have to walk up to 2 miles in mid-April, or about ½ mile in mid-summer. Still, this is a destination

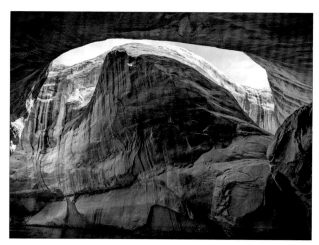

Cathedral in the Desert

that can easily be done in one day from Bullfrog or Halls Crossing, even in a houseboat.

The next closest location is the iconic Cathedral in the Desert. Unless the lake is eventually drained, this idyllic oasis of peace and quiet may never again be experienced in its full glory. Old 8mm movies taken before the lake was flooded show the way it was, but you would really need to have been there in person.

Approaching and entering Cathedral in the Desert is bordering on a spiritual experience. Others have devoted much effort to document it and I'd rather let them speak. James Kay, in particular, has done spectacular photography for a seminal book: *Resurrection - Glen Canyon & a New Vision for the American West*.

Even though the lake level varies from year to year, it almost always reaches lowest pool in mid-April, before returning to its highest level in July due to snowmelt. After that it starts slowly losing elevation. To photograph the Cathedral under conditions close to its past glory, you should plan your visit around this short time frame in April.

Cathedral in the Desert is located at the navigable end of Clear Creek Canyon, which means that a small craft can go at anytime of the year up to the waterfall, right by the Cathedral. An unofficial rope anchored to the rock inside the waterfall's gully allows the intrepid to climb to the next level and explore more of Clear Creek. The distance is approximately 35 miles downstream from Bullfrog to the Escalante, about 3 miles to Clear Creek, then 1½ miles up Clear Creek. This is a multi-day trip by houseboat (minimum 2 days), but an easy day-trip for a speedboat. The light is excellent in the early morning, with crystal clear reflections on the approach and good reflected light inside the cathedral proper. An ultra-wide angle lens is recommended.

Heading south from the mouth of the Escalante River, you'll be passing Hole-in-the-Rock Bay at

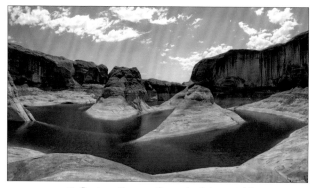

Reflection Canyon from the lake, midday

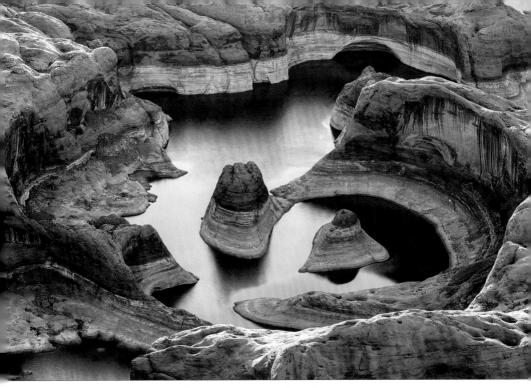

Reflection Canyon aerial, early morning

about 4 miles. Time permitting, you can easily scramble up the narrow gully to the rim of Hole-in-the-Rock in less than 90 minutes round-trip (see *Canyons of the Escalante* chapter).

Another 6 miles brings you to the confluence with the San Juan River, on your left, and 1 more mile to the mouth of Reflection Canyon, on your right. From here, it's a mere 5 minutes to a couple of island rocks jutting out prominently between a gracious snake-like curve formed by the lake. This iconic location yields spectacular photos under the right circumstances. Although the best views are from the rim, which is not accessible by boat, for sheer enjoyment and when photography is not the primary goal, the easiest way to see Reflection Canyon is by houseboat or speedboat. If you are on a house boat, visiting Reflection can only be part of a multi-day trip. However, you can get there from Bullfrog by speedboat in a long day, or take two days to enjoy early morning and late after-noon light. Make sure with the outfitter that your boat has enough gas in the tank to make it here and back, as speedboats are major gas guzzlers.

From a small craft, you can easily access and climb a slickrock slope to gain some elevation for your shot. However, the beautiful snake-like shape of the lake around the island rocks (making the rocks stand out in the center) is only vis-ible when the lake level is low. This requirement is not as critical as in the case of Cathedral in the Desert, so you have a bit more leeway planning your trip in early spring. The S-curve is also not as prominent as when photographed from the rim—the latter is only accessible via a strenuous 16-mile round-trip hike (see *Reflection Canyon* section in *Chapter 7 - Canyons of the Escalante*).

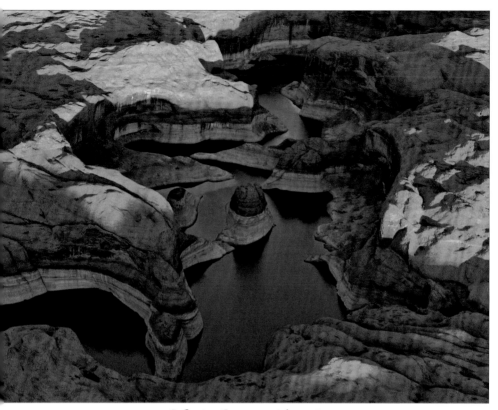

Reflection Canyon aerial, sunrise

A good alternative is to photograph Reflection Canyon from the air, at low altitude, which allows different, but spectacular and varied compositions. As "unmanned aircraft" are officially banned over National Parks, Monuments, and Recreation Areas, drones are not an option, at least legally. An ultralight aircraft would be a terrific way to get close and capture amazing photos, but this option is mostly limited to owner-pilots. A small plane offers fantastic views and it's relatively easy to find a commercial pilot in Page, AZ (see *Photographing the Southwest: Vol. 2 - Arizona*). It's generally a cheaper option than a helicopter, albeit not quite as versatile for photography. The flight from Page to Reflection Canyon is a short 15 to 20 minutes.

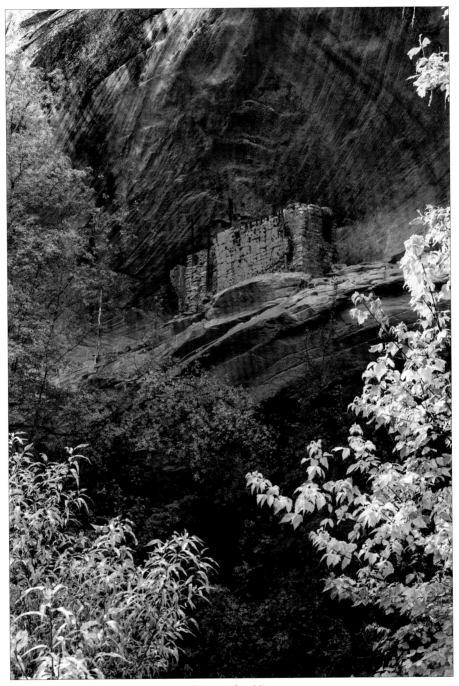

Ruin with a View

Chapter 11

AROUND BLANDING

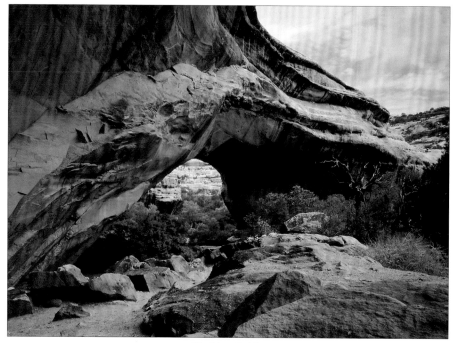

Kachina Bridge

Introduction to Cedar Mesa

Cedar Mesa is a vast plateau south of the Abajo Mountains, extending all the way to the dramatic cliffs of Muley Point, where it drops abruptly. From east to west, it stretches from the Comb Ridge to Natural Bridges National Monument before gradually descending along White Canyon toward Lake Powell. What defines Cedar Mesa from a photography standpoint is its rich Ancient Puebloan heritage. Nowhere in the Southwest can such a concentration of vestiges from the Puebloan civilization be found. Countless canyons harbor dwellings, granaries, rock art and artifacts, all silent witnesses of a once vibrant civilization. It is not an exaggeration to say that one could devote a lifetime to the exploration of Cedar Mesa; some archaeologists have done so. This area exercises a fascination on many visitors, as it combines the joy of hiking in relative solitude along beautiful mesas and canyons, with the excitement of the search for clues of the Puebloans presence and the elation of discovery. Hiking and photographing Cedar Mesa can be an enormously rewarding experience on a deeply personal level.

Cedar Mesa is both immense and very accessible, served by good paved roads and numerous dirt or slickrock tracks, and dotted with many hiking trails. Once out of the car, however, one feels like walking in the footsteps of the Puebloans.

Many excellent books exist to guide us around and interpret the Cedar Mesa environment and history for us. They remind us that we have a collective responsibility in treading lightly and leaving this fragile landscape and heritage intact, out of respect for those who once lived here as well as for future generations. In the internet age, the dissemination of information and the use of GPS have made finding once obscure ruins or rock art panels a much easier task. Use this information responsibly: enjoy and leave no trace. For my part, as elsewhere in this book, I have purposely limited the information I provide on rock art.

A day hiking permit is required for many of the sites described in this chapter. This permit (which is not subject to a quota) can be purchased for a day, a week, or even a year. It can be obtained from the Kane Gulch Ranger Station (open only mornings) or at the main trailheads. For longer trips, an overnight backpacking permit must be secured, available exclusively from the Kane Gulch Ranger Station. A specific walk-in permit (subject to quota) is required to visit Moon House and can also be obtained solely from the Ranger Station.

For more information, consult :
www.blm.gov/ut/st/en/fo/monticello/recreation/permits/grand_gulch_and_cedar.html

The locations selected for this chapter are introduced in the following order: sites north of UT-95 from east to west, sites east of UT-261 from north to south, and finally sites west of UT-261, also from north to south.

Edge of the Cedars State Park Museum

The little town of Blanding makes an excellent base for exploring Cedar Mesa, if you are looking for the comforts of civilization, hence the name of this chapter. There are good motels, some restaurants, as well as markets and gas stations. While in Blanding, I suggest you pay a visit to the Edge of the Cedars State Park Museum. The park has very informative exhibits providing a good introduction to the Ancestral Puebloan civilization, as well as modern Navajo and Ute artifacts. Behind the museum is a rebuilt structure and a kiva from a pueblo which was inhabited from AD 825 to 1125.

Getting there: To get there from downtown Blanding is a bit like following the yellow brick road as you are guided to the museum by a series of Puebloan icons painted on the surface of the paved road.

Time required: At least 1 hour.

Tower House

Tower House is one of the most photogenic two-storied, fortified ruins on the northern Comb Ridge and it is quite easy to visit. It is tucked in under an alcove, with a second, mostly dilapidated small structure close by.

From the suggested car park, descend into the drainage below near the potholes, which may or may not contain water. The large toadstool on the left

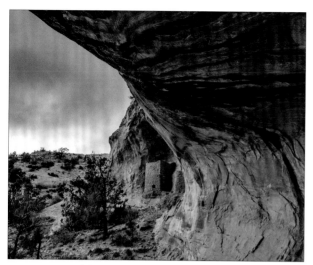

Tower House © Ron Flickinger

side of the drainage makes a good landmark—from here it's only a ten-minute walk down to Tower House at 37°34'51" 109°39'08". Most people should have no trouble descending cautiously into the drainage but if you don't feel comfortable doing so, walk west 300 feet to find an easier descent.

Photo advice: Tower House is best photographed in late afternoon with a medium to super wide-angle.

Getting there: From the junction of US-191 and UT-95 about 3 miles south of Blanding, drive 6.3 miles west on UT-95 and turn north on signed and paved Cottonwood Road. Drive 1 mile and turn west (left) on CR-228. Continue 4 miles on this well-graded dirt road and turn left at 37°35'02" 109°39'18". Drive about 500 feet on the spur road to a circular carpark with a couple of caprock hoodoos at 37°34'58" 109°39'16". If you have a high clearance vehicle, there is a good alternative road 0.2 mile past the first one, leading to a car park in 800 feet. From here, walk about 400 feet southeast and locate the cairned trail going down into the canyon. You'll see the ruin to your left as you walk down. This trail is easier to find from the bottom, so it's a good alternative for going back up.

Time required: About 2 hours from the beginning of Cottonwood Road.

Nearby location: The Posey Trail follows the top of the Comb Ridge, offering great views of the side of the ridge and the valley below, especially at sunset. Continue on CR-228 for 0.6 mile, leaving the Comb Ridge dugway on the right to the ATVs, and proceed straight another 1.2 miles to a carpark with an excellent view.

Over & Under Ruin

This 'double-decker' ruin is easily accessible and also easy to observe and photograph from atop a long sloping sandstone ridge. The high viewpoint provides an original perspective, with the ruins tucked in at the end of a long box canyon. The ruins proper are quite dilapidated and not too interesting to shoot at close range so I don't particularly recommend going down the steep slope, as it is a bit tricky. If you want to do so, pick a spot further down on the ridge where the incline is a bit more forgiving.

Photo advice: From the viewpoint on top, use either a wide-angle lens to capture the entire box canyon—with its nice mix of colorful deciduous and conifer trees in the fall—or a medium-range zoom to isolate the ruins.

Getting there: From its junction with UT-95 about 6.3 miles east of US-191, drive 5.2 miles on Cottonwood Road,

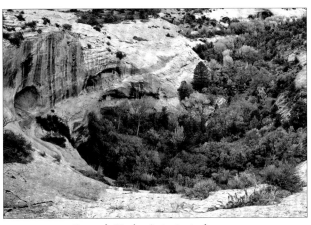

Over & Under Ruin in its box canyon

then bear left on Elk Mountain Rd. for another 5.5 miles to a car park on the left at 37°39'05" 109°40'16". Passenger cars should park here. 4WD vehicles can go a bit further south, but there is no real point as this is a short trail. From the car park, follow the track for 0.2 mile, then continue on the slickrock another 800 feet or so until you find a good view of the ruins below.

Time Required: About 2½ hours from UT-95 to photograph the ruins from above. About 1½ hours more to go down and make your way to the ruins through the thick vegetation.

Target Ruin

Target Ruin (a.k.a. Bulls Eye Ruin) is one of the most attractive Ancestral Puebloan sites in the northern Butler Wash area and it's another easy to visit spot. It is similar to its Butler Wash Ruins neighbor, described in the next section, but you can observe the ruin almost at eye level, instead of from a viewing platform. I also find Target more visually interesting than the big Butler Wash Ruins. Target Ruin is actually located in Butler Wash, while the neighboring Butler Wash Ruins are in a tributary. The site gets its name from a bull's-eye symbol painted on a back wall, visible only by climbing high on the opposite hillside.

From the trailhead, follow the well-worn path through the tallgrass and tree canopy. Note that after a rain storm the tallgrass could be flattened by the ensuing flood. After a tad over ½ mile, you'll pass a side canyon with a short dryfall and a hiker's trail on the right side. Don't take it! Instead continue less than 0.1 mile inside the wash and look for a short but steep sandy slope to the left, exiting the canyon around 37°31'55" 109°38'13". Continue about 0.1 mile on an easy to follow trail ending in a dryfall, where the ruins are located.

Photo advice: The promontory directly facing the ruins makes a good

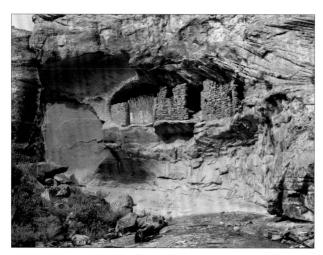

Target Ruin

vantage point to photograph them with a less severe angle than from the canyon floor. A moderate wide angle works best.

Getting there: The car park is located on the north side of UT-95 near mile marker 111.1, about 10.2 miles from US-191 and just past the Upper Butler Wash bridge. There is a BLM sign-in register, but no fee is required. There is a permanent pit toilet at the large Butler Wash ruins car park located a short distance further and a social trail connects the two trailheads, adding 0.4 mile to the round-trip.

Time Required: About two hours.

Nearby location: There are more ruins upstream along Butler Wash, albeit not anywhere near as photogenic. The closest ones are in Ballroom Cave, less than ½ mile upstream from where you entered/left the Target Ruin side canyon. The alcove is very deep and impressive, but the ruins proper are unremarkable. More ruins follow after that, all of them on the west side.

Butler Wash Ruins & the Comb Ridge Cut

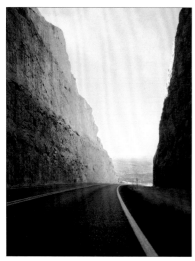

Crossing the Comb Ridge Cut

About 10.5 miles from the start of UT-95 on US-191, or a short 0.3 mile past the Target Ruin car park, you'll find the large Butler Wash parking area on the right hand side of the road. An easy 1-mile round-trip trail takes you to an overlook with a good view of a nice balcony-shaped dwelling perched inside a grotto in the canyon below. Butler Wash looks its best in mid-morning. The dwelling is then evenly illuminated and the light is not yet too harsh. Earlier than that, you'll need to warm up the scene and later in the afternoon you'll be shooting against the light.

About 2½ miles further west on UT-95, you'll enter an enormous man-made cut in the ridge before the road opens up into the valley. You are passing through the great retreating cliff face of the Comb Ridge, stretching almost a hundred miles from north to south. Along with the Cockscomb and the Waterpocket Fold, the Comb Ridge is one of the big three anticlines traversing the Colorado plateau. From here, the views of the Abajo Mountains to the north and the Henry Mountains to the north-west are spectacular. As the road makes a blind curve through the cut, stopping is prohibited and you should park well before the beginning of the curve to take photographs from above. Coming from the east, as you descend into Comb Wash valley, don't miss the small pullout on the left side of the road at 37°30'43" 109°39'48". It is a great vantage point with a fantastic view over miles of the ridge to the south.

The west-facing cliff consists mostly of Wingate sandstone, with a bit of Navajo sandstone on top. It glows a rich red in the late afternoon sun and that's the best time to photograph it.

Mule Canyon

Mule Canyon is an outstanding location both for leisurely hiking and photography of small Puebloan dwellings and granaries.

The Mule Canyon system consists of two different arms, separated by about ½ mile at their entrance. Both the north and south forks extend for roughly 5 to 6 miles. They are both easy level walks with few obstructions along a shallow stream, often dry or reduced to a trickle. They offer pleasant walks in solitude, inside sunny canyons with shallow walls. Both harbor nice ruins almost every mile or so, which are easy to spot and get to and fun to photograph.

The south fork of Mule Canyon is by far the most popular with photographers as it contains the striking "flaming ceiling" ruin which has become an icon of the Colorado Plateau (see "House on Fire" image on next page). From the trailhead, head west up-canyon, following the mostly dry stream. After about 1 mile, you'll skirt a bend and find House on fire to the right. It is located under a cliff overhang, part of a small set of ruins and granaries just 20 feet above the canyon floor (37°32'38" 109°44'41"). After photographing the ruins, walk inside the small passageway to the left and look above for some handprints.

Photo advice: The best time to photograph House on Fire is in late morning, to take advantage of the light bouncing from the slickrock slope below the ruins. This side of the canyon remains in the shade until late morning with no reflected light on the ruins. Later in the day, direct sunlight washes out the "flames".

Getting there: The two canyon trailheads are located on an unmarked county road (SJC-263) on the north side of UT-95), about 19.5 miles from the beginning of UT-95 on US-191. It's 9 miles from the junction with UT-261 if you're coming from the west. It is also ½ mile east of the signed Mule Canyon Ruin exhibit (a reconstructed kiva of no great interest). You'll find a self-registration station near the entrance of the county road to pay your fee. Park about 0.3 mile

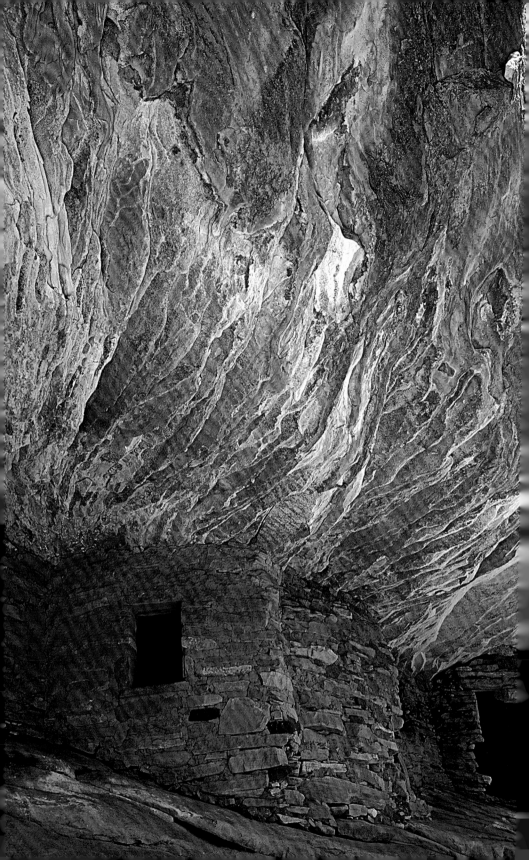

after leaving UT-95 for House on Fire in the south fork. There is a large car park for the north fork almost a mile from the road.

Time required: About 2 hours to photograph House on Fire in the south fork of Mule Canyon; 5 to 6 hours to visit the entire length of each arm.

Arch Canyon Viewpoint

Arch Canyon is a massive box canyon, twelve miles long and several hundred feet wide, a favorite of ATVers. This convenient viewpoint allows you to peer into the canyon from a great height and even photograph the first of two spectacular arches: Cathedral Arch and Angel Arch (the latter not to be confused with the more famous Angel Arch in Canyonlands Nat'l Park). This is truly a great viewpoint requiring no effort, yet it's surprising how few people seem to be aware of it.

Photo advice: A moderate wide angle will allow you to photograph a bird's eye view of the canyon encompassing both rims. To shoot Cathedral Arch, you'll need the long end of a medium telephoto. Arch Canyon is at its best in late afternoon, but beware the contrast which can be brutal in a wide angle view. Too close to sunset and you'll have huge shadows projecting onto the other rim. A cloudy day would probably work best. Follow the rim near the car park to the northwest (left) for almost 900 feet to the best open view of Cathedral Arch.

Getting there: The first mile is common with the Mule Canyon access road (see previous section). At about mile 3 from UT-95, a section of the track with loose white rock could give some trouble to passenger cars; just be cautious. At mile 4.6, take the right fork. At mile 5.3, the track makes a sharp and not obvious hairpin to the right—be sure not to go straight. At mile 6, take the right fork and continue less than 0.2 mile to the car park.

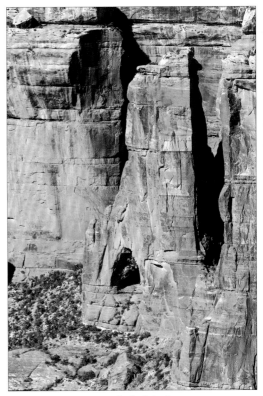

Cathedral Arch

Opposite page: House on Fire in Mule Canyon

Natural Bridges National Monument

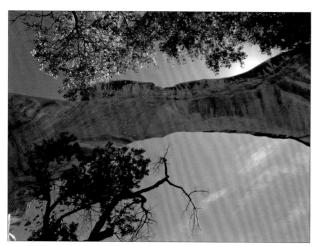

Sipapu Bridge makes for an interesting shot from below

Although not as spectacular as Arches, this park has a personality all its own. However, it only reveals its beauty and interest to those with enough time and willingness to do some hiking. Natural bridges are eroded by the action of water flowing from rivers, as opposed to arches, which are eroded by wind and sand.

The three gigantic natural bridges named Sipapu, Kachina, and Owachomo are spectacular. Because of their particular geological origin, they are set deeply inside canyons, instead of being in the open like arches. This makes the bridges difficult to photograph from the top of the canyon, but if you take the time to go to the bottom you'll be rewarded by superb views of these huge bridges.

The three bridges are located on a 9-mile one-way loop road. Sipapu Bridge is the longest, with a span of 286 feet, and is arguably the most elegant of the three. Forget the viewpoint close to the road, however, because the bridge appears

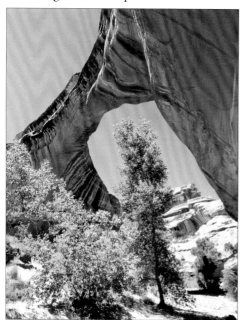

Side view of Sipapu Bridge

totally lost among its whitish Cedar Mesa surroundings. Instead, take the 1.2-mile round-trip hike down into the canyon and you'll reach the bridge in less than ½ hour, including a brief stop halfway down the trail on a ledge providing a photogenic view of the bridge below. It's a 500-foot elevation drop, so it's fairly steep in places and you'll be using ladders. Sipapu is a nice mid-morning view and there are some spectacular angles looking up to the bridge from the bottom of the canyon. The canyon walls provide nice reflected light.

Kachina Bridge, being just a bit shorter than Sipapu, is most notable for the thickness of its span. Just under 100 feet thick, it resembles a gigantic rock muscle stretched 130 feet above your head. The trail leading to Kachina Bridge from its overlook is a tad longer than Sipapu's. However, elevation gain is only 400 feet and the hike feels markedly easier. An added benefit is the presence of a kiva and pictographs behind a small talus south of the bridge.

If you have at least 3 hours available, I strongly recommend hiking the 5.6-mile loop between Sipapu and Kachina. The section at the bottom of White Canyon is an easy level walk alternating between a sandy path and the dry bed of the beautiful canyon. It's a unique opportunity to day hike inside a wild Cedar Mesa sandstone canyon in a relatively safe environment. On the way to Kachina, a few hundred yards past the confluence with Deer Canyon, look for ruins up on a ledge on the right side of White Canyon. The Horse Collar Ruin granaries are somewhat hidden at the back of this ledge. When you arrive under Kachina Bridge, don't proceed straight into the canyon. Instead, turn immediately to the left to locate the path leading to the Kachina Bridge trailhead. On the other side of the road, a good path will bring you back to the Sipapu parking area in less than 2 miles, passing through a pinyon and juniper forest.

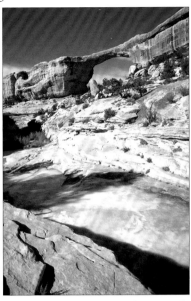

Owachomo Bridge with frozen creek

From the road, Owachomo Bridge is easy to reach and photograph, which is a good reason for not missing it, though it is dwarfed in comparison with the other two. If you're not in great shape, but still want to see a nice bridge, Owachomo is for you!

Photo advice: White Canyon consists of a very ancient, light-colored Cedar Mesa sandstone, which is difficult to expose on a sunny day. You'll have to find a way to isolate the bridges, preferably against the sky, to convey the true measure of their size and the feeling of power, which they project when close. There is only one way to do this, and that's by descending into the canyon. If your time is limited, you're most likely to do so at Owachomo, where the bridge is located only a few minutes from the road. In that case, don't stop when you arrive at the bridge, but continue under it and to the left, descending towards the creek flowing below. The creek makes a nice foreground and the angle you'll get from below provides an easy exposure of the bridge throughout the day.

Getting there: From Mexican Hat and US-163 by way of UT-261, with the added bonus of the beautiful viewpoints of Mokey Dugway and Muley Point, or by the superb UT-95 leaving from either Blanding or Hanksville. About 2 miles west of the junction of these two roads, you'll find the short UT-265 leading to the park's entrance.

Time required: 2 to 5 hours in the park, depending on the hikes you choose.

Moon House

Located in McLoyd Canyon, Moon House is one of the most unique and interesting Puebloan ruins in the entire southwest. It is not easy to get to, however, and there is a quota on daily visitation (more on this below). The complex was built in the mid-1200s A.D. According to BLM literature, it is believed that Moon House was used as a religious center due to a higher concentration of kivas than the surrounding canyon system.

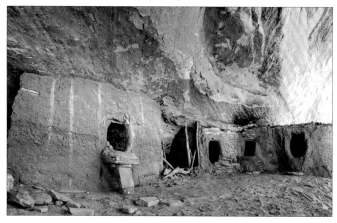

Moon House dwellings

Moon House has a striking setting in the canyon, forming a long string of dwellings and granaries below a gigantic boulder, with an equally large balanced rock on top. The complex has an inner and outer section, with two walls that provided protection from intruders. The center room in the primary structure is painted with white, with a crescent moon on one wall and a full moon on the facing wall, hence the name. This is a feature otherwise unknown in southwest Puebloan dwellings.

As of this writing, visitation is limited to 20 individuals per day (12 by reservation and 8 walk-ins) and you need a specific permit. Things change, so be sure to check the web site: http://www.blm.gov/ut/st/en/fo/monticello/recreation/permits/grand_gulch_and_cedar/Moonhouse_Permits.html

From the rim of McLoyd Canyon, you will see Moon House across the canyon. Look for cairns marking the route down. The hike is about 1.3 miles round-trip. The slope is steep in places, so exercise caution. Part of the way down, there is a five-foot pour-off with a pile of rocks at the bottom to aid your descent. Proceed to the canyon bottom and continue a short distance up canyon to find the north side trail leading up to the cliff and the ruins. Once there, please obey the warnings not to touch the walls or enter the rooms. After visiting and photographing, you can follow the ledge to the northwest for a while past the huge balanced rock or you can explore the ledge to the southeast for ¼ mile to find more well-preserved ruins.

Getting there: Note that this is a long and rough road, with nasty sections of slickrock as well as extensive sections of clay that can become impassable when wet. Passenger vehicles should not attempt the drive; a high-clearance vehicle is a must. Before you leave, ask the Ranger about the condition of the final 1-mile track leading to McLoyd Canyon. Permit in hand, drive 10 miles south on UT-261 from UT-95 (or 6.2 miles from the Kane Gulch Ranger Station) to signed Snow Flat Road. Turn left, and drive west for 8.2 miles until you come to the spur leading north to the canyon. As of this writing, there is a trail register on the left side of the track. After registering, decide whether to drive or hike to the rim, knowing that hiking will add less than 30 minutes (each way). This 1.3-mile clay track is narrow, winding, and sometime deeply rutted so you don't want to get stuck there. On the other hand I have had no problem driving it in an SUV.

Time Required: 4-6 hours from UT-261, depending on time spent photographing the ruins and whether you hike or drive the spur track.

Fallen Roof Ruin

Road Canyon is a very pleasant canyon, quite verdant and open, and it contains some of the most remarkable Ancestral Puebloan dwellings, granaries and kivas on the Cedar Mesa plateau. You won't have to go far either, because arguably the most photogenic dwelling, which I like to call "Fallen Roof Ruin", is located less than 45 minutes from the trailhead. In recent years, it too has become an icon of the Colorado Plateau.

To get to the ruins from the trailhead, follow the well-trod 0.3-mile footpath taking you northeast to an easy entry point into a side canyon. Descend the steep route to the side canyon. If you don't see a cairn when you reach it, mark this point on your GPS or build a visual cue so you can find this turnoff when you get back. Getting out could otherwise be a problem, especially late in the day after several hours of exploration. Continue east-northeast for a while until the side canyon meets Road Canyon. Take your bearings at this junction also and turn right, proceeding eastward into Road Canyon on a now fairly obvious trail. A few hundred yards from the last turnoff, a tall hoodoo comes into view on the left side. Start looking up from this point on. The first ruin, the highly photogenic Fallen Roof Ruin, is not hard to find, but it does not jump out at you either, as it is perched more than a hundred feet above the canyon floor (37°23'46" 109°52'21"). Access to the ruin is easy, requiring only a bit of climbing on slanted slickrock, leaving the trail about 150 yards after passing the tall hoodoo.

Note that you may find the initial side canyon badly obstructed after particularly heavy rains. If that's the case, use the bypass trail starting immediately at the entrance of the side canyon. Instead of going down-canyon, climb up on the north side on an easy to follow footpath. This route completely bypasses the side canyon from the top, dropping you down into Road Canyon ½ mile later. There is an easy descent on a steep 10-foot wall of slickrock but there are plenty of holds and no rope is needed.

After photographing Fallen Roof Ruin, stay high above the canyon and continue northeast until the end of the same narrow ledge to reach several interesting granaries in just a few minutes.

Tread lightly near the ruins. Do not go inside or touch the walls with your

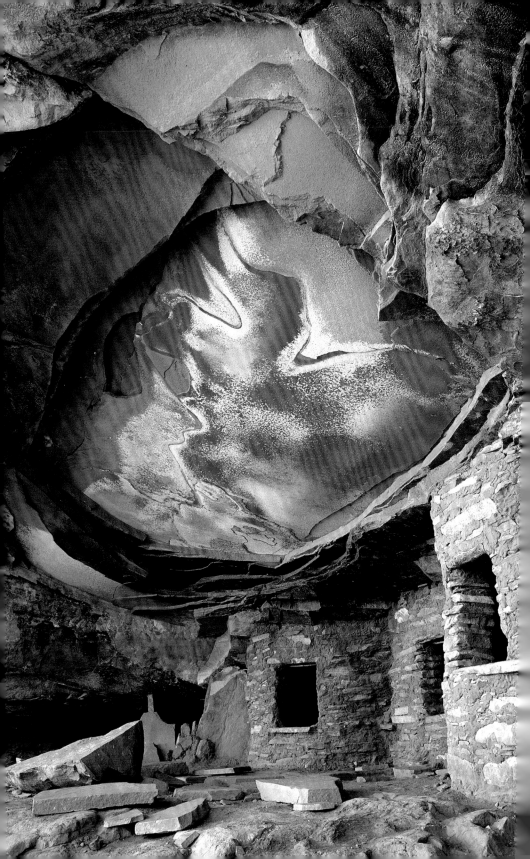

hands or remove anything. It is a privilege to visit such a lovely canyon and you should leave no trace of your passage.

Photo advice: The best light is in mid-morning, when Fallen Roof Ruin is still in shadow. Part of the ruin is in full light from midday to mid-afternoon; you can nonetheless get acceptable results during that time frame on an overcast day. A vertical composition with a wide angle works best to encompass the entire alcove, with its pterodactyl-like pattern revealed on the collapsed ceiling.

Getting there: On UT-261, about 13.5 miles south of UT-95, turn left on Cigarette Spring Road (CR-239). Past the self-register/fee station, located about 1 mile from the turnoff, drive straight ahead until you reach an unmarked spur road 2.4 miles further on your left. Turn onto this road, going north for a couple hundred feet until you find an obvious pullout and a small trail marker (37°23'26" 109°53'19").

Time required: About 3 hours round-trip from UT-261 to photograph the first two sets of ruins. A half day to enjoy more of the canyon at a relaxed pace.

The Citadel

The Citadel is an apt name for this unique Ancestral Puebloan structure, obviously built with protection in mind. As you will see when you visit, it is unlikely any enemies could have approached it easily. Access is via a narrow passage on a land bridge with a considerable drop-off (approx. 500 feet) on each side. Additionally, the steep canyon walls prevented any attempt to approach from the canyon floor. The structure proper is built under the rim of a dominating rock formation at the end of a stone peninsula jutting into Road Canyon. The only access then was the narrow land bridge which was likely guarded and attackers would have been seriously exposed. Although the Puebloans who thrived in this area from 200-1300 A.D. are believed to have been mostly peaceful, defensively positioned ruins such as the Citadel, suggest they needed to protect themselves from enemies. Anthropologists believe this situation resulted as game animals were hunted to scarcity and the soil became depleted, thereby causing fierce competition for food. The ruin itself is in particularly good condition, leading me to think that the BLM or some other entity had a hand at restoring it.

From the trailhead, the trail essentially follows the south rim of Road Canyon. After about 1.5 miles the trail turns to slickrock, with enough cairns to make it easy to follow. Before it dead-ends above the canyon, there are at least two large cairns to your left that you'd have a hard time to miss. There may be more by the time you read this but these two large piles of rock should still be there because they both provide relatively easy access to the next level below. Now it's time to climb down. I don't think any able-bodied person would have trouble negotiating the scramble, using solid grips and exercising caution. Next comes what may be the hardest part for some. To get to the beginning of the peninsula where the

Opposite page: Fallen Roof Ruin in Road Canyon

Citadel is located, you need to walk almost 300 feet on wide but sloppy slickrock with considerable exposure on your left. The angle of the slope is not steep and it can be walked normally, but if you are afflicted by fear of heights, the sheer drop to your left may make you very uncomfortable. Past that tricky part, you have one more easy descent to the next lower level to start crossing the land bridge. The latter is quite wide and shouldn't present any problems despite the impressive drop on both sides. In only a couple of minutes you'll arrive at the base of the rocky outcrop sheltering the impressive structure for a final very easy ascent.

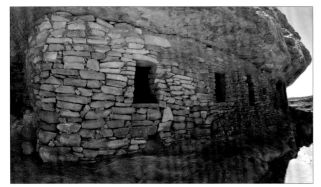

The Citadel

Photo advice: Sunny, mid-day light is lethal for a wide, all-encompassing image of the peninsula. You would need to go in late afternoon to catch the best light. For the Citadel ruin proper, it's possible to take good, tight shots during daytime by paying attention to where the shadows are falling. If you want to include the rock and the sky above the dwelling your best bet is to shoot for exposure blending or HDR. A very wide angle will be an asset to photograph the citadel, but you can get very good results by stitching vertical shots—preferably using focus-stacking, given the limited depth-of-field due to your close proximity to the stone work.

Getting there: From UT-95, follow UT-261 south about 13.5 miles to Cigarette Springs Road. Turn left (east) on Cigarette Springs Road as if going to Fallen Roof Ruin. From UT-261, drive 6 miles and turn left on a narrow, well-used, but rocky track (not for passenger cars), following it for less than a mile until it ends.

Time required: Allow 4 to 5 hours round-trip from US-261.

Introduction to Grand Gulch

Grand Gulch is the Mecca of Indian ruins and rock art on the Cedar Mesa plateau. During springtime and autumn, it attracts many visitors, particularly small groups, eager to explore easily accessible ancient Puebloan ruins while enjoying a laid-back backpacking experience in a pleasant canyon. The combination of moderately difficult terrain and a high concentration of well-preserved dwellings, granaries and rock art makes it a very rewarding trip.

Walking the entire length of the canyon from the main entry at Kane Gulch to the San Juan River is 53 miles and few people tackle such a daunting trip. Most people concentrate on the upper part of the canyon, which offers several exit points. This makes it easier to plan two to five-day trips. If you want to enjoy the wilderness experience without roughing it too much, there are accredited outfitters offering increasingly popular llama trips. I recommend these llama trips strongly to photographers, for they remove the burden of carrying camera equipment on top of your backpacking gear. If you are a large format photographer, this may well be your only option. If you want to see Grand Gulch without backpacking, it can be done with moderate effort on consecutive day-hikes.

From Kane Gulch, a 10-mile round-trip hike from the ranger station brings you to the confluence with Grand Gulch and good ruins at Junction Ruin and Turkey Pen Ruin. Bullet Canyon is a very rewarding entry point for short incursions into the Gulch. From the Bullet Canyon trailhead, Perfect Kiva and Jailhouse Ruin make a moderate, under 10-mile round-trip. Bullet Canyon can also be combined in a longer loop including Sheiks Canyon (see next two sections). A couple of hundred yards inside Sheiks Canyon from Grand Gulch, the Green Mask site has excellent pictograph panels and is located about 1.5 miles upstream from Bullet inside Grand Gulch. An easier 10.6-mile day-hike in the central section of Grand Gulch is to the Big Man pictograph panel (37°27'16" 110°06'24"), reached by the well-maintained Government Trail and an easy up-canyon hike before a short climb to the panel.

Arguably one of the best ruin complex in Grand Gulch, Split Level House is named for two connected dwellings located at different levels under an alcove, also sheltering a small kiva, granaries and pictographs. It is located 10 miles from the Kane Gulch trailhead and 13 miles from the Bullet Canyon trailhead, requiring an overnighter.

Getting there: The Kane Gulch trailhead is just across the road from the Ranger Station on UT-261, about 4 miles south of its junction with UT-95. To reach the Government Trailhead, drive south on UT-261 about 13.5 miles from UT-95 to a dirt road heading west (just opposite signed Cigarette Spring Road). Follow it for 2.6 miles, taking the right fork at the junction. Continue for 3 miles and again take the right fork for 1.9 miles. Take the road heading northwest to your right for about 1.5 miles to the Government trailhead (information kiosk at 37°24'59" 110°05'06"). Most of this road requires high clearance with the last 0.5 mile being the hardest part. You may want to park just before the descent to the trailhead. All these clay roads become impassable during and after a rain.

Nearby location: Owl Creek Canyon and Fish Creek Canyon are a popular

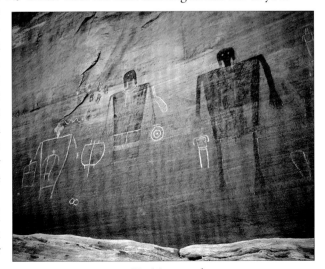

Big Man panel

backpacking destination, usually done as a two-day loop. Or you may want to plan a quick jaunt into Owl Canyon to photograph a kiva and three granaries just below the rim, only 0.8 mile round-trip from the trailhead. The well-signed 5.2-mile road to the trailhead (37°28'27" 109°48'32") is located 1 mile south of the Kane Gulch Ranger Station (or 5 miles from UT-95).

Sheiks Canyon

Sheiks Canyon is one of the least frequented tributaries of Grand Gulch. Sheiks is relatively short, being only 3.5 miles in length to Grand Gulch, but the last half-mile is tricky, with a very steep descent where it wouldn't take much to twist an ankle.

Highlights of Sheiks Canyon include an attractive ruin referred to as Yellow House, near the beginning of the canyon, Wall Ruins, about a mile downstream, and of course the Green Mask site, located just before the junction with Grand Gulch. And yes the Green Mask site is right after the difficult descent, which partially explains why a lot of folks prefer visiting it while on a Grand Gulch tour.

The Green Mask site really does have a very unique pictograph of a mask with some green color, but this anachronism of the Southwest—while definitely a trophy shot for hardcore rock art enthusiasts—is of marginal interest as a photographic subject. The real wonder of this site is the superb Breech Birth panel, located less than a couple hundred feet downstream.

Photo advice: For Sheiks, be sure to bring a telephoto zoom if you want to photograph the Green Mask proper, as it is located high on the alcove-shaped wall. The Breech Birth panel, on the other hand, requires only a moderate wide-angle, as you're right in front of it.

Getting there: From the Bullet Canyon trailhead (see next section), head north for 1.4 miles to a smaller track branching west for 1.7 miles to the

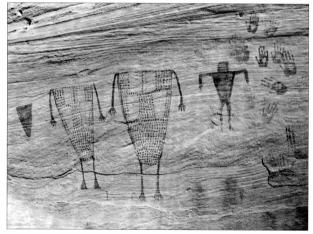

Sheiks Canyon trailhead at 37°26'57"109°59'00". The last 0.3 mile is rather rugged and cars and small campers should park before the rocky section. Others park on the slickrock just before the trailhead.

Time required: The three major sites of Sheiks Canyon can be seen in a 7-mile round-trip consuming 5-6 hours, including photography.

Breech Birth panel at the Green Mask site

Bullet Canyon

Bullet Canyon is the most popular tributary of Grand Gulch, providing a rewarding backcountry experience with numerous Ancestral Puebloan sites below stunningly beautiful Cedar Mesa sandstone. It is also very easy to hike, with a few obstacles that are easily negotiated.

Bullet Canyon's star Puebloan attractions are the so-called Perfect Kiva and Jailhouse ruins, the latter named for an unusual lattice window resembling prison bars. The lower end of Bullet has a quasi-perennial spring and several good camping spots.

Most people do Bullet Canyon as a day-hike; the 15-mile round-trip to the confluence with Grand Gulch is a long but relatively easy day-hike during the spring and fall months. Summer is very hot with temperatures in the hundreds and no guarantee that the two springs at the end of Bullet are flowing. Winters can be bitterly cold and the days are too short for a day-hike. Also, the presence of ice could make the trip dangerous.

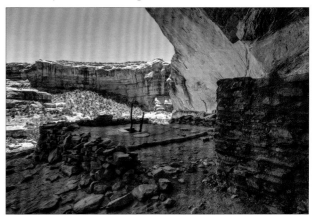

A fair number of people also backpack the classic Bullet to Kane Gulch route (or vice-versa) into Grand Gulch for a wonderful three to four-day backcountry experience.

Bullet's Perfect Kiva © *Charles Wood*

I highly recommend the Sheiks-Bullet loop with a car shuttle. The two combine well into a long 14-mile day hike, more challenging than the Bullet in-and-out, but also more rewarding. This can also be done as an overnighter, but beware the difficult rocky section in Sheiks Canyon.

Photo advice: Bullet Canyon offers a large variety of subject matter, in turn calling for a wide range of focal lengths. While a standard zoom will work in many situations, such as shots of the canyon, detail shots of wooden structures, rocks, and interesting artifacts such as metate, pottery shards, etc., it will not adequately cover some of the most interesting subjects: cramped interiors, such as ruins in the Jailhouse alcove and especially the Perfect Kiva, require a very wide angle. A standard zoom may also not be enough at the long end, for distant shots of petroglyphs or granaries high on the cliffs or extractions of small mammals or reptiles, if you are into that. My equipment for this kind of trip is a very wide zoom, one (or two) small primes covering the normal range, and a medium telephoto zoom. In addition, you'll need a tripod (it doesn't have to be big) for shots inside the Perfect kiva. But beware, what's important above anything else is your water! If weight is an issue, sacrifice the big zoom first.

Getting there: The trailhead for Bullet (37°25'51" 109°56'58") is located 1.1 miles along a good dirt road heading west from UT-261 between mileposts 21 and 22, about 11 miles from UT-95. The road is unmarked (as of this writing) but easy to locate. If hiking the full Sheiks-Bullet loop, the best strategy consists of parking one car at the Bullet trailhead and driving the second vehicle to Sheiks Canyon. You will do the loop in the easiest direction and you'll save yourself the extra 3-mile return to your car.

Time required: A long day.

Slickhorn Canyon

To the south of Grand Gulch, Slickhorn Canyon drains a number of tributaries all the way to the San Juan River. Although less visited and dryer than its more famous brethren, it has a high concentration of pristine ruins that make it worthy of a visit.

In this section, I propose a half-day circuit specially tailored to photographers. It requires a bit of Class IV scrambling and routefinding skills. Backpackers or large individuals may have trouble with a few obstacles I'll point out below.

From the car park, walk down into the mostly dry creek for about 1.6 miles until you arrive at a huge dryfall. Locate the bypass trail to the left and climb until you reach a bench just below the rim: there is a short exposed section on slickrock, but it's easily negotiated. Continue along the bench high above the canyon floor for about 0.3 mile. Looking directly across the canyon, you'll notice a large caprock with two small ruins; both have openings that help in spotting them. Make a note of it as you will pass by this caprock on the return leg of this trip. Look for the cairns signaling the descent to rejoin the canyon. The descent is very steep but particularly well cairned. Be very careful if you carry a large photo pack and heavy tripod. You'll reach the canyon floor in about fifteen minutes. Continue

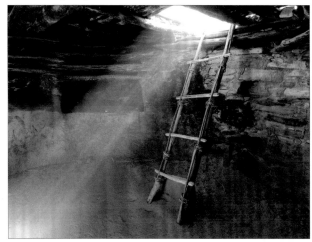

downcanyon for a short while and look up to spot ruins under a large alcove. The steep cairned hiker's trail leading to the Perfect Kiva starts near 37°22'40" 110°02'12". The Kiva is best lit in the morning and early afternoon and the little ruin next to it is quite photogenic. Shoot the latter first before the sun gets to it. You can descend into the Kiva on a ladder similar to the

Slickhorn's Perfect Kiva

original—which you can see at the Edge of the Cedars Museum in Blanding. Be sure not to step on the roof of the Kiva! It is not a large Kiva and inside you'll need the widest angle available. On a sunny day you'll have a nice beam of light, further highlighted by a constant draft produced by the clever air suction scheme built by the Ancient Ones to reduce smoke.

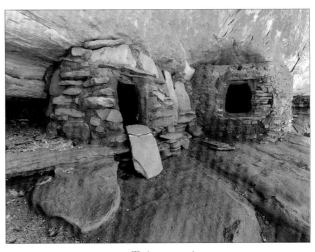

Twin granaries

After your visit, proceed along the bench 200 yards in a down-canyon direction toward a tree cluster and follow the cairned route climbing to a higher bench. You'll soon come to a narrow crack which you have to ascend. It is too narrow for chimneying so you'll need to use upper body strength to lift yourself up and out of the crack. Remove your pack/tripod and hand it to the next in line in your party—you do have a hiking buddy, right? Once past this obstacle, it is an easy hike to the aforementioned caprock and its beautiful little ruins. Once again you'll need a very wide angle lens. To return to your car, locate the steps between the caprock ruin and the bigger ruin to the right and start climbing, this will be your last little obstacle before reaching the rim. Continue on the slickrock, contouring a little gully and you'll soon find a hikers's trail following the canyon upstream. From here it is a level and fast return to your car. I do not recommend using this hiker's trail as an approach as it could be difficult to locate the proper way down to Perfect Kiva.

Getting there: From UT-261, take the good unmarked Point Lookout Road opposite Cigarette Springs Road. After 2.6 miles, continue straight, leaving the signed Government Trail to your right. Continue 1.7 miles and turn right onto the 0.4 mile track leading to the Slickhorn-1 carpark at 37°23'23" 110°00'30".

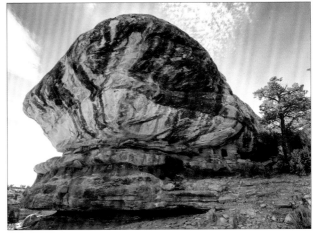

Slickhorn's Caprock Ruin

Overleaf: Caprock ruin on Cedar Mesa Plateau

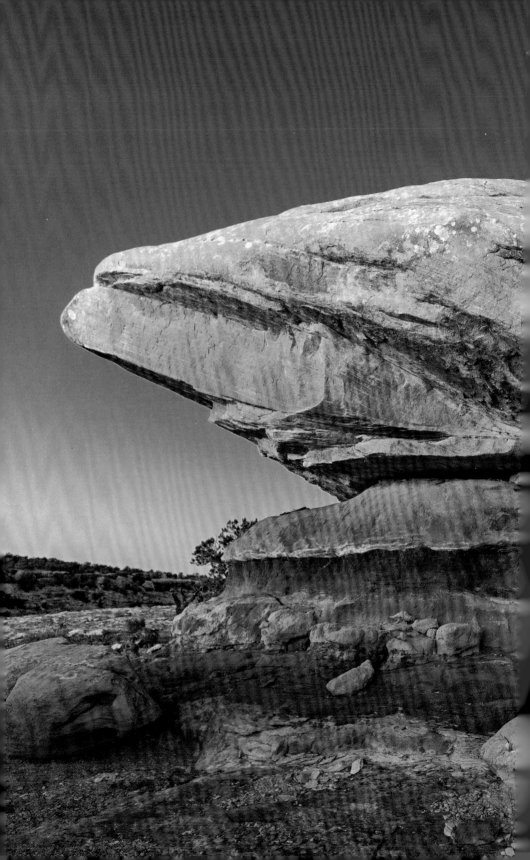

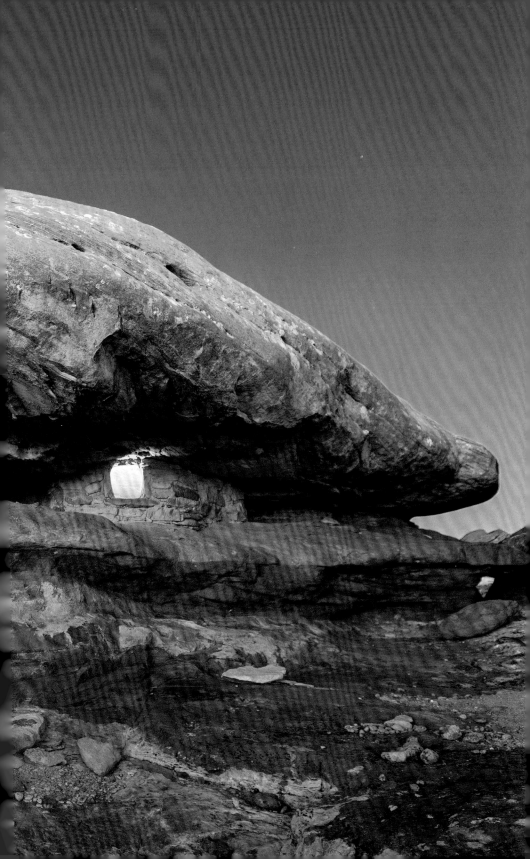

Nearby location: Continuing about 5.7 miles south on Point Lookout Road from its junction with the Slickrock 1 spur brings you to a car park on the left. High clearance SUVs can safely navigate to this car park. From there you can easily walk to the rim of an unnamed canyon in 15 to 20 minutes. There is no established trail going down into this canyon, but this is a great place for camping and exploring the rim on your own. There is a nice caprock ruin close to the rim.

Mokey Dugway & Muley Point

About 23 miles south of UT-95 on UT-261, you reach the edge of the plateau at a place called Mokey Dugway. This is where the paved road suddenly turns into graded gravel. Here, at an altitude close to 6,000 feet, you have a spectacular view of the Valley of the Gods about 1000 feet below. Monument Valley is also visible in the distance.

For even better viewpoints, take the dirt road heading west to Muley Point immediately before starting the descent from the plateau. There are two viewpoints: the first one, at about 3.7 miles, yields wonderful views of the goosenecks of the San Juan River. The second one, at about 5 miles, marks the end of the road and affords a closer and more open view of Monument Valley, as well as an almost 360° panorama, including Navajo Mountain, the Henrys, the Abajos and Sleeping Ute Mountain.

Returning to Mokey Dugway on UT-261, you descend an amazing portion of road, carved into the flanks of the cliff during the 1950s for the use of local uranium miners. It's an all-gravel road with almost 3 miles of hairpin turns descending steeply to the bottom, but it's wide and doesn't present any problems for a passenger car as long as you drive slowly. The pavement resumes as you near the bottom and in about 7 miles you reach US-163, where you can continue your trip southwest toward Mexican Hat and Monument Valley or northeast toward Bluff and Moab.

Photo advice: The views from the viewpoints are so incredibly vast that it is easier and probably more interesting to simply admire them than to photograph them. If you want to photograph Monument Valley in the distance, you'll need a long telephoto, using a small aperture if you include the badlands in the foreground. It is best to shoot at sunrise, when Monument Valley and the badlands are in better light. The view is often too hazy, but you could get a good shot after a rain, with some nice clouds or a dramatic sky.

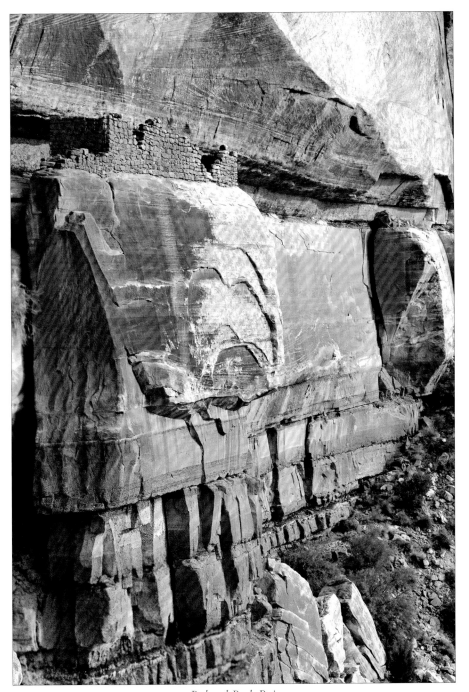

Pedestal Rock Ruin

Chapter 12

AROUND BLUFF

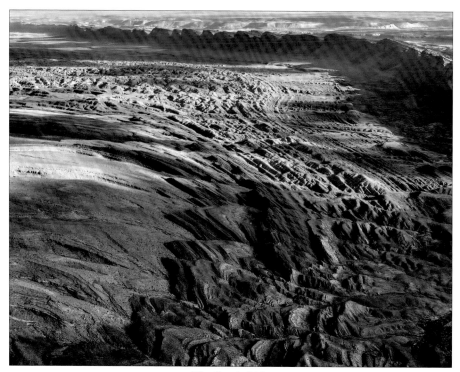

The Comb Ridge

Bluff

Bluff might be a tiny little town but it has a lot going for it. Surrounded by the red cliffs that gave it its name, the town proper has a lot of character, with its atypical Victorian style stone houses and its spectacular Twin Rocks. Good lodging and its central location between Moab and Monument Valley make it an excellent stop for the night, as well as a great base for exploring the Comb Ridge and surrounding areas. It has a good airstrip and it is the starting point for the San Juan River boat trips. May I add that it doesn't have the zoo atmosphere of Moab, nor the high prices of Monument Valley.

Starting with the town proper, you'll find nice Victorian houses on Mulberry Street, which runs parallel to the highway. They were built at the end of the 19th century by the same Mormon pioneers who founded the town following their epic Hole-in-the-Rock odyssey (see *Canyons of the Escalante* chapter).

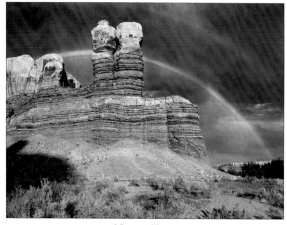

Navajo Twins

This expedition is recounted in a very interesting video that can be seen at the Bluff Fort's visitor center. There is also a small museum focused on the Mormon Pioneers as well as a reconstructed version of the old compound, complete with wagons and little cabins arranged in a defensive square, tastefully furnished and decorated by the locals with historical accuracy. The "Fort" is located on Main Street and access to the visitor center is on Black Locust Ave.

The Twin Rocks (a.k.a. Navajo Twins) located near the trading post of the same name, look good from both sides. The photo is somewhat cliché, but as you can see on my image, a bit of dramatic sky can make it fun to shoot.

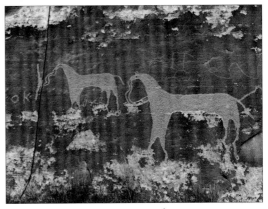

Horse panel

A couple of hundred yards past the Twin Rocks Café on Twin Rocks Drive, you'll find a gravel road leading in about ½ mile to a car park and trailhead. The trail leads north along the creek. This is a very pleasant hike of less than ½ mile to a superb modern Ute/Navajo panel depicting horses in lovely, fluid lines. I'd rather not give a GPS waypoint, but the panel is easy to locate by scanning the ridge high up, close to the vertical cliff. You can find it with the naked eye or, better, a pair of binoculars. There are social trails leading to the panel, but you should be careful ascending and descending as the ground is very loose and it would be easy to twist an ankle.

Nearby location: Traveling westbound from Bluff, 0.8 mile before the junction of US-163 and 191, the road to Sand Island Recreational Area leads to a wall with many petroglyphs at the western edge of the recreational area. However, the most photogenic panel is at the eastern edge and can be reached in an easy 10-minute walk along the cliff from a small parking area. Sand Island is also a launching pad for rafting trips on the San Juan River. Wild Rivers Expeditions offer a 26-mile one-day rafting trip to Mexican Hat. The rare rapids won't delight thrill seekers, but photographers can expect beautiful scenery—especially near Mexican Hat. The trip stops at the impressive Butler Wash Petroglyph Panel as well as at the River House cliff dwelling (see *River House* section).

The Wolfman Panel

The Wolfman Panel is a stalwart "must check" location in the quest for trophy shots many of us unabashedly engage in. It's a very rewarding one too, considering the ease of access. It's actually quite an original panel and it's sad that it has resisted the ravages of time fairly well, only to be marred by bullet holes.

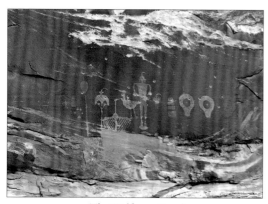

The Wolfman Panel

Photo Advice: The Wolfman Panel is best photographed in the morning, when it's shaded. A polarizing filter will help if you're there when it's in full sun.

Getting there: From Bluff Fort, drive 4.2 miles west on US-191 and continue straight ahead on US-163 for 0.9 mile. Turn right onto CR-262 (a.k.a. Butler Wash Road). Open the gate, pass through and close it behind you. Continue for 1 mile and turn left onto the spur road just before the cattle guard; the parking area is a short 500 feet from here. Walk west/southwest to the rim, locate the cairns marking the descent at about 37°16'33" 109°38'46" and ease down south on the sloping ledge. Cross the gully to arrive on a flat ledge, close to the panel at 37°16'29" 109°38'46".

Nearby location: There is a fairly good size cliff dwelling almost across the canyon facing the descent, but it is hard to reach due to the dense vegetation.

Pedestal Rock Ruin

Pedestal Rock Ruin is a Puebloan structure spectacularly perched on top of a tall rock face. The "pedestal" is actually part of the cliff but looks like it is separated from it, creating a very unique view.

With some effort, you can reach a level platform close to the ruin by climbing the highly-eroded steep hillside to the left (looking at the ruin), which is a combination of very loose sandy and rocky terrain that could become a serious ankle-buster if taken too casually on the downhill. Be very cautious and do your best to minimize further erosion.

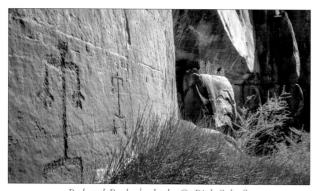

Pedestal Rock & glyph © Rick Schafer

Photo advice: From the above-mentioned platform, you can create a striking shot of the ruin with two petroglyphs in the extreme foreground. Look for the petroglyphs close to the bottom. You'll need a polarizer to bring out detail and you may want to further enhance three-dimensionality in post-processing.

You may also need to shoot several frames—focusing them for stacking, especially if you shoot APS or larger format with inherent poor depth-of-field. Alternatively, a small-sensor camera would allow you to take a single shot, using a small aperture. Pedestal Rock is best photographed in late afternoon.

Getting there: From US-163 about 5.1 miles west of Bluff Fort, turn right onto CR-262 (aka Butler Wash Road). Drive a little over 4 miles and turn east (right) on an unmarked track. Follow it southwards for 0.4 mile to a car park at 37°18'45" 109°37'28". From here walk south cross-country following the cliffs at a distance for almost 0.6 mile, often crossing gullies. Follow the cliff when it angles southeast to the foot of Pedestal Rock at 37°18'19" 109°37'20".

Time required: About 2 hours from the turnoff on Butler Wash Road.

The Procession Panel

The Procession Panel is a large and highly unusual petroglyph panel: a 15+ foot conga line of tiny marching figures following large animals entering a big circle. The ±3.5-mile round-trip hike is quite easy but it requires that you pay attention in order not to miss the panel. From the trailhead, use social trails to cross Butler Wash through the thick vegetation. After reaching the slickrock, follow the cairns on a gentle slope, heading west toward a reddish sandstone ridge. The panel is located on a side cliff facing southwest, opposite the red ridge and close to the edge of Comb Ridge. After reaching the top of the slope, descend to a spot between the red ridge and a large, colored side cliff to your right. Continue up along this cliff to the panel at 37°21'02" 109°38'55".

There is much subject matter to pick from on the Procession Panel and you have a choice of shooting wide-angle or extracting interesting detail. It's best to be there during the first part of the morning, when the panel is still in the shade.

After you're done shooting, take a short walk to the top of the ridge to enjoy great views of Comb Wash to the west. Just don't expect great pictures.

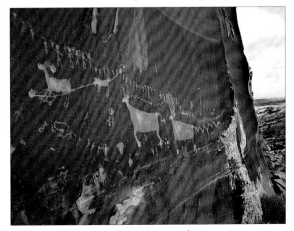

Getting there: From US-163 about 5.1 miles west of Bluff Fort, turn right on Butler Wash Road. Drive about 6.6 miles to a spur road on the west side (left), leading to the trailhead in 200 feet at 37°21'04" 109°37'44".

Time required: About 3 hours r/t from the trailhead, including the side trip to the ridge top.

Procession panel

Monarch Cave

Monarch Cave is among the largest ruins in the Cedar Mesa area. It boasts a picturesque setting, tucked under a long alcove adorned with spectacular streaks of desert varnish and overlooking a lush box canyon. The precariously perched ruins overlook a pool of water that must have provided irrigation for crops. Monarch Cave is also known as Hidden Pool Ruins. It's interesting to note the unusual presence of round rooms with a bunch of little openings in the masonry, likely used to defend against intruders. The ruins proper have become very unstable in recent years and are off-limits, as of this writing. Please obey all BLM warnings to avoid damaging the ruins or ending up injured.

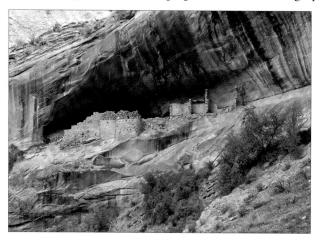

Monarch Cave

Photo advice: Monarch Cave offers a great shot with a medium telephoto from an obvious vantage point above the canyon floor. On a sunny day, it's better to come in the afternoon to avoid having the ruin and alcove partly lit, partly in the shade.

Getting there: From the previously mentioned Butler Wash Road gate, about 5.1 miles west of Bluff Fort on US-163, drive north 7.2 miles and turn left on the spur road leading to the car park a few feet from Butler Wash (37°21'31" 109°37'50"). After crossing Butler wash, the trail follows the canyon floor through overgrown vegetation for ¾ mile until Monarch Cave comes in sight. From here simply ascend the slickrock slope to the right until you find a suitable viewpoint.

Time required: 2+ hours round-trip from the trailhead.

River House & the Butler Wash Panel

River house (a.k.a. Snake House) is a small but nice Puebloan dwelling tucked under an alcove near the confluence of Butler Wash and the San Juan River. What makes this ruin special, however, is the spectacular pictograph of a snake above the dwelling to the right. This snake is at least 8 feet long.

The Butler Wash Petroglyph Panel is a huge panel, with a number of large striking anthropomorphic figures pecked into the dark part of the desert varnish at the bottom of a tall, straight cliff. You definitely get a sense that the artist who did the big figures had some real talent.

Photo advice: Early morning works best at River House, to avoid having the ruins partly in the shade. The glyphs at the Butler Wash Panel are carved on highly reflective desert varnish and are facing south, so they can appear faint to the naked eye under bright sunshine. The solution is obviously a polarizing filter to remove the glare. This works quite well as you can see on my image. A normal lens to short telephoto works well here.

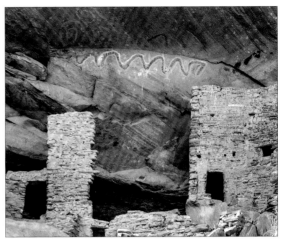

The big snake above River House

Getting there: From Bluff Fort, drive 4.2 miles west on US-191 to the intersection with US-163, continuing straight on US-163 for 3.1 miles to mile marker 38.3. Take the dirt track to the left (south) and drive 3.9 miles to a fork, crisscrossing the sandy wash several times. Take the left fork, ascending a steep range that requires 4WD for traction. At the top, take the right fork and continue ¾ mile to the River House, passing the remnants of the Barton Trading Post along the way. River House is on the cliff side (north) and easy to see from the road. Do not drive this road after a rain, or you could get stuck.

After you've photographed River House, continue on the dirt track for another 1.3 miles to a shady car park at 37°13'56" 109°40'19", close to the Butler Wash Petroglyph Panel. From here, it's a short 700 feet to the panel. As of this writing, the last ¾ mile to the Butler Wash panel is on a narrow sandy track surrounded by overgrown tamarisk and you risk damaging your paint by continuing, especially with a full size SUV. You'll be the judge to see if it's passable or if it's preferable to park before the tamarisk, and walk the extra distance.

Time required: 3 to 4 hours from the beginning of the track.

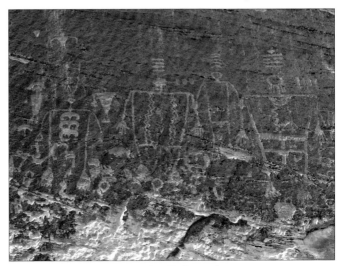

Butler Wash panel

Valley of the Gods

Driving UT-261 from US-163, just before ascending the Mokey Dugway (see *Around Blanding* chapter), you'll see a track heading east and forming a loop around the area known as the Valley of the Gods. After a moderately spectacular portion in the vicinity of the Bed & Breakfast, you'll encounter imposing monoliths and buttes strewn about the valley. Although reminiscent of those found at Monument Valley, they do have their own flair. Though quite beautiful, Valley of the Gods doesn't offer the same photographic variety as the latter. The main advantage of the Valley of the Gods is that it is much less visited and an impression of solitude reigns here. You'll truly have the impression that you are embarking on an adventure, which is not the case in the highly controlled world of the Monument Valley Tribal Park. I particularly like the northern side of the valley, where the road abruptly turns south behind one of the tallest monoliths. I call this particular spot the Rincon and I like to park here and explore on foot. This area, located about 8 miles from either entry of the track, has by far the best views in the entire valley.

Photo advice: These 'gods', immense monoliths rising high into the sky, won't disappoint you. If you arrive past mid-afternoon, when the rocks take very warm colors, take the track from its western entrance in order not to have the sun against you. From sunrise to early morning, take it from the opposite direction, you'll get good light and even better views.

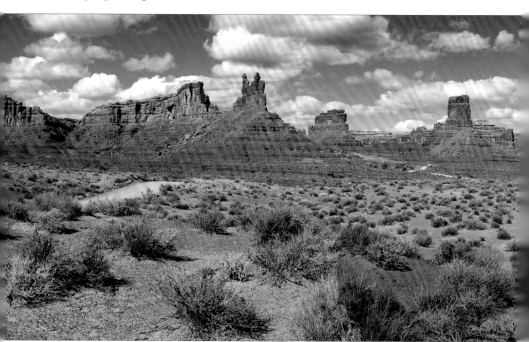

Valley of the Gods

Getting there: The west entrance is at the foot of the Mokey Dugway on UT-261, less than 7 miles from the junction with US-163, and almost 4 miles north of Mexican Hat (or 20 miles west of Bluff). The southeast entrance is on US-163, 8 miles northeast of Mexican Hat (or 16 miles west of Bluff) and about 4 miles from where it branches off UT-261. Using caution, the 16-mile dirt road is generally passable for passenger cars except during or after inclement weather.

Time required: At least 1 hour just to drive the dirt road; 2 hours to do it at a more leisurely pace taking photos.

Goosenecks of the San Juan

At the southern end of UT-261, there is a small but interesting Utah State Park, often ignored by travelers who are either in a great hurry to get to nearby Monument Valley or in a euphoric state from visiting it.

Here, the San Juan River has cut out four successive bends over 1,000 feet in depth in a shale core, twisting and turning for almost 7 miles in a space of less than 2 miles. This view is more remarkable for being odd than for sheer beauty. You are presented with a geological phenomenon that defies the imagination.

Photo advice: The Goosenecks make for eye-catching pictures no matter what size of wide-angle lens you have. There's no way you can get them all into one single shot, unless you shoot from a drone or a small aircraft. Alternately, you can stitch together several vertical images to make a panorama.

Getting there: On UT-261, about 1 mile from US-163 or 6 miles from the foot of Mokey Dugway, take SR-316 heading southwest for about 3½ miles until you reach the viewpoint at the edge of the plateau. Camping is allowed.

Time required: A detour of less than 1 hour round-trip from US-163.

Mexican Hat Rock

I'll be the first to admit that photographing Mexican Hat Rock is a bit cheesy, but it's really tempting to stop and gawk, especially the first time there. Judging by the number of cars that pull off for a close-up view and a quick snapshot, the temptation is universal.

Photo advice: If you are in a position to pick your timing, the second half of the afternoon offers the best light on the rock.

Getting there: Less than 2 miles north of the Mexican Hat township, a well-graded dirt road leaves US-163 to wind around the southern side of Mexican Hat Rock, allowing you to pick up the view you prefer.

Time required: 30 minutes.

Overleaf: Goosenecks of the San Juan

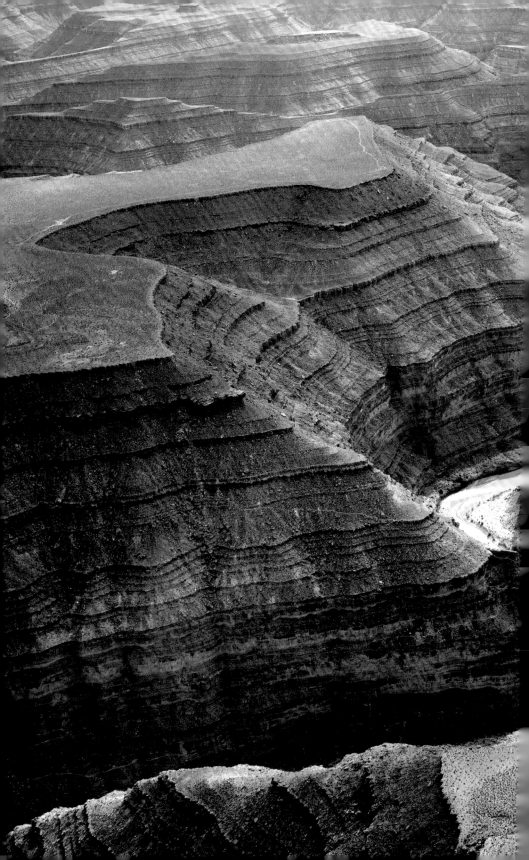

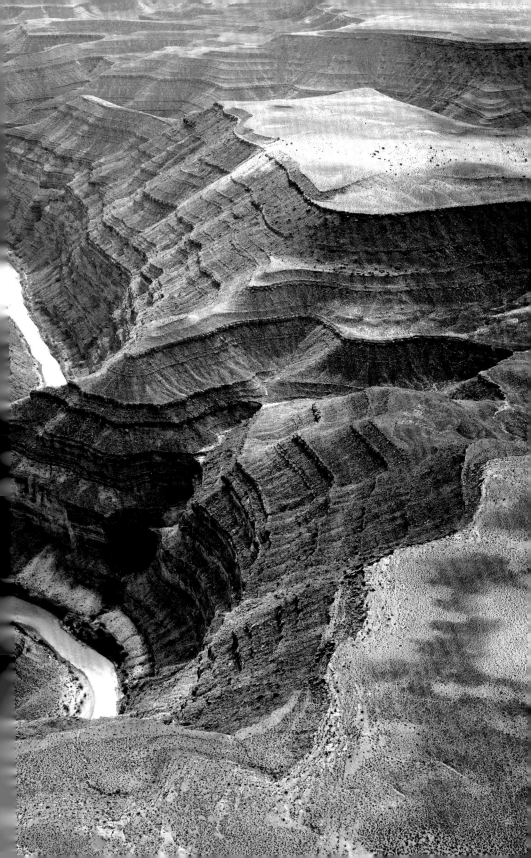

The Raplee Anticline (a.k.a. Lime Ridge)

Coming from Bluff or heading north out of Mexican Hat, one can't help but be mesmerized by the colorful upfolds of the hogback to the east. This hogback, known locally as the 'Indian Blanket' or 'Navajo Rug', bears the official name of Raplee Anticline. The remarkable patterns, exposing three hundred million years of erosion, form the western flank of the large Monument Upwarp—a great limestone mass from an ancient seabed extending to the Comb Ridge to the east and bisected by the San Juan River.

Photo advice: As with the nearby Goosenecks, photographing the magnitude of the Anticline from the ground is a challenge due to a scarcity of vantage points. Interesting views come shortly after you pass the turnoff to Mexican Hat Rock, coming from Mexican Hat. From here you can shoot the rock with the Raplee upfolds in the background.

Good views can also be found on the Mexican Hat Rock spur road near the river. From US-163, take the Mexican Hat Rock road for 0.3 mile, then the left fork for 0.4 mile to reach a high viewpoint before descending closer to the San Juan. A short walk toward the shore reveals two large upfolds partially hidden behind the meander to the southeast. There is also a photogenic view from above the San Juan River on the north side of a gully located ½ mile northeast of the spur road leading to Mexican Hat Rock. To get there, drive 2.7 miles from the gas station in Mexican Hat on US-163 to a pullout on the east side; walk back 0.2 miles along the road, cross the fence, then walk along the gully for 0.3 mile

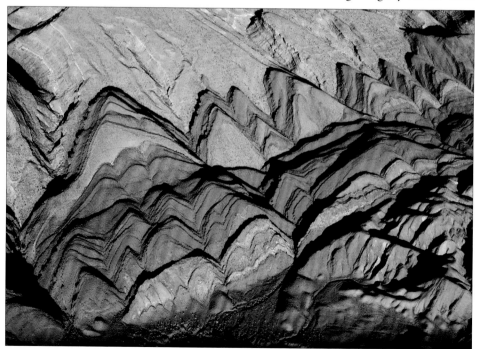

Raplee Anticline

to the rim above the San Juan. This spot is best in mid- to late afternoon and a medium telephoto allows you to include the river forming a nice ribbon of light in the foreground.

If you are on a rafting trip from Bluff to Mexican Hat (or longer), there are good views as you exit the anticline and again, after the commotion of shooting Mexican Hat Rock has died down in the raft, as you float toward the second meander.

On a day without haze, it's worth driving up UT-261, trading proximity for elevation to shoot with a medium telephoto.

Mile 13 to Monument Valley

Although Monument Valley is largely in Arizona and is covered in *Photographing the Southwest – Volume 2,* this iconic viewpoint known as Mile 13 is way inside Utah and I thought it would be a nice teaser to include it here.

The classic shot depicted in my two photos has been used for countless movies, commercials, print ads, calendars, you name it. To many younger movie buffs, it was the place where *Forrest Gump* decided to stop running, but it was first revealed to me in James William Guercio's classic *Electra Glide in Blue*, starring Robert Blake. And what a shocker it was to see him on his Harley in this larger then life setting.

Photo advice: From Mile 13 on, the highway becomes a giant leading line to the distant monuments in your composition. You don't have a lot of room for creativity here. Whether you stand on the road (be careful!) or the shoulder, the highway will be a strong element in your shot. In the accompanying images, I show you both sunset and sunrise illumination. As you can see, this subject works very well both ways. Morning or late afternoon shots can also be successful here with the right clouds as supporting elements.

There is another teachable moment to the comparison, illustrating the difference between a single shot with a wide angle lens (sunset picture) and a stitch of several telephoto shots taken vertically (sunrise picture). It's easy to see how the compression generated by the telephoto shots makes the Monument Valley monoliths look more imposing.

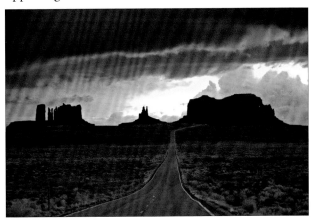

Mile 13 sunset

Overleaf: Sunrise on Monument Valley from Mile 13

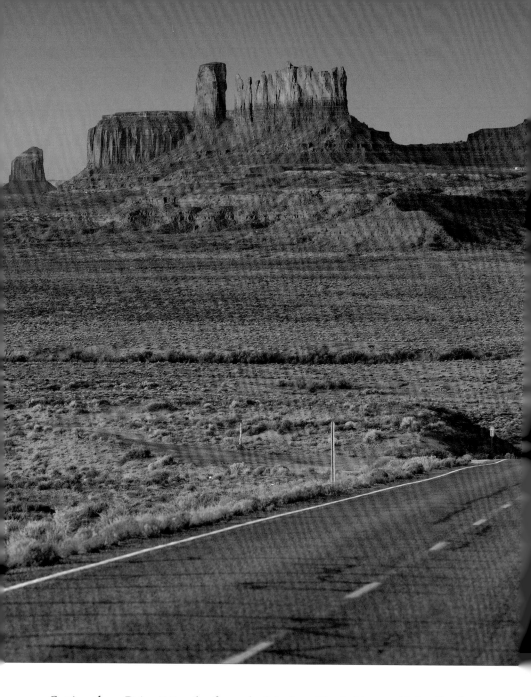

Getting there: Drive 7.7 miles from the Mexican Hat bridge or 12.8 miles from the turnoff to Monument Valley Tribal Park and look for milepost 13 and several dirt pullouts on the north side of US-163.

Time required: Allow at least 30 minutes to come from your lodging in Mexican Hat or the tribal park, or 45 minutes from Bluff, so you can have plenty of time to scout and prepare.

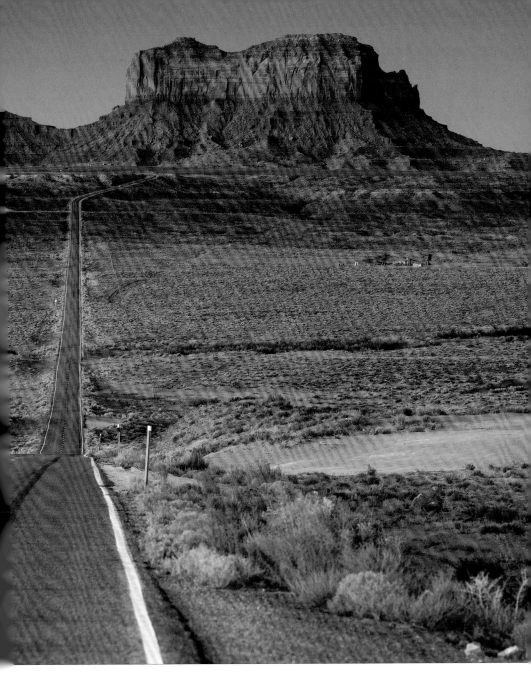

Seventeen Room Ruin

This large cliff dwelling must have housed quite a number of people in its heyday. In 1875, part of a group called the Hayden Survey, commissioned to explore and map the American West, found a large Ancestral Puebloan ruin in a north-facing alcove immediately south of the San Juan River, in the vicinity of Bluff. The ruin, likely dating from the late 1200's, was dubbed "Casa del Eco".

This name has not stuck, however, and today the ruin is called most commonly Seventeen Room Ruin. Depending on how you decipher the layout of the ruin, the count is actually between 14 and 18 rooms. The ruin proper is nothing to rave about, but the setting under the vast alcove overlooking the San Juan River Valley is truly outstanding. Also, the location is atypical due to its north-facing orientation—most cliff dwellings face south to catch the warm sunlight in winter. The ruin is located on the Navajo Reservation, so a hiking permit for the San Juan River and Four Corners Area must be obtained from Navajo Parks and Recreation, Four Corners Monument office, located on US-160, approximately 6 miles north of Teec Nos Pos, AZ and about 48 miles from Bluff!

The obvious way up is to ascend the hill on the right side of the alcove. Although very few visitors come here and few people are even aware of its existence, the dirt path shows severe signs of erosion. Please use the rocky trail further to the right which is on more solid ground.

Photo advice: The lack of direct sun due to the northern orientation goes a long way in eliminating contrast issues. Obviously, in a setting like this an ultrawide is an asset, but there is always the possibility of stitching.

Getting there: This is the tricky part. The bridge which provided quick and easy access to the site (only 3 miles east of Bluff) was severely damaged by a flood in 2007. It was subsequently decided to cut it loose from its moorings to prevent boating accidents. It is not likely to be rebuilt in the foreseeable future. As a result, one must make a rather convoluted drive to reach it. From the junction

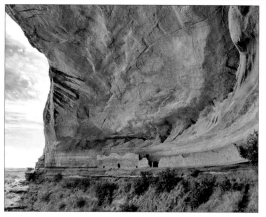

Seventeen Room Ruin

of US-163 and US-191 west of Bluff, drive about 7.5 miles on US-191 and turn left on CR-441. Drive about 6.8 miles northeast to an intersection with five different tracks. Take the one on the left, almost at a right angle; this is CR-438. Continue for about 4.8 miles, going north first before turning west following the San Juan River. Park away from traffic near the big alcove.

Time required: 3 to 4 hours from Bluff.

The Recapture Pocket

It's a mystery to me that this wonderful playground hasn't been talked about more, in print and on the web. In less than thirty minutes from Bluff, you find yourself in a fantasyland of brownish goblins, hoodoos, and other stone creatures with fantastic shapes. The Recapture Pocket is also a particularly nice place to camp; you can explore at sunset and sunrise and even do some nighttime photography. You could even go with a passenger car, or at least come close enough, as you'll be on gravel roads most of the way.

There are three groups of formations, each with its own interest. The first two are very close together. The image I picked to illustrate this section is from the first group, which is very dense and has taller standalone spires. The second group has the most striking setting, tucked as it is at the end of a playa with eroded cliffs in the background forming a semi-circular amphitheater. This group has a greater variety of shapes and forms and more space between them. The last group, farther to the north, is smaller and sparser and by the time you have thoroughly explored the first two groups, you may have had your fill of spires and pillars.

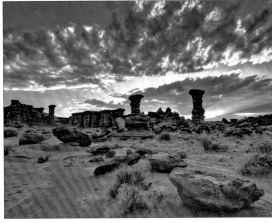
Recapture Pocket

Getting there: From its junction with US-191 east of Bluff, take UT-162 for 4.9 miles and turn left on an unmarked gravel road. Drive 1 mile and make a left (west) at this junction. This is Trading Post Rd., although it's unmarked. Continue almost 0.5 mile and turn right (north) onto unmarked Bluff Bench Rd. Drive about 0.8 mile, still on gravel. Take the sandy left fork, continuing 0.3 mile to reach the first group of formations. The second group is located 0.3 mile further at the end of its dry sand playa. To reach the third group, return to the fork where you had turned for the first two groups, turn left (north) for 0.9 mile and turn right just past the slickrock patch and storage tanks for another 0.3 mile.

Time required: About 2 hours for a quick visit of the first two groups, 3 hours or more to thoroughly enjoy the place.

Montezuma Canyon

Montezuma Canyon is a pleasant drive along a wide and verdant canyon that sees few visitors. The canyon runs roughly between Hatch Trading Post to the south and Monticello to the north, with the possibility of coming from Blanding via Perkins Road. The well-maintained mostly dirt road follows the course of Montezuma Creek. Although the creek is dry much of the year, it is prone to flash-flooding, so watch out during the monsoon season. Most of the road is graded and suitable for passenger vehicles, although this may not hold true following wet weather. There are no established hiking trails, campsites, or facilities of any kind. Bring lots of water, make sure you have a full tank of gas, and pay close attention to road junctions and signs.

Photo advice: Montezuma Canyon is home to a number of Ancestral Puebloan sites representing several periods and cultures. Keep your eyes open for cliff dwellings and rock art panels; they are difficult to locate.

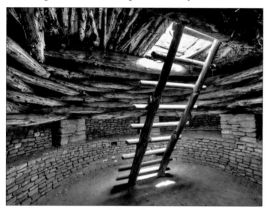
Three Kiva

About 0.7 mile past the junction with Perkins Road coming from the south (or 6.6 miles south of the Three Kivas site when coming from the north), you can observe several panels strewn along the cliff, including a nice hunting scene with buffalo and elk, a horse's head, and within a short walk, four cranes. Look for a car park on the west side of the road.

The most prominent (and official) photogenic attraction is the nicely restored kiva at the Three Kiva Pueblo site; it makes for a good photo in mid- to late-afternoon light with some nice sun rays. As with most kivas, a very wide angle is a must and a tripod is highly recommended. Three Kiva Pueblo is about 7.3 miles north of the junction with Perkins Road at 37°33'54" 109°15'07".

About 2.5 miles north of Three Kiva and just past the mouth of Bradford Canyon, you'll find the Bradford Canyon Ruins—11th century cliff dwellings in fairly good condition. Look for the car park on the north side of the road at 37°35'08" 109°16'09".

Arguably the most photogenic ruin on the road is the Honeycomb Ceiling ruin. Although I am not providing a GPS waypoint, it is located approximately halfway on Montezuma Canyon Road, northeast of the Bradford Canyon junction and south of Devil Canyon. Be very careful climbing to the ruin; it is steep and the ground is loose. A very wide angle is needed; don't try dangerous acrobatics if you don't have one.

Further north, there are a couple of modern 'cave dweller' homes that are quite unique, both very visible from the road coming from the south, but easily missed coming from the north. Respect the owner's privacy and stay on the road if you are taking pictures.

Getting there: From Bluff Fort, drive 11 miles north on US-191 and turn right (east) on UT-262 (a.k.a. Hovenweep Rd.). Drive 8.4 miles to a junction, and turn left for another 6.6 miles to Hatch Trading Post, an interesting place and your last chance for bathroom, food, and drinks.

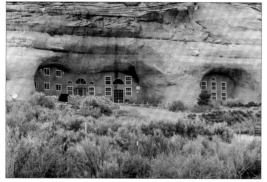
Modern Cliff Dwellings

Exiting from Hatch, go left and continue straight past the junction, heading north. This is the beginning of CR-446 (a.k.a. Montezuma Canyon Road). About 9 miles further north, be sure not to miss the right turn on CR-146 (a.k.a. Montezuma Creek Road) at the junction with Perkins Road, which comes from Blanding at 37°29'51" 109°14'01".

From Blanding, turn east on East 500 S which becomes Perkins Road (CR-206). Drive almost 21 miles and turn left on Montezuma Creek Road (CR-146).

From downtown Monticello at the intersection with US-491, continue 5.1 mile south on US-191 and turn left on an unmarked road. This is the beginning of Southbound Montezuma Creek Road (CR-187).

Time required: Plan on no less than 3 hours, more if photographing extensively.

Hovenweep National Monument

Located on the expansive Cajon Mesa, which is part of the Great Sage Plain of southeastern Utah and southwestern Colorado, Hovenweep National Monument protects some of the most interesting examples of pre-Columbian stone architecture in the Southwest, including its unique "towers".

Hovenweep's photographic interest lies primarily in the rich colors of the sandstone walls of its towers, contrasting with pure blue skies, beautiful fluffy clouds during the Monsoon season, and the snow-capped peaks of Sleeping Ute Mountain in winter. Although the remaining structures are only partially standing (Hovenweep was abandoned circa 1300 ACE), they are all interesting and well worth photographing.

Hovenweep National Monument consists of five distinct groups of ruins. The Square Tower group is the largest and most easily accessible and we will concentrate on this one. It is located only 300 yards from the small Ranger Station and Museum. Following the easy 2-mile loop around the canyon will let you visit all the interesting ruins of this group. This pleasant trail stays mostly on the rim, except for a small portion in and out the canyon. The first part of the walk takes you past some interesting structures resting atop the canyon walls. These are easily photographed from various vantage points. Hovenweep Castle is the most visible landmark for the outstanding masonry work of its remaining walls. The "Castle" was actually part of a larger structure bordering the canyon rim, which is now totally gone. As you turn around the bend, Square Tower comes into view. This three-story high tower rests upon a large boulder, which makes it quite unique.

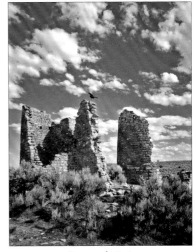

Raven & Ruin

Overleaf: Honeycomb Ceiling ruin

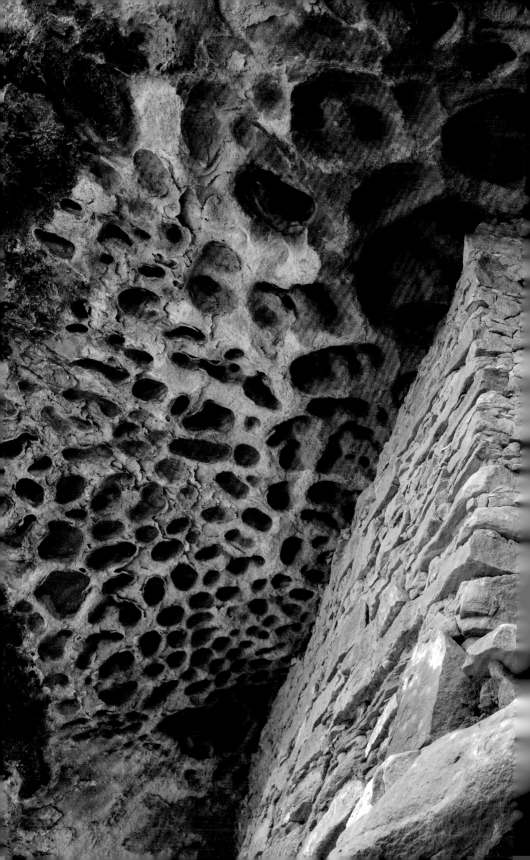

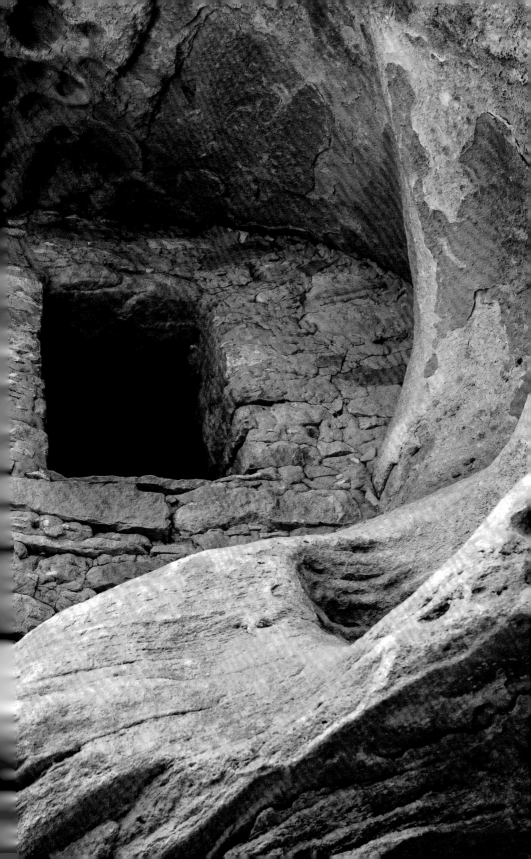

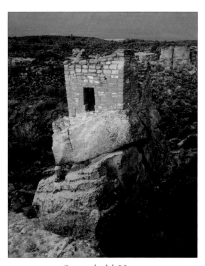

Stronghold House

You'll then pass by Hovenweep House, Rim Rock House, and the Twin Towers, before crossing the canyon. At the end of the loop, Stronghold House is the most outstanding landmark on this trail. It's named for its lack of an easy entrance, which led archaeologists to believe it may have been used for defensive purposes.

On the Colorado side of the monument is the Holly Group, once home to an estimated 150 people. This group contains five structures; the most noticeable of which is the two-storied Holly Tower, built on a tall, narrow boulder.

Photo advice: You'll get plenty of good angles by moving around the structures in mid-morning or mid-afternoon and by concentrating on the strong detail of the masonry work. I have created stronger images this way, rather than by blasting the towers in strong evening light, losing much of the detail to the intense color. I also encourage you to seek snow or clouds to add more interest to your images.

Getting there: From Bluff Fort, drive 11 miles north on US-191 (from Blanding south on US-191 for about 15 miles) then east on UT-262 for 8.5 miles. Turn left on UT-401 for 16 miles (passing Hatch Trading Post), then left on UT-413 for 6 miles to the entrance of the park on your right.

Time required: Up to 2 hours to walk the 2-mile loop, taking your time to photograph the main structures.

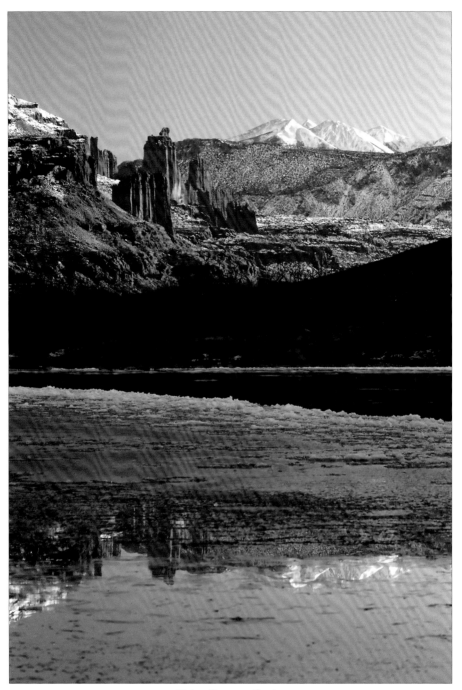

Fisher Towers reflection

Chapter 13

AROUND MOAB

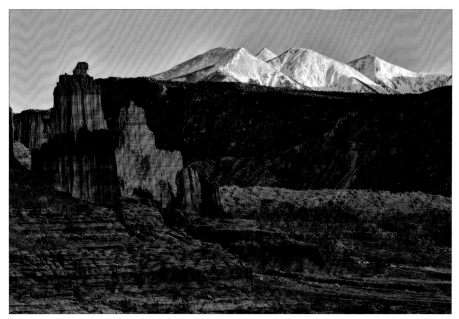

Fisher Towers & La Sal Mountains in winter

Introduction to Moab

If there's one town in the Southwest that has changed drastically in the last thirty years, it's Moab. I knew Moab when it was still a big village with a couple of stray motels, a few odd restaurants... and definitely no liquor. Today, with dozens of motels, Moab has become a tourism Mecca, attracting visitors from all over the world. They buy cool T-shirts proclaiming "New York, Paris, London... Moab" and relax after a long day of hiking, climbing, rafting, four-wheeling, or mountain biking, in one of the several micro-breweries in town.

Moab is the jumping-off spot par excellence for the two scenic giants of the Colorado Plateau that are Arches and Canyonlands Nat'l Park. However, the area around Moab contains a number of remarkable sites outside the parks that would be a shame to miss. This chapter deals with those sites that don't quite have the stature of National Parks or Monuments, but can be just as fascinating and full of photographic opportunities. If you need some inspiration, be sure to check out Tom Till's exquisite photography in his gallery on Main Street.

Potash Road

Scenic Byway 279 (a.k.a. Potash Road) begins off US-191, about 1.3 miles past the Colorado River Bridge north of Moab.

This highly scenic road follows the right bank of the Colorado River below steep Entrada sandstone cliffs adorned with desert varnish. Indian petroglyphs cover the canyon walls at some signed points and rock climbers from all over the world show off their skills on the slickrock. This road provides access to landmarks such as Poison Spider Mesa and Corona Arch (see next two sections) as well as to the main put-off and staging area for Colorado River trips in Canyonlands Nat'l Park and Cataract Canyon. After the pavement ends, you reach Thelma & Louise Point (remember the last scene of the movie…), the Shafer Trail, and the White Rim Road (see *Canyonlands-Island in the Sky* chapter).

The road gets its name from the vast potash extraction site it serves; the plant is located about 1 mile before the end of the 17-mile paved road. The basins are a few miles further on a rough dirt road, where high-clearance is recommended. At the Potash site, water from the Colorado River is pumped into underground galleries where it dissolves potash salts, which are then aspirated back to the surface and into large evaporation basins. On paper, it doesn't sound really exciting for the landscape photographer. However, the colorful basins display a spectacular palette, ranging from turquoise to deep dark blue and offer a shocking contrast with the red Entrada of the surrounding cliffs. To photograph this surreal sight, drive at least 5 miles past the end of the paved road to the farthest basins and find a slickrock ridge or a knoll close to the road to climb on for a better view. The best light is in late afternoon when it is evenly distributed on the whole scene. The evaporation basins can also be seen, albeit more distantly, from Hurrah Pass, accessible by high-clearance vehicle from Kane Creek Road (see *Along Kane Creek* section). Another distant view of the basins is from Dead Horse Point State Park (see *Canyonlands-Island in the Sky* chapter) and Anticline Overlook (see *Canyonlands-Needles* chapter).

Poison Spider Mesa

I highly recommend a short hike up Poison Spider Mesa for the great telephoto view it provides over the fantastic jumble of rocks and fins known as "Behind the Rocks", spread on the other side of the Colorado River. The challenging 4x4/mountain bike track has deteriorated so much since the previous edition that you must now hike it from the car park.

Photo advice: You can get good shots of the Behind the Rocks fins and coneheads by hiking about a mile on the dirt track then climbing up one of the steep slickrock hills near 38°32'06" 109°36'46". Be extra careful doing so!

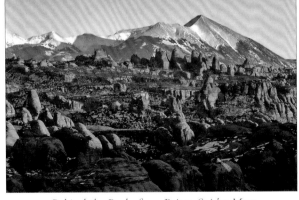

Behind the Rocks from Poison Spider Mesa

A long telephoto will yield spectacular results shortly before sunset, with the extraordinary rocks lit up by the sun and the La Sals as a backdrop.

Getting there: Follow Potash Road (SB-279) for about 6 miles from the beginning of the road off US-191 and exit at the Dinosaur Tracks sign. All vehicles but the most rugged Jeeps should stop at the parking area.

Corona Arch

This is an easy and very rewarding 3-mile round-trip hike to two spectacular arches: massive yet elegant, Corona Arch and lovely Bowtie Arch, along the way.

Corona Arch is one of the prettiest arches in the Moab area, thanks to its graceful span and an unobstructed view from both sides. Some people like to call it "Little Rainbow Bridge" and its shape is reminiscent of the well-known landmark near Lake Powell (see *Around Page* chapter in *PTS Volume 2*). Corona Arch has always been a magnet for rappellers, and more recently rope swingers. As of this writing, the BLM is considering banning these activities after several accidents occurred and to protect this outstanding geologic formation.

Photo advice: Afternoon works best to photograph Corona Arch from the slickrock bench. You can also walk under it and photograph it from the other side if you come around mid-morning.

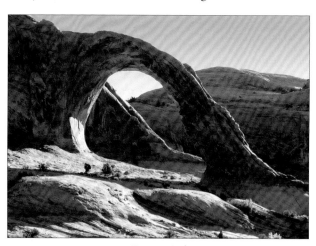

Corona Arch

Getting there: Drive 10 miles from US-191 on Potash Road (SB-279) until you reach the signed car park. The well-maintained trail climbs gently at first and makes use of safety cables and small ladders, although it's never dangerous or difficult, toward the end to reach the slickrock bench where the arches are located.

Time required: 1½ to 2 hours.

Courthouse Wash Rock Art

On your way out of Moab, consider a brief stop along US-191 just north of town to observe an interesting Barrier style panel. The 50-foot Courthouse Wash panel is located within the southern confines of Arches Nat'l Park, displaying a juxtaposition (sometimes a superposition) of anthropomorphs and abstract figures. Unfortunately, the pictographs are quite faint, having been vandalized in the past, which makes them hard to photograph.

To find the panel, drive out of town past the Colorado River bridge and pull out at a large car park on the right side of US-191 (at milepost 129, immediately after crossing Courthouse Wash). Walk east, crossing the mouth of Courthouse Wash and, still walking along US-191, bear southeast uphill to the base of the cliff. You'll find the panel less than ½ mile from where you parked.

Time permitting, you can hike up Courthouse Wash as much as you like toward the inside of the park, following the pleasant perennial stream bed with its cottonwoods and willows.

Time required: 1 hour round-trip from downtown Moab for the rock art panel.

The Colorado Riverway

You'll drive this outstanding Scenic Byway (UT-128 a.k.a. SB-128) if you come from Colorado on I-70, on your way to Moab. If you come from US-191 either north or south of Moab, you will miss it, so I strongly recommend that you take at least an afternoon to enjoy this beautiful route. It's a 30-mile one-way drive from the turnoff with US-191 north of Moab to the site of historic Dewey Bridge, burnt down in 2008, where you can turn around.

This road provides superlative views as it follows the twists and turns of the Colorado River through Professor Valley, winding its way at the foot of red canyon walls alternating with wide-open areas offering tantalizing glimpses of the La Sal Mountains. You can include side trips to Negro Bill Canyon (well-known for its 4½-mile round-trip hike leading to Morning Glory Natural Bridge), Castle Valley and its impressive mesas reminiscent of Monument Valley, pretty Onion Creek Canyon, Mary Jane Canyon, and the magnificent Fisher Towers, all very photogenic locations. All the beautiful scenery along this stretch of road is better lit after the middle of the afternoon and through sunset.

In spring and summer, you'll see commercial raft trips floating down the Colorado River. There are no real rapids there, just a quiet float suitable for

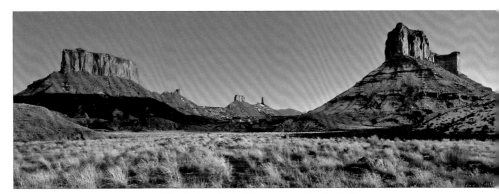

The Priest & the Nuns, near Castle Valley

families. These half-day trips are more rewarding for the beautiful scenery than for their thrills, but they do provide a taste of the better multi-day trips down river from Potash Road to Cataract Canyon. If you're interested in a more challenging experience, consider joining a one or two-day rafting trip on Westwater Canyon, which offers a rough 17-mile descent of the Colorado River with many rapids. Outfitters in Moab and Green River offer this trip.

Professor Creek (a.k.a. Mary Jane Canyon)

This is a rather long hike to a very photogenic double waterfall, split by a chokestone, deep inside a slot canyon. From the car park, just follow the trail in and out of the wash and into the narrows. The trail follows Professor Creek for about 4 miles with many shortcuts in the shallow first half. You'll be wading in ankle-deep water as you get close to the waterfall. The flow will be at its peak in the spring; the water could be a little cold but not freezing. Summer is great for a refreshing hike.

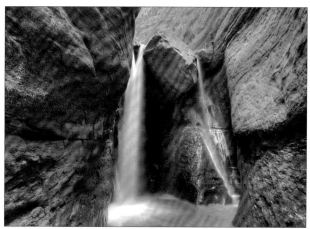

Professor Creek's waterfall © Tom Till

Photo advice: The canyon is not very deep at the waterfall. Arrive late enough to avoid direct light on the walls. The light on the red walls of the slot is at its best in early afternoon in late spring. Late afternoon is pretty good too. A tripod is a must for best depth-of-field and angel hair effect.

Getting there: From the bridge at Moab, take UT-128 for 18.4 miles to a dirt road on the right. Follow the road for 2.2 miles past a cluster of teepees, to the car park at 38°41'01" 109°21'20".

Time required: About 4 hours round-trip, not counting the drive.

The Fisher Towers

Driving from Moab on UT-128 through Professor Valley, you'll reach the amazing Fisher Towers, rising almost a thousand feet high on your right, at the far end of Richardson Amphitheater. These monoliths are extremely photogenic, especially at sunset, when the dark brown and purple walls become almost completely red for just a few minutes. In the entire Colorado plateau, you'd be hard put to find a spot more red than this one at sunset. Don't miss the interesting little group of goblins and chimneys to the right of UT-128, just after passing the track leading to the Towers.

From the trailhead close to their base, follow the 4½-mile round-trip cairned trail going up and down around the Towers. There are plenty of great views along the way. However, don't look any longer for The Cobra—a cap rock formation popular with rock climbers and photographers that collapsed during summer 2014. After about 1½ miles, you reach the base of the Titan, which is the tallest tower. You can backtrack at this point, but I recommend that you follow the trail to its very end, where you'll eventually reach a ridge with a fantastic 360° panoramic view. From there, you can see and photograph the Towers with the shiny ribbon of the Colorado winding in the background, the very colorful badlands of Onion Creek Canyon on the backside, and Castle Rock in the distance. Use hiking boots and exercise caution near drop-offs if the trail is slippery after a rain. In summer, take lots of water as the entire trail is in full sun in the afternoon.

Photo advice: The Fisher Towers look their best in late afternoon. If you hike the entire trail, start in mid-afternoon in summer or shortly after mid-day in the wintertime. Plan on being back before sunset to shoot the red monoliths from short social trails near the parking area or from pullouts on UT-128.

Better yet, you can get an excellent shot of the Towers from the river with a medium to long telephoto lens. To get this shot, continue north on UT-128 for about 3¾ miles after the turnoff to the Fisher Towers and park at the official pullout on the left, shortly past the cattle guard. Although there are other pullouts, I find this one to be the best. The BLM has built a short ramp leading to a slightly elevated platform with just the right angle for an awesome view of the distant Towers and the La Sal mountains in the background. Getting the reflection of the Towers on the Colorado River is another matter: You need to cautiously descend to the edge of the river, about 450 feet upstream from the ramp, and shoot from there. When the river is low, look for a flat rock near the bank to put your tripod legs on. A polarizing filter is helpful in controlling the amount of reflection. Be there about 45 minutes before sunset to minimize the shadows at the bottom of the Towers and on the Colorado River. The Towers glow an astonishing bright red just before sunset. The high contrast is even better in winter and spring, when the La Sals are capped with snow.

Some local photographers have also produced beautiful shots of the Fisher Towers with a full moon in the background. If you shoot the Towers just before they are in shadow, you can keep the exposure within a couple of f/stops over the entire picture and get a perfectly exposed moon in the deep blue sky.

Getting there: At the north end of Moab, just before the bridge, take UT-128 and drive 21 miles northeast from US-191 (or 5½ miles past the Castle Valley turnoff) along the Colorado River. The 2.2-mile track leading towards the Fisher Towers trailhead is marked and generally in good condition for passenger cars.

Time required: About 1½ hours for a short hike; 4 hours including the described hike and pre-sunset shot by the river.

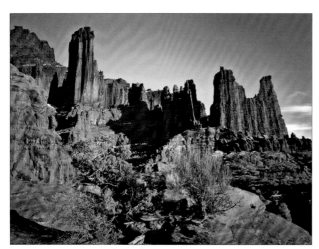

The Fisher Towers at sunset

Nearby location: If you've got a high-clearance vehicle, try a 1-hour foray by car into beautiful Onion Creek Canyon, following a perennial stream just south of the Fisher Towers. This is an outstanding backway, extremely scenic and with a high fun factor as you'll be crossing and recrossing the creek about two dozen times in shallow waters. The canyon gets quite narrow after a couple of miles and you'll find yourself constantly looking up at the impossibly red sandstone walls and tall spires. Drive almost 7 miles to where the canyon opens up into a valley and return the same way. This dirt road is well signed on UT-128, about 20 miles from US-191 and less than 1 mile before the Fisher Towers turnoff. I suggest that you do this drive prior to visiting the Fisher Towers to avoid the narrow canyon being totally in shadow and to reserve the late afternoon light for the Towers.

The Entrada Bluffs

At the burnt-down Dewey Bridge, about 30 miles from the beginning of UT-128 near Moab, a well-maintained dirt and gravel road leads to the Entrada Bluffs area, providing scenic views along the way. For those with time on their hands, a 4WD vehicle, and adequate driving skills, two rough 4WD roads lead south to a couple of spectacular viewpoints over the Colorado River and surrounding canyons. A topo map is essential for these two drives.

Getting there: From the south end of Dewey Bridge, drive southeast for 1.3 miles on the well-graded Entrada Bluffs Road leading to the Kokopelli Bike Trail and angle right on the faint 4WD track leading toward the electric poles. This road is known as the Pole Rim Trail; it leads in about 5 miles to a dead-end, close to the rim above the Colorado River. The main challenge is a steep ascent about ½ mile from the beginning, followed by an even steeper drop-off on slickrock. This is actually more scary than it looks, because traction is good in dry weather. If you can clear this obstacle, you should have no problem the rest of the way. Follow the road as it appears on the topo map. At the point where the road angles sharply northwest, make sure you don't stray off the main track or you could find yourself in a cul-de-sac. You can actually drive another ¼ mile past the point where the road ends on the topo. From here, walk north off-trail for about

20 to 30 minutes to avoid the higher cliffs obscuring the view of the Fisher Towers. Find here a suitable foreground for a terrific shot of the Colorado River with the Richardson Amphitheater, the Fisher Towers and the La Sal Mountains in the background.

After returning to the Entrada Bluffs Road, turn right, continuing toward the Kokopelli Bike Trail. About 4 miles past the turnoff to Pole Rim Trail (or about 5.3 miles from Dewey Bridge), you'll find a dirt road to your

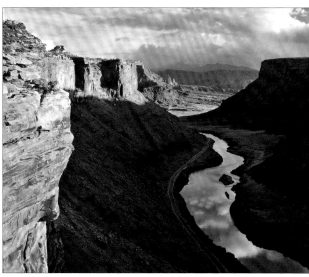

Pole Rim view © Denis Savouray

right. This rough 4WD high-clearance road leads southward in about 4 miles to the ledge of Top of the World Mesa. As its name suggests, this location offers a superb panoramic view above Professor Valley and the east side of the Fisher Towers. The view from the ledge is quite reminiscent of what you see from the end of the Fisher Towers trail, albeit somewhat behind the Titan and the Towers proper.

Photo advice: The second part of the afternoon works best to photograph the Colorado River from Pole Rim; you may need an ND Grad filter if the light is bright. Top of the World is best in the early morning because in late afternoon you'll be shooting against the light.

Faux Falls

A very photogenic waterfall in the Moab vicinity, Faux Falls is so-named because it is entirely man-made (the project was completed in the early 1980's). Man-made or not, the appearance is remarkably natural and the combination of water and red rock is very appealing. The water creating the falls is channeled from Mill Creek through a pipeline, ending up in Kens Lake (actually just a reservoir) which you'll pass to your left along the way.

Photo advice: Be there at least one hour prior to sunset because the sun disappears quickly behind the Moab Rim. The juxtaposition of the background rocks and the falls is the prime attraction, but there are also some nice cascades below the main falls. The best light for Faux Falls is in late afternoon. By all means, avoid the week-ends, especially in summer. Wildflowers may be present during springtime along with the strongest flow of water. Speaking of flow, you should inquire about it in Moab before driving to Faux Falls. In a dry year, Faux Falls may be totally devoid of water. On my last trip there, I saw two mountain goats so you may want to keep a telephoto handy.

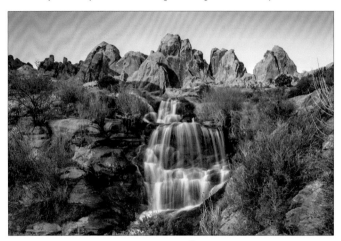

Faux Falls

Getting there: From Moab at Kane Creek Blvd. (where McDonald's is located), drive south on US-191 for approximately 7.2 miles and turn left (east) at the sign for the La Sal Mountain Loop Road. Drive 0.5 mile and turn right (south) on Spanish Valley Road continuing for 0.6 mile to a fork; follow the left (east) branch for 0.8 mile and turn onto Kens Lake Road on the left (east). Continue on this road for 1 mile, passing the first campground entrance, and at the next fork make a left. Drive another 0.2 mile and soon after passing the second campground entrance, take the spur road heading to your left with a sign "Trail to the Falls" and follow it for 0.4 miles to the trailhead at 38°28'49" 109°24'46". This last stretch has been improved in recent years and is now drivable by passenger cars, with caution. The main falls are only 200 yards distant on a good trail with a gentle climb, and are easily noticeable from the trailhead.

Time required: A couple of hours there and back from Moab.

The La Sal Mountain Loop

This great 62-mile loop from Moab offers a remarkable variety of landscapes, from alpine mountains to canyons. Along the 36-mile section between US-191 and UT-128, a number of viewpoints let you photograph the summits, the pine forests, the canyons above Moab, and the Moab fault in the background. It's hard to beat that. The loop rejoins the Colorado Riverway just past the lovely little community of Castle Valley, at the foot of the towering monoliths of Castle Rock and the Priest and the Nuns.

Photo advice: The preferred route is from the south, as the descent into Castle Valley is spectacular. The view of Castle Valley from a viewpoint 19.6 miles from US-191 is best in the afternoon, when the Priest & the Nuns are getting very good light. This trip can be combined with a late afternoon arrival at the Fisher Towers (see section by that name).

Getting there: From Moab at Kane Creek Blvd., drive 7.2 miles south on US-191 to catch the clearly marked loop on the left. From the north, take UT-128 just before the bridge over the Colorado River and drive almost 16 miles to the Castle Valley sign, where you turn right. The road is entirely paved, but the upper part of the loop is closed or impassable in winter.

Time required: At least 2½ hours for the complete loop.

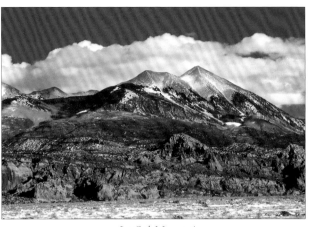

La Sal Mountains

Tukuhnikivats Arch

Tukuhnikivats Arch is an outstanding little arch, located at the southern tip of the area called Behind the Rocks, southeast of Moab. It has a very unusual square shape on one side and a rather rough texture. It makes a great photo, framing the La Sal Mountains in the background. On your way to the arch, you'll pass on the left side of the track some outstanding fins and beehives of Entrada sandstone, in the shape of conical skulls.

Photo advice: A wide-angle lens is required to frame the arch completely, as there is very little room to walk around it. Don't go ultrawide or the La Sal Mountains will appear very small in the background. This is an excellent sunrise and late afternoon location.

Getting there: Follow US-191 south for 12.3 miles from Kane Creek Blvd. in Moab. You'll come across a dirt road leading off to the right. Watch out as this dirt road is not posted on US-191 and is easy to miss. However, there is a small sign on the road itself indicating Pritchett Arch and a large signpost with a topo map of the area can be found a bit further.

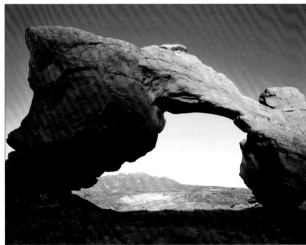

Lovely Tukuhnikivats Arch © Denis Savouray

The road soon branches at 0.4 mile, with the left fork going toward Pritchett Arch as well as the northern section of Behind the Rocks. Take the right fork and head north for about 1.2 miles. When the dirt road begins to bear left, look to your right for a spur track heading north. Unless you drive a rugged 4WD—a must for this very rough track—park here. Follow the track toward the north for about 1.2 miles until it ends. Looking northwest, spot the small opening of Tukuhnikivats Arch (38°27'17" 109°27'10") high on your left. It looks very small from the bottom, but don't let this discourage you; it's not that small once you're there. The trail becomes very steep in the last 300 yards and could be dangerous if you hike alone.

Time required: 2½ hours round-trip from US-191.

Nearby location: See an arch without leaving your car? Easy enough. About 25 miles south from downtown Moab, you'll find Wilson Arch right next to US-191. But if you want to climb to the arch to admire the beautiful view of the Abajo Mountains, prepare yourself for a rough ascent (about 150 feet of elevation gain in just 600 feet of trail). The descent on the slippery slickrock is even more difficult. Be extremely cautious and wear shoes with good traction. Sunrise and early morning is the best time to photograph the arch and get a nice red glow under its span. Mid to late afternoon works too but the arch is going to be directly lit.

The Olympic Torch

The Olympic Torch, a.k.a. Elvis' Hammer, is a spectacularly tall hoodoo, perched at the edge of a deep valley off the Porcupine Ridge.

The Torch is visible from Sand Flats Road as you come from Moab, but it is

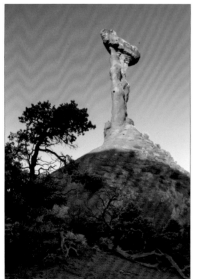

not its best side. From the road, it looks massive and rather mundane—one more big rock in a land of many. But climb to get close to it and it reveals a delicate profile that sets it apart.

The hike to the Torch is not easy for several reasons: It is never in sight during your ascent, which makes finding it a bit tentative the first time; brush and low branches force you to take many detours; and there is a deep depression, not visible from the road, preventing you from following a straight route.

This is not a shoot you should try alone if you have little experience with route finding. Although I provide GPS waypoints, do not rely exclusively on these. Study your map, look at the terrain ahead of you, and have a good idea of where the Torch is hiding before you leave.

The Olympic Torch

There is no trailhead. Start at 38°34'52" 109°22'18" aiming for 38°34'44" 109°22'25" to ensure that you will safely bypass the deep depression to the west. You now have line of sight to the high point on the route, at 38°34'43" 109°22'30", from where you finally see the torch about 300 yards away. On your way back, you can make a short detour and climb the left arm of a small circular bowl at 38°34'42" 109°22'16'. Stretching to look to your left, you get an interesting angle on a formation I call the Elephant Man.

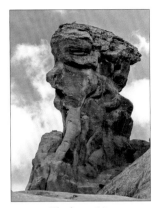

Elephant Man

Photo advice: The Torch is best photographed in the early morning. Sunrise light reaches the Torch quite late, so you'll be fine if you arrive a tad after sunrise. There isn't much scouting to be done; just find a spot less than 200 feet east of the torch.

Getting there: From Milt's Stop & Eat on 4th E St., drive 12.5 miles on Sand Flats Road. There is no fee if you tell the guard you are just passing through for a day hike up in the mountains. Find a spot where you can safely park near the starting point, making sure you are completely off the road and the ground is solid under your car

Time required: 2½ to 3 hours round-trip from your car; add about 45 minutes each way for the drive.

Nearby location: Castle Valley Overlook offers a great view of the entire Castle Valley from the Porcupine Rim, including Round Mountain, the great monoliths of the Parriott Mesa, the Priest & Nuns, as well as the Book Cliffs in the distance. To reach the overlook, continue on Sand Flats Rd. for 1.1 miles then turn left on the overlook road for another 0.6 mile to the car park. The last thousand feet are very rough; unless you have 4WD, I suggest you park there and walk.

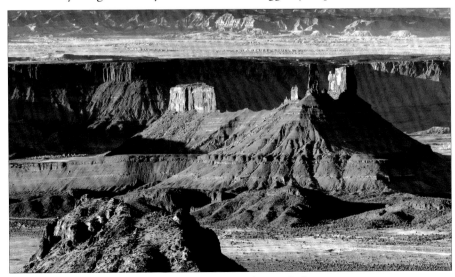

Castle Valley from the Overlook

Along Kane Creek

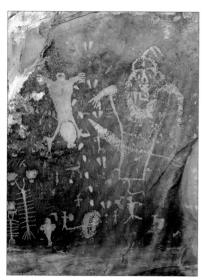

The Birthing Scene

Kane Creek Road runs parallel to Potash road for a while, on the opposite bank of the Colorado River, before making the transition from paved to graded. It offers a number of sites that are either next to the road or accessible without too much effort. There are three very popular sites. The first one you encounter is Moonflower Canyon, a wide panel with a large number of glyphs from different eras. Much of the art has suffered decades of damage at the hand of vandals, but I still would include it in this short tour for the sake of a single anthropomorph, quite elegant in its simplicity with its triangular shape and head ornament. This individual glyph offers a good representation of the Barrier Canyon Style and can be somewhat isolated in a photograph.

The second one is the Birthing Scene, a striking panel with wonderfully whimsical characters. I particularly love the post-Barrier style anthropomorph next to the creature giving birth.

The third one is the beautiful Owl panel, consisting of several petroglyphs including a large armless anthropomorph and an owl with a surprisingly modern shape. It requires an easy hike and a bit of a climb on loose rock, but nothing drastic. From the trailhead, follow the 4WD/mountain bike track down to the wash and up on the other side. At the end of the second switchback, 0.5 mile into the hike, locate the trail ascending the gully in a northerly direction below the cliff. It's easy to find and the climb is not difficult. Once you reach the ledge, circumnavigate the edge of the cliff and walk east along the ledge until you reach the panel, at about 0.8 mile from the start. For your safety and to avoid getting lost, I recommend that you spot the panel from the trailhead before starting your

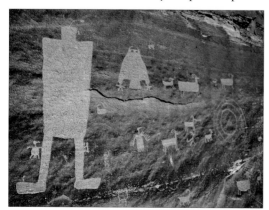

The Owl panel

hike; the large anthropomorph is visible to the naked eye, although quite small, to the left of a huge, but shallow alcove, looking northeast.

There is of course plenty more rock art on the walls, side canyons, and boulders surrounding Kane Creek, some of it quite beautiful, much of it of a confidential nature and beyond the scope of this book. Further information can be found from sources on the web if you are a serious rock art aficionado.

After returning from the Owl panel, drive another 7 easy miles, following Kane Spring canyon, before ascending a rougher road (high-clearance SUV required) for another 1.7 miles to Hurrah Pass. From this high vantage point, you can enjoy nice views of the Colorado River and the Potash basins.

Photo advice: A wide to standard lens is adequate, but I shot the Owl picture with a super wide.

Getting there: From the McDonald's on South Main St. in Moab, drive 0.8 mile on Kane Creek Blvd. to the junction with 500 West. Go left at the stop sign and continue 2.3 miles to Moonflower Canyon. The site is on the side of the road. For the Birthing Scene, continue another 2.9 miles, park at the nearest pullout (additional pullouts are available further up), and walk back down to 38°31'19" 109°36'9.5". Glyphs are carved on all sides of the large boulder located a few feet below the road, creek-side.

The starting point for the Owl panel is the trailhead for the Amasa Back/ Cliffhanger 4WD and mountain bike trail. You could leave your car at one of the Birthing Scene pullouts 0.2 mile further, or sooner at the large official parking area for loading/unloading bikes and ATVs for the Amasa Back Trail, but it involves an additional 1 mile walk round-trip along the road to get to the Amasa Back trailhead. If you have 4WD, you could park directly at the trailhead, but be warned that it's a severe incline with some loose rocks and there is very little room to maneuver.

Time required: From downtown Moab, 1½ hours for a whirlwind visit of the first two sites; 3 to 4 hours including the Owl panel, and at least 1½ hours more if going up Hurrah Pass.

Around Monitor & Merrimac

This section covers a large swath of land west of US-191 and on either side of UT-331. The latter is the road leading to the Island in the Sky district of Canyonlands National Park from US-191 (see chapter by that name), about 8.3 miles from the Colorado River Bridge north of Moab. I chose to name the section after Monitor & Merrimac Buttes for two reasons: their location is more or less at the center of our area of interest, and the fact that they are a well-known landmark that anybody who has been to Island in the Sky will immediately remember.

Let's begin with the buttes proper. Monitor & Merrimac are the two very large monoliths you can observe as you drive toward Island in the Sky on UT-331. You'll find the signed viewpoint as you come out of the second hairpin, about 4.5 miles from the junction with US-191. The buttes are quite a startling view the first time one lays eyes on them, but somehow despite the grandiose view they don't make for a good composition, even with a telephoto. You have to get closer.

If you want solitude and have routefinding experience, you can hike your way cross-country to either butte, starting from the north fork of Seven Mile

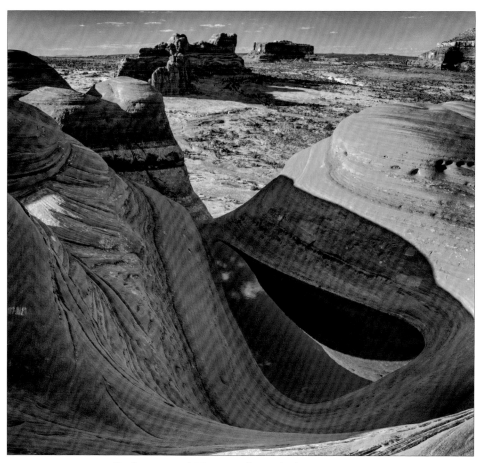

Looking toward Merrimac from a high vantage point

Canyon. Drive back 1.3 mile from the official viewpoint and park at a pullout on the south side of UT-331 next to a cattle guard. Walk down 100 feet east to the culvert and cross to the north side under the highway. Coming from US-191 on UT-331, drive 3.2 miles to the pullout by the fence and boulders on the north side of the road. The wash is not accessible from this side of the road; you must cross the highway and take the culvert to reach the north fork.

If you have a 4WD SUV and don't mind a lot of mountain bikes, ATVs, and Jeeps, you can reach Merrimac Butte with a bit of cautious driving. The track starts from signed Mill Canyon Road on the west side of US-191, about 4.4 miles north of the UT-331 turnoff. There is an excellent orientation panel showing roads and trails for the whole area.

From this point, it is about 4 miles to the photogenic Determination Towers, and another 1.4 miles to the western base of Merrimac Butte. Park here and walk around. A lot of 4-wheelers and bikers come here to tackle a favorite spot called Wipeout Hill, so it could be busy, but it's the best spot to photograph both buttes together.

Back on UT-331, about 2.7 miles from the junction with US-191, park on a pullout along the north side of the road and follow a social trail to the rock wall. Look for the small, intricate Intestine Man pictograph. It is high on the wall and hard to spot, especially in bright sunshine.

This pullout is also the trailhead for the south fork of Seven Mile Canyon. The south fork offers a long but easy hike inside a wide sandy wash, with some good rock

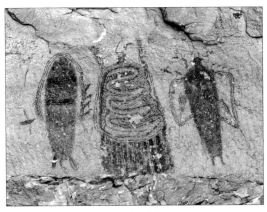

Intestine Man

art. Binoculars will help spotting the art which is sometimes high on the cliff side and hard to see.

The Gemini Bridges are a unique natural landmark that's worth seeing in the vicinity if you have a 4WD SUV to drive the 7.6 miles to the trailhead on Gemini Bridges Road, which begins 1.2 miles south of UT-331 on US-191. There is an easy 0.2 mile foot trail from the car park to the Bridges. Unfortunately there is no worthwhile shot from the rim. From the top, you can marvel at the gaping hole between the bridges, but there is no photograph there. You can skirt around the rim to the left, descend to a promontory, and shoot the one bridge closest to the canyon, but it fails to show the two bridges. Still I recommend that you see the Bridges from the top and enjoy the easy, rather crowded loop road.

For a more interesting view from below, drive 3.6 miles on the signed Bull Canyon trail, which leaves from the Gemini Bridges Road 5.3 miles from US-191 (about 2.3 miles east of the Gemini Bridges car park).

Perhaps the most photogenic feature accessible from the Gemini Bridges road is a tall spire called The Bride, as well as other spires at the end of Bride Canyon. The spur to Bride Canyon is about 4 miles from US-191, a little before the Gooney Rock landmark. The car park for the spires is about 0.6 mile up canyon.

Getting there: In addition to the indication I'm providing, I recommend you carry a GPS (preferably a tablet and a topo App) and one of the excellent 4WD trail guidebooks for the area.

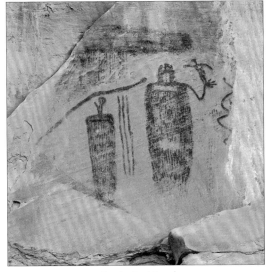

Snake in Mouth

The Secret Spire

There is nothing secret about the Secret Spire. It has been a classic destination for novice 4-wheelers for decades, and for good reason: it is a spectacular

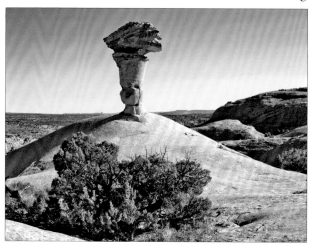

formation and an easy drive on a very good road, making for a fun outing in late afternoon. The area is quite remote and sees few people outside of week-ends and the main 4x4 jamborees, adding to the enjoyment of the place.

Photo advice: Morning and afternoon will work, with a preference for the afternoon when the spire's best side is lit. For a more creative alternative to the classic view, I suggest framing the spire

The Secret Spire

through a tiny little arch on the small knoll just east of the spire.

Getting there: From the Colorado River Bridge north of Moab, drive about 8.3 miles northbound on US-191 and take UT-313 toward Island in the Sky for about 8.5 miles. Turn right on a wide dirt road and right again after 1.5 miles, continuing for 5 miles to a Y. Take the left fork. After 2 miles, the road skirts around the southern tip of a spectacular promontory called The Needles and a large squat mesa comes into view to reassure you that you are on the right track. Continue another 2.6 miles past The Needles, ignoring a couple of spur roads to your right, to an obvious pullout on your left (38°41'20" 109°57'35"). Under normal conditions, the entire dirt section should be passable by a passenger car driven cautiously, but an SUV is recommended. From the car park, walk south and follow the 4WD track. If you have 4WD, you can get a bit closer to the spire, which is at 38°40'60" 109°57'47", but there is a lot of slickrock to cross and it's only a short ½-mile walk, anyway.

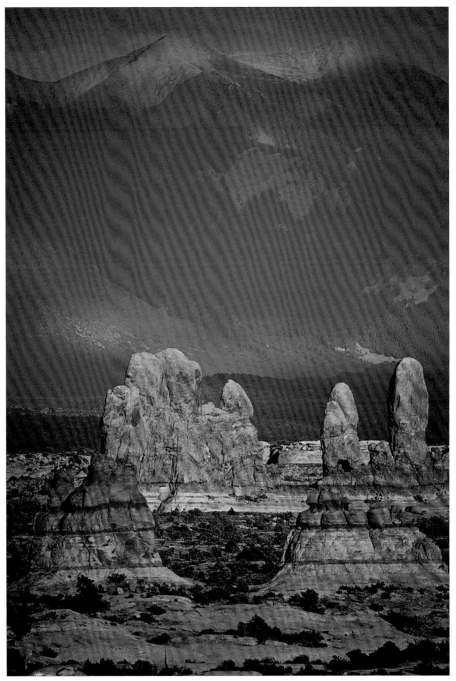

Pillars of the Earth

Chapter 14

ARCHES NATIONAL PARK

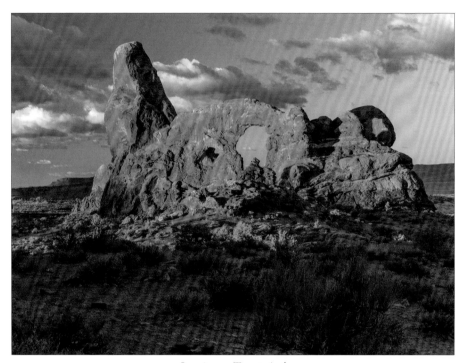

Sunrise on Turret Arch

Introduction to Arches National Park

Almost everything has been written about Arches National Park in traditional guidebooks. What more can be said? That it's only been forty years since it was an isolated and little visited spot? That there was only a simple dirt track when Edward Abbey was a ranger here and wrote his seminal work, Desert Solitaire? Today, you're practically assured of finding a crowd rivaling that of the Grand Canyon, especially during the summer and on weekends.

Located just 5 miles north of downtown Moab, this relatively small National Park is incredibly spectacular and exercises a particular attraction on visitors from all over the world, not only for its extraordinary concentration of arches, but also for its fantastic monoliths and fins with the La Sal Mountains in the background. The park can be visited year-round, but spring and fall are the best seasons. Summer is very hot and the long hours of bright sunshine make it difficult to photograph the park. Winter can be magical after a fresh dusting of snow.

It's possible to see the main sights in one day, as the very scenic paved road is only a 45-mile round-trip, including short side attractions. However, you should spend at least two days in the park if you want to do most of the rewarding hikes and photograph the highlights at the best time of day. The park is open 24 hours a day, so you'll have no problem being in the field before sunrise or for a moonlight walk, even if you stay in Moab instead of the park's campground.

Park Avenue & the Courthouse Towers

After driving 2.2 miles up the high cliff past the Visitor Center and taking in the spectacular view of the Moab Fault, the Park Avenue viewpoint will be your first contact with the unique landscape of Arches Nat'l Park. The best light is in mid-morning or from mid-afternoon on. It is fun to shoot Nefertiti's Head and its beacon-like neighbor on top of the west cliff with a long telephoto. Where the 1-mile trail, pleasantly descending between the high walls of Park Avenue, meets the main Park road at the Courthouse Towers viewpoint, you'll find the very photogenic Three Gossips. Nearby, the Courthouse Towers is in shadow from early spring to early summer. However, that's also the season when wildflowers appear in front of the butte called "The Organ" for a glorious photo made famous by Tom Till and many times imitated.

Nearby location: The Petrified Dunes are interesting Navajo sandstone formations, located close to the road and offering photogenic compositions, provided you're there at the right time.

Before sunrise, park at the Petrified Dunes pullout, 2.4 miles past the Courthouse Towers viewpoint, and walk in the direction of the dunes. Once there, walk a little bit more into the heart of the dunes or until you come to a spot that seems picturesque and where you can't see your car. The sun rises behind the La Sal Mountains and directly lights the Great Wall, a series of rock faces several miles long that glow bright red with the appearance of the first sun rays. You can photograph these red walls with the petrified dunes in the foreground. Although less vital in the digital age, a graduated neutral density filter is helpful in preserving detail on the dunes, while still correctly exposing the walls.

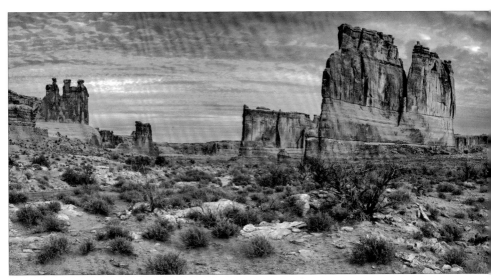

Courthouse Towers at dawn

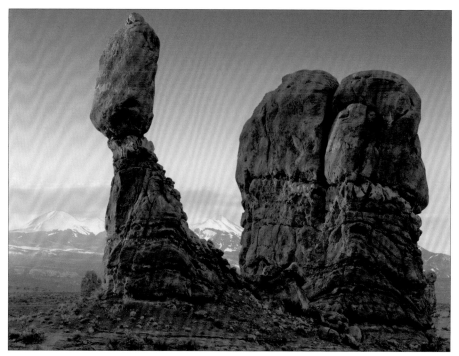

First light on Balanced Rock

Balanced Rock

Often photographed, always beautiful, Balanced Rock is a geological rebel, defying the unstoppable forces of erosion. Unfortunately, it is bound to lose its fight at some point and be toppled over like the rest. This will undoubtedly happen very soon in geological time and could even happen soon in our own narrow human scale of time. So, don't wait. Record its beauty for the sake of your children, before it disappears forever! Balanced Rock is located about 9 miles from the Visitor Center. You can see it close up by walking the ¼-mile loop.

Photo advice: You can shoot it at close range with a wide-angle lens, but I prefer the other side of the road using a medium range zoom, isolating it against a back-

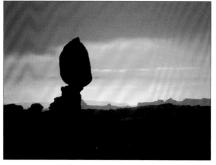

drop of the La Sal Mountains. Sunrise or late afternoon are best. Night photos under a full moon give great results and are fun to shoot. From this spot, I also like to shoot the tall pillars located near the Windows, using a long telephoto (see photo on chapter's front page). There is also a good shot of Balanced Rock at sunset from the intersection of the Windows and Garden of Eden roads, also with a powerful telephoto.

Balanced Rock at dusk

Eye of the Whale

Eye of the Whale is an interesting side trip. From the main park road at Balanced Rock, turn left (west) onto the Willow Flats Road. After 0.8 mile, turn right on the spur road and continue 1.9 miles to the trailhead on your left. A high-clearance vehicle is required on this road. Walk to the arch on the well-trod ¼-mile sandy trail and ascend it from the right side. From below the glowing

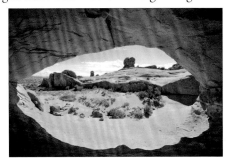

red span, you'll need an ultra-wide lens to capture the entire arch opening with the first ridge of Herdina Park in the background. There is an almost permanent draft blowing through the opening of the arch: erosion in progress. To understand how the arch got its name, you'll need to descend on the other side and walk to the sandy hill. You'll then discover the oblong shape of the cetacean eyelid with the eye looking back at you.

Eye of the Whale

The Windows

This section of the park has a series of impressive arches that are easy to reach. From the parking area at the end of a 2½-mile side road, start your walk in the direction of Turret Arch and the North and South Windows. Near the South Window, a spur trail lets you make a loop around the backside of the Windows; very few people use it and it's a real place for photography. Unfortunately, one can no longer shoot the iconic photo of Turret Arch at sunrise, framed within North Window's opening, as access to the viewpoint is currently off-limits. Continuing past Turret Arch and South Window, you'll come to a group of very interesting monoliths.

Back at the parking area, walk or drive to the Double Arch car park, from where you can walk right under the twin spans of this monumental arch.

If you are lucky enough to be at Arches in summer during the full moon, a midnight walk around this section of the park can be very rewarding. The heat radiating from the ground and currents of cool air mix in a delicious swirl around you

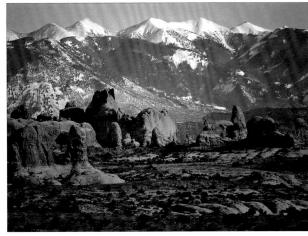

The Windows in winter

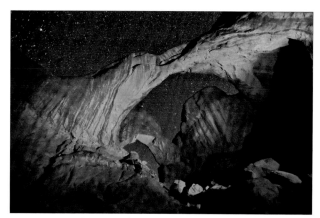

Double Arch & night sky © Charles Wood

and the rock formations of the Windows take on a fantastic quality.

Time required: About 1½ hours.

Nearby location: On a short side road off the main road, Panorama Point provides a bird's-eye view of a good deal of the park, very lovely at the end of day, but too vast to be photographed with much success. You can, however, get a good morning view of Balanced Rock and also of the Devil's Garden with a medium range zoom or long telephoto.

Wolfe Ranch Petroglyphs

Most visitors stopping at the Wolfe Ranch parking area are anxious to be on their way to Utah's most prominent of icons: Delicate Arch. Few visitors go out of their way to look at these almost modern petroglyphs. This is sad, because it is an interesting panel.

The small but well-preserved panel illustrated the way of life of local Ute tribes. Bighorn sheep, horses and riders are featured prominently on the panel. It is easy to assume that tribal artists endeavored to represent scenes of hunting.

Photo advice: The panel is well lit and surrounded by vegetation. I find it beautiful, because of its simplicity, and a perfect subject for imaginative photography. The immediate area surrounding the mural is cordoned off, but the panel is close enough for standard lens or short telephoto photography.

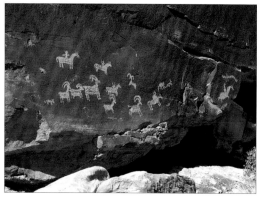

Ute petroglyphs at Wolfe Ranch

Getting there: At the Delicate Arch parking area, about 1.2 miles east of the main park road, follow the main trail past Wolfe Ranch. After a hundred yards or so, you'll come to a small wooden bridge. Immediately after the bridge, you'll find a small trail to the left. Follow it for another 200 yards until the panel comes to view. You can continue on this trail to meet the Delicate Arch trail.

Delicate Arch

Arches National Park, and the State of Utah, wouldn't be the same without the extraordinary symbol of Delicate Arch. What sets this arch apart is not its size, but its incredibly graceful shape and stunning location above a curving slickrock basin with the La Sal Mountains in the background.

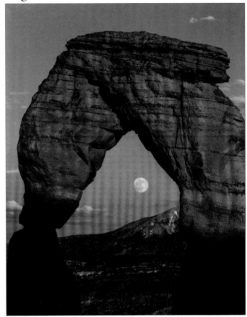

Delicate Arch is not so easy to get to and that's just as well because it somewhat limits foot traffic, which is already very high. You can reach it by taking a trail that's about a 3 mile round-trip, half of which is marked by the footprints of previous visitors on the slickrock as well as by strategically-placed cairns. Though it may be easy to climb to Delicate Arch during the day—count on about 45 minutes one way—exercise extreme caution when descending after sundown and bring a flashlight. It's easy to take a bad fall if you tend to shuffle along and not lift your feet sufficiently.

Visiting Delicate Arch in the middle of the day is not advised. This is partly because the climb is quite hard and can be strenuous if the temperature is high, but also because the arch doesn't reveal all its splendor until late afternoon. In any case, Delicate Arch is the perfect hike to end your day in the park.

Delicate Arch at sunset © Tom Till

Photo advice: The best season for photographing Delicate Arch is winter, when the arch is entirely basked in sunset. Also, you'll have fewer people walking by or parking themselves in front of the arch, as is often the case in the other seasons. In late spring, a small amount of shadow becomes visible at the bottom and by July, half of the arch is in shadow at sunset. Keep this in mind and don't arrive too late so you can avoid that nasty black shadow, even if you have to settle for less red on the arch. In summer, you'll be better off leaving the trailhead at least 1½ hours before sunset. You can get information at the Visitor

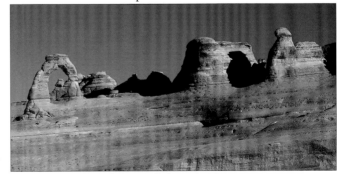

Delicate Arch from the Viewpoint

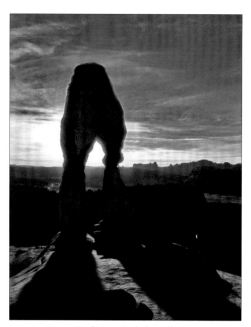

Delicate Arch backlit

Center or in town as to when the sun will set and then determine the best time to climb to it. There aren't many angles to use at sunset. Backlit shots taken from the extreme left of the arch aren't very satisfactory and the view directly down the axis of the arch is only suitable for family photos. The best vantage point is from the edge of the rock ledge encircling the arch, where the trail comes out. Try positioning yourself so that the highest peaks of the La Sal Mountains are profiled on the horizon between the base and the summit of the arch, a height of about forty feet. The peaks are frequently adorned with a rosy veil during the last moments of sunset when the arch is lit up in red. If you can, stay a while after sunset to capture the residual lighting in the clouds and just to appreciate this sublime spectacle while the rest of the crowd hurries toward the parking area.

Nearby location: Past the Delicate Arch trailhead at Wolfe Ranch, the road continues for one mile to a distant viewpoint of Delicate Arch. It's quite interesting to go there to see how precariously the arch rests on the plateau. You reach the upper viewpoint at the end of a moderately difficult 1-mile round-trip trail. This hike should preferably be made before mid-afternoon, otherwise the arch will be in shadow. The view of the arch and the cirque from the ridge, with a 200-foot drop-off below you, is startling. From here, a medium range zoom will isolate the arch perfectly. A wide-angle lens is necessary for a panoramic view of the cirque.

The Fiery Furnace

About 2.5 miles past the Delicate Arch road turn-off, on the east side of the main park road, the huge sandstone fins of the Fiery Furnace form a maze of confusing narrow canyons and dead-ending passageways, with a number of arches peppered here and there to make things even more interesting. Notwithstanding the biblical reference that the early Mormon pioneers might have found appropriate, the Fiery Furnace gets its name, as you might have guessed, from the fiery red glow of reflected light on the narrow passageways between the fins. Ironically, the Fiery Furnace is the coolest place to be in Arches when it's hot, because you're almost constantly walking in the shade and there is always a light draft running through it.

Hiking the Fiery furnace is not easy: you must climb uneven sandstone, walk along narrow ledges above drop-offs, use hands and feet to scramble through narrow cracks. Nevertheless, it can be done by anyone in reasonably good physical condition. As many individual hikers have gotten lost or injured in this labyrinth over the years, I strongly recommend that you join a

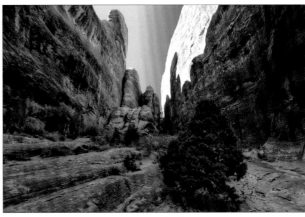

Between the fins

guided walk. It's easy to lose your way—there are no cairns and GPS units are unlikely to produce a reliable track—so first-timers, people with a poor sense of direction, anybody not endowed with a good memory of places they've been to, and those who are not comfortable hiking on rough terrain should definitely sign up for the Ranger-led visit. Nevertheless, it is possible to venture alone into this area after buying a permit at the Visitor Center (up to seven days in advance) and following a 20-minute video orientation, but you'll miss several interesting highlights. During the guided tour, the Park Ranger will show you hidden arches, such as Surprise Arch and Skull Arch, and explain basic facts concerning the geology and ecology of the park, such as the difference between an arch and a bridge, Entrada and Navajo sandstone, and the usefulness of cryptobiotic crust.

You'll need a reservation for the Ranger-led tour. Tours are led twice a day from mid-March to late-November, weather permitting, with groups limited to twenty people. Except in November, when tickets can be bought at the Visitor Center, reservations can only be made online on the www.recreation.gov web site,

up to six months in advance and at least four days before the date of the hike. Be sure to reserve weeks in advance as this is a popular activity across all age groups. If you don't have a reservation, check for potential cancellations at the desk; you might not get one for the same day, but if you are in the Moab area for a little while and your schedule is flexible, you might nab one for a few days later. If your attempt

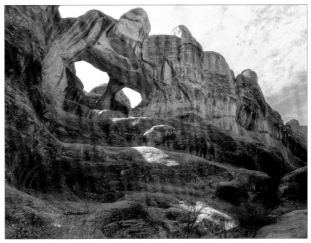

Skull Rock in Fiery Furnace

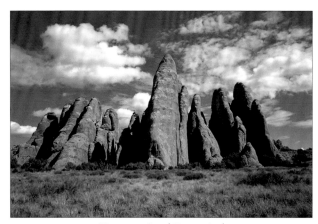

Fins near Sand Dune Arch

to secure a reservation for the Ranger-led hike was not successful, note that a few Moab outfitters are authorized to offer a similar guided tour. You'll pay a premium, but you'll also stand a better chance of finding a spot.

Photo advice: As your group may have as many as twenty bodies who must move together, it is not an ideal situation for photography. However, nothing prevents you from returning on your own the next day, retracing your steps; perhaps an hour before a scheduled guided tour. If everything goes according to plan, you'll have plenty of time to shoot before the group catches up with you. If you get lost or something happens to you, stay put or retrace your steps and wait for the guided tour to arrive.

During the hike inside the Fiery Furnace, don't bother with anything else than a wide-angle! There is often quite a bit more light inside the Furnace than in most slot canyons. If you don't have time to do the guided walk, you can descend for a short distance towards the fins to photograph them with a medium or long telephoto lens and compress the perspective. This works better from late afternoon until sunset. From the parking area, the fins can also form a good foreground with the La Sal Mountains behind them.

Time required: The Ranger-led tour lasts about 3 hours at a relaxed pace and you'll cover a distance of approximately 2 miles.

Sand Dune Arch & Broken Arch

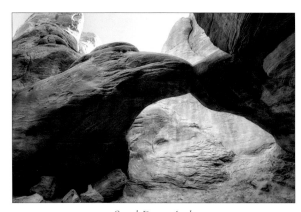

Sand Dune Arch

About 1½ miles before the northern end of the park road, don't miss the very short walk to Sand Dune Arch. It's a peculiar sight, hidden as it is between the walls of huge fins. It is difficult to photograph, but you'll be rewarded along the way by a great shot of a group of symmetrical fins, especially in late afternoon. Broken Arch is also nice and it's an easy flat walk. Consider continuing on the 2-mile loop trail, going through the campground and passing through narrow joints between the fins before returning to the Sand Dune Arch parking area.

The Devil's Garden

Located at the end of the scenic road, about 18 miles from the entrance of the park, the Devil's Garden loop is a real pleasure, arguably one of the most rewarding half-day hikes of the Colorado Plateau. It's a moderately difficult, but spectacular, walk. On your way to superb Double-O Arch, you'll be passing by Pine Tree Arch, Landscape Arch (the longest in the park), and Navajo Arch. Wall Arch is no more, having collapsed in August 2008. Past the spur trail to Navajo Arch, you'll climb high on a narrow ridge providing excellent views of the fins below.

From Double-O Arch, you can do the extension to Dark Angel—a solitary monolith overlooking Salt Valley. Nearby, you can see a little-known but interesting site of Indian petroglyphs. For this short detour, with Dark Angel behind you, walk cross-country toward the southwest for about 700 feet to reach the edge of a low cliff. Exercising caution, find your way along a ramp to the foot of the cliff and follow it to your left, bearing southeast. Look for the petroglyphs that are spread over several hundred yards. Return the way you came.

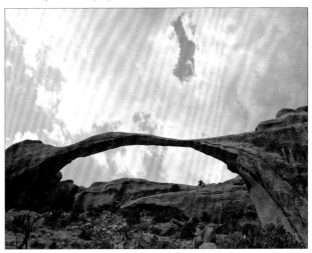

Landscape Arch © Tom Till

Back at Double-O Arch, you can retrace your steps to the trailhead or return by the more difficult Primitive Trail, which is beautiful and less crowded. The Primitive Trail is a cairned route passing through canyons formed by fins and sandstone slabs, with some sections on steeply slanted ground (slippery when wet). Pay close attention to the cairns to avoid getting sidetracked. The whole loop, including all side trails (except the Indian petroglyphs) and returning via the Primitive Trail, is 7.2 miles round-trip. You can shorten the hike by a mile by returning the way you came instead of taking the Primitive Trail. Bring hiking shoes, a hat, and lots of water on this trail. If you want to capture the best light on Landscape Arch and avoid the extreme heat of the day—especially in summer when it's cooking—you should begin the hike early in the morning. If you do it in mid- to late-afternoon, however, you'll have the advantage of good light on the most beautiful side of Double-O Arch and the nearby fins.

Photo advice: The best season to photograph Landscape Arch is in late spring and early summer, when there are no shadows on the arch in early morning. The

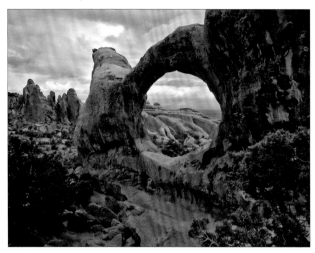

view in complete sunshine is only available in mid-morning during the rest of the year. In 1991, a large block of rock fell from the 306-foot long span of Landscape Arch, causing the National Park Service to close the trail under the arch. The fence, which was put up to prevent people from venturing under the arch, severely limits your ability to frame Landscape Arch artistically. The best vantage point to photograph the arch against a background of sky is at

Double-O Arch

the end of the short spur. Double-O Arch is one of the most spectacular arches in the Southwest. To photograph it, pass through the lower opening of the arch and climb the slickrock on the other side until you find a suitable location. A wide-angle lens is necessary to capture the entire arch. This side is in the shade in the morning and is best lit from mid-afternoon on, as are most of the fins in the Devil's Garden area.

Time required: 4 to 5 hours for the complete loop. Add almost an hour for the detour to the Indian petroglyphs near Dark angel.

The Klondike Bluffs

The Klondike Bluffs area offers a nice easy hiking experience coupled with some great sights and photography, away from the increasing stream of visitors. Outside of the season, it is entirely possible to spend a couple of hours in the Klondike Bluffs and never see a soul.

Although massive Tower Arch gets most of the attention, another striking landmark in the Klondike Bluffs area is the formation group known as the Marching Men, consisting of spires of various thickness and height aligned one behind another, very much like a soldier troop on the march. The pleasant loop from the trailhead near Salt Valley Road is 3.4 miles round-trip and takes at least two hours, depending on the time you devote to photography.

Photo advice: Photography inside the Klondike Bluffs is generally best in late afternoon. To photograph the Marching Men in the best possible light, plan on returning from Tower Arch about 45 minutes before sunset and find a suitable location at the top of the sand dune where all the Marching Men appear in your line of sight from a slightly dominant position. This location requires a short telephoto. Alternately, you can walk down toward the middle of the last sand dune and photograph the group from below with a moderate wide-angle to standard lens.

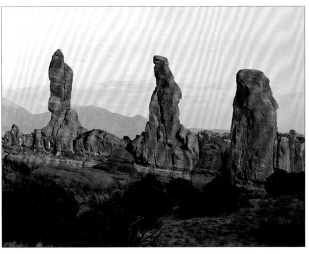

The Marching Men

Getting there: The easiest and most common way is to come via Salt Valley Road; its turnoff is on the main park road, 1 mile before the Devil's Garden area. This dirt road is usually in good condition, although it can be quite sandy in places or even impassable after a rain. After about 7.2 miles, you'll see a first spur road to your left. This sandy 4WD road leads in about 3.3 miles to a parking area very close to Tower Arch. But a nasty ramp needs to be negotiated around mile one. Also, if you use this road, you'll miss the hike through the beautiful scenery of the Bluffs, including the Marching Men. Instead, take the next road to the left (300 feet further), leading in 1 mile to the main trailhead; it is passable by 2WD vehicles. If you came to Tower Arch using the first sandy 4WD road, you'll encounter the Willow Flats 4WD road, returning to the main park road opposite Balanced Rock. Note that this is a very sandy and difficult road. Every year visitors get stuck on it and have to be pulled out.

Returning to Salt Valley Road, it's relatively easy to leave the park by continuing north on this road for 11 miles until the intersection with Thompson Road. Turning left, you'll then reach US-191 in about 1.2 miles and turning right you can reach Thompson in 7½ miles to visit the Sego Canyon rock art site about 3½ miles further (see *Along I-70* chapter). I have driven the northern section of Salt Valley Road in a 4x4 and feel it would

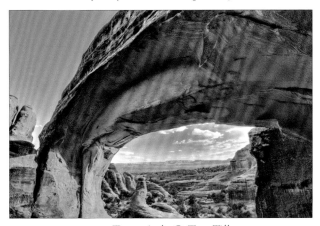

Tower Arch © *Tom Till*

present no difficulties for a high-clearance vehicle in dry weather. As always, get directions in town or at the Visitor Center and find out the exact condition of the road. One good rain could have washed it out.

Nearby location: If you leave the park from the north via Salt Valley and Thompson Road, consider stopping at the Copper Ridge Sauropod Track site. It has some fossil tracks of a brontosaur and carnivores from the Jurassic period, unfortunately difficult to photograph. To get there, leave US-191 at milepost 148.7, about 4 miles south of the Thompson Road turnoff (8½ miles south of Exit 182 on I-70 at Crescent Junction or 20 miles north of the Colorado Bridge near Moab). Cross the railroad tracks on the east side of US-191 and follow the dirt road—suitable for passenger cars in dry weather—for about 2 miles to a parking area. The tracks are about 300 feet up the hill to the east.

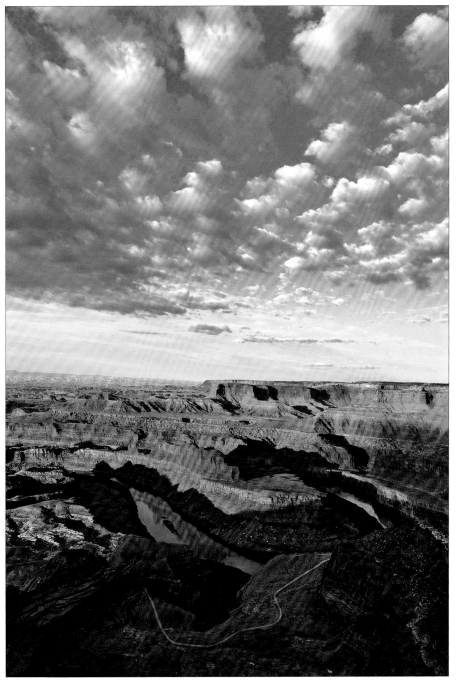

Dead Horse Point sunrise © *Philippe Schuler*

Chapter 15

CANYONLANDS – ISLAND

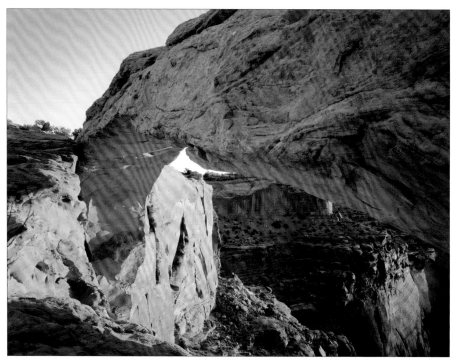

Mesa Arch at sunrise

Introduction to Island in the Sky

I heartily recommend Canyonlands National Park to those who love sweeping canyon panoramas, river goosenecks, outstanding rock formations and wish to escape the Grand Canyon crowds. I have recommended and continue to recommend this park to innumerable visitors. They return unanimous in their opinion that some of the views are as vast and impressive as those of Grand Canyon.

Just thirty years ago, this park received only 10,000 visitors a year and had no paved roads. Today, though not as heavily visited as Arches, it's become a destination of choice for tourists, 4x4 enthusiasts, mountain bikers, hikers and certainly for photographers. Madison Avenue and Hollywood have also discovered it, and you can see it in more and more movies, TV ads and music videos. Let's hope it won't have a negative impact on the park in years to come.

Canyonlands National Park consists of three districts separated by the two rivers merging in its center: the Colorado River and the Green River. Each district has its own distinct flavor: to the north, Island in the Sky and Dead Horse Point form a vast peninsula overlooking the canyons and is easy to visit. To the southeast, the Needles district is particularly remarkable for the diversity of its geological features—pinnacles, arches, grabens and canyons—requiring a lot of hiking or 4-wheeling. To the west, the Maze is wild and desolate and visiting its intricate network of canyons and mesas is only for the most adventurous, with mountain bikes, rugged 4x4 vehicles, or backpacking from the Colorado River.

Lacking bridges on the rivers, these three districts are separated by hours of driving. Just to get a glimpse of the three districts, one needs several days; several visits are a more realistic approach to enjoy some of the many trails. To gain a true perspective of the vastness of the park and understand its geography, geology and diversity, you would need to fly over it. Given the extreme temperatures that affect this region, the best time to visit is undoubtedly spring and the first part of autumn.

Due to the specific character of each of the three districts, as well as the huge distances separating them, each is described under its own chapter. The present chapter concentrates on Island in the Sky which is the most accessible, as well as the most visited, of the three districts in the park. A scenic road provides easy access to expansive views from a high mesa top (reaching 6000 feet of elevation) overlooking dozens of miles of canyon country. This paved road is UT-313, heading southwest 8.3 miles from the river bridge north of Moab. The Visitor Center is located about 21 miles further and the road continues for another 12 miles until it dead-ends at Grand View Point Overlook.

Dead Horse Point State Park

Even if you do not have much time, don't miss Dead Horse Point State Park for an outstanding panorama of the area. This small park, located near the entrance to Canyonlands National Park (Island In The Sky), offers the prototypical view of the American West canyons, as pictured in many ads and movies.

Photo advice: The best location is at Dead Horse Point Overlook, at the very end of the road, a few hundred yards past the narrow neck. It offers two panoramic views: to the southwest, the bend of the Colorado River with its superb mesa at the center and, on the opposite side, a view of the canyons with the La Sal Mountains in the background. From the parking area, the choice of views is limited. Walk on the Rim Trail around the viewpoint and pick a foreground you like which will best show the depth of the canyon and the immensity of the terrain. A moderate wide-angle lens is ideal for the river bend. For the panorama of the canyons and the La Sal Mountains, you can give free rein to your imagination, if you have a zoom. Any focal length will highlight something different. The bend is best photographed in the early morning, with the sun rising on the left, but sunset is equally beautiful. It's also a good idea to photograph the bend before sunrise or after sunset to avoid strong shadows and catch the alpenglow. In fact, it's so awe-inspiring that even mid-day photos can be impressive with a polarizer. On the other hand, for the panorama of the canyons, a morning or evening light is essential to best render depth and contrast. With a bit of luck and patience, the high clouds will be basking in the last gleams of sunset and the snowy peaks of the La Sal Mountains will be a vivid pink. For a slightly different view of the eastern canyons, you can also walk to Basin Overlook, about halfway between Dead Horse Point Overlook and the Visitor Center.

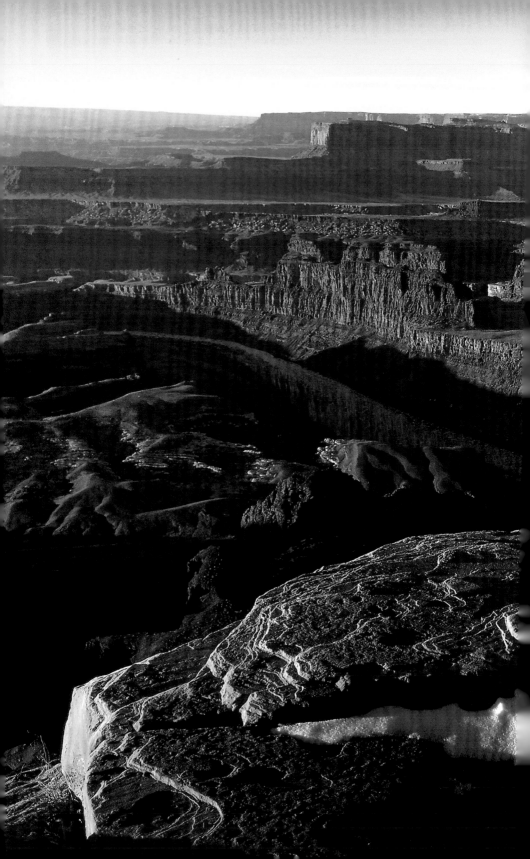

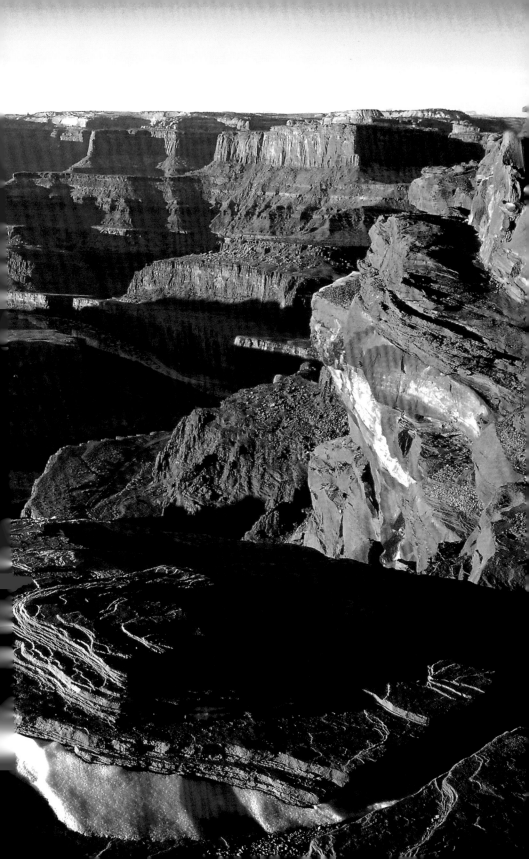

Getting there: The turnoff to Dead Horse Point State Park is on UT-313, 14.6 miles from US-191 and before the entrance to Island in the Sky. From the turn-off, drive 8 miles to Dead Horse Point Overlook at the very end of the road.

Time required: About 1½ hours round-trip to get there from Moab and 1 hour on location. However, you will most likely want to visit this place at the same time as Island in the Sky. The complete circuit of the viewpoints—to Grand View Point, including the side roads—can be done in a long half day at a hurried pace, though that will mean sacrificing taking pictures at either sunrise and/or sunset and missing interesting sites such as Aztec Buttes and False Kiva.

Nearby location: If you have a high-clearance vehicle, you can return to Moab by way of Long Canyon Road and Potash Road (SB-279). You'll find Long Canyon Road 6.3 miles from Dead Horse Point Overlook (or 1.6 miles from UT-313). After a tad over 3 miles on a good gravel road, you reach Pucker Pass, offering a nice open view with the canyons below and the La Sals in the background. From here on, the road becomes rough for about 4.4 miles and somewhat steep in places, as you descend slowly through an impressive landscape of huge sandstone cliffs. At one point, you'll pass under a huge boulder that has fallen from the cliff, forming a sort of arch with just enough room for your SUV to get through. Look for a beautiful horse hoof-shaped arch to the left at the junction with Potash Road. Long Canyon Road is passable most of the time, except after heavy rains; be sure to inquire about its condition at the Visitor Center.

Marlboro Point

Marlboro Point lies in the shadow of Dead Horse Point, at the southern edge of the Big Flat plateau. While the view is nowhere near as panoramic as its world-famous big brother's, it offers a photogenic view over twin spires and a flat butte jutting out between the middle and east forks of Shafer Canyon. Their close proximity places them at a middle point between your foreground (i.e. the rim) and the distant cliffs of Island in the Sky, allowing you to construct a nicely layered photograph with great depth. You can pick several spots along the rim, all within a very short distance, and try a limited variety of compositions as well as different foregrounds, such as white rocks or green vegetation.

Camping is not allowed at the viewpoint proper. However, you're free to camp anywhere else on BLM land, as long as it's away from the road. You can also use the developed alternatives at Dead Horse Point or Willow Flats.

Photo advice: You'll want to shoot Marlboro Point at and before sunrise, so arriving early is essential. A moderate wide-angle is ideal for this location.

Getting there: From US-191, drive 14.6 miles on UT-313. Instead of turning left for Dead Horse Point, continue straight south 1.2 miles on Island in the Sky Road and take the unmarked dirt road on the left (east). Continue on this road through the deserty Big Flat plateau. After 1.9 miles, a track to your right (south) leads in about 2 miles to the roomy car park close to the rim. You'll need at least high clearance and good tires as this track is rocky with slickrock steps in places. Stock SUVs non 4WD should park before the end of the track when the steps get too difficult. From the car park (at 38°29'43" 109°46'10"), walk 250 feet to the rim.

Time required: From the beginning of the dirt road, allocate 1 hour each way, to be safe. Coming from Moab, count on about two hours.

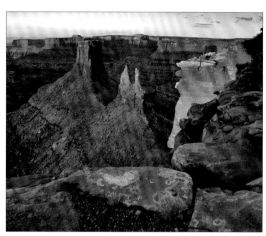

Marlboro Point

Moses & Zeus

The Taylor Canyon Rim is Marlboro Point's counterpart on the west side of the Island in the Sky Road. The two locations share several similarities: proximity to each other, somewhat identical distance from the park road, outstanding scenery, and spectacular formations just a short distance from the rim, making them a great focal point drawing the eye in an otherwise distant photo.

The main difference is, of course, that Moses & Zeus is a late afternoon to sunset shot, being on the other side of the Island.

There are also minor logistical differences: Taylor Canyon Rim is more remote and sees far fewer visitors, so you have to be even better prepared. More importantly, it requires an almost 3-mile round-trip hike with 800 feet of elevation change. Be sure to take enough water for this tough hike.

After parking your vehicle at the National Park boundary, continue on the old Jeep road about 1 mile until it ends, then walk cross-country northwest toward 38°28'34" 109°54'06". This puts you very close to Moses & Zeus with an excellent side view of the monoliths and Taylor Canyon in the background. You can then walk south/southeast along the rim for slightly different compositions.

Getting there: From US-191, drive 14.6 miles on UT-313. Instead of turning left for Dead Horse Point, continue straight south 2.5 miles on Island in the Sky Road and turn right (west) on the unmarked dirt road. Follow it for almost 5 miles to the park boundary at 38°28'59" 109°52'32". Road condition is very unpredictable and is susceptible to change after any substantial rain. I have been on this trail twice over the years and during my last visit I found very deep ruts as well as high slickrock steps between mile 2.4 and mile 2.7 that would make it impassable to most stock SUVs.

Time required: About 4 hours, from the paved park road.

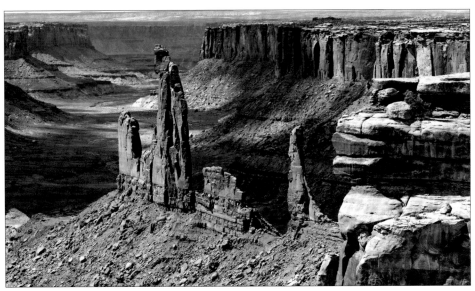

Moses & Zeus from Taylor Canyon Rim

Mesa Arch

Mesa Arch is located about 6 miles south of the Island in the Sky Visitor Center, or 0.3 mile north of the junction with Upheaval Dome Road. It offers an outstanding photographic opportunity, which has become a "classic" of the Southwest. If you go during the day, you'll see the entire superb spectacle of these immense canyons framed through a magnificent arch perched on the edge of a precipitous drop... really pretty, you say. Yes, but there's more still if you're willing to pay the price: you'll have to get up well before dawn to catch it at its very best for a truly magical photograph.

Start by getting the precise time of sunrise for that day. Mesa Arch has become an extremely popular sunrise location for photographers, so plan on arriving at the parking area no less than 1 hour before sunrise to increase your chances of landing a good spot. Only a handful of early arrivals have the luxury of picking a prime spot. If you are late, you'll have to plant your tripod legs wherever space is still available. From Moab, count on almost 1 hour travel time to get there. The short trail takes only 15 minutes. This should give you enough time to find a good spot and get ready. The atmosphere can get a little tense on busy mornings, when latecomers try to squeeze in and 'handheld-shooters' look for spots below (or in front of) the firmly ensconced tripod shooters. My recommendation is to visit Mesa Arch in winter and early spring, when the crowds are more sparse. It also offers softer light on the sandstone in the foreground, as the sun rises to the right, instead of behind the La Sal Mountains.

When the sun makes its appearance, far beyond the canyons, the underside of the arch will glow a vivid red, offering an absolutely sublime spectacle. Regardless of the season, it's always possible to frame the sun inside one of the arch's pillars.

You'll get the best results by spot metering on the sky just above the arch. As a general rule, a clean northern sky is as neutral as a gray card and can be metered on accurately. Do not meter under the bridge where the light is too intense and would severely underexpose your picture. If your camera doesn't have spot metering, just trust your metering system and add ½ f/stop overexposure—but not more—to be safe. You'll have a good 15-minute window of opportunity to photograph the underside of the arch basking in intense red light, gradually turning orange and yellow on the edges. Work briskly, the first five minutes are the most intense. You'll have a hard time containing your excitement in the face of such a magnificent spectacle. For the grand finale, position yourself so the sun appears masked just behind the edge of the arch and bracket a couple of stops on each side.

You'll get great results with lenses ranging from ultrawide to moderate wide-angle. The latter will allow you to get better detail of the canyons through the arch and of the La Sal Mountains in the distance.

If you back up about 70 feet, a hillock will let you shoot partially through the arch with a short telephoto, compressing the perspective of the canyons and La Sal Mountains with the incandescent arch at the top.

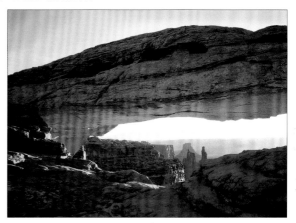

A tripod is mandatory to maximize depth of field. An artistic blur of the foreground or background would kill the impact of this classic landscape composition. Mesa Arch can also be photographed at the end of the afternoon with the sun

Mesa Arch sunrise

lighting the front of the arch and the canyons in the distance. The accent is then on the contrast between the strongly lit arch and the blue sky.

Grand View Point & White Rim Overlook

At the very end of the main park road, about 12 miles south of the Visitor Center, Grand View Point offers a breathtaking panorama and you won't regret the miles you've traveled to get to this spot. From the parking area's vista point, your eye encompasses hundreds of miles of canyon country, with the spectacular white-capped spires of Monument Basin in the foreground; you can even improve on this view by taking the easy 2-mile round-trip trail leading to the tip of the plateau. The view from the end of the trail includes even more territory to

Overleaf: Mesa Arch at sunrise

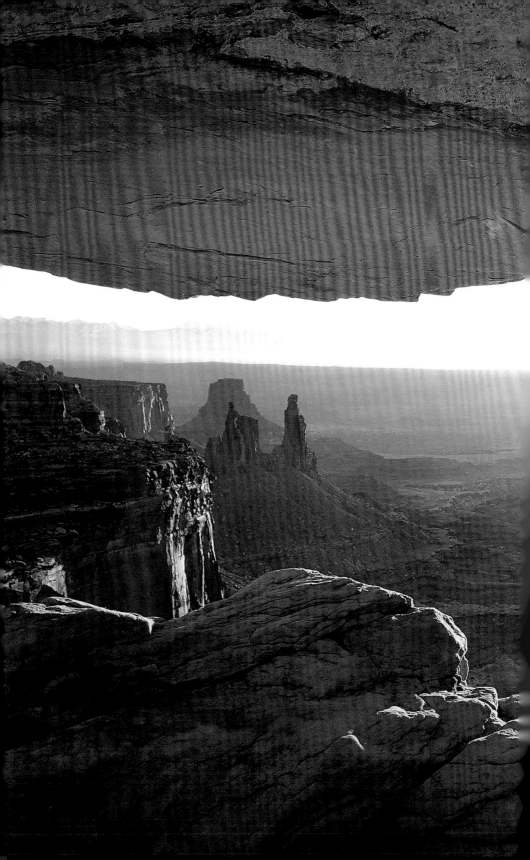

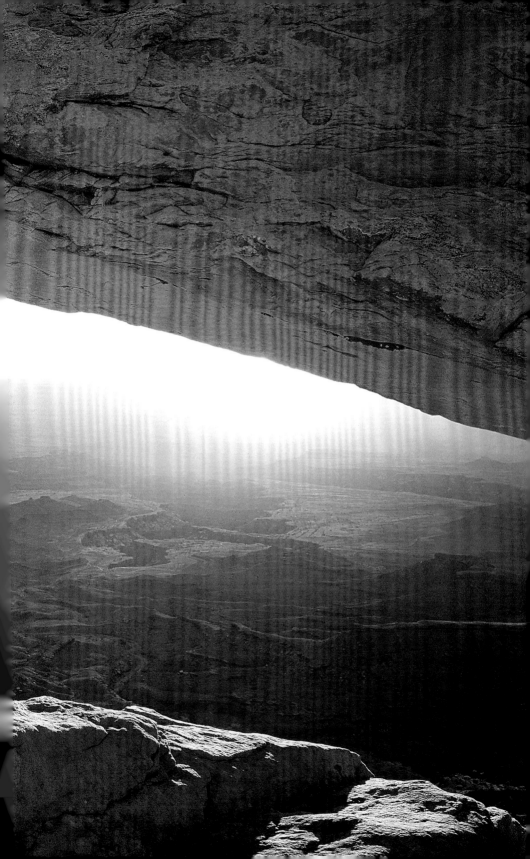

the northeast, as well as a closer view of Junction Butte, just ½ mile away. Due to the immensity of the landscape, it's not an easy task to capture this view, unless you have a truly spectacular sky or you crop a panoramic view without the sky. You can also zoom in on a specific spot, such as Monument Basin. This view is best just before sunset.

For an even better view, drive back almost a mile north towards the Visitor Center, stop at the picnic area and hike the 1.8-mile round-trip trail leading, at the right fork, to the lesser-known White Rim Overlook. This easy trail is quite interesting in itself and the overlook is a great early morning location with an outstanding view of Gooseberry Canyon and Monument Basin.

Green River Overlook & Murphy Point

If you're on the Island toward the end of the afternoon, go to the Green River Overlook or to Murphy Point, set up your tripod and get ready to capture

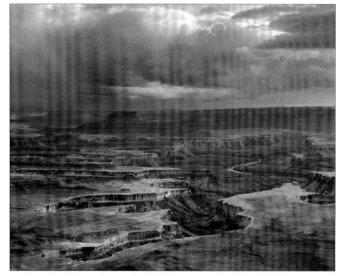

another grandiose vista.

The popular view from the Green River Overlook is a no-brainer. From Grand View Point Road, take Upheaval Dome Road for 0.3 mile, turn left on the 1½-mile road to the large parking area, then walk 400 feet to a fantastic view of Soda Springs Basin. This is a great evening location, when no haze is present. You may want to walk northwest along the rim for a little while to look for locations

Green River Overlook at sunset © Tom Till

that inspire you, but you can't go wrong just staying at the main viewpoint. There are some small bluffs slightly to the left of the overlook, with a great view and plenty of space for your tripod. Camping at nearby Willow Flats campground is very convenient to get an early morning start for other Island in the Sky locations, such as nearby Mesa Arch.

Murphy Point, whose trailhead is on Grand View Point road about 2.4 miles south of the junction with Upheaval Dome Road, also offers a great panoramic view of the western side of the White Rim with a closer view of Soda Springs Basin, the Murphy Hogback and the tip of the Island-in-the-Sky to the distant south. Like the Green River Overlook, it is a great place for sunset photography, but the 3.6-mile round-trip jaunt deters many and you're likely to have the place to yourself.

Aztec Butte

Aztec Butte has a small but very photogenic concentration of Ancient Puebloan dwellings and granaries. Given that it's only a 2-mile round-trip hike from the road, you shouldn't miss it.

From the trailhead, follow the good trail until you reach the base of the butte, climb the steep slickrock face to the top and take the trail to the right, passing the rather mundane top ruin. The path then continues toward the back of the butte, just under the rim, where you'll find a series of alcoves and granaries, but the best is yet to come. Continuing the loop around the butte, you'll arrive on its northwestern side at an unusual granary built inside an eroded sandstone alcove supported on each side by pillars. Unfortunately, part of the wall of the granary has recently collapsed and it is not as photogenic as it used to be. Continue around the butte to rejoin the trail descending on the slickrock. The second butte is worth a quick visit to see two more granaries.

Photo advice: This unusual granary is facing northwest and the best time to photograph it is in mid-afternoon. Closer to sunset, the right pillar of the alcove causes the dwelling to be in the shade. A moderate wide angle works perfectly to capture the ruin with the horizon showing through the left pillar.

Getting there: On the road to Upheaval Dome, park at the signed Aztec Ruin trailhead, about 0.8 mile from the junction with Grand View Point Road.

Time required: 1 to 1½ hours.

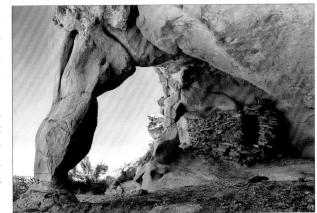

Aztec Butte ruin © Philippe Schuler

False Kiva

False Kiva is a hauntingly beautiful photographic location, originally made popular by Tom Till. Hidden under a vast alcove at the edge of Island in the Sky, False Kiva has all the ingredients of a great Canyon Country shot. It consists of a low circular ruin forming an ideal foreground to a classic Canyonlands grand scenic, with the silhouette of Candlestick Butte balancing the shot beautifully. Although False Kiva is not featured in the park's literature, its increased popularity no longer guarantees that there won't be any other souls during your visit. But being there by yourself reinforces the beauty and serenity of the place.

Despite its circular shape, the ruin is not a kiva. There are, however, multiple traces of the passage of the Ancient Ones, who knew and used this location. The first part of the hike, down to the rim, is a very good trail, with the dryfall easily bypassed thanks to a cairned path. The second part, down from the rim to the beginning of the climb to the ruins, is now a real trail, well cairned and made much safer.

Photo advice: The best time to photograph False Kiva is in the second part of the afternoon, when the cliffs to the southwest and Candlestick Tower in the background take on a superb golden hue. You may get good results by waiting until sunset and shooting an ambiance picture where the ruins are not in full sun. The ruins themselves receive less light as they are tucked in under the alcove and in full shadow before sunset. At that time, you'll need a 3-stop ND Grad filter to maintain detail in the ruins while keeping the background correctly exposed. Or you can try a polarizer if you have a fairly good blue sky in the background.

As far as lenses are concerned, anything wide will do. A super wide angle will let you frame the entire alcove, at the expense of the background which will look quite distant. A moderate wide angle will give you a more natural perspective but will only include part of the alcove. Experiment and find your own way.

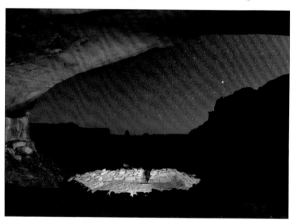

False Kiva at night

I have paid several visits to False Kiva over the years, including at night, each time in the hope of coming back with something different, but at least I feel I have made my peace with this wonderful location. I have experimented with a number of techniques, including stacking a couple of ND Grads, shooting HDR, shooting for stitch and using opposite angles. I have also tried different light sources, from flashlights to iPads, and using reflected light from the alcove's ceiling. So many factors are at play, it is hard to predict what will happen.

There are some rules you should be aware of before you go. Due to the increased popularity of False Kiva in recent years, the NPS has come up with a policy regarding protection of the site. Although most of the regulations concern commercial photography and filming permits, three rules stand out for the general public: 1) do not trespass over the taped area at the back, where Puebloan artifacts are protected; 2) walking inside the Kiva circle is prohibited; 3) the rock walls at the back are part of the ruin and are not to be used to sit on or place gear on. Please abide by these rules. Do not disturb the site in any way and leave only footprints (where allowed), so False Kiva can remain open to visitation and other visitors may enjoy this very special place.

Access to the Kiva is still permitted 24 hours at the time of this writing. Nevertheless, there is an ongoing review of the impact of visitation on the site, so I suggest you check with the Rangers before you go.

Getting there: On the road leading to Upheaval Dome, park at the pull-out for the Alcove Spring trailhead, 3.6 miles from the junction with Grand View Point Road. Walk back about 250 yards in the direction of Grand View Point Road and look to the right for a well-trod footpath leading west.

Follow the sandy footpath for about ten minutes to the edge of a dryfall/small cliff. Bypass the cliff by descending on the slickrock to the left. There are a few cairns present during this brief off-trail section. The visible trail resumes at the bottom and you reach the edge of the rim about 5 minutes later. A steep trail to the right leads down some talus. This trail has been greatly improved in recent years. It is now cairned and easy to follow but still a bit treacherous due to loose rock underfoot. The trail eventually levels out as you reach the foot of a massive alcove. As you continue on the ledge toward the northern end of the alcove, look to your right for a footpath angling back and ascending the slope diagonally toward the southern end of the alcove. The steep ascent on small loose stones is brief and yields no clue of the presence of the False Kiva, which you discover at the last second, upon reaching the hidden platform.

Time required: 1½ to 2 hours round-trip to appreciate and photograph the site.

Nearby location: On the east side of the pull-out, you'll find the trailhead for the Alcove Spring Trail, leading in 5.5 miles to Upper Taylor Canyon and the 1.8-mile loop trail around the bottom of Moses and Zeus spires. You can also reach the Moses and Zeus loop trail by 4WD from the White Rim Road via the 5-mile long Taylor Canyon Road (see the *White Rim* section).

Upheaval Dome

Located at the end of the 5-mile Upheaval Dome Road beginning at Grand View Point Road, this geologic phenomenon, which looks more like a crater than a dome, is quite interesting to observe. In and around the crater, the various geologic layers of the park are particularly well displayed and easy to observe because of the angle of the walls. It's a perfect opportunity for a little refresher course on the geology of the plateau and to learn to distinguish between the colors and the strata of the various sandstone formations.

Overleaf: False Kiva

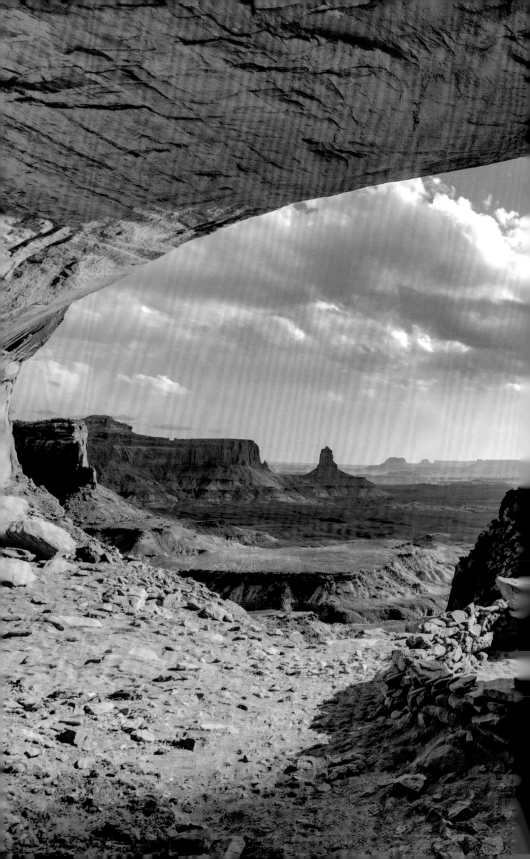

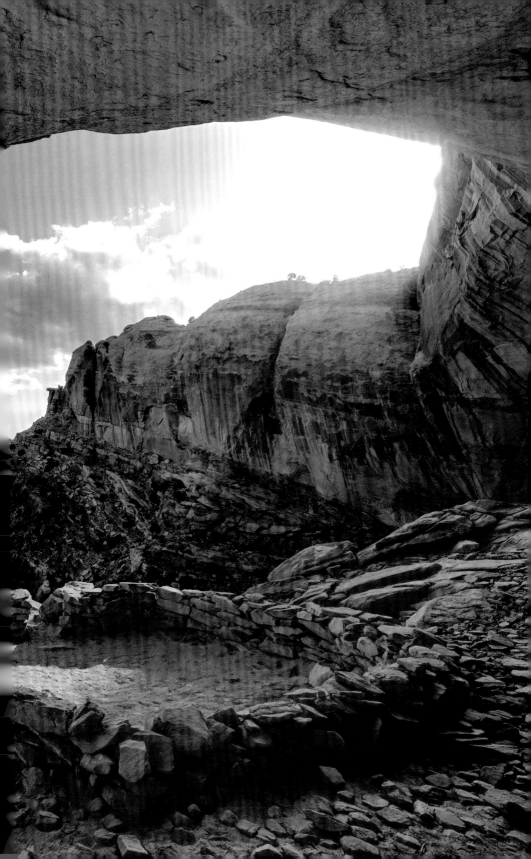

An easy 2-mile round-trip trail leads to two successive overlooks from the edge of the crater. The first overlook is the better one to shoot from, although it's difficult to photograph the crater successfully, anyway.

Nearby location: Driving back 0.8 mile from the Upheaval Dome parking area, you can also take the easy 1-mile round-trip trail to the top of Whale Rock, from where you have good views of the dome in the earlier part of the day.

The Shafer Trail

Branching off Island in the Sky Road about a mile north from the Visitor Center, the 5.3-mile long Shafer Trail lets you descend, amongst superlative views, onto the White Rim plateau a thousand feet below. There, it joins with Potash Road to the left and the White Rim Road to the right. Originally an old cattle road used by ranchers since the late 1800's, it was enlarged in the fifties during the uranium boom. You can observe its spectacular switchbacks carved right into the flank of the steep canyon cliffs from the Shafer Trail viewpoint, located about ½ mile south of the Visitor Center.

A high-clearance vehicle is advised to descend the scary-looking, but not technically difficult, Shafer Trail and get a close-up view of the Colorado River and the famous White Rim Road. Needless to say, this trail must only be driven in dry weather, very slowly, and using low gears.

Even when the Shafer Trail has been recently maintained and is in good condition, high clearance is still mandatory for a foray on the White Rim Road

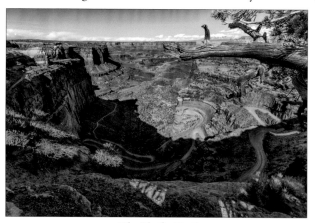

The Shafer Trail

and/or to return to Moab via the 14-mile unpaved Potash Road. The latter has become much rougher in places in recent years.

The Shafer Trail can be easily integrated into a highly scenic loop drive, starting and ending in Moab. In the course of one day, you can watch sunrise at Dead Horse Point or Mesa Arch, visit Island in the Sky including some of the short hikes described

above, descend the Shafer Trail and spend some time on the beginning of the White Rim Road, at least as far as Musselman Arch. All this before returning to Moab by way of Potash Road and SB-279, passing Thelma & Louise Point along the way. A memorable day by any standards, amply justifying the rental of a 4WD vehicle for the day in Moab if you don't have one.

The White Rim Road

To visit the extraordinary White Rim in greater depth, you'll have to allow for a multi-day trip to cover the 100 miles of this popular loop. There are some steep rocky spots, so a 4WD vehicle with low gear is necessary. This road is a favorite of vehicle-assisted mountain biking groups, so you might want to consider this option as an alternative to driving. Most of the time, the road winds along the edge of the rim of the flat plateau halfway between the Island in the Sky mesa and the Colorado and Green rivers. It's an unforgettable trip and, all in all, not too difficult to accomplish.

A quota system is in effect for all camping trips, so it's necessary to make your reservation early (up to four months in advance at https://canypermits.nps.gov). Only a few permits are issued every day, based on the small number of primitive campsites along the road.

In spring or early autumn, you can do this trip at a relaxed pace without suffering from summer's heat or icy winter nights. On this arid plateau, where wood fires are allowed, nighttime temperatures drop well below freezing by November and remain so until early March.

Photo advice: Drive down the Shafer Trail (see previous section) until it meets with the White Rim Road (to the right). About 1.3 miles past the junction, follow the short Gooseneck Trail for an outstanding overlook above the Colorado River. About 2 miles further, you'll find the turnout to Musselman Arch, a flat span above the basin below. Look for the nearby Standing Rocks, which can be reached by walking up the rim from the arch. Almost 8 miles further, the rough 3.8-mile Lathrop Canyon Road provides the only access to the Colorado River, and is mostly used by commercial river float operators.

The most interesting section of the White Rim is without doubt Monument Basin, reached about 15 miles further. There, you'll drive at the edge of the rim, with great views above huge pillars capped with white rocks. Monument Basin is best photographed from late afternoon to sunset.

Past the 1.3-mile spur road to the White Crack campsite (a favorite of people doing the White Rim Road in two days), the western side of the trail offers outstanding views of the Green River and the great monoliths of the Maze: Ekker Butte, Cleopatra's Chair, Buttes of the Cross, and more. Beyond the Murphy Hogback and Soda Springs Basin, Turk's Head is an outstanding shot requiring a very wide angle to frame the entire

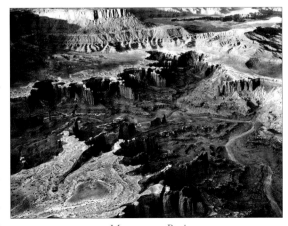

Monument Basin

gooseneck of the Green River. As you go past Candlestick Tower, you'll come level to the Green River at Potato Bottom and, after a steep climb, reach the spectacular location of Fort Ruin, smack in the middle of a great gooseneck. Take the 4.2-mile round-trip trail crossing the narrow mesa high above the river to the remnants of an Ancient Puebloan tower before descending to an old cabin on Fort Bottom.

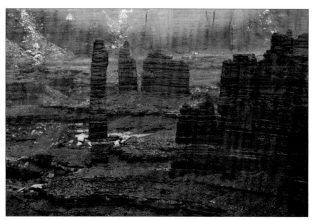

Monument Basin sunset © Synnatschke Photography

Getting there: The Colorado River side of the White Rim starts at the bottom of the Shafer Trail, or the end of Potash Road (see respective sections). The Green River side is reached from signed Mineral Canyon Road, leaving UT-313 12.2 miles from the junction with US-191.

Time required: 2 to 3 days for the entire loop in a 4x4 vehicle. Mountain bikers need an extra day. From the Shafer Trail (or Potash Road) you can drive to Gooseberry Canyon or even Monument Basin and back in one extra-long summer day if you begin at sunrise. From Mineral Canyon Road, you can visit Fort Bottom and Taylor Canyon in one day.

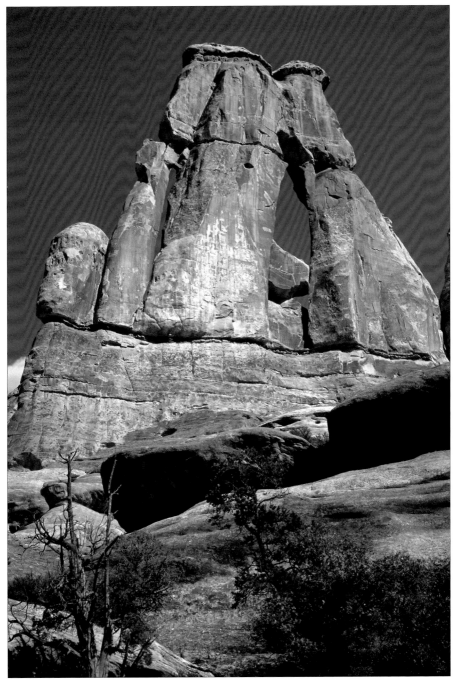

Druid Arch

Chapter 16

CANYONLANDS - NEEDLES

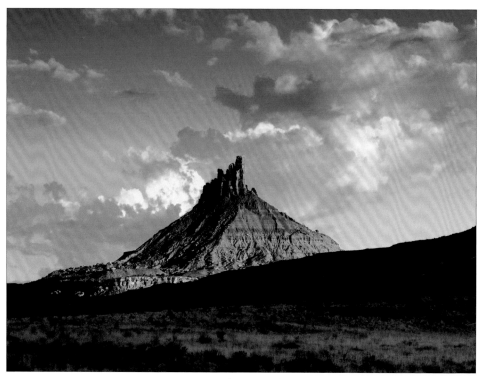

Six-Shooter Peak

Introduction to the Needles

The Needles district is much less visited than Island in the Sky. One reason is distance, as it is a cul-de-sac with only one way in and out, far away from the amenities of town. Another is that there is little to see from the scenic road proper—not even viewpoints like at Island in the Sky. The main attractions of this district can only be explored by day hiking, backpacking and 4-wheeling. The Needles area has a wonderful network of trails, all well signed at the trail-heads and junctions, and made easier to follow thanks to many cairns along the way. Those with enough time and who are not discouraged by the effort will not regret their visit to the Needles. They'll discover a wide variety of geological features, including colorful spires rising hundreds of feet above the ground, many mushroom-like sandstone formations, massive arches, grabens and canyons. Add to this abundant rock art and alcove dwellings left by the early inhabitants.

The most practical way to visit the Needles is to camp at Squaw Flat, which fills up quickly during the high season. This will let you photograph these extraordinary needles in the early morning, while the light is at its best, beginning a long and rewarding day of exploration in the area. If you can't camp, you can always resort to staying in a motel in Moab or Monticello, but it makes it considerably harder to be on location during the golden hour.

Moab offers all the advantages of modern civilization as well as a central location for exploring the surrounding parks, but it is 75 miles (about 1½ hours) from the Visitor Center. Monticello can save you time as it is only 49 miles away. Also, this small town at the foot of the Abajo Mountains has a bit of an alpine flavor, which is quite pleasant. Regardless of your starting point, you turn off US-191, almost opposite an interesting monolith called Church Rock, for the last 35 miles leading to the Needles' Visitor Center on UT-211. The turnoff is about 40 miles south of downtown Moab and 14 miles north of Monticello.

From Monticello, you can also take the fully-paved Harts Draw Road and get some nice but distant views of the park down the northern side of the Abajo Mountains before catching up with UT-211, 2.7 miles before Newspaper Rock. The winding Harts Draw Road shaves about 5 miles off the trip, but almost no time. Past Newspaper Rock, UT-211 becomes particularly scenic as it follows the superb red cliffs of Indian Creek Canyon. With the right light and little wind, there is an interesting photo opportunity of the cliffs reflected in a little lake located on the right side of the road, 7½ miles past Newspaper Rock.

If you go to or from the Needles before sunrise or after sunset, watch out for deer that often cross the road between Newspaper Rock and US-191, as well as on Harts Draw Road.

Newspaper Rock

After passing by the base of the Abajo Mountains, UT-211 enters the lovely, shallow canyon of Indian Creek, along which you'll stumble upon Newspaper Rock State Park, about 12.3 miles from US-191. Even if you aren't a fan of Indian pictorial rock art, you really should stop to see these remarkable petroglyphs carved in the rock, very close to the road. A couple of them have been found to be 1,500 years old, but the majority were carved more recently over a period of several hundred years. This is one of the largest panels of petroglyphs you will find on the Colorado Plateau. These petroglyphs are very easy to photograph at any time of the day, but are better lit in the afternoon.

Time required: 10 to 20 minutes.

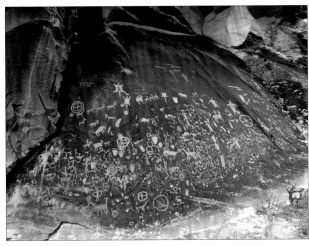

A cornucopia of glyphs at Newspaper Rock

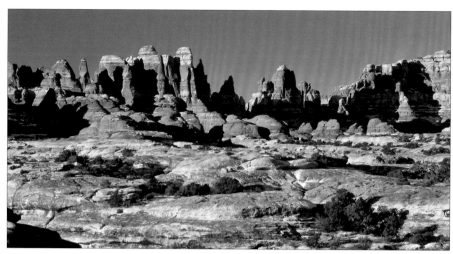

Needles panorama at sunrise

Nearby locations: About 1.9 miles from Newspaper Rock, 0.2 mile past mile marker 5, you'll see a large pullout on the west (left) side of the road. This is the trailhead for Shay Canyon, another interesting and easy-to-visit Fremont-style rock art site, with a bountiful mix of anthropomorphs and animal figures; a favorite of photography workshops. You are at eye-level and very close to most of the glyphs, so a moderate wide angle works best. On a sunny day, a polarizer will help bring out detail. Cross the creek and walk southwest about 700 feet to the north (right) side of the canyon. You'll find the panels scattered along the base of the cliff. Count on an hour, at a relaxed pace, with plenty of time for photos.

The Indian Creek rock art site is located a short distance from mile marker 4 and has some very nice petroglyphs. There is a pullout on the east (right) side and some of the glyphs can be seen from the road. Follow the hiker's trail to the base of the cliff. Note that you are in Indian Creek Recreation Area, a world-renowned climbing location.

The Scenic Drive

The Scenic Drive winds for about 13 miles round-trip from the Visitor Center through red rock country with some distant views of the spires. The first stop along the road is Roadside Ruin, a nice Ancestral Puebloan granary only a couple hundred yards from the road. About 1.7 miles further, the Wooden Shoe Arch Viewpoint offers good shots of the distant cliffs at sunset. Further to the east, after about a mile on a side gravel road leading to the Salt Creek area, you reach Cave Spring. This pleasant and easy trail, only 0.6 mile round-trip, leads to a grotto near a perennial creek where you'll find some pictographs and a well-preserved cowboy camp with original items left by the last occupants. The trail passes two ladders and continues on slickrock with good views of the surrounding area.

At the junction of the Scenic Drive and Elephant Hill Road, you'll find a lovely prairie, making a good foreground for the Needles in the early morning.

About 2 miles farther, the short Pothole Point loop contains a group of water holes carved into the slickrock by erosion. These potholes are quite interesting when they are filled with water and you can see myriads of tiny organisms swimming in them. Nearby, you can see some nice examples of cryptobiotic soil along the trail. Be sure not to step on it, as it literally takes decades to regenerate.

About ¼ mile before the end of the road, the 2.4-mile Slickrock Trail makes a loop along the mesa top overlooking the canyon. The best viewpoint is at the end of the trail, where Junction Butte and the Island in the Sky district are in full view. If you don't want to walk all the way, the first viewpoint on the Slickrock Trail—a short ½ mile from the start of the trail—offers a panoramic view of the cliffs with the La Sal Mountains in the background. At sunset, there are miles of cliffs that glow red while the snowy peaks are tinted pink. Big Spring Canyon Overlook, at the very end of the road, is not spectacular but offers an easy access to a lovely canyon, if you prefer not to do too much walking.

Elephant Hill

A mostly gravel road leads in 2.7 miles from Squaw Flat to the Elephant Hill car park. There, you'll find the famous 4x4 track of the same name, as well as the foot trail heading south to Chesler Park and Druid Arch. From the highest point on this gravel road, you can get a beautiful panorama of the Needles district. A few hundred yards after the "blind curve" sign, you'll see a small slickrock hill to the right. You can easily climb on it for an excellent view of the entire area, including the Needles. The view is particularly majestic at sunset with a medium to long telephoto. Watch out for the cryptobiotic soil, however.

The challenging Elephant Hill 4x4 track is only for specially equipped vehicles and carries a substantial risk of vehicle damage. No behemoths there either, the Squeeze Play section is very narrow. This track requires excellent mastery of driving on slickrock and of your vehicle's reactions. Elephant Hill is not the only difficult spot on the track; sections such as the Silver Stairs have some rock steps that are at least as challenging. On the other hand, you can also do

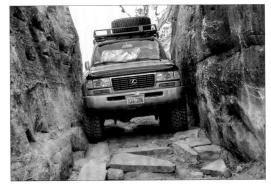

Elephant Hill's Squeeze Play

this route on foot for a short distance up from the car park, as there are good views of the Needles after you've crossed Elephant Hill. It's also entertaining to see 4x4 drivers negotiating the slickrock grades. The Elephant Hill 4WD track leads in 3.3 miles to Devil's Kitchen and its very nice campground, surrounded

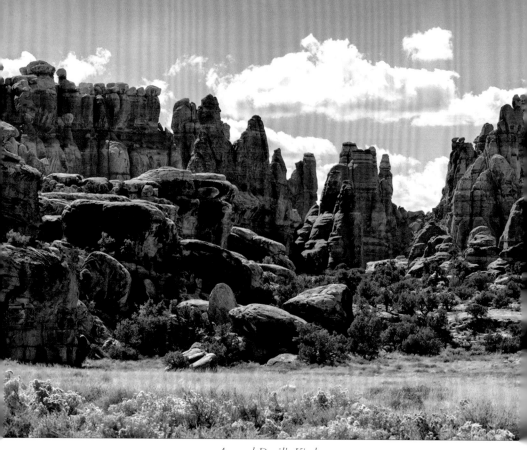

Around Devil's Kitchen

by huge spires. To return to the Elephant Hill car park, continue 0.7 mile northwest to Devil's Lane and head north 1.5 miles to New Bates Wilson Camp via the above-mentioned Silver Stairs section. There, instead of turning right to finish the loop, you can continue northwest 3 miles to an overlook on the confluence of the Green and Colorado rivers. Arriving at Devil's Lane after leaving Devil's Kitchen, you can also head south 3.4 miles to the Grabens area, past the challenging 4WD section of SOB Hill, to reach the west side of Chesler Park and the Joint Trail (see next section).

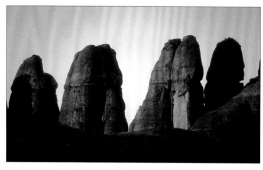

First light on Needles formations

Time required: The minimum loop of almost 9 miles from the Elephant Hill car park can be accomplished in half a day with the proper vehicle. It is best to devote two days to this trip, camping at Devil's Kitchen along the way. You can then visit Chesler Park from its western access and take a side trip to the Confluence Overlook on your way back.

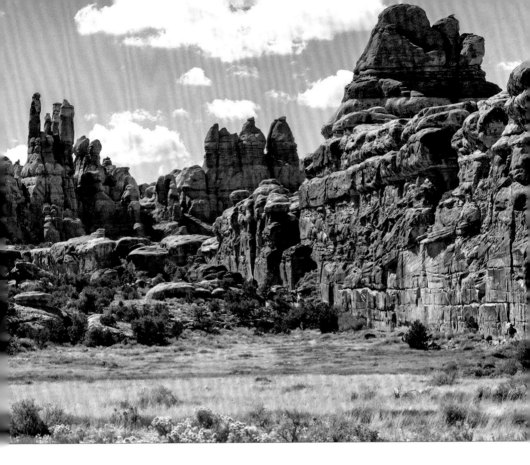

Chesler Park

This outstanding group of spires, with strongly colored horizontal striations, is located beyond the needles that are visible from the Scenic Drive and the Elephant Hill gravel road. The ancient spires of Cedar Mesa sandstone are located in the center of a remarkably verdant basin surrounded by a circle of needles. The tall grasses in the park form a beautiful foreground and a singular contrast with the large spires.

Located on a saddle at the northern edge of the basin, the Chesler Park Viewpoint can be reached on a beautiful slickrock trail sometimes only recognizable by cairns. It's a 6-mile round-trip from the Elephant Hill parking area, requiring about 3 hours. The last 200 yards, on a slope nicknamed Fat Man's Misery, are moderately challenging.

If you don't mind adding another 1½ hours to your hike, walk back down Fat Man's Misery and take the nice trail to your left, leading to Devil's Kitchen and passing at the foot of several beautiful needles. This allows you to return to the car park by way of the Elephant Hill 4x4 track. If you are considering driving it later, it's a good way to gauge the infamous rock steps and make sure you and your vehicle will be able to make it.

However, if you really want to get the most out of Chesler Park and take photos in late afternoon light, you'll have to descend into the "park" from the

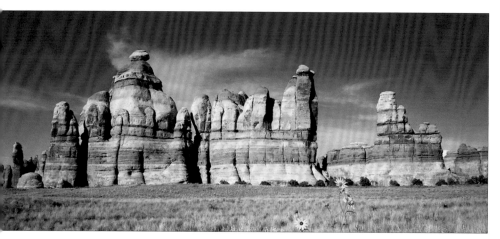

Exquisite Chesler Park in its tallgrass setting

viewpoint. From there, walk the 5-mile loop around it in a clockwise direction, passing through the Joint Trail—a narrow crack in the rock about 60 feet deep and ¼ mile long located at the southern tip of the loop. The entire loop from the Elephant Hill trailhead is about 11 miles, using the shortest route. This may seem a bit long, but once in the "park" proper you'll progress rapidly, about half the time over flat ground. The entire loop can be completed in 6 to 7 hours, leaving enough time for pictures, rest, and enjoying the scenery.

Another possibility is to walk into Chesler Park near campsite CP2 and turn left (east) to descend into Elephant Canyon. From there, you can return north to the parking area or hike south to Druid Arch (see next section).

Watch out for the heat and possible dehydration if you do these hikes in summer. Even in late afternoon, the heat is still intense.

Photo advice: Best early in the morning for the view of the Needles from the beginning of the trail and from Chesler Park Viewpoint, but afternoon is preferred for photographing the spires from the south. You can get distant pictures of the spires from the viewpoint just before the east entrance of the Joint Trail. To do this, follow the cairns on the slickrock and climb on a small ridge overlooking the "park", with some red round rocks on white sandstone making a beautiful foreground. For the closest views of Chesler Park's spires, follow the side trail toward campsites CP3, 4 and 5 until you find a suitable spot.

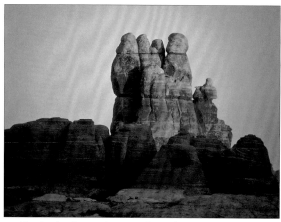

Sentinels of stone line up along the Needles horizon

Druid Arch

Druid Arch is one of the most striking arches of the Colorado Plateau, definitely worthy of the top five. It would certainly be yet another overused icon of the Southwest if it were more accessible. As it is, the shortest 11-mile round-trip hike discourages many visitors. For those who are ready to put in a reasonable effort, however, Druid Arch is a fantastic photo destination. From the Elephant Hill trailhead, the mostly level walk follows the Chesler Park Viewpoint trail for about 2 miles before reaching a fork. At this junction, the sign indicates two ways to reach Druid Arch: the shorter one takes you southward directly to the arch via Elephant Canyon. The other one leads first to the Chesler Park Viewpoint, then into the "park" close to campsite CP2, where you turn left to descend into Elephant Canyon and rejoin the direct trail to Druid Arch. If you don't mind hiking an additional 1.5 miles, I highly recommend this second alternative, which allows you to combine a visit to Chesler Park and Druid Arch into one hike for a small additional effort. Walking in Elephant Canyon on sand or slickrock is rather easy and not much different from any other walks in the Needles area. The upper part of the canyon reveals awesome views as you penetrate deeper inside the needles. There is one easily negotiated dryfall and a fixed iron ladder to be climbed in your final approach to the arch.

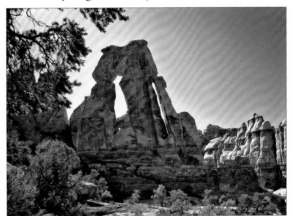

Druid Arch from the upper viewpoint

Photo advice: If you get to the arch in the morning, continue up the steep cairned trail until you reach a large platform on the northeast side of the arch. This is the best vantage point for morning photography of the arch. A moderate wide-angle lens will work best. In the afternoon, the arch is backlit from this point. Retrace your steps, descending to the wash between the ladder and the dryfall. Follow the wash to the southwest, skirting the arch until you end up on the opposite side. Climb on the slickrock to find some good vantage points.

Time required: 6 to 8 hours for the entire loop, depending on which way you decide to hike.

Horse Canyon

Horse Canyon is open to limited 4WD traffic, subject to obtaining a day-use permit by prior reservation or at the Visitor Center. The access track leaves south of the Cave Spring trailhead (see *Scenic Drive* section above). After 0.4 mile, you encounter the locked gate (for which you receive the combination on the day of your permit) and 2.3 miles further, you reach the junction of Salt Creek and Horse Canyon.

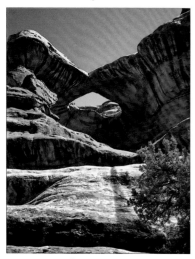

Paul Bunyan's Potty

Take the left fork for Horse Canyon. The track goes on for about 7 miles. Under normal conditions, it is not very challenging but there are some deep pockets of sand in places. However, in recent years the track has often been closed due to flooding. It's costly to fix and not very productive, given the relatively small percentage of visitors who come here. In about a mile, you'll pass below Paul Bunyan's Potty, a pothole arch with a suggestive streak of desert varnish flowing through and out of it. A normal lens or short telephoto will capture it perfectly. A mile further, a 0.7-mile spur track leads to Tower Ruin, a nice ruin located under an alcove, high on the cliff. A short trail leads to the base of the ruin where you can catch a better glimpse. Do not climb into the ruin; instead, use a medium telephoto to capture it. Continuing about 3.6 miles on the main track, you'll find a small side canyon to your right; its entrance is soon blocked for vehicles. Walk about 0.7 mile in the wash to find the somewhat hidden Thirteen Faces Panel to your right.

Almost a mile further on the main track, look for the 1.2-mile round-trip spur trail leading to lovely Castle Arch. ¼ mile further, where the track ends, dedicated arch hunters can see Fortress Arch at the end of a 1½-mile round-trip footpath.

Time required: About 1½ to 2 hours for a visit to Paul Bunyan's Potty and Tower Ruin. A good part of the day to drive the entire track and back, and do the hikes.

Salt Creek

The Salt Creek thru-hike is the quintessential Needles District backpacking trip: about 28.5 miles from Cathedral Butte to Cave Spring road or 30 miles to Squaw Flat. Three to five days of easy hiking, solitude, and pure bliss in a serenely beautiful environment! Arches, hoodoos, Indian ruins, rock art, handprints, pioneer cabin, luxurious vegetation, big sky day and night (mostly), great campsites, water aplenty: Salt Creek has it all!

I'll begin with a brief discussion of trip planning. This trek is best done northbound, starting from the southern trailhead near Cathedral Butte. If you like to take your time to explore or if you are unable to get an early start (if you are using a shuttle to bring you to the trailhead, for instance), you should plan on taking 4½ days, spending the first night at SC1 or SC2 and the second night at SC3, which is a strategically located campsite for photographers. With an early start, it's also easy to do the trek in 3½ days, spending the first night at SC3 (which is about 9 miles from the trailhead). There is lots to see on that first day, though, so you wouldn't be able to linger much. Your next night will be at the Angel Arch Camp (at-large camping) and the final night at Peekaboo Camp or close by.

In terms of logistics, the good news is that Salt Creek normally runs year-round and water is available at crossings, so there is no need to burden yourself with gallons of water. Do verify this with the Rangers before leaving, however. You will still need to filter all water and/or treat it. On the downside, bear-resistant containers are now required for backpacking in Salt Creek and human waste must be packed out by campers staying at Peekaboo Camp. Backpacking requires a permit and advance reservations for SC1 to SC4 campsites. As of this writing, reservations are available no more than four months, and no fewer than 48 hours, prior to your permit's start date. Walk-in permits may also be available for the next day, but don't count on it. It is best to reserve your backcountry permit well in advance at https://canypermits.nps.gov. April and May, as well as September and October, are traditionally the busiest months, with late October having a particular appeal because of fall colors and mild temperatures.

I will now describe a typical 3½-day Salt Creek thru-hike. After a steep descent from the Cathedral Butte trailhead (you lose 800 feet in the first mile), the trail levels gradually and becomes quite flat after 1¾ miles when you officially enter the National Park and a spectacular area of tallgrass and tamarisk. A tad more than 2 miles further, the first major landmarks are Kirk Cabin and the view of Kirk Arch to the west. A couple of hundred feet past the cabin, you'll find the signed spur trail to campsites SC1 and SC2. About 1.5 miles past the cabin, as you are almost done crossing the mouth of the Big Pocket, look for a faint social trail to your right about 120 feet past the main Big Pocket trail. Follow this trail the best you can for about 400 feet, then aim northeast for the tip of the cliff through thick and thorny vegetation to a panel of hand prints. Back on the main trail, continue 0.2 mile and look for an unmarked but well-defined social trail to the left. This is the trail for the Big Ruins. The trail is easy to follow, crossing the

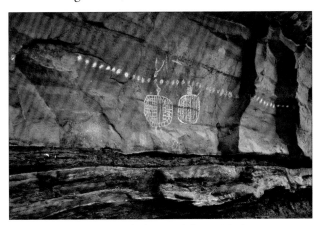

Peekaboo Glyphs © Philippe Schuler

creek after 600 feet and continuing for 0.3 mile to vantage points from where you can photograph the long row of about twenty dwellings and granaries tucked high under a ledge, truly a spectacular sight. There is no access to the ruins proper. Returning to the main trail, Wedding Ring Arch's perfect oval span comes into close view on the east side after about 0.4 mile. Almost 0.7 mile further (or about 1.1 mile past the Big Ruins trail), you'll come to a well-trod trail to your left. About 500 feet away, just past a squash patch, you'll reach an alcove with granaries and many handprints, further on your left. You'll want to spend some time here photographing the negative handprints and pointillist patterns. The next major landmark is the All-American Man, about 1.3 mile further on the east side (about 8 miles from the trailhead). This unique and colorful red, white, and blue pictograph is located in a small cave about 20 feet above ground, right by the trail. It can be photographed from the ground at an odd angle. Although there is no sign saying so, the Park Service frowns on people climbing the narrow crack to the cave.

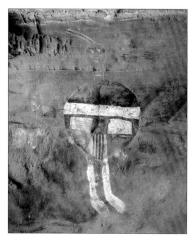

All-American Man

About 700 feet beyond this landmark, the trail climbs steeply through a crack in a fin, emerging high on the other side before descending in the vast valley. Then, in 0.7 mile the trail passes close to the nice "modern style" Four Faces panel. It is best photographed in late afternoon when it is uniformly lit. From here it's a short 0.2 mile to the junction with the signed SC3 campsite spur, so it's easy to return to the panel if you are there too early. The creek normally flows strongly near the panel, so it's also where you'll refill water bottles and bladders.

Day 2 to Angel Camp is an easy day so there is no need to rush, unless you want to return to the Four Faces panel before it gets hit directly by the sun. Your first stop is at the small falls of Upper Jump, a short 0.3 mile from the campsite. From here, the trail follows the creek course one meander after another, sometimes through thick vegetation. About 2.2 miles further, look up to your right to spot several ruins located along a ledge where you can easily climb. There is also a pictograph panel at the western end of the ledge.

In 2.7 miles, after passing campsite SC4 and numerous small arches on the ridge tops, you'll see the signed trail to Angel Arch on your right. Continuing a bit further north in Salt Creek, you'll arrive at Angel Arch Camp (at-large camping, no reservation required), which will be your base for the night. It is the closest place to camp for the Arch, as camping in Angel Arch Canyon is not allowed. Angel Arch Camp has plenty of flat and shaded ground, so you don't have to worry about room should other parties be present. Angel Arch is a sunrise and early morning photographic location, so I suggest that you visit it the next day. In the morning, you'll need to leave at least one hour before dawn to catch alpenglow and scout for a shooting location to your liking. In recent years the rains have seriously impacted the trail, making the 1½-mile approach to the viewpoint difficult at night, with only headlamps. A full moon would be helpful here. The classic, and arguably best way to photograph spectacular Angel Arch is from the viewpoint, including Molar Rock—a precariously top-heavy rock in the shape of a tooth—in the foreground. It is possible to hike and scramble another

0.5 mile up to arrive below the spectacular span for close-up shots and a nice overview of Angel Arch canyon. However, it is not as photographically rewarding as from the viewpoint.

Back at Angel Arch Camp in Salt Creek, you'll have time for breakfast, and possibly a nap, before breaking camp. I am suggesting the nap because the rest of your day will be a long 7.5-mile hike to Peekaboo Camp in Lower Salt Creek, walking along a former Jeep track closed to vehicular traffic for many years. The walking is level and easy, with plenty of meanders on the menu, and patches of deep sand here and there. You'll be constantly following or crossing the mostly dry bed of the creek, with usually shallow water during springtime in the upper part of the creek. Watch out for the extremely aggressive deerflies that patrol the Salt Creek bed during spring and summer. The hike in Lower Salt Creek is not as beautiful as in Upper Salt Creek or trails around Elephant Hill and Squaw Flat.

The official campsites at Peekaboo Camp are reserved for 4WD traffic, but you are allowed to stay there when the 4WD road from Cave Spring is closed (which has been a regular occurrence in recent years). In any event, at-large camping is permitted in the vicinity, as long as you stay away from the creek.

For your final half-day, you must have decided beforehand where to leave your car. If you parked at the locked gate south of Cave Spring Road, it is just an easy (but rather unexciting) 3.3-mile walk, roughly following the 4WD track in the wash. If you parked at Squaw Flat trailhead/campground, it is a much more difficult 5-mile route along the Peekaboo Trail, with extended sections of high slickrock benches yielding spectacular views.

Less than six hundred feet from the Peekaboo official campsites and next to a slickrock window, this trail passes along very photogenic Fremont pictographs representing shield-like figures.

If you don't have enough time to do the above-described thru-hike or if you cannot arrange a shuttle between the northern and southern trailheads of Salt Creek, there are other opportunities for shorter and partial hikes limited to Upper Salt Creek or Lower Salt Creek.

For Upper Salt Creek, a first option to reach Peekaboo Camp is to take the road leaving south of the Cave Spring trailhead (see *Horse Canyon* section), driving the 4WD track for 2.3 miles past the locked gate, followed by another mile in the right fork of Salt Creek past the junction with Horse Canyon. This last mile inside the wash is a very narrow track with a perennial shallow stream, running through tallgrass. It

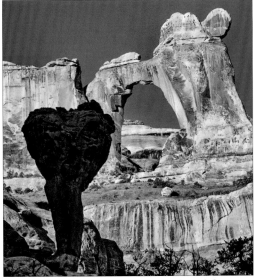

Angel Arch, with Molar Rock on left

often gets flooded during the monsoon and well into fall, causing its closure. The second option is to park at the locked gate and hike 3.3 miles to Peekaboo; the foot trail is always open. Your third option is to hike the nicer, but longer, 5-mile Peekaboo Trail from Squaw Flat.

Driving to Peekaboo and back can take 1½ to 3 hours depending on conditions, but is more rewarding combined with a foray into Horse Canyon, at least as far as Tower Ruin. With a car shuttle, hiking from Squaw Flat to the locked gate south of Cave Spring Road via Peekaboo, or vice versa, can be easily done in one day. Many people prefer a longer trek including other trails in the Needles district (such as Big Spring, Squaw Canyon, and Lost Canyon) with a stop at Peekaboo.

If your goal is to photograph Angel Arch and your time is limited, there are two alternatives when the 4WD road to Peekaboo is open. The least desirable from a photographer's standpoint is the almost 20-mile marathon from Peekaboo to the arch and back in one day, hitting it at the worst possible time for light. A much more reasonable alternative is to light-backpack about 8 miles to 'at-large' Angel Arch Camp on the first day, do the 3-mile round-trip to the arch for dawn, and return to Peekaboo in the afternoon.

From the Cathedral Butte trailhead, it is possible to do an incursion into Upper Salt Creek down to the Four Faces or Upper Jump and back in one very long day, but it is a demanding 19-mile round-trip only very strong hikers should undertake. A round-trip to Angel Arch from Cathedral Butte requires a minimum of two days, with a night at Angel Arch Camp. You would have to hike almost 15 miles the first day and 18 miles the second day, so this is not for everybody.

Photo advice: Backpacking with camera equipment forces you to decide on a strategy to balance your photographic needs with the logistics of carrying your gear. Many photographers, including myself, may find it difficult to adequately carry their usual equipment. My recommendation for backpacking trips and very long day hikes is to take a mirrorless camera with either a fixed lens or a short zoom and a very lightweight tripod or monopod. As camera bodies become more miniaturized, you should be able to carry your camera/lens combo in your pants' pocket or in a waist bag. If you absolutely need your dSLR, it should fit in a shoulder or hip bag with a short zoom or a medium-wide prime. I'm not saying you shouldn't carry your big boy camera in your backpack, but you'll be a lot happier if you have it at hand without having to take off your backpack every time you want to shoot. One thing I would not sacrifice is a small tripod. You will need it to shoot Angel Arch at dawn.

Getting there: To reach the northern Peekaboo Camp trailhead, start from Squaw Flat campground or from the road south of Cave Spring. To reach the southern Cathedral Butte trailhead, take the signed Beef Basin Road, 14 miles southeast of the park entrance or 8 miles north of Newspaper Rock on UT-211, and drive it about 17.2 miles to the trailhead spur at 37°57'01" 109°42'20".

Opposite page: Angel Arch & Molar Rock on right, at sunrise

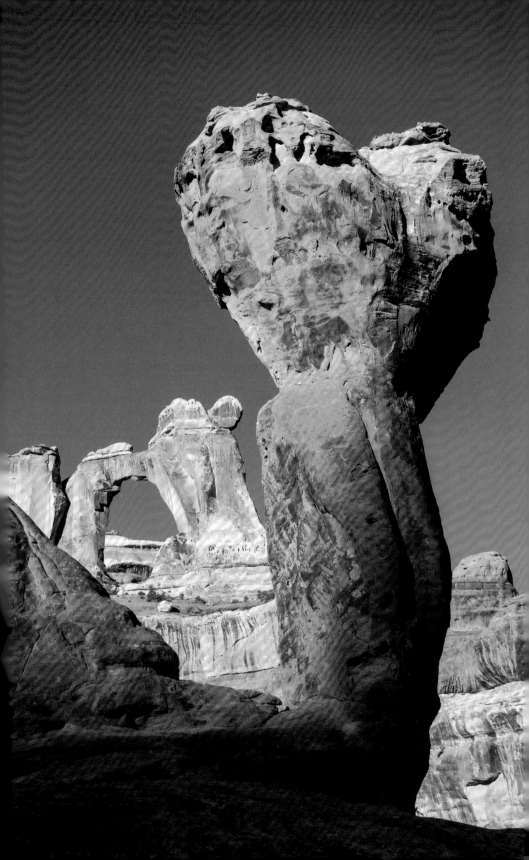

Davis Canyon

Davis is a beautiful canyon and a trove of Ancient Puebloan ruins. I would heartily recommend it to anyone except for the deep sand that requires a high-clearance 4WD vehicle. AWD SUVs with low clearance incur a real risk of getting stuck in the deep sand toward the end of the track. If you've never driven in deep sand, the most important thing to remember is to keep your momentum and not stop. The first part of the road inside the very wide dry wash is quite easy and fun to drive.

Park at the park boundary at the end of the track, sign the register and hike southwest into this pristine area to your heart's content. There are no arches in Davis Canyon, but many Puebloan dwellings, granaries, and pictographs waiting to be spotted and explored. At the very least, look for the well-preserved Five Faces pictograph panel which is about 1/3 mile from the trailhead, somewhat hidden on a ledge on the north side of the canyon. Camping is allowed only outside the park boundary. Be sure to close all gates behind you.

Photo advice: The striking silhouettes of North and South Six-Shooter Peaks yield great photos at sunrise about a mile or two into the track, with a medium telephoto.

You can get right in front of the Five Faces panel by following a small bench leading to its left side. A wide-angle is then needed. This will give you a much better photo than the telephoto shot you can take from the mouth of the small rincon leading to the panel.

Getting there: From UT-211, turn on signed Davis Canyon Road, about 14 miles north of Newspaper Rock or 7.7 miles east of the park's entrance station. Drive south about 8 miles to the fence at 38°04'01" 109°40'55". Most of the road is essentially tracks in the wash and is easy to follow, except in the last part, where it makes a turn to the west and meanders between trees around 38°04'36"

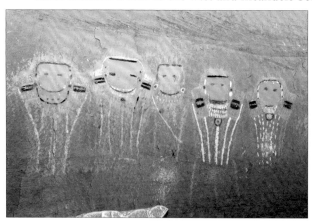

The Five Faces

109°40'14". From here to the fence, it is very sandy and requires 4WD.

Time required: You can easily spend a day in Davis Canyon, following tracks and finding beauty in each and every side canyon. A short foray to photograph the Five Faces panel and immediate surroundings would take up to 4 hours from UT-211.

Lavender Canyon

You may be wondering why Lavender Canyon Road makes such a long detour via Davis Canyon when your topo map indicates a more direct route? Some years ago, a prominent outdoor magazine published an article on the ten best places for car camping in America. One of them was Lavender Canyon! Lavender may be a great place for camping, but its remoteness and notorious quicksand make it a potential hazard for unsuspecting visitors. Hundreds of people flocked Lavender in the months following publication, seriously impacting the environment, creating incidents with the local ranchers and in a few instances requiring costly rescues. The NPS ended up closing the access route through private property, relocating it about 3½ miles to the northwest, closer to South Six Shooter Peak, and instigating a permit/quota system.

Lavender Canyon is popular for its beautiful canyon walls, arches, lush vegetation and solitude. Although it is within the limits of high-clearance 4WD SUVs under optimal conditions, Lavender should only be tackled by experienced and well-prepared visitors due to the deep sand and occasional patches of treacherous quicksand one may encounter. Two cars, a tow strap, and a shovel for each participant would just about eliminate any risks (I also carry a sandtrack and an inflatable jack to facilitate self-recovery). However, the wash becomes incredibly narrow for the last 2 miles of the track, about 1 mile after passing the park boundary, and your paint job may be given a rough treatment by the surrounding vegetation.

After the initial 3 miles common to Davis and Lavender canyons, the signed Lavender Canyon Road (the turn-off to the east is at 38°06'48" 109°38'15") follows a wide sandy wash passing through BLM and private land and crossing three gates (remember to close behind you). About 1.6 miles after the turnoff, and 0.1 mile after crossing the third gate, there is a treacherous second crossing of Lavender Creek; flash floods can occur after strong rains, cutting deep into the soft sandy banks and making the track dangerous or impassable. Hopefully, this situation will have been remedied by the time you read this. Things settle down after that and the track ambles leisurely along the Lavender Creek streambed. After about 13 miles from UT-211, the wash enters a spectacular canyon of blond Cedar Mesa sandstone, announcing what's awaiting ahead. Two miles later, you reach the locked gate at the park boundary at 38°01'04" 109°39'52". Camping is not allowed inside the Park, so this is a good place to camp as you are on BLM land.

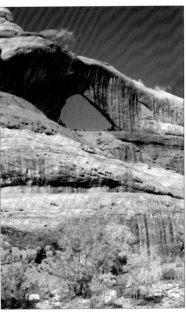

Cleft Arch

With your permit, you received a combination for the lock (this combination is changed frequently) allowing you to open the gate and continue driving into the canyon. By now, you're used to the routine of opening and closing gates.

Shortly after entering the national park, you'll encounter Natural Arch and Caterpillar Arch to your right, high on top of the canyon walls, but easy to spot. Indian ruins are also visible on the left side of the track. The area is remarkably pristine and riparian and Lavender Creek is usually a trickle once in the park. The wash becomes progressively narrower and the road ends shortly after passing Cleft Arch, a massive arch with beautiful streaks of desert varnish, about 4 miles from the park entrance. You can continue on foot in the east fork another half mile past the arch until you reach the end of the canyon, at the foot of Cathedral Mesa. Lavender Canyon is an absolutely awesome adventure!

Photo advice: Cleft Arch is best photographed from a small rise to the southwest. A short telephoto works best. Turn around and enjoy a great view of the end of the canyon, with Cathedral Butte in the distance.

Getting there: Follow the directions for Davis Canyon (see previous section). About 3 miles into the drive, in the wide wash section, keep your eyes open for a small sign pointing to Lavender Canyon on the left. This bypass eventually rejoins the old Lavender Canyon Road about 1.6 miles ahead.

Time required: When planning your trip, count on between 2 and 4 hours, depending on conditions, just for the round-trip drive. Also, don't forget to allo-

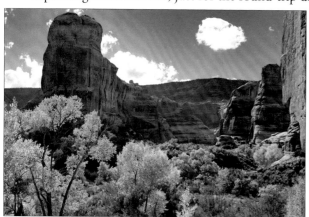

cate extra time to pick up your permit at the Needles Visitor Center. Your time inside the park is up to you, but it's easy to spend the day in Lavender. During my last visit, the track became impassable about 0.5 mile inside the park and I had to walk the rest. If this is the case during your visit, count on 2 to 3 hours to walk to Cleft Arch and back, at a relaxed pace.

Lavender Canyon fall colors

Cathedral Point (a.k.a. Big Pocket Overlook)

With its commanding position at the tip of Cathedral Mesa, this high overlook is without a doubt the best viewpoint to photograph the spectacular southern end of the Needles. The 180° view encompasses the colorful spires of Upper Salt Creek, the meadow-like Big Pocket, and the white meanders of Upper Lavender Canyon.

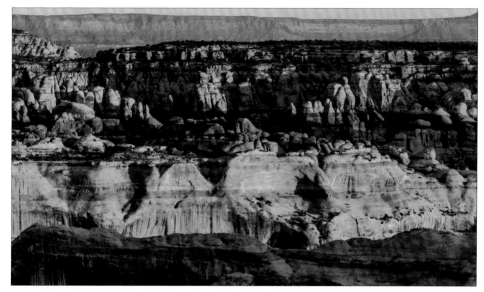

Cathedral Point

Photo advice: This is a fantastic location at both sunset and sunrise, shooting Lavender in late afternoon to sunset and Salt Creek and Big Pocket at sunrise. This makes it a prime spot for remote camping if you're going to backpack Salt Creek (as the Cathedral Butte trailhead is very close) or visit the Beef Basin (you are already on the way). I recommend a medium wide-angle for the 'grand scenic' shot, as well as a long telephoto to extract some of the distant Needles formations.

Getting there: From Newspaper Rock's parking area on UT-211, drive almost 8 miles to the signed Beef Basin Road turnoff, shortly after passing a large pond on the right side of the road. You'll know you're on the right road when you see the information kiosk on the left, showing the climbing routes of the Indian Creek Corridor. Drive 16.7 miles to a road on the right, to the northwest of massive Cathedral Butte. To avoid any confusion with other dirt roads in the area, the turn is at 37°57'29" 109°42'09". From this junction, drive 2.1 miles to a T, close to the end of the peninsula. The track requires high-clearance 4WD after 0.7 mile, due to slickrock steps. At the T, you have three choices: about 100 feet to the left, you have a great view over Salt Creek; continuing straight 200 feet, you have a more encompassing view of Salt Creek, including the Big Pocket; driving right 0.2 mile leads to a close view of the meanders of Upper Lavender Canyon.

Time required: A 30-minute drive each way from the junction with the Beef Basin Road, plus 1 hour to scout the area and shoot. More is better and an overnighter is highly recommended.

Nearby location: Sparks Wall Ruin is a tall and attractive, fortified, double-decker ruin rebuilt by volunteers high on a cliff of Bridger Jack Mesa. It is located next to the Sparks Wall climbing routes in the Indian Creek Corridor.

You can see the ruin from the car park, located on a short spur track to your right, about 3.8 miles from UT-211 on Beef Basin Road. There is a faint social trail leading up to the base of the climbing routes, with a 10-foot vertical climb aided by a log at the end. This route takes you to the left of the ruin which is not so photogenic. Instead, continue past the car park and make your own way up through the scree and boulders, aiming for the right of the ruin where a little ledge allows you to catch the ruin's best profile. This is a very steep hike on loose soil, so be careful not to slip or twist an ankle.

The Beef Basin

Continuing east on Beef Basin Road (CR-107) past Cathedral Butte, the spur road to Cathedral Point, and the trailhead to Salt Creek, the county-maintained road usually does not present too much difficulty for SUVs with good tires and sufficient clearance. It's a good idea, though, to inquire about the state of the road before setting out. The higher sections of the road are usually snowed-in during winter and muddy when the snow melts. Early summer and early fall are the best time to go, before and after it gets too hot. Once you get off the county road, leaving the higher elevation to descend into the Beef Basin, be ready for a lot of sand. Some low-clearance SUVs may struggle if the sand is deep after a long dry spell. Mostly, the potential danger of the Beef Basin is its remoteness, so be well prepared.

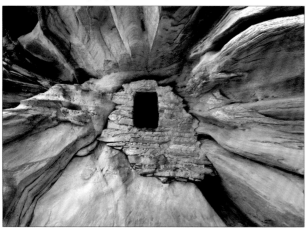

The Beef Basin consists of a number of lower elevation meadows, or 'parks'. The main draw is its high concentration of Indian ruins, peppered all over, but hard to find. Michael Kelsey has done a great job documenting the area in his book, *Hiking, Biking & Exploring Canyonlands National Park & Vicinity,* I highly recommended it for an in-depth exploration of the area.

Little Granary © Rick Schafer

Getting there: To get to Beef Basin, take the signed Beef Basin Road, about 14 miles southeast of the Needles District entrance or almost 8 miles north of Newspaper Rock on UT-211. Drive it about 25 miles and take a dirt road to your right at 37°54'21" 109°14'27" descending into House Park.

Photo advice: I will point out a couple of attractive ruins that are particularly photogenic. About 9.2 miles past the aforementioned waypoint, leave House

Park Road at 37°58'47" 109°52'24" and take signed Beef Basin Road to the right toward Middle Park. After 1.5 miles, turn right at 38°00'04" 109°52'27" on a spur road leading to a car park on the left in 0.8 mile. From here, walk northwest along the well-trod path to a wonderful little granary tucked inside the cliff. There are other granaries along the cliff, walking east from the car park. I wouldn't have mentioned this precious spot but for the fact that Moab outfitters now run 3-day tours of the Needles including the Beef Basin ruins.

Back at the last junction, turn right toward Ruin Park. Drive 1.3 miles and turn left on the short spur to Tower Ruin, a well-known landmark of Ruin Park. 4.6 miles past the last junction is the infamous Bobby's Hole leading to the Grabens area of the Needles district. This road is only for modified 4WD vehicles and starts deteriorating near the end of Pappys Pasture, so you'll have ample warning.

Returning to the county-maintained road at 37°54'21" 109°14'27", you can either return the way you came to UT-211 or continue south where it joins Elk Mountain Road, leading through the Bears Ears to UT-275 and Natural Bridges National Monument.

Time required: About 5 hours from UT-211 to explore Middle Park and Ruin Park and back. From my unofficial campsite at Cathedral Point/Big Pocket Overlook, it took about 7 hours to UT-275.

Canyon Rims

Canyon Rims Recreation Area encompasses three major viewpoints on the vast Hatch Point plateau. They are reached via a long but well-maintained road that dead-ends at the Anticline Overlook, a cool 76-mile round-trip from US-191.

The Needles Overlook is the first viewpoint encountered. The view from the Overlook is spectacular because it is such an incredibly vast panorama; however, for this very reason, it doesn't lend itself well to photography. The Colorado River is not visible and the Needles district is very distant, even with a telephoto.

The Anticline Overlook gets much closer to recognizable landmarks of Island in the Sky. The best views are of the long ridge of the anticline, with Hurrah Pass and Kane Gulch to the east. It makes for an interesting sunset shot, but not a great image. You can also shoot the Potash evaporation ponds, which are quite close—not everybody's cup of tea, but I've seen some nice photos of these from

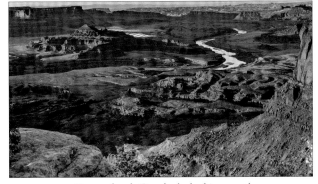

Canyonlands Overlook, looking north

this viewpoint. On your way back from Anticline Overlook, after about 2.6 miles, look for a surprising arch shaped like a wine glass. The aptly named Wine Glass Arch is on the southern edge of a butte on the west side of the road (38°25'45" 109°36'37"). The arch is fairly small and you'll need to get close to it to get a decent picture.

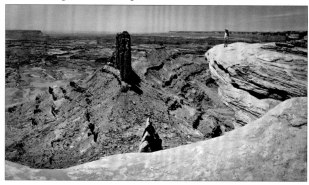

Canyonlands Overlook, looking southwest © Philippe Schuler

I left the best for last because it requires a 4WD approach and it takes much longer to visit, especially if the track is in poor condition. Canyonlands Overlook is a great sunrise/sunset location with a couple of nice viewpoints. The track has deteriorated in recent years; as of this writing, you can drive a stock SUV easily to 38°24'14" 109°41'35". For the last mile to the edge of the peninsula, you'll need high-clearance 4WD, with beefier tires than stock, and you may need to do a bit of road building. Alternatively, you can just walk to the picnic area at 38°24'16" 109°42'32" in about twenty minutes.

Photo advice: From the north rim near the picnic area, you can shoot a vast panorama including Pyramid Butte, the Colorado River, and the Lockhart Basin. For the best sunset shot, walk south about 600 feet to the west rim, where you can shoot a big monolith known as the United Nations Tablet, looking southwest. For sunrise, you can shoot a closer view of the Tablet with an interesting foreground from the south rim, roughly ½ mile south of the picnic area.

Getting there: Drive about 32 miles south of Moab on US-191 and turn right (west) on the signed Needles/Anticline Overlook paved road. Coming from the south this turnoff is 6.8 miles north of UT-211. Continue 15 miles to a junction. For the Needles Overlook, continue left (west) on the paved road for 6.8 miles. For Anticline Overlook, continue straight (north) on the excellent gravel road for another 16.5 miles. The road to Canyonlands Overlook starts 1 mile past the turnoff for the Hatch Campground (or 7 miles from the Anticline Overlook), to the west. The Canyonlands Overlook track is mostly signed and obvious. The first viewpoint is reached at 5.3 miles and the picnic area at 6.3 miles.

Time required: 2½ hours for a quick visit to the Needles Overlook and Anticline Overlook. Add at least a couple of hours for the Canyonlands Overlook or camp there to shoot at sunset and sunrise.

❖ ❖ ❖

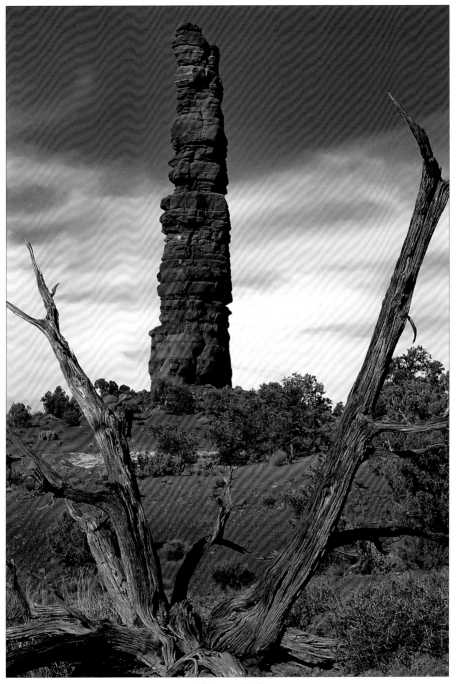

Chimney Rock

Chapter 17

CANYONLANDS – THE MAZE

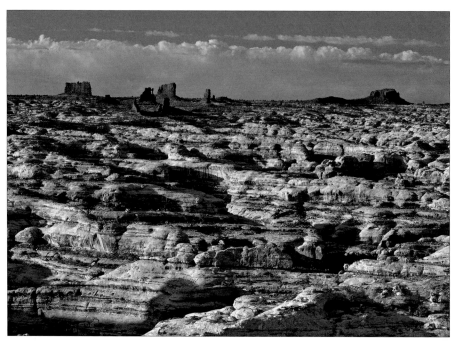

Sunrise on the Maze

Introduction to The Maze

As the name implies, the Maze is an intricate network of canyons. However, it also contains an amazing variety of fascinating rock formations spread out over a vast, wild and rugged area. As Canyonlands National Park's most remote and difficult to access district, the Maze sees relatively few visitors. If you are adventurous, as well as looking for solitude and quiet, the Maze is for you. With the exception of the Horseshoe Canyon detached section, which can be visited in one day, you will need at least four days to explore the Maze if you are coming by 4WD or from the Colorado River—more if you're backpacking or mountain biking deep inside the canyons. Spring and fall are the best seasons to explore the Maze. During wintertime, snow conditions often force access route closures. In summer, the heat can become unbearable and there is no water along the trails. Regardless of the season, avoid rainy weather at all cost; it turns the clay roads into a quagmire and you could get stuck for days on end.

The Maze district of Canyonlands is arguably one of the most remote areas in the continental U.S. and visiting it requires careful preparation. You have two options to visit the Maze on your own: driving the rough tracks with a 4WD vehicle, or coming/returning from/to Moab by jet boat on the Colorado River and backpacking from Spanish Bottom at the confluence with the Green River.

In the first scenario, you need a rugged, preferably lifted, 4x4 in tip-top mechanical condition. A short wheelbase is recommended and so are rugged mud-terrain tires with as many plies as possible. Large SUVs don't do well in the Maze, especially in some difficult sections like Teapot Canyon. You would most likely make it—although the stock tires may not—but you would risk inflicting serious damage to the undercarriage, bumpers, mud flaps, running boards, etc. For additional security, you need a couple of extra tires, a tire repair kit and plugs, a high-lift jack (I use an ARB exhaust jack), a good compressor, and a recovery strap plus a couple of sandtracks and shovels. Further, you need chains for all tires if there is a chance of snow, extra gas, lots of water, topographic maps and other necessities as you see fit for an extended 4x4 road trip requiring total self-sufficiency. Needless to say, you also need good 4-wheeling skills. A vehicle rescue from the Maze could cost you in the neighborhood of $2,500; not an outlandish figure when you consider that the Doll House is located 100+ miles from the nearest town, mostly on a wretched trail. Oh, and don't forget the compulsory port-a-potty (not required for backpackers).

In the hiking/backpacking scenario, you make arrangements with an outfitter to take you by jet boat from the Potash Road boat ramp to Spanish Bottom and pick you up on your return day. For any kind of hiking or backpacking inside the Maze, especially with photographic equipment, you need to be in good physical shape, as some of the hikes are long and strenuous. Most are on primitive trails, with exposure to cliff edges and steep routes requiring some scrambling and no fear of heights. Even if you are in good shape, you may experience a lot of discomfort if you are not used to carrying weight over long distances. A rope or a couple of 30-foot slings are necessary to lower packs in some difficult passages.

Any overnight trip to the Maze requires a backcountry permit, which has to be reserved well in advance if you go in spring or early autumn. This is especially true for car camping, as there are very few authorized campsites. Reservations are done on the web at canypermits.nps.gov/index.cfm. During the off-season, you could possibly get a campsite by checking directly with the Hans Flat Ranger Station. If you don't enter the Maze via Hans Flat, you must have a pre-reserved permit in your possession.

One final piece of advice: bring some friends, preferably in a second vehicle— the more arms to push, the better. Do not venture into the Maze alone or without leaving specific details of your whereabouts. If you have neither the vehicle(s) nor the partner(s) for this trip, but have a grand or more to spare, you may consider hiring an outfitter to take you into the Maze. Let them wreck their vehicle and enjoy yourself free of concerns in one of the world's greatest wilderness.

Getting there: The following information applies to driving a vehicle to all locations described in the next sections. There are three access routes to the various landmarks of the Maze. The most common way is to take UT-24 to the Hans Flat turnoff, located about 0.6 mile south of the Goblin Valley Road turnoff (see *Around Hanksville* chapter). This is about 19 miles north of Hanksville or 25 miles south of I-70 if coming from Green River. Follow the good graded dirt road for 24 miles. At the roofed signpost, follow the right fork for another 21 miles to the Hans Flat Ranger Station. The left fork leads in 7 miles to Horseshoe Canyon's trailhead. There are often pronghorns visible a short distance from the road in this area. Except during and after a rain, these roads are passable by passenger car. However, about 2½ miles southeast of Hans Flat Ranger Station (at the North Point Road Junction), a 4WD becomes necessary, whether going west to Panorama Point or south toward the turnoff to the Flint Trail.

After descending the steep switchbacks of the Flint Trail, you can either head northeast to the Maze Overlook or, if you want to visit the Land of Standing Rocks and the Doll House, go southwest, then northeast, traversing an extremely rough section around Teapot Rock. This section has some technically difficult spots and is extremely hard on tire walls and your vehicle's undercarriage. Over the past decade or so, I have observed a trend toward deterioration of the 4WD roads in the park. Drought, stronger monsoon rains, and lack of adequate budget combine to make this trend the norm for the foreseeable future.

An alternate way to visit the southern part of the Maze is to enter from the south on the usually well-maintained county road, leaving from UT-95 near Hite. This road is located about halfway between the Colorado River bridge and the Dirty Devil River bridge and is easy to miss. It allows you to make relatively good speed for the first thirty miles to Waterhole Flats and to avoid the switchbacks of the Flint Trail. However, this can lead to a false sense of security as it leads you smack into Teapot Canyon where things become suddenly hellish. Teapot Canyon is by far the most infamous section of road in the Maze—there is another short one just before arriving at the Doll House. In my opinion, it would also be sad to miss the Flint Trail, which is a road of legend and part of the fun of visiting the Maze, much as the Shafer Trail is part of the White Rim Road experience. However, even if you enter the Maze from the north by Hans Flat, you can also exit via this southern route. Gas is available at the Hite Marina.

A third way into the Maze is from Green River via a graded dirt road heading to Horseshoe Canyon (see section below).

Horseshoe Canyon

Horseshoe Canyon is a detached section of Canyonlands National Park, located northwest of the Maze and much easier to access. It protects a series of outstanding early Barrier-style pictographs, located inside a very scenic canyon. By a strange quirk of history, this canyon, formerly known as Barrier Canyon, has lost its original name while vesting it to a style of rock art associated with the Fremont culture of the Late Archaic period (prior to the advent of agriculture). The crown jewel of Horseshoe Canyon is a large and well-preserved panel of intricately beautiful human and animal figures known as the Great Gallery, stretching over 120 feet of smooth slickrock wall. Most of the figures are life-size and some of them are over seven feet tall. They have large tapered torsos, no appendages and are quite ghostlike in appearance. A few figures are decorated with various patterns or surrounded by small birds and animals. Many have theorized that the figures are depictions of shamans in drug-induced spiritual states. Some people even believe that they represent visiting space aliens. Upon close examination, you'll notice that some of the figures not only consist of pigment applied onto the rock, but that the rock itself is intricately pecked around the silhouette. One phenomenon you will easily notice is the fact that some of the figures are pock-marked, leading some archaeologists to theorize that objects could have been thrown at them during rituals. The issue around the age of the mural has long been a subject of controversy. It was first said to be two to four thousand years old, but recent studies using cutting-edge luminescence dating techniques point to a range of one to two thousand years. Regardless of your own interpretation of these pictographs, there is little doubt that the Great Gallery is the most spectacular panel of rock art in North America, as well as an unforgettable experience.

The Great Gallery stretches out on a ledge located about 15 feet above ground. The area is cordoned off and, unless a park ranger is present, you'll need to admire and photograph the panel from a distance of about 30 feet, which makes it easy to capture either large portions of the panel or to focus on specific figures or groups of figures with a telephoto. To guarantee that you can observe and photograph the figures at close range, as well as listen to an interesting interpretation, you'll need to join a ranger-led hike. Such hikes are usually held in the spring, based on staff availability (call the Hans Flat Ranger Station for more information).

The hike from the trailhead at the top of the mesa to the Great Gallery is about 7 miles round-trip, but can feel longer than that when the weather is hot. It takes approximately 4 to 5 hours to accomplish, with enough time at the panels for observation, photography and rest. By hiking out early in the morning, you'll be able to take advantage of the best lighting conditions at the Great Gallery, as well as avoid the hottest part of the day as you climb back up to the plateau, which lies 750 feet above the canyon floor. It is a long climb—over a mile—and if you do it in mid-afternoon, it will be extremely hot. In late afternoon, however, the cliff will be partially in the shade.

At the bottom of the mesa, the canyon itself is absolutely gorgeous, with many cottonwoods providing welcome shade along the way. All through the hike, you'll be following a stream that usually seems to run with at least a small trickle of water, although it becomes frozen in winter.

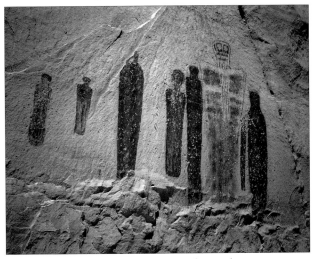

The Great Ghost... and Friends

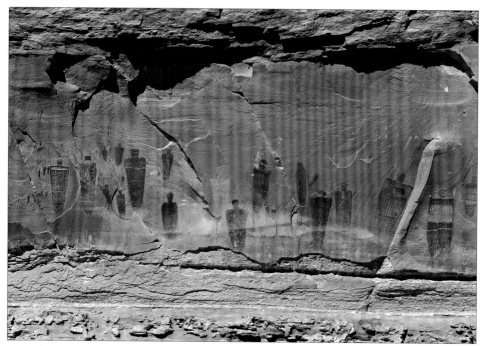

Wall of Spirits

There are other pictograph panels along the way to the Great Gallery. The first one is easily spotted on your left, less than 20 minutes after the descent, and is called the High Gallery; you'll know why when you see it. The canyon is fairly wide and you'll need to cross the stream bed and walk on a trail to the right in order to visit the easily missed Horseshoe Shelter panel, a bit further up. About ½ mile further, you'll encounter a huge alcove on the right side that makes for a nice resting spot, especially if you are hiking in the sun. Look for a few small pictographs toward the back of the alcove, unfortunately marred by some graffiti. If you look at the roof of the alcove, you will also note marks that seem to have been made by globs of wet mud thrown at the rock.

Continuing on 1¼ miles upstream, you'll eventually reach the main panel of the Great Gallery, to your right.

Photo advice: As with all other large rock art panels of the Southwest, it's up to you to photograph what you want, from the wide scene encompassing the whole panel to the minutest detail.

Anything from a moderate wide-angle to a telephoto will work well at the Great Gallery. If no Ranger is present to unlock the fence, a long telephoto will be useful to isolate some particularly interesting anthropomorphs, such as the one with the tiny birds perched on its shoulder. Of course, you will want to photograph the Great Ghost, a large figure with a mysterious, ghostly appearance and intricate detail in the head. You'll find it to the left of the main panel, under a shallow alcove. Many of the other figures on the panel look like tapered mummy-like blobs of pigment with broad shoulders and two spots representing the eyes. On the whole, the "Gallery" gets its impact from the number of figures and size of the panel, so moderate focal lengths will work best. Use different angles to impart some variety to your shots.

If you hike-in very early in the morning, you will have the ethereal experience of seeing the figures gradually illuminated by the soft morning light. On the other hand, if you end-up photographing the figures in bright sunlight, you may want to use a polarizing filter to eliminate glare.

Getting there: From either Hanksville or I-70 west of Green River, take UT-24 to the Hans Flat turnoff (about 0.6 mile south of Goblin Valley road) and turn onto the graded dirt road. Follow it for 24 miles until your reach a fork with a roofed signpost. Now bear left and continue east for about 5.2 miles, then turn right and drive 1.8 miles to the car park and primitive campground near the top of the mesa. Alternately, there is a direct 45-mile graded dirt road from Green River to the above-described last junction; it leaves from Airport Road, south of town, and takes about the same time as using UT-24. If you come all the way from Moab, count on approximately 2½ hours driving time.

Time required: Allow the good part of a day for Horseshoe Canyon, including driving time both ways, especially if you come from Moab. If you're not going to explore other parts of the Maze, it's possible to visit Goblin Valley State Park in mid to late-afternoon of the same day (refer to the *Around Hanksville* chapter).

Nearby location: Perched high on the rim of Two Mile Canyon, on the west side of the Green River, impressive Colonnade Arch (a.k.a. Five Hole Arch) consists of multiple spans forming several grottoes. It is best visited in the afternoon after returning from the Great Gallery. You can create unusual images looking out through the pillars from the back of the grottoes with a wide or ultrawide lens.

From the Horseshoe car park, drive back to the last junction and turn right. Continue 5.3 miles and turn right for another 4.6 miles to a car park at 38°34'34" 110° 05'24". High clearance is required for the last road. Walk north/northwest on the slickrock and in less than a thousand feet, you'll find an old road. Follow it past a fence for another 0.7 mile and angle east toward the rim for ¼ mile at 38°35'09"110°04'37". Then descend to the next level down and walk north to the arch at 38°35'10"110°04'36". On your way back from the arch, continue southwest along the rim to shoot the strange sand castles of Crocodile Rock at 38°34'50" 110°04'56". Allow about 2 hours for the hike only.

Panorama Point

Panorama Point affords a fantastic panoramic view of the northern Maze area and Island in the Sky, as well as close views of the Orange Cliffs. However, much like its Needles Overlook counterpart on the east side, the view is too distant to get interesting photographs. Telephoto views rarely give any quality results because of the haze that usually blankets the area. If you are pressed for time, you can pass this viewpoint without regret and head toward the Maze Overlook instead—although it's much farther. On the other hand, it is also the easiest way to catch a glimpse of the Maze, as it is only an hour's drive from Hans Flat Ranger Station by 4WD, without any technical sections along the way.

Getting there: 2½ miles south of Hans Flat Ranger Station, take the marked track leading east for less than 7 miles, then follow the right fork for another 1.6 miles to the overlook. The left fork leads in about 2 miles to the base of Cleopatra's Chair, a huge monolith dominating the whole area.

The Maze Overlook

This is without question the best vantage point over the Maze. You sit above the extraordinary labyrinths of Cedar Mesa sandstone and are relatively close. The impressive group known as the Chocolate Drops is right in front of you, less than a mile away—a last remnant of organ-shale rock capping the sandstone and looking much like a row of nuclear submarine kiosks. The Land of Standing Rocks can be seen in the distance to the south, but close enough to yield good images with a medium-range zoom, if no haze is present. Elaterite and Ekker Buttes are also fairly close and spectacular. This is a great spot to camp, relax and admire the Maze at its best. Late afternoon is the best time for photography. Approximately thirty minutes before sunset, you'll loose direct light over the Maze, but you'll get great colors in the sky if you have some clouds to the east. At dusk, you could have a nice alpenglow. Early morning is very good for shooting in the direction of the Land of Standing Rocks. The side light brings out much detail in the maze of canyons at your feet. Don't wait too long: an hour after sunrise, the Maze will appear flat and the opportunity will be gone!

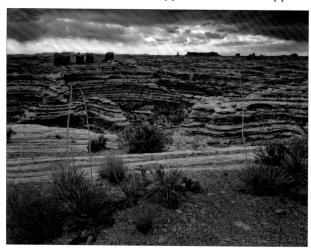

A very steep trail descends into the canyon bottom, leading to four different backpacking trails. One of these allows you to do a half-day trip to the Harvest Scene (see section below).

Getting there: About 12+ miles south of Hans Flat Ranger Station, go left and down the steep switchbacks of the Flint Trail for the 16-mile 4WD drive to the overlook. It takes about 3 hours one way from Hans Flat Ranger Station.

Clearing storm over the Chocolate Drops

The Harvest Scene

The Harvest Scene is one of the largest and most intriguing group of pictographs on the Colorado Plateau. This Late Archaic panel derives its name from unique scenes of harvest depicting the life of the early hunter-gatherers who traveled through these canyons. At least that is the official explanation. Altogether, there are a dozen or so figures on the main panel, spread over roughly forty feet. They are smaller and less impressive than those of the Great Gallery. One striking difference is the lack of a foreboding ghostlike appearance in these figures. No wide torsos here, but some fairly elongated bodies. The horns on the heads of several figures suggest masks used in some shamanistic ritual. The fact that they have feet but no arms, also contributes to make them a bit more human-like. There are more pictographs along the cliff, to the left of the main panel, but they are less interesting.

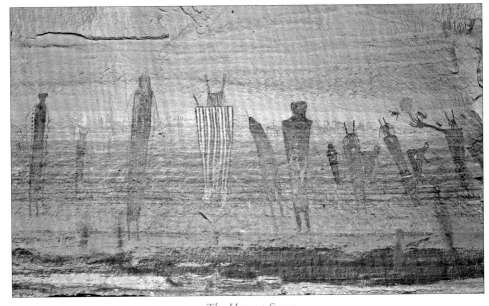

The Harvest Scene

Photo advice: Unfortunately, the panel is quite exposed to sun and wind erosion and the pigments have become faint, making it difficult to see and photograph without a soft light. If you are there in the middle of the day and the sun is shining directly on the panel, it will be difficult to bring out much detail, even with a polarizer. The best light occurs late in the day, when the sun is just leaving the panel. Early morning works too, before the sun hits the panel.

Photographing the panel is up to your imagination, however I would like to draw your attention to the large figure to the left, reminiscent of a telephone pole as well as to the interesting anthropomorph on the far right of the panel. Both isolate well vertically.

Getting there: There are two ways to get to the Harvest Scene, which is located in Pictograph Fork Canyon. The most interesting way is via the shorter but much more exposed Maze Overlook Trail (see previous section for access to the trailhead), which winds its way 600 feet down a steep cliff. This cairned route is quasi-technical in places, requiring that you negotiate a series of moki steps, a narrow crack, and a short vertical climb with exposure. It is not overly difficult if you are agile and not afraid of heights, but the short vertical climb could be a real issue for some. A rope or a couple of 30-foot slings will help greatly to lower your gear if you carry a camera backpack and a tripod. I suggest stashing a water bottle at the bottom of the cliff for later. Once in the Maze, follow the surprisingly verdant canyon to the south (left at the base of the cliff and around the eastern side of the Chocolate Drops) on a partly cairned path. Despite the cairns, do not venture inside the Maze without map, compass and a GPS. While walking, take regular bearings to be sure to find your way back. There are several small groups of pictographs visible along the way; some are very high up the canyon walls, so keep looking. The entire round-trip from the trailhead is about 5.5 miles. Starting at daybreak, you can be at the Harvest Scene in about 1½ hours, before the sun hits the panel. My recommendation, however, is to start in mid-afternoon and come back shortly before sundown, catching good light at the panel and possibly a light breeze on the way back up. Incidentally, you'll find that climbing back up is easier than coming down.

The other way to get to the Harvest Scene is the longer but easier 9-mile loop starting from Chimney Rock in the Land of Standing Rocks.

Nearby location: Returning to the Maze Overlook from the Harvest Scene, a short detour brings you to Triple Flush Arch: three arches stacked on top of the other above an alcove. Shooting from an appropriate angle at the base of the cliff, you can get the alcove (which has nice desert varnish) and all three openings in your picture. It's best to be there in the morning to ensure you won't have to deal with high contrast. Returning from the Harvest Scene, continue north past the canyon leading to the Maze Overlook ascent. Walk about 0.3 mile in the wash, then angle east (right) 300 feet to the arch at 38°14'06" 109°59'24".

The Land of Standing Rocks

One great way to observe and photograph the vast area known as Ernie's Country is by walking down the Golden Stairs, a moderately steep 2-mile hike down a sheer cliff composed of many different rock strata, hence the name Golden Stairs. If you're part of a group, you could arrange for your party to drop you at the Golden Stairs picnic area, located at the end of a 1-mile spur not far from the bottom of the Flint Trail. You could then take a leisurely walk down this spectacular path and then on to Land of Standing Rocks Road towards the Fins, where you can rendezvous with your friends after they have negotiated the infamous road around Teapot Rock.

Walking down the Golden Stairs offers great opportunities to see a formation called the Mother and Child, best photographed from the beginning of the trail in early morning, as well as the fins of Earnie's Country.

The Fins are beautiful and the backdrop of the Needles across the Colorado River make the scene very photogenic from the Land of Standing Rocks road, especially in mid-afternoon. Look for Cave Arch, easily located with the naked eye in front of the Fins.

After the jarring of Teapot Canyon or the sheer drop of the Golden Stairs, you'll be happy to enjoy a relatively smooth drive through the

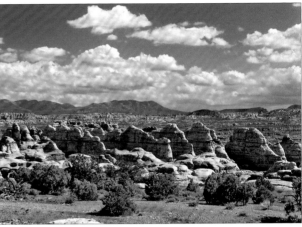

The Fins of Earnie's Country

Land of Standing Rocks, with its spectacular and photogenic monoliths. These include The Wall, Lizard Rock, the Plug and Chimney Rock. The Wall campground is a great place to stay and shoot from during the golden hour.

Getting there: The Land of Standing Rocks is about 35 miles from Hans Flat, past the switchbacks of the Flint Trail and the infamous section around Teapot Canyon. Count on 5 hours driving time.

The Doll House

This is a great location for photography, but also one of the most remote. The Doll House is almost 88 miles from UT-24 on dirt and rocky roads and 65 miles by boat from Moab. But what a place; it's a bit like the Needles district, with a whimsical flair thrown in. Rocks on pot, you might say.

There are three very scenic camping spots dispersed throughout the Doll House area. You'll need to pick the one you want when you reserve your permit. Campsite 3, at the top of a very steep slickrock hill is located 0.7 mile to the southwest of the Doll House and has a good panoramic view. From the other two campsites almost nested in the Doll House, just wander amidst the formations and seek

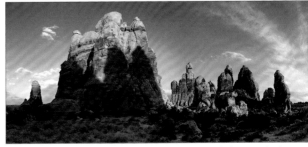

Panorama from above Campsite 1 © Philippe Schuler

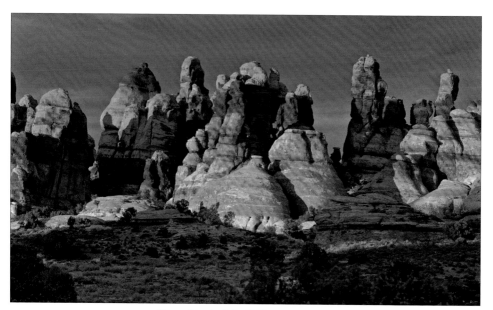

The whimsical Doll House at sunset

inspiration, you won't have difficulty finding it. I strongly recommend the 2-mile round-trip walk on the Granary Trail, south of the Doll House. It goes through a couple of interesting joints, as on the Joint Trail in Chesler Park (see *Needles* chapter), before reaching the lovely and aptly-named Surprise Valley, a verdant "graben" that is a refreshing site in this universe of stone. The trail ends at a cluster of four granaries, which are worth a picture if reflected light is present.

Photo advice: The Doll House is best photographed in late afternoon and at sunset. Take a general view from the vicinity of Campsite 3 with a medium tele-photo, then wander on foot inside the Doll House proper. There is a good sunset spot just over Campsite 1. At sunrise, walk a ¼ mile down the Spanish Bottom trail to be on the sunrise side, in front of huge formations. You'll be using a wide-angle most of the time

Getting there: The Doll House is located 5 miles past Chimney Rock at the very end of the Land of Standing Rocks Road (see above section). It is 42 miles from Hans Flat Ranger Station and about 6 hours driving time.

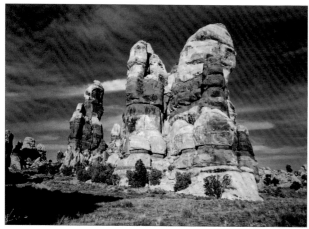

Doll House in early morning

The best way to reach the Doll House from spring to fall is by jet boat from Moab. A private trip with an outfitter is doable in one day, as the jet boat needs about 2 hours to cover the 50+ miles from the Potash Road boat ramp to Spanish bottom and about the same time on the way back (if no stops). The boatman waits for you as you climb to the top for a quick foray into the Doll House. In

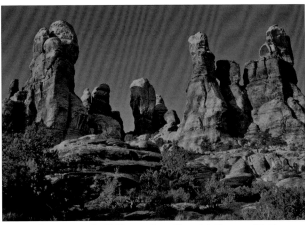

Sunrise on Doll House from Spanish Bottom Trail

this scenario, you'll be there in the middle of the day and the light will be very crude. Besides, you will not have enough time to enjoy the place thoroughly and it could be frustrating. The view down the Spanish Bottom Trail is superb, but even more so is the view of the Doll House from the Colorado River as you come within a mile from Spanish Bottom on the jet boat.

A better solution is to arrange a trip whereby a jet boat drops you off at Spanish Bottom and picks you up the next day or several days later. You need to carry all your water, camping gear, and camera equipment up and down the trail, which gains 1,200 feet of elevation in only 1.2 miles on a rocky talus slope. This is not a fun experience but not a problem either, if you are in good shape. If your schedule is flexible, you can arrange being dropped off and picked up on days the outfitter is going out anyway (usually to pickup canoeists paddling to the confluence of the Green and Colorado rivers and returning to Moab by jetboat). This translates into considerable savings compared to a private trip. Tex Riverways, among others, offers this kind of arrangement. If you join a multi-day Cataract Canyon trip, you stand a good chance to be able to do a quick trip to the Doll House, as many trips stop at Spanish Bottom for the night. If you arrive in mid-afternoon, you can hike up and back the steep Spanish Bottom Trail in less than 3 hours and have a quick peek at this unique place.

Above Canyonlands

Although a scenic flight above Canyonlands National Park is by no means limited to the Maze district, I chose to include it in this chapter because for many people it is the only way to get an idea of this highly inaccessible part of the park. A flight can easily be arranged from Moab, Blanding, Monticello, Cortez, or Telluride. Another possibility is to fly back from Hite to Moab at the end of a multi-day rafting trip, as offered by some outfitters. Most of the time, two or three people are necessary to book a scenic flight.

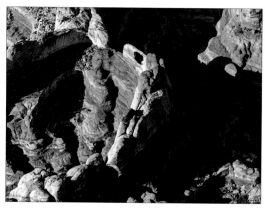

Arch & shadow

Seen from a small aircraft, the Canyonlands landscape is nothing but extraordinary. A 1-hour flight is enough to view many parts of the three districts: The Needles, with its amazing Grabens, Chesler Park, Salt Creek, the confluence of the Green and Colorado, Cataract Canyon, all of the fantastic formations of the Maze described in this chapter, the mesas of Island in the Sky and Dead Horse Point, and more.

If you only take one small plane trip in the course of your journey through the Southwest, make it this one. You won't regret the money spent.

Photo advice: A short telephoto is well suited to aerial photography of the Canyonlands at the lowest elevation allowed. Little or no depth-of-field is required, but you will of course need to keep the vibrations of the aircraft and your own movements in check. With the always improving quality of high ISO, an aperture of f/4 or f/5.6 (wider if you have to shoot through a window) and a minimum shutter speed of 1/500 sec. represents the best compromise for sharpness and resolution. Just set these two parameters and let the camera pick the ISO automatically. If you have a short gyro-stabilized zoom, it will work give you an additional two to three stops to compensate for the movement of the plane. Check beforehand to see if the pilot will allow you to open your window. Some pilots charge an additional fee for this extra "service". If you're shooting with the window closed, place the lens as close as possible to the glass to avoid reflections;

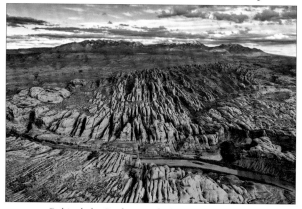

Behind the Rocks aerial © Momo Vuyisich

a polarizing filter can be helpful but may compromise your shutter speed with low ISO. In any case, disengage the autofocus and manually set the focus to infinity. Early morning or the end of the day is great for color and depth but could be too contrasty, so a soft light is preferred. Such a trip works well in winter when the sun is mostly at a low angle, even close to midday.

APPENDIX

Maps

The maps are classified by scale, beginning with the largest and most general.

Large scale road maps: The best general road map is without doubt the Indian Country Guide published by the American Automobile Association (AAA). This remarkable guide/map is a sheer pleasure to read and use. It contains a surprising amount of dirt and gravel roads, with very accurate mileage and it does an excellent job of referencing little-known locations. Unless you intend to do some heavy-duty hiking or four-wheeling, this map is quite sufficient for an ordinary car-based tour of the "Grand Circle". The only locations in the present guide not covered by AAA's Indian Country Guide are part of the San Rafael Swell north of Interstate 70 (Wedge Overlook, Buckhorn Draw, Nine Mile canyon) and Pine Creek/Cathedral Gorge. They are adequately covered by the AAA Utah and Nevada maps. You can obtain these maps from any AAA office and many of the bookstores in the National Parks and Monuments, as well as some gas stations.

Detailed road maps: Southeastern Utah and Southwestern Utah maps are published by the Utah Travel Council. Roads and tracks are indicated in a very precise fashion. These maps can prove very useful when used in conjunction with the Indian Country map, especially to find less important 4WD trails.

National Park and Monument miniguides: These wonderfully concise mini-guides are packed with all the essential information about the parks, their history, geology and fauna. You can get them at the park entrances or at Visitor Centers. Each has a detailed map of the highlights of the park to help you find your way around on roads and trails. For Grand Staircase-Escalante Nat'l Monument, you'll need the Visitor Information brochure; it includes a map introducing a very convenient numbering system that greatly helps in identifying and navigating the numerous backcountry roads in the area (including the southern part near US-89).

National Park topographic maps: If you plan on adventuring along the trails and roads in distant parts of the national parks, the topographic maps of the Illustrated Trails series, printed on waterproof paper, are extremely well made and highly recommended. I always use them for hiking in the parks.

Topographic maps for mobile devices: Downloadable 7.5' USGS topo maps in the palm of your hand! The ultimate tool to know exactly where you are at any given moment and monitor your progress on remote roads and trails. I use Phil Endecott's Topo for iPhone and iPad, but there is a wide choice of others.

Maps on CD-ROM: A fantastic resource to plan your trip beforehand, the maps print spectacularly well and you can mark your intended route. Great to enter way points in your GPS. Delorme, Maptech, and others make topo mapping software on CD-Rom. National Geographic's Topo! State Series was particularly good, but is no longer available new.

Other web resources: topoquest.com and others allow you to display and print, at no charge, small portions of topographic maps, using GPS coordinates. Many other sites, such as trimbleoutdoors.com, alltrails.com, trails.com, arcgis.com, etc., offer a more sophisticated interface and better printing, for a fee.

mapper.acme.com allows instantaneous switching between satellite, topo, and navigation maps.

Earthpoint.us/topomap.aspx allows you to use topographic maps in a Google Earth layer.

4x4 topographic maps: Fran Barnes' maps in the Canyon Country series are old but still excellent, if you can find them. They are U.S. Geological Survey topo maps with numerous superimposed 4x4 tracks. They are extremely practical for four-wheeling in the Moab/Arches/Canyonlands area.

Lake Powell and its 96 Canyons Boating and Exploring Map: Stan Jones' fantastic map, traced by hand before the age of computers. Now maintained by Steve Ward. I treasure mine, signed by Mr. Lake Powell.

Selected Bibliography - Guidebooks

You have a wide selection of materials from which to choose among the traditional guidebooks. Here are some of my favorites:

Non-Technical Canyon Hiking Guide to the Colorado Plateau by Michael Kelsey, ISBN 978-0944510278; a remarkable resource for fit people wanting to explore remote places of the Colorado Plateau. Truly a monumental work. To be used responsibly and according to the author's warnings and disclaimers. Hiking times are underestimated for almost everybody. Use maps with caution and not as your primary source of information.

Hiking and Exploring the Paria River by Michael Kelsey, ISBN 978-0944510261; excellent reference; comments for the Canyon Hiking Guide to the Colorado Plateau apply to this one and the next one too.

Hiking, Biking and Exploring Canyonlands National Park by Michael Kelsey, ISBN 978-0944510292, the latest great resource by the seminal author.

Utah's Favorite Hiking Trails by David Day, ISBN 978-0966085815; great descriptions of a large number of Utah trails; highly recommended.

Canyonlands National Park Favorite Jeep Roads & Hiking Trail by David Day, ISBN 978-0966085822; a classic for exploring Canyonlands Nat'l Park.

Favorite Hikes In & Around Zion National Park by Tanya Milligan & Bo Beck, ISBN 978-1892540829: excellent, a must-have for southwestern Utah.

Hiking Guide to Cedar Mesa by Peter Francis Tassoni, ISBN 978-0874806809; excellent resource if you can find it, with an abundance of GPS points.

Canyoneering 3: Loop Hikes in Utah's Escalante by Steve Allen, 978-0874805451; excellent resource for novice canyoneers.

Zion: Canyoneering by Tom Jones, 978-0978961404; excellent resource for advanced canyoneers; compulsory reading for the Subway 'from the Top'.

Guide To Moab, UT-Backroads & 4-Wheel Drive Trails, by Charles Wells; ISBN 978-1934838068; a must have for 4-wheeling in the Moab area.

Utah Trails Southwest Region by Peter Massey & Jeanne Wilson, ISBN 978-1930193109; part of an excellent series; a must have for 4-wheeling in Utah, more practical to use than their huge Backcountry Adventures Utah.

Utah Trails Central Region by P. Massey & J. Wilson, ISBN 978-1930193314

Utah Trails Moab Region by P. Massey & J. Wilson, ISBN 978-1930193093

Journey to the High Southwest by Robert Casey, ISBN 978-0762740642; remarkably endearing and thoroughly documented.

Utah Byways by Tony Huegel, ISBN 978-0899972633; nice to have in the glove box for good description of the Scenic Backways.

Hiking the Southwest's Canyon Country by Sandra Hinchman, ASIN: B001TK3Q6A; excellent hiking guide to the Southwest, very complete.

Hiking Zion and Bryce Canyon NP by Erik Molvar, ISBN 978-0762782765; excellent hiking guide to these major parks.

Hiking Grand Staircase-Escalante & the Glen Canyon Region by Ron Adkinson, ISBN 978-0762760619; excellent hiking resource.

Exploring Canyonlands and Arches by Bill Schneider, published by Falcon Press, ISBN 1-56044-510-6; good hiking resource.

Canyon Country Off-Road Vehicle Trails (a collection) by Fran Barnes; very old, but still very good, if you can find them in Moab or online.

Guide to Rock Art of Nine Mile Canyon by M. and J. Liddiard, no ISBN; a useful booklet for finding rock art panels in the canyon.

Canyon Country Geology for the Layman and Rockbound by F. A. Barnes, ISBN 1-891858-18-1; one of many highly informative and easy-to-read guidebooks by Mr. Barnes. Highly recommended.

National Geographic's Guide to the National Parks of the USA ASIN 1426208693, an excellent primer for beginning travelers, very well illustrated.

Selected Bibliography - Other Recommended Reading

I cannot recommend too highly the following works, which I consider quintessential to a good understanding of various aspects of the Southwest. Reading these books during a trip in the American West reinforces the pleasure of discovery.

The Southwest Inside Out by Thomas Wiewandt and Maureen Wilks, ISBN 978-1879728066; highly-innovative and approachable presentation of the natural features of the Southwest. Remarkably illustrated. Outstanding photography.

Resurrection - Glen Canyon & a New Vision for the American West by Annette McGivney & James Kay, ISBN 978-0-898867-71-8, a glimpse into the past and future of Glen Canyon, superbly photographed by James Kay. A must-have.

Mormon Country by Wallace Stegner, ISBN 978-0803293052; a fundamental work on the colonization of Utah by the Mormons; impartial, remarkably documented, and an easy read. It would be a shame to visit Utah without knowing or understanding the remarkable saga of the Mormon pioneers.

Architecture of the Ancient Ones by A. Dudley Gardner and Val Brinkerhoff, ISBN 978-0879059552; outstanding photography.

Cliff Dwellers of Cedar Mesa by Donald Rommes and William Lipe, ISBN 978-0-937407-226; outstanding photography.

Standing Up Country by Gregory Crampton, ISBN 978-1887896153; a great resource on the human history of the Colorado Plateau, richly illustrated.

The Exploration of the Colorado River and its Canyons by John Wesley Powell, ISBN 978-1420946482; Powell's extraordinary journals of his expedition, prefaced by Wallace Stegner. Seminal work. You'll be in awe of the Man.

Centennial by James Michener, ISBN 978-0449214190; a remarkable book, describing the conquest of the Western frontier through the fascinating saga of several characters and families over centuries.

Desert Solitaire by Edward Abbey, ISBN 978-0671695880; the classic among the numerous books by Abbey, the rebel ranger, at once libertarian and redneck. Abbey depicts his love of the desert with a fine sensibility. It's the perfect accompaniment for a trip to Arches and Canyonlands.

The Dark Wind by Tony Hillerman, ISBN 978-0062018021; one of a series of fun novels with a cool Navajo cop as its reluctant hero. An excellent introduction to Navajo culture in the guise of a lively story. A must-read when on the Big Rez! Don't be ashamed of the "white guy" syndrome. If you get hooked on Navajo and Hopi culture, you'll naturally step up to more serious works.

RATINGS

Using a scale of 1 to 5, the following ratings attempt to provide the reader with an overall vision of each location, in order to facilitate comparisons and choices. Obviously, the ratings alone don't tell the whole story about a location and should always be used in conjunction with the explanations of each section.

The ratings are assigned on the basis of four different criteria: overall interest of a location, based mostly on its scenic value (or its beauty and interest in the case of rock art and ancestral dwellings), photographic potential for those of you who happen to carry a camera :-) and level of difficulty to access each location with your vehicle and/or on foot"

Rating	Scenic Value
—	Of no particular interest
♥	Mildly interesting, visit if nearby and/or time permitting
♥♥	Scenic location, worthy of a visit
♥♥♥	Very interesting, scenic or original location
♥♥♥♥	Remarkably scenic or rewarding location - a highlight
♥♥♥♥♥	World-class location - absolutely tops

Rating	Photographic Interest
—	Of no particular photographic interest
♦	Worthy of a quick photo
♦♦	Good photo opportunity
♦♦♦	Good photographic potential and scenic subjects
♦♦♦♦	Outstanding photographic potential, highly original or scenic subjects
♦♦♦♦♦	World-class photographic location, "photographer's dream"

Rating	Road Difficulty
—	Paved road, accessible to all normal-size vehicles
▲	Dirt road accessible without difficulty by passenger car (under normal conditions)
▲▲	Minor obstacles; accessible by passenger car with caution (under good conditions)
▲▲▲	High-clearance required, but no major difficulty
▲▲▲▲	High-clearance 4WD required, some obstacles, no real danger
▲▲▲▲▲	High-clearance 4WD required, some risk to vehicle & passagers, experienced off-road drivers only

Rating	Trail Difficulty
—	No or very little walking (close to parking area)
♣	Easy short walk (<= 1 hr r/t), for everybody
♣♣	Moderate hike (1 to 3 hr r/t) with no major difficulty or short hike with some minor difficulties
♣♣♣	Moderate to strenuous (3 to 6 hr r/t) and/or difficulties (elevation gain, difficult terrain, some risks)
♣♣♣♣	Strenuous (> 6 hr r/t) and/or globally difficult (elevation gain, difficult off-trail terrain, obstacles, risks)
♣♣♣♣♣	Backpacking required or for extremely fit dayhikers

Warning: Road Difficulty ratings are for normal, dry conditions. Driving conditions can change dramatically during or after a rain, even more so on clay roads or roads that follow the course of a wash. As an example, the popular and well-used Cottonwood Canyon Road—rated 2 in difficulty—can become impassable after a rain and stay so for days on end, even with 4WD. Severe weather can drastically alter conditions for extended periods of time. When the road was last maintained also has a huge impact on its condition and can alter the rating by 1 level in either direction. Always check current road conditions with local authorities before you leave.

Location	Page	Scenic Value	Photo Interest	Road Difficulty	Trail Difficulty
1 Around St. George					
Snow Canyon - Trails along Scenic Road	24	♥♥♥♥	♦♦♦♦	—	♣♣
Snow Canyon - UT-18 Overlook	25	♥♥♥	♦♦♦	—	—
Red Mountain	26	♥♥♥	♦♦♦	—	♣♣
Santa Clara River Reserve	28	♥♥	♦♦	—	♣♣
Gunlock Mesa	29	♥♥♥	♦♦	♠	♣♣
Yant Flat	31	♥♥♥♥	♦♦♦♦♦	♠♠♠	♣♣♣
Red Cliffs	36	♥♥	♦♦	—	♣
Kanarra Creek	37	♥♥♥	♦♦♦	—	♣♣♣
Parowan Gap Petroglyphs	38	♥	♦♦	—	—
Pine Park	39	♥♥	♦♦♦	♠♠	♣
Cathedral Gorge	41	♥♥♥	♦♦♦	♠	♣
2 Inside Zion					
Towers of the Virgin	45	♥♥	♦♦♦	—	—
Watchman (from the bridge)	46	♥♥	♦♦♦	—	—
Pa'rus Trail	46	♥♥	♦♦	—	♣
Court of the Patriarchs	47	♥♥♥	♦♦♦	—	♣
Emerald Pools	47	♥♥	♦♦	—	♣♣
Angels Landing	48	♥♥♥♥♥	♦♦♦	—	♣♣♣♣
Hidden Canyon	50	♥♥	♦♦	—	♣♣♣
Observation Point	50	♥♥♥♥	♦♦♦	—	♣♣♣♣
Photo Point	52	♥♥♥	♦♦♦	—	—
Temple of Sinawava & Riverside Walk	53	♥♥♥	♦♦	—	♣
Virgin Narrows	56	♥♥♥♥♥	♦♦♦♦	—	♣♣♣
Canyon Overlook Panorama	59	♥♥	♦	—	♣
Zion Plateau	60	♥♥♥♥	♦♦♦	—	—
Many Pools	61	♥	♦	—	♣
Checkerboard Mesa	61	♥♥	♦	—	—
East Rim Trail	62	♥♥♥	♦♦	—	♣♣♣♣
Deertrap Mountain	63	♥♥♥	♦♦♦	♠♠	♣♣♣
Kolob Terrace Road	64	♥♥♥	♦♦	♠♠	—
Subway from the "Bottom"	66	♥♥♥♥	♦♦♦♦♦	—	♣♣♣♣
Subway from the "Top"	70	♥♥♥♥	♦♦♦♦♦	—	♣♣♣♣♣
West Rim Trail	72	♥♥♥♥	♦♦♦♦	♠♠	♣♣♣♣
Kolob Canyon Viewpoint	74	♥♥♥	♦♦	—	—
Taylor Creek	76	♥♥	♦♦♦	—	♣♣
3 Around Zion					
Smithsonian Butte & Gooseberry Mesa	78	♥♥	♦♦	♠♠♠	—
Water Canyon	81	♥♥♥	♦♦♦	♠♠♠	♣♣
White Domes	82	♥♥♥	♦♦♦	♠♠♠	♣♣♣♣
Pipe Spring	83	♥	♦	—	—
Parunuweap Canyon (hike & canyon)	84	♥♥♥♥	♦♦	—	♣♣♣♣♣
Coral Pink Sand Dunes	86	♥♥♥	♦♦♦	—	♣
Red Canyon Slot	88	♥♥	♦♦	♠♠♠♠	♣
4 Around Bryce Canyon					
Sunrise & Sunset Viewpoints	91	♥♥♥♥♥	♦♦♦♦♦	—	—
Inspiration Point & Bryce Point	91	♥♥♥♥	♦♦♦♦	—	—
Navajo & Queen's Garden Trails	92	♥♥♥♥	♦♦♦	—	♣♣
Peek-a-Boo Trail (from the Rim)	94	♥♥♥♥	♦♦♦	—	♣♣♣
Fairyland Viewpoint & Trail	94	♥♥♥♥	♦♦♦	—	♣♣♣
Mossy Cave	95	♥♥♥	♦♦	—	♣
Yovimpai Point & Rainbow Point	96	♥♥♥	♦♦	—	♣
Red Canyon	96	♥♥♥	♦♦♦	—	♣♣
Cedar Breaks National Monument	98	♥♥♥	♦♦	—	♣
Twisted Forest	99	♥♥♥	♦♦	♠♠♠	♣♣♣

Location	Page	Scenic Value	Photo Interest	Road Difficulty	Trail Difficulty
5 Along the Paria					
Cottonwood Canyon Road	102	♥♥♥♥	♦♦♦	♠♠	—
Round Valley Draw	104	♥♥	♦	♠♠♠	♣♣♣
Grosvenor Arch	105	♥♥	♦♦	♠♠	—
Cottonwood Narrows	105	♥♥	♦♦	♠♠	♣
Lower Hackberry Narrows	107	♥♥	♦♦	♠♠	♣♣
Yellow Rock	107	♥♥♥♥	♦♦♦♦	♠♠	♣♣♣
Hackberry Heights	110	♥♥♥	♦♦	♠♠	♣♣♣♣
Wahweap Hoodoos	111	♥♥♥♥	♦♦♦♦	♠♠	♣♣♣
White Rocks	113	♥♥♥	♦♦♦	♠♠	♣♣♣
Rimrocks Hoodoos	115	♥♥♥	♦♦♦	—	♣
Old Paria	117	♥♥♥	♦♦	♠♠	—
Wire Pass (+ foray in Buckskin Gulch)	118	♥♥♥♥	♦♦♦	♠♠	♣♣
Edmaier's Secret	119	♥♥♥	♦♦♦	♠♠	♣♣♣
Paria Canyon to Buckskin Gulch	121	♥♥♥♥	♦♦♦	♠	♣♣♣♣
Cobra Arch	124	♥♥♥	♦♦	♠♠♠	♣♣♣
6 Along Scenic Byway 12					
Kodachrome Basin State Park	128	♥♥♥	♦♦♦	—	♣♣
Skutumpah Road	129	♥♥	♦♦	♠♠♠	—
Willis Creek	130	♥♥♥	♦♦♦	♠♠♠	♣♣
Johnson Canyon	130	♥♥	♦♦♦	—	♣♣
Escalante Petrified Forest	131	♥♥	♦	—	♣♣
Smoky Mountain Road	132	♥♥	♦♦	♠♠♠♠	—
Horizon Arch	133	♥♥♥	♦♦	♠♠♠	♣♣♣
Hell's Backbone Road	134	♥♥	♦♦	♠♠	—
Death Hollow (via Escalante Trailhead)	135	♥♥♥	♦♦	♠	♣♣♣♣
Escalante to Boulder (SB-12 & Hogback)	136	♥♥♥♥	♦♦	—	—
Old Sheffield Road Hoodoos	137	♥♥	♦♦	—	—
Boulder Mail Trail (to Death Hollow)	137	♥♥♥	♦♦	♠♠♠	♣♣♣♣
Escalante Natural Bridge	139	♥♥♥	♦♦	—	♣♣
Hundred Handprints	140	♥♥♥	♦	—	♣♣
Phipps Arch	141	♥♥	♦♦	—	♣♣♣
Lower Calf Creek Falls	143	♥♥♥♥	♦♦♦	—	♣♣
Upper Calf Creek Falls	144	♥♥	♦♦	♠	♣♣
Around Boulder Mountain	144	♥♥♥	♦♦	—	—
Burr Trail (Boulder to Long Canyon)	145	♥♥♥♥	♦♦♦♦	—	—
Little Death Hollow	147	♥♥♥	♦♦	♠♠♠♠	♣♣♣
7 Canyons of the Escalante					
Hole-in-the-Rock Road	150	♥♥	♦	♠♠♠	—
Cedar Wash Arch	151	♥♥	♦	♠♠	♣
Zebra & Tunnel Slots	152	♥♥♥	♦♦♦♦	♠	♣♣♣
Red Breaks	154	♥♥♥	♦♦♦	♠♠	♣♣♣♣
Volcano	156	♥♥♥♥	♦♦♦	♠♠	♣♣♣
Little Valley	158	♥♥	♦♦	♠♠♠	♣♣
Devil's Garden	159	♥♥♥♥	♦♦♦♦	♠	♣
Choprock Canyon	161	♥♥♥	♦♦♦	♠♠♠	♣♣♣♣
Neon Canyon	163	♥♥♥♥	♦♦♦♦	♠♠♠	♣♣♣♣
Dry Fork, Peek-a-Boo & Spooky Slots	165	♥♥♥♥	♦♦♦	♠♠♠	♣♣♣
Coyote Gulch (loop Crack in the Wall - Jacob Hamblin)	168	♥♥♥♥♥	♦♦♦♦	♠♠♠♠	♣♣♣♣
Coyote Gulch (Crack in the Wall to Red Well)	168	♥♥♥♥♥	♦♦♦♦	♠♠♠♠	♣♣♣♣♣
Sunset Arch	173	♥♥♥	♦♦♦♦	♠♠	♣♣
Dance Hall Rock (amphitheater & top)	174	♥♥♥	♦♦	♠♠♠	♣
Broken Bow Arch	175	♥♥♥	♦♦♦	♠♠♠	♣♣
Reflection Canyon	176	♥♥♥♥	♦♦♦♦	♠♠♠	♣♣♣♣♣
Hole-in-the-Rock	178	♥♥	♦	♠♠♠	♣♣

Location	Page	Scenic Value	Photo Interest	Road Difficulty	Trail Difficulty
8 Capitol Reef					
Panorama & Sunset Points	181	♥♥♥	♦♦♦	♠	♣
Sulphur Creek	182	♥♥	♦♦	—	♣♣♣
Fruita Oasis	182	♥♥♥	♦♦	—	♣
Cohab Canyon & Overlooks	184	♥♥♥	♦♦	—	♣♣
Scenic Drive (including Capitol Gorge)	184	♥♥♥♥	♦♦♦	♠	—
Hickman Bridge	185	♥♥	♦	—	♣♣
Navajo Knobs	186	♥♥♥	♦♦	—	♣♣♣
Cathedral Valley Loop	186	♥♥♥♥	♦♦♦♦	♠♠♠	—
South Desert & Bentonite Hills	188	♥♥♥	♦♦	♠♠♠	♣
Upper Cathedral Valley	189	♥♥♥♥	♦♦♦♦	♠♠♠	♣
Lower Cathedral Valley	191	♥♥♥	♦♦♦	♠♠	—
Caineville Badlands (off UT-24)	192	♥♥	♦♦	—	—
North Caineville Mesa (from top)	193	♥♥♥	♦♦♦	—	♣♣♣
Waterpocket Fold / Nottom-Bullfrog Rd.	195	♥♥	♦♦	♠♠	—
Strike Valley Overlook	196	♥♥♥♥	♦♦♦	♠♠♠	♣
Upper Muley Twist	196	♥♥♥♥	♦♦	♠♠♠	♣♣♣
Halls Creek (Brimhall Bridge)	197	♥♥	♦♦	♠♠♠	♣♣♣♣
9 Along Interstate 70					
Interstate 70 Corridor & San Rafael Swell	200	♥♥♥	♦♦♦	—	—
Fremont Indian State Park	201	♥♥	♦♦	—	♣♣
Rochester Rock Art Panel	201	♥♥	♦♦	♠	♣
Moore Cutoff Road - Snake Panel	202	♥	♦	—	—
Nine Mile Canyon	203	♥♥♥	♦♦	—	♣
Wedge Overlook	204	♥♥♥	♦♦	♠♠	—
Buckhorn Draw	204	♥♥♥	♦♦♦	♠♠	—
Head of Sinbad	205	♥♥♥	♦♦♦	♠♠♠	—
Dutchman Arch	206	♥	♦	♠♠♠	—
Lone Warrior	207	♥	♦	♠♠	—
Swasey Cabin	207	♥	♦♦	♠♠	—
Eagle Canyon Arch	208	♥♥	♦♦	♠♠	♣♣
Family Butte	208	♥♥	♦♦	♠♠♠	♣
San Rafael Reef - Spotted Wolf Canyon	209	♥♥♥	♦♦♦	—	—
Black Dragon Wash	210	♥♥	♦♦	♠♠	♣
Crystal Geyser	211	♥♥	♦♦	♠♠	—
Sego Canyon	212	♥♥♥	♦♦♦	♠	—
10 Around Hanksville					
Factory Butte	214	♥♥	♦♦	♠	—
Goblin Valley State Park	215	♥♥♥♥	♦♦♦♦	—	♣
Little Wild Horse Slot Canyon	219	♥♥♥♥	♦♦	♠♠	♣♣
Wild Horse Canyon	221	♥♥	♦♦♦	♠	♣♣
Wild Horse Window	222	♥♥	♦♦	♠	♣♣
Temple Mountain Pictographs	223	♥	♦	—	—
Crack Canyon	223	♥♥♥	♦♦♦	♠♠	♣♣♣
Burr Point	225	♥♥♥	♦♦	♠♠	—
Arsenic Arch	225	♥♥♥	♦♦	♠♠	♣♣♣
Little Egypt	226	♥♥	♦♦	♠	♣
Leprechaun Canyon	227	♥♥♥	♦♦	—	♣♣
Hog Springs & Panel	228	♥♥	♦♦	—	♣
Pedestal Alley	229	♥♥	♦♦	♠♠	♣♣
Out of Bullfrog on Lake Powell	229	♥♥♥♥♥	♦♦♦	—	—
11 Around Blanding					
Edge of the Cedars State Park Museum	235	♥♥	♦	—	—
Tower House	235	♥♥	♦♦	♠	♣♣
Over & Under Ruin (from viewpoint)	236	♥♥	♦♦	♠	♣
Target Ruin	237	♥♥♥	♦♦	—	♣♣
Butler Wash Ruins	238	♥	♦	—	♣

Location	Page	Scenic Value	Photo Interest	Road Difficulty	Trail Difficulty
Mule Canyon - House on Fire	239	♥♥	♦♦♦♦	▲	♣♣
Arch Canyon Viewpoint	241	♥♥♥	♦	▲▲▲	—
Natural Bridges - Sipapu & Kachina Loop	242	♥♥♥	♦♦♦	—	♣♣♣
Natural Bridges - Owachomo Bridge	243	♥♥	♦♦	—	♣
Moon House	244	♥♥♥♥	♦♦♦	▲▲▲	♣♣
Fallen Roof Ruin	245	♥♥♥	♦♦♦♦♦	▲▲	♣♣
Citadel	247	♥♥♥	♦♦	▲▲▲	♣♣♣
Government Trail to Big Man Panel	249	♥♥♥	♦♦♦	▲▲▲	♣♣♣
Sheiks Canyon	250	♥♥♥	♦♦♦	▲▲▲	♣♣♣♣
Bullet Canyon	251	♥♥♥	♦♦♦	▲	♣♣♣♣
Slickhorn Canyon	252	♥♥♥	♦♦♦	▲	♣♣♣♣
Point Lookout	256	♥♥	♦♦♦	▲▲▲	♣♣
Mokey Dugway & Muley Point	256	♥♥	♦	▲	—
12 Around Bluff					
Bluff - Horse Panel	258	♥♥	♦♦	▲	♣♣
Sand Island Panels	259	♥♥	♦	—	♣
Wolfman Panel	259	♥♥	♦♦	▲	♣♣
Pedestal Rock Ruin	260	♥♥♥	♦♦	▲▲	♣♣
Procession Panel	261	♥♥♥	♦♦	▲▲	♣♣♣
Monarch Cave	262	♥♥	♦♦	▲▲	♣♣
River House & Butler Wash Panel	262	♥♥♥	♦♦	▲▲▲▲	♣
Valley of the Gods	264	♥♥♥	♦♦	▲▲	—
Goosenecks of the San Juan	265	♥♥♥	♦♦♦	—	—
Mexican Hat Rock	265	♥	♦	▲	—
Raplee Anticline (a.k.a. Lime Ridge)	268	♥♥♥	♦♦	—	—
Mile 13 to Monument Valley	269	♥♥♥♥♥	♦♦♦♦♦	—	—
Seventeen Room Ruin	271	♥♥	♦♦	▲	♣
Recapture Pocket	272	♥♥♥	♦♦	▲▲	—
Montezuma Canyon	273	♥♥♥	♦♦♦	▲	♣
Hovenweep National Monument	275	♥♥♥	♦♦	—	♣
13 Around Moab					
Potash Road - SB-279 (paved)	280	♥♥	♦♦	—	—
Potash Road (dirt road) to Shafer Trail	280	♥♥♥	♦♦	▲▲▲	—
Poison Spider Mesa (from parking)	281	♥♥	♦♦♦	—	♣♣♣
Corona Arch	282	♥♥♥	♦♦♦	—	♣♣
Courthouse Wash Rock Art	282	♥♥	♦	—	♣
Colorado Riverway	283	♥♥♥	♦♦	—	—
Professor Creek (a.k.a. Mary Jane Canyon)	284	♥♥	♦♦	▲	♣♣♣
Fisher Towers	284	♥♥♥♥	♦♦♦♦	▲▲	♣♣♣
Onion Creek	286	♥♥♥	♦	▲▲▲	—
Entrada Bluffs	286	♥♥♥	♦♦♦	▲▲▲▲	♣
Faux Falls	287	♥♥	♦♦	▲▲	♣
La Sal Mountain Loop	288	♥♥♥	♦♦	—	—
Tukuhnikivats Arch	289	♥♥	♦♦♦	▲▲	♣♣♣
Wilson Arch	290	♥♥	♦♦	—	♣♣
Olympic Torch	290	♥♥♥	♦♦♦	▲▲	♣♣♣
Along Kane Creek	292	♥♥♥	♦♦	▲	♣
Monitor & Merrimac from Seven Mile Wash	293	♥♥♥	♦♦	—	♣♣♣
Monitor & Merrimac from Mill Canyon Road	294	♥♥♥	♦♦	▲▲▲	♣
Seven Mile Canyon - South Fork	295	♥♥	♦♦	—	♣♣
Gemini Bridges Loop	295	♥♥	♦	▲▲▲	♣
Secret Spire	296	♥	♦	▲▲	♣
14 Arches NP					
Park Avenue & the Courthouse Towers	299	♥♥♥	♦♦♦	—	♣
Balanced Rock	300	♥♥	♦♦♦	—	—
Eye of the Whale	301	♥	♦	▲▲▲	♣
The Windows	301	♥♥♥♥	♦♦♦♦	—	♣

Location	Page	Scenic Value	Photo Interest	Road Difficulty	Trail Difficulty
Wolfe Ranch Petroglyphs	302	♥♥	♦♦	—	♣
Delicate Arch (top)	303	♥♥♥♥♥	♦♦♦♦♦	—	♣♣
Delicate Arch (from viewpoint below)	304	♥♥♥	♦♦	—	♣
Fiery Furnace	304	♥♥♥	♦♦	—	♣♣
Sand Dune Arch & Broken Arch	306	♥♥	♦♦	—	♣
Devil's Garden	307	♥♥♥♥	♦♦♦	—	♣♣♣
Klondike Bluffs	308	♥♥♥	♦♦♦	▲▲▲	♣♣
15 Canyonlands - Island in the Sky					
Dead Horse Point	313	♥♥♥♥♥	♦♦♦♦♦	—	♣
Long Canyon	316	♥♥♥	♦♦	▲▲▲	—
Marlboro Point	316	♥♥♥	♦♦♦	▲▲▲	—
Moses & Zeus Viewpoint	317	♥♥	♦♦	▲▲▲▲	♣♣♣
Mesa Arch	318	♥♥♥	♦♦♦♦	—	♣
Grandview Point & White Rim Overlook	319	♥♥♥	♦♦♦	—	♣
Green River Overlook & Murphy Point	322	♥♥♥	♦♦♦	—	♣♣
Aztec Butte	323	♥♥	♦♦	—	♣♣
False Kiva	323	♥♥♥	♦♦♦♦	—	♣♣♣
Upheaval Dome (overlooks)	325	♥♥	♦	—	♣
Shafer Trail	328	♥♥♥♥	♦♦	▲▲▲	—
White Rim Road	329	♥♥♥♥♥	♦♦♦♦	▲▲▲▲	♣♣
16 Canyonlands - Needles					
Newspaper Rock	333	♥♥♥	♦♦	—	—
Shay Canyon Panels	334	♥♥	♦♦	—	♣
Roadside Ruin	334	♥	♦	—	—
Cave Spring	334	♥♥	♦	▲	♣
Pothole Point Loop	335	♥	♦	—	♣
Slickrock Trail	335	♥♥	♦♦	—	♣♣
Elephant Hill (2WD road & uphill hike)	335	♥♥	♦♦	▲	♣
Elephant Hill (full loop)	335	♥♥♥♥	♦♦♦	▲▲▲▲▲	♣♣
Chesler Park Overlook	337	♥♥♥	♦♦	▲	♣♣
Chesler Park (full loop)	337	♥♥♥♥	♦♦♦♦	▲	♣♣♣♣
Druid Arch	339	♥♥♥♥	♦♦♦	▲	♣♣♣♣
Horse Canyon	339	♥♥♥	♦♦♦	▲▲▲▲	♣♣
Salt Creek Thru-hike (from Cathedral Butte)	340	♥♥♥♥	♦♦♦♦	▲▲▲	♣♣♣♣♣
Upper Salt Creek to Upper Jump	341	♥♥♥♥	♦♦♦♦	▲▲▲	♣♣♣♣♣
Lower Salt Creek to Angel Arch	343	♥♥♥♥	♦♦♦♦	▲	♣♣♣♣♣
Cave Spring Road to Peekaboo Camp	344	♥♥	♦	▲▲▲▲	♣♣
Squaw Flat to Peekaboo Camp	344	♥♥♥	♦♦♦	—	♣♣♣
Davis Canyon - 5 Faces	346	♥♥	♦♦	▲▲▲▲	♣
Lavender Canyon	347	♥♥♥♥	♦♦	▲▲▲▲▲	♣♣
Cathedral Point (a.k.a. Big Pocket Overlook)	348	♥♥♥♥	♦♦♦	▲▲▲▲	—
Beef Basin	350	♥♥♥	♦♦	▲▲▲▲	—
Canyon Rims - Needles Overlook	351	♥♥	♦	—	—
Canyon Rims - Anticline Overlook	351	♥♥♥	♦♦	▲	—
Canyon Rims - Canyonlands Overlook	352	♥♥♥	♦♦	▲▲▲	♣♣
17 Canyonlands - The Maze					
Horseshoe Canyon	356	♥♥♥♥	♦♦♦♦	▲▲	♣♣♣
Colonnade Arch	359	♥♥♥	♦♦	▲▲▲	♣♣♣
Panorama Point	359	♥♥	♦	▲▲▲▲	—
Maze Overlook	360	♥♥♥	♦♦♦	▲▲▲▲	—
Harvest Scene	361	♥♥♥	♦♦	▲▲▲▲	♣♣♣♣
Land of Standing Rocks	362	♥♥♥	♦♦♦	▲▲▲▲▲	♣
Doll House & Surprise Valley (via 4WD road)	363	♥♥♥♥	♦♦♦♦	▲▲▲▲▲	♣♣
Doll House & Spanish Bottom (via jet boat)	365	♥♥♥♥	♦♦♦♦	—	♣♣♣
Above Canyonlands	365	♥♥♥♥♥	♦♦♦	—	—

INDEX

A not so brief blip about the Author

I was born in Paris, France. Thanks to an open-minded family, I attended school in Paris, London, Barcelona, and several cities in Germany. I hold degrees in modern languages and international business.

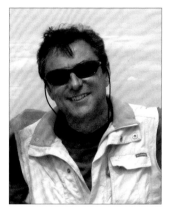

A couple of years after college, I did the best thing a young person can do to widen his or her horizons and gain an understanding of our world and its wonderful diversity: I set out on a 20-month trip around the world, photographing extensively.

From 1976-1981, I lived in Tokyo, becoming a permanent resident of Japan and teaching at Sophia University. During this time, I also worked as a freelance photographer and pursued my research on the origins of Sumo and its ties with the Shinto religion, resulting in *Sumo – Le Sport & le Sacré*, published in 1984. My years in Japan have had a profound influence on my life, my philosophy, and my photography.

I immigrated to the United States in 1982, settling on Southern California to create Graphie Int'l, Inc.—a firm specializing in software rights acquisition, as well as creation and management of corporate subsidiaries of European firms. Constant exploration and photography of the Southwest resulted in the publication of *Land of the Canyons* in 1998. In 1999, I permanently switched the company's focus to book publishing under the *Photo Trip USA Publishing* imprint, spending a great deal of my time on the road writing and photographing my award-winning *Photographing the Southwest* series.

In addition to my duties overseeing the publishing of new award-winning books and authors, I do a fair amount of world travel and sell my photography at a limited number of high-end art festivals, where I greatly enjoy interacting with patrons. I have served for a number of years as a member of the jury and artist advisor for the prestigious, #1-ranked in the nation, La Quinta Arts Festival.

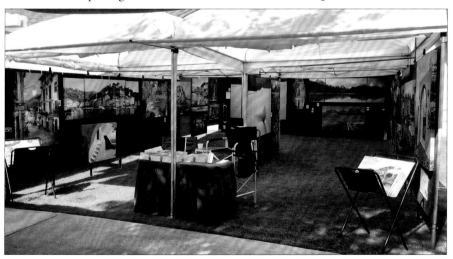

OTHER TITLES IN THE SERIES

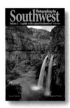

Photographing the Southwest: Volume 2 - Arizona (2nd Ed.)
A guide to the natural landmarks of Arizona
by Laurent Martrès
272 pages
ISBN 978-0-916189-13-6

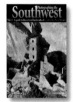

Photographing the Southwest: Volume 3 (2nd Ed.)
A guide to the natural landmarks of Colorado & New Mexico
by Laurent Martrès
272 pages
ISBN 978-0-916189-14-3

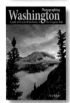

Photographing Washington
A guide to the natural landmarks of the Evergreen State
by Greg Vaughn
320 pages
ISBN 978-0-916189-19-8

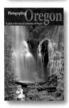

Photographing Oregon
A guide to the natural landmarks of Oregon
by Greg Vaughn
304 pages
ISBN 978-0-916189-18-1

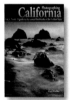

Photographing California: Volume 1 - North
A guide to the natural landmarks of the Golden State
by Gary Crabbe
432 pages
ISBN 978-0-916189-20-4

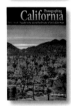

Photographing California: Volume 2 - South
A guide to the natural landmarks of the Golden State
by Jeff Sullivan
ISBN 978-0-916189-21-1
Available mid-2015

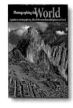

Photographing the World
A Guide to photographing 201 of the most beautiful places on Earth
by Tom Till
336 pages
ISBN 978-0-916189-22-8